Intermedial Studies

Intermedial Studies provides a concise, hands-on introduction to the analysis of a broad array of texts from a variety of media – including literature, film, music, performance, news and videogames, addressing fiction and non-fiction, mass media and social media.

The detailed introduction offers a short history of the field and outlines the main theoretical approaches. Part I explains the approach, examining and exemplifying the dimensions that construct every media product. The following sections offer practical examples and case studies using many examples that will be familiar to students, from Sherlock Holmes and football, to news, vlogs and videogames.

This book is the only textbook that takes both a theoretical and practical approach to intermedial studies. The book will be of use to students from a variety of disciplines looking at any form of adaptation, from comparative literature to film adaptations, fan fictions and spoken performances. The book equips students with the language and understanding to confidently and competently apply their own intermedial analysis to any text.

Jørgen Bruhn is Professor of Comparative Literature at Linnæus University, Sweden. His main interests include intermedial studies, ecocriticism and climate emergency studies.

Beate Schirrmacher is Associate Professor of Comparative Literature at Linnæus University, Sweden. She has published on the intermedial relation of literature and music. Her current research explores the truth claims of media.

Intermedial Studies
An Introduction to Meaning Across Media

Edited by
Jørgen Bruhn and Beate Schirrmacher

Cover images: © Getty Images

First published 2022
by Routledge
2 Park Square, Milton Park, Abingdon, Oxon OX14 4RN

and by Routledge
605 Third Avenue, New York, NY 10158

Routledge is an imprint of the Taylor & Francis Group, an informa business

© 2022 selection and editorial matter, Jørgen Bruhn and Beate Schirrmacher; individual chapters, the contributors

The right of Jørgen Bruhn and Beate Schirrmacher to be identified as the authors of the editorial material, and of the authors for their individual chapters, has been asserted in accordance with sections 77 and 78 of the Copyright, Designs and Patents Act 1988.

The Open Access version of this book, available at www.taylorfrancis.com, has been made available under a Creative Commons Attribution-Non Commercial-No Derivatives 4.0 license.

Trademark notice: Product or corporate names may be trademarks or registered trademarks, and are used only for identification and explanation without intent to infringe.

British Library Cataloguing-in-Publication Data
A catalogue record for this book is available from the British Library

Library of Congress Cataloging-in-Publication Data
Names: Bruhn, Jørgen, editor. | Schirrmacher, Beate, editor.
Title: Intermedial studies : an introduction to meaning across media / edited by Jørgen Bruhn and Beate Schirrmacher.
Description: Abingdon, Oxon ; New York : Routledge, 2022. | Includes bibliographical references and index.
Identifiers: LCCN 2021032911 | ISBN 9781032004662 (hardback) | ISBN 9781032004549 (paperback) | ISBN 9781003174288 (ebook)
Subjects: LCSH: Intermediality. | Mass media and literature. | Mass media and the arts. | Intertextuality.
Classification: LCC P99.4.I58 I55 2022 | DDC 302.2--dc23/eng/2021107
LC record available at https://lccn.loc.gov/2021032911

ISBN: 978-1-032-00466-2 (hbk)
ISBN: 978-1-032-00454-9 (pbk)
ISBN: 978-1-003-17428-8 (ebk)

DOI: 10.4324/9781003174288

Typeset in Bembo
by Taylor & Francis Books

Contents

List of illustrations vii
List of contributors ix

PART I
Introducing intermedial studies 1

1 Intermedial studies 3
   JØRGEN BRUHN AND BEATE SCHIRRMACHER

2 Media and modalities – Film 28
   SIGNE KJÆR JENSEN AND NIKLAS SALMOSE

3 Media and modalities – Literature 42
   PEDRO ATÃ AND BEATE SCHIRRMACHER

4 Media and modalities – Music 56
   SIGNE KJÆR JENSEN AND MARTIN KNUST

5 Media and modalities – Computer games 69
   PÉTER KRISTÓF MAKAI

6 Media and modalities – News media 86
   KRISTOFFER HOLT AND BEATE SCHIRRMACHER

PART II
Intermedial analysis: The three fundamental intermedial relations 101

7 Media combination, transmediation and media representation 103
   JØRGEN BRUHN AND BEATE SCHIRRMACHER

Contents

8 Intermedial combinations — 106
   MATS ARVIDSON, MIKAEL ASKANDER, LEA WIERØD BORČAK,
   SIGNE KJÆR JENSEN AND NAFISEH MOUSAVI

9 Transmediation — 138
   JØRGEN BRUHN, ANNA GUTOWSKA, EMMA TORNBORG AND
   MARTIN KNUST

10 Media representation: Film, music and painting in literature — 162
   JØRGEN BRUHN, LIVIU LUTAS, NIKLAS SALMOSE AND
   BEATE SCHIRRMACHER

PART III
Applying intermedial perspectives — 195

11 Introduction to Part III — 197
   JØRGEN BRUHN AND BEATE SCHIRRMACHER

12 The intermediality of performance — 198
   PER BÄCKSTRÖM, HEIDRUN FÜHRER AND BEATE SCHIRRMACHER

13 Truthfulness and truth claims as transmedial phenomena — 225
   JØRGEN BRUHN, NIKLAS SALMOSE, BEATE SCHIRRMACHER AND
   EMMA TORNBORG

14 Media modalities of theatrical space — 255
   HEIDRUN FÜHRER AND JANNEKE SCHOENE

15 Transmedial storyworlds — 265
   MIKAEL ASKANDER, ANNA GUTOWSKA AND PÉTER KRISTÓF MAKAI

16 Intermediality and social media — 282
   SIGNE KJÆR JENSEN, NAFISEH MOUSAVI AND EMMA TORNBORG

17 A toolkit for the intermedial analysis of computer games — 309
   PÉTER KRISTÓF MAKAI

   Index — 329

Illustrations

Figures

8.1	*Fun Home* (Bechdel 2007, p. 120)	111
10.1	Corpse of Che Guevara, 10 October 1967 (Photo by Freddy Alborta/Bride Lane Library/Popperfoto via Getty Images/Getty Images)	189
10.2	*Lamentation of Christ* by Andrea Mantegna (1430–1506) (Photo by Jean Louis Mazieres. CC BY-NC-SA 2.0)	190
16.1	Screenshot of the first YouTube video, 'Me at the Zoo', posted by YouTube co-founder, Jawed Karim, in 2005	292

Tables

2.1	Media and modalities – Film	38
3.1	Media and modalities – Literature	53
4.1	Media and modalities – Music	66
5.1	Media and modalities – Computer games	75
6.1	Media and modalities – News media	96
10.1	Different representations of cinema in literature	174
16.1	Transmediation from a source media product to a GIF	301

Boxes

1.1	Terms to get you started	4
1.2	Medium specificity and transmediality	12
1.3	The three Peircean sign relations briefly exemplified	23
2.1	Overview of the development of technical media for displaying film	29
3.1	Embodied reading	46
5.1	Interpretative frameworks for making sense of games	76
5.2	The paratexts of computer games	79
8.1	Comics terms explained	108
9.1	Adjustment strategies	140

9.2	Prestige adaptation	143
9.3	From transmediation analysis to opera adaptation	155
9.4	Word and tone in opera	156
10.1	The LP and the concept album: Technical medium of display and qualified medium	167
12.1	Performativity	200
12.2	Bodily performance: Orality and gestures	202
12.3	Poets	205
14.1	Ancient Greek theory of theatre	258
14.2	The body as subject and object	260
16.1	YouTube and the tension between democratization and commercialization	286
16.2	What is a vlog?	289
16.3	Authenticity	290

Contributors

Mats Arvidson is Associate Professor (Docent) of Musicology and Senior Lecturer in Intermedia Studies at The Department of Arts and Cultural Sciences, Lund University, Sweden. His main research focus is intermedial music and sound culture and its relation to narrative structures.

Mikael Askander is an Associate Professor of Intermedia Studies, at Lund University, Sweden. His research is focused on literature, popular culture and digital aspects.

Pedro Atã is a Postdoctoral Research Fellow the University of the Free State, South Africa. He researches the semiotics of surprise and creativity in media and technology, and has published on intersemiotic translation in dance, music, and arts, and improvisation in poetry.

Per Bäckström is an Affiliate Professor in Comparative Literature, and project leader for the implementation of open science, Linnæus University, Sweden. He researches intermediality across media types, often in avant-gardist genres.

Lea Wierød Borčak, International Postdoc at Linnæus University, Sweden, has published work on intermedial song analysis, hymnology and community singing.

Jørgen Bruhn is a Professor of Comparative Literature at Linnæus University, Sweden. His main interests include intermedial studies, ecocriticism and climate emergency studies.

Heidrun Führer works as Associate Professor at the Department of Arts and Cultural Sciences within the Division of Culture Management and Intermediality at Lund University, Sweden. Her research field is ekphrasis, theatre, performativity, advertising and popular culture.

Anna Gutowska is a literary scholar and screenwriter whose interests include adaptation studies and Neo-Victorianism. She works as Assistant Professor of English Literature at the University of Kielce in Poland.

Kristoffer Holt is Associate Professor at the Department of Media and Journalism (MJ), Linnæus University, Kalmar, Sweden and Docent in Political

Science with Mass Communication, Åbo Akademi University, Vaasa, Finland. His field of research includes alternative media, media criticism, media and religion, political communication and media history.

Signe Kjær Jensen has a background in Musicology and holds a PhD in comparative literature. She works as Lecturer at Linnæus University, Sweden. Her research interests centre on music and sound as parts of intermedial and multimodal media constellations.

Martin Knust is an Associate Professor of Musicology. Educated in Germany in musicology, philosophy and theology, he has been employed at universities and music colleges in Germany and Sweden, among others, and specializes in opera and music theatre, north European composers and music in political journalism.

Liviu Lutas is a Professor of French at Linnæus University, Sweden, with special interests in narratology, intermediality and ecocriticism in film and literature.

Péter Kristóf Makai recently completed his research project as a KWI International Fellow at the Institute of Advance Study in the Humanities in Essen, Germany, on the transmediation of theme parks in video games and the role of theming in board games. As a Craaford Postdoctoral Research Fellow at Linnaeus University he studied the communication of biological evolution in a transmedial context. He received his PhD in English Literature and Literary Theory in 2016. In addition, he also published in the field of Tolkien Studies, science fiction and fantasy studies.

Nafiseh Mousavi holds a PhD in comparative literature and works as Lecturer at Linnæus University. Her research interests include narratives of migration, intermediality and comics.

Niklas Salmose is an Associate Professor of Literatures in English at Linnæus University, Sweden. As a member of the Centre for Intermedial and Multimodal Studies at Linnæus he has published extensively on intermediality, cross-modal aesthetics, ecocriticism and on nostalgia.

Beate Schirrmacher is an Associate Professor of Comparative Literature at Linnæus University, Sweden. She has published on the intermedial relation of literature and music and her current research explores the truth claims of media.

Janneke Schoene is an art historian, cultural researcher and art mediator. Based at Lund University, Sweden, and Münster University, Germany, Janneke's research focus is on performance art and performativity, 'immaterial art' and forms of display, art and (auto)biography/auto-fiction.

Emma Tornborg holds a PhD in Comparative Literature and works as a lecturer at Malmö University and Karlstad University, Sweden. Her research interests include poetry, intermediality, ecocriticism and children's literature.

Part I
Introducing intermedial studies

1 Intermedial studies

Jørgen Bruhn and Beate Schirrmacher

Even if you have never heard the term intermediality before, you may still be familiar with the phenomenon. You have no doubt often compared a film adaptation with the novel it is based on, and you probably listen to audiobooks. On social media, you sometimes create and share memes or GIFs with your friends, and as a child your parents perhaps read picture books to you.

Intermedial studies is interested in the interaction of similarities and differences between media and the changes that may occur in communicative material when it is transported from one media type to another. It is also interested in how the differences between media types are bridged by similarities on other levels. The strange thing is that despite having no knowledge of or training in intermedial studies most people are very good at using and understanding intermedial relations, though of course not many of them would be able to use academic terminology to describe what they are doing, nor would they be interested in doing so.

One of the reasons why people navigate effortlessly in these communicative environments is that all communicative situations and all media types are multimodal: they draw on different forms of resources for meaning-making. When we speak to someone face-to-face, we not only understand the words they use but draw on intonation, body language, speech rhythm and the surrounding context to make sense of what we hear – and we do this without even thinking about it. This is not just true concerning face-to-face communication: even when we communicate across temporal and spatial distances when studying scientific articles, reading novels, or watching movies, there is never only one form of meaning-making involved. As you are reading this very text, in a print version or online, you are not only responding to the meaning of the written words, but the layout and typography also provide you with various kinds of visual information that facilitate reading and following the line of argument. If you are reading a printed copy, you are evaluating tactile and auditory information, and the weight distribution between your hands informs you that you are at the beginning of a longer text. If you are reading an e-book, the physical information found in a printed book has to be replaced by visual indicators. Thus, as media scholar W.J.T. Mitchell has pointed out, all communication involves all our senses. There are no purely visual, textual, or auditory media. All media products are, therefore, mixed and heterogeneous rather than 'monomedial'. Intermedial studies explores this

DOI: 10.4324/9781003174288-2

heterogeneous relation between different forms of meaning-making, either within a particular media product or between different media types. A summary of the main terms used in intermedial studies is provided in Box 1.1.

> **Box 1.1 Terms to get you started**
>
> **Media**: the material-based tools that are needed to communicate across time and space.
> **Intermedial studies** analyses the interaction within and between different media; traditionally, the research objects have been artistic phenomena.
> **Multimodal studies** is, like intermedial studies, interested in the internal mix of modes inside each media product.
> **Media studies** has traditionally been more focused on mass media, journalism and pedagogical contexts – and its approach is often closer to a social scientific approach.
> **Media product**: a specific communicative object or event, for example, a Penguin copy of Jane Austen's *Pride and Prejudice*, an article on global warming in *The Guardian* or a letter, an email or a spoken remark to a friend.
> **The technical medium of display** refers to the material object or entity that allows access to basic and qualified **media types**.
> **Basic media types** such as text, organized sound, or images are used as the communicative 'building blocks' in many different media
> **Qualified media types**: when we speak of the news media, the arts, or genres such as the novel and the documentary, we are talking about media types in a way that is qualified and is defined by context, convention and history and by our experience of many individual media products.

Defining intermedial studies

The term intermediality has gained popularity and influence despite the confusion about whether the term 'intermediality' denotes an *object* of study, a *method* of study, or a *theory* about a category of objects. The concept of intermediality opens up for all three of them. In the following, however, we will be careful to distinguish between intermedial studies as the method and theory of study and intermediality of media products as the object of study.

Historically, intermedial research has been particularly interested in artistic media products and focusing on relations between media types such as texts and images, words and music, or on media transformations that in some way or other cross and challenge conventional media borders. Intermedial studies has been very good at demonstrating these relations – but perhaps not so good at demonstrating how to analyse them in practical ways. In order to compare and analyse intermedial relations within particular media products, this book presents different kinds of medial relations, and tools to analyse them, which will allow you to describe, analyse and compare a huge variety of different media products in relation to each other. Our perspective is different from the classic intermedial approach, which deals mostly with artistic objects in that it is not only relevant for artistic media products but offers a method that can be applied to all forms of communication and analysis. Throughout this book, the choice of case studies and topics demonstrates that an intermedial perspective is not only relevant for artistic media products.

But what is the point of such an intermedial perspective? As previously mentioned, we can read and understand picture books, we can resend a funny GIF in an online thread, and we can apprehend the relation between words and photographs in newspapers without knowing anything about intermediality. But if you want to discuss, understand and compare these intermedial relations, terminology and useful analytical tools are needed. These should allow you to address similarities and differences and see how they relate to each other.

Intermedial studies is important, because academic disciplines such as literary studies, art history, musicology and even film studies do not provide the tools to analyse and interpret these intermedial relations. The analytical tools used within a discipline risk falling short when an attempt is made to analyse media products that go beyond the conventional borders of art forms and media types. And while film studies, theatre studies, comics studies, opera studies and media and communication studies have developed tools and terms to some extent to analyse their respective kinds of media, these disciplinary frameworks seldom address or discover similarities and differences between different forms of media types.

Intermediality emerged as a field of research in the late 1990s early 2000s. However, the interest in the relations between different forms of communication dates back far longer. It had previously been explored under the labels of, for instance, interart, adaptation studies, word and image studies. There has been a long debate in Western thinking, sometimes explicit, sometimes under the radar, about relations between different art forms and media, but from an institutional point of view the discussion has been scarce, and methodologies have not been developed. Innumerable artists, for example, have worked and continue to work with more than one medium, and it is probably the rule rather than the exception to do so, but traditional research in the different disciplines has not focused on this aspect. For instance, literary history abounds with writers who 'also' painted, who 'also' were skilled musicians or composers. There might have been an awareness of but not the analytical tools available to grasp how the knowledge and practice in one medium informs the work in another. Following the academic tradition of organizing study into different disciplines and therefore into different university divisions, we have left it to musicology to understand music and comparative literature departments to understand written literature, even though large portions of the history of music have to do with words and a lot of texts that are studied in literary studies are meant to be performed. For a long time, film studies as well as film directors were intensely interested in what they considered to be the 'cinematic' aspects of film (meaning the visual aspects) and neglected the fact that they were dealing and working with an audiovisual media type. But questions such as what makes some stories easy to narrate in many different media and why it is so difficult to make certain scientific ideas appealing to children and easy for them to understand were too seldom understood as general, intermedial questions: that is, questions with a structural similarity that could be approached by applying just one broad theory.

These are exactly the kinds of questions that intermedial studies wants to ask, though. How can we analyse translations and transformations that exist not between languages but between different media types? How can we move from a superficial value judgement of liking or disliking a film adaptation to a level where we can describe and discuss how certain aspects of the narrative were changed? Can we perhaps even start discussing why such changes are made? We could consider questions such as how does a text succeed in getting us to 'see' mental images and 'hear' mental sounds when all we have in front of us are lines of black letters on a paper or a screen? And how can still images convey a sense of movement? How can we analyse and discuss the relation between texts and images in a children's book, comics, newspaper articles and internet memes? Can we compare multimodal communication on a theatre stage with the performance of YouTubers? Our argument is that understanding the heterogeneity of different media products increases our understanding of how medial choices shape, form and support what is communicated.

Traditions of media studies

There are various ways to define what media are and how we use them. Below is a very rough and brief outline of some of the most important ones.

The academic field of **media and communication studies** explores the history and effects of various media, primarily mass media, often with a focus on the content side of communication. Media and communication studies has a social scientific background – it is more interested in the role of media in relation to societal questions (news, ideologies, political impact, societal communication). The content and impact of particular media in a particular social context are explored in empirical studies or from different theoretical perspectives.

Other media-related fields focus on different forms of interrelation, mixedness and heterogeneity. Examples of such fields are media archaeology, intermedial studies and multimodal studies, which are based on some of the same assumptions – namely that communication takes place in the complex interaction between different media, mixed media and different resources. But scholars who use these different theoretical approaches seldom work together and common terms or ideas are seldom developed. This is partly because although the objects of study are quite closely related, they are approached from different perspectives and with different analytical foci.

The tradition of **media archaeology** originated in German cybernetical and philosophical approaches. The often controversial, even provocative, ideas of

German literary and media scholar Friedrich Kittler (1943–2011) played a decisive role. He mostly investigated the technical forms that support media content, demonstrating and developing Marshall McLuhan's (1911–80) famous idea that the 'medium is the message'. This means that all communication must be understood, at least partly, as being significantly influenced by the physical device that communicates it, the historical development of the device, and the ideologies underlying the historical conditions.

The broad field of **media studies**, also McLuhanesque in its approach, investigates mass media and art from the fundamental idea that all meaning has a relation to the medium's form, which includes thinking philosophically about mediation. Mitchell and Hansen's *Critical Terms for Media Studies* is an anthology of such contemporary media studies, and it discusses and exemplifies aesthetics, politics and communicative approaches (Mitchell and Hansen, 2010).

Multimodal studies tend to focus on the complexity of the integration of different modes (understood as different means of communicating such as speech, colour or typography) within media products and in relation to a social context. The oral communication that takes place during face-to-face communication involves numerous 'semiotic resources', such as intonation, facial expression and body language, and each can be examined and understood in greater detail. Multimodal studies often draws on insights from linguistics to understand the generation of meaning potential.

Intermedial studies touches upon similar questions. Intermedial studies draws attention to the technical media of display and media technology, which are explored in media archaeology. Like media studies, intermedial studies is interested in the aesthetic and philosophical aspects of media. Intermedial studies considers the interaction of different forms of meaning-making on interfaces, which is similar to what multimodal studies is interested in. The focus of intermedial studies thus overlaps with other approaches to the mixedness of media. Intermedial studies, however, does not tend to focus on only one of these levels but investigates how these levels interact and lead to the formation of what we call qualified media types. Intermedial studies explores how media technology and material qualities form our idea of media and vice versa.

The aim of this book

This book, built upon several ideas developed in different traditions within the study of media, is meant to demonstrate how to describe, analyse and discuss a large number of communicative forms across the conventional media borders. We will provide tools to understand media that are involved in the communication of fictive as well as of factual narratives and the role of media in artistic and self-reflexive communication as well as knowledge-based communication. In short, we hope to introduce tools that enhance intermedial literacy. This book provides a kind of analytical toolbox of intermedial studies that offers:

- An introduction to the central terms and methodologies of intermedial studies.
- Analytical methods that will facilitate analyses of media products in different media types.
- A large number of short case studies exemplifying theory and method.

Our aim is not so much to offer the reader a set of clear-cut typologies and labels, nor do we want to conduct long theoretical discussions or provide thorough historical contexts. There is a large body of intermedial research that already does that. Our main aim is not to give a detailed overview of different traditions and introduce all the complex terminological discussions taking place in intermedial studies as a research field.

In this book, we focus on an intermedial analytical method. We want to introduce a set of tools that will enable you to critically analyse and dissect the different layers of mediation in specific media products and that – if you wish – will enable you to compare different media products that are found in the contexts of different qualified media types.

This aim for our readers is mirrored in the composition of the book. We begin with theory, move on to analytical method and end with specific societal, historical and cultural questions, demonstrating that the intermedial approach is a useful tool that helps us to provide answers to these questions. The book, consequently, is divided into three main parts: a theoretical but very general introduction, where the necessary intermedial concepts will be introduced. The main theoretical ideas explained there will be exemplified in five substudies in which we demonstrate how our understanding of film, literature, computer games, music and news is formed and shaped by the material, sensorial, spatiotemporal and semiotic aspects of the media types involved.

The second part of the book deals with the different intermedial relations: media combination on the one hand, and media transformations in the form of transmediation and representation on the other hand. These are necessarily different phenomena but instead different perspectives that can often be brought to bear upon the same media product. We will present and discuss these intermedial relations with some main cases supported by a broader variety of minor examples.

In the third part of the book, we will demonstrate how the intermedial approach can contribute to better understanding specific cultural and communicative phenomena in order to reflect upon or even respond to current phenomena and societal challenges. We will also discuss how intermedial theory can contribute to neighbouring disciplines such as performance studies, and we will describe the construction of transmedial storyworlds that span different qualified media. Finally, we will offer intermedial perspectives on contemporary media types such as social media and computer games. As will become clear through this book, the intermedial analytical aspects are not only interesting or useful for academic purposes or for creating communicative 'literacy'. Intermedial studies, in particular in the format that we want to advocate here, has a distinct relevance when it comes to better understanding and possibly responding better to some of the societal challenges that are marring the world at the time of writing. The burning question of global warming, for instance, has several medial aspects to it: most people's knowledge of the climate crisis is gained through media transformations. We seldom read scientific articles on climate change but receive current research by way of newspaper articles, documentaries, Hollywood blockbusters, or even poems – with different effects, of course. The question of 'fake news' and spreading of disinformation in digital media highlights that we need more knowledge concerning exactly how and when we perceive a media product as truthful. By providing tools to analyse how the material qualities of media of display and basic media types convey certain truth claims and how we evaluate truthfulness differently in different qualified media types, intermedial studies can contribute to media literacy.

The intermedial toolbox

What is a medium?

When we talk about media in everyday conversations, we are mostly referring to mass communication channels for news, sports and entertainment. That is, we are referring to the technical devices which enable communication across time and space and the social institutions that provide it, like television and radio, or perhaps more personal devices, such as a computer or a smartphone. News media keep us updated on important events and social media enable us to be social in spite of being apart.

Medium is Latin for 'in between', and a medium can be seen as a mediator, something that enables communication across time and space. Media are the material aspects of human communication. News informs us about recent events. Literature can provide existential insights. Architecture not only provides shelter but also communicates social power relations. Fashion communicates ideas about the human body and about social norms. In the 1960s, Marshall McLuhan was already defining medium as 'any extension of man'. Thus, the list of material objects that can function as a medium is endless and it involves even other physical phenomena like light or sound waves, and our own bodies. In other words, once we become interested in the material aspect of human communication, media suddenly turn out to be everywhere. And anything and everything can be used as a medium. White pebbles on a beach are not usually a medium, but the white stones that Hansel, in the fairy tale by the Brothers Grimm, drops as he goes into the woods are definitely a media product, conveying a simple but important message: 'We came this way'.

There is not much point in asking what a medium is (and what it is not); it is more productive to investigate the ways in which objects and phenomena can function as media products. How do material objects facilitate human communication? And how do the material aspects of medium shape what is communicated?

With an intermedial toolbox we will have a useful perspective and terminology that we can use to understand text–image relations in comics or in newspaper articles, or the relations between the lyrics and a melody in both pop music and opera. We can discuss how diegetic media representation is used to represent narrative conflicts; we will also be able to pay attention to the material characteristics of literature, which are so often overlooked – the letters, typography, paper – and the impact of these elements on how we make sense of literary text. In short, we will be much better equipped to discuss a large number of phenomena that we seldom notice when we consume media products but which still deeply affect their reception. Marshall McLuhan famously said that 'the medium is the message'. We formulate more or less the same idea differently (and much less catchily): media are the invisible but crucial basis of human communication, and the material aspects of media shape what is communicated and what can be communicated.

Therefore, all communication is dependent on material objects, that is, different kinds of physical phenomena that we can perceive with our senses (including sound or light waves). The choice of media defines what and how we communicate. This is one of the main reasons why intermediality is a helpful toolbox. At a historical moment when digital media provide a technology through which we can easily switch between and combine media, it is easy to overlook the complex transformations and combinations inherent in such operations. We are not always aware that every choice, change or medium actually forms 'the message' that we want to bring across. This is yet another reason why we need to be 'media literate': because we live in contemporary media-saturated societies, we must be able to critically navigate and discuss and even partly produce media products.

History of intermedial studies and traditions

Although intermedial *studies* is a fairly new research discipline, intermediality as a phenomenon (defined as the interaction within and between different media types) has always existed, because all communication is multimodal and all communication employs different forms of media. This has not always been noticed.

The qualified media type of Greek drama from the fifth century BC, for instance, has been investigated in literary studies and classics departments primarily as *texts*, with remarkably little focus on the multimodal integration of speech, gestures, music and dance, as well as architectural space and ritual contexts. The orchestral suites of the German composer Johann Sebastian Bach (1685–1750) are compilations of dance music but are today often perceived as an example of instrumental art music that you primarily listen (and maybe not dance) to. And if we enjoy and even memorize a poem by the American poet Gertrude Stein (1874–1946), the poem is not only made by the meaning of the words but by how they sound and look. For aesthetic effects, the literary avant-garde plays with the material aspects of language, and advertising can use similar means to reach economic ends.

All media are internally multimodal and externally interrelated with each other. However, whether intermedial and multimodal aspects are acknowledged and encouraged or are instead criticized or perhaps even suppressed depends on the time and context. Therefore, mediated communication is also formed by ideas, ideologies and conventions. In Ancient Greek, for example, the word *mousike* refers to both what we would call poetry and what we would call music (song) today. In the centuries that followed the Ancient Greek period, these have been increasingly conceptualized as different qualified media types. And when Bob Dylan (b. 1941) was awarded the Nobel Prize in Literature in 2017, the decision was difficult to accept for those who insisted on a conventional border between literature and music. To others, the same decision highlighted the idea that poetry should be performed.

One way of looking at the history of discussions about intermedial aspects of Western art is to track the ideals of homogeneous art forms as opposed to heterogeneous art forms. Historical discussions about this can be traced far back in European cultural history and the issue was mainly seen as a question of aesthetics, albeit with important ideological undertones. From an intermedial perspective, we can see how these discussions and concepts about the relation between different art forms includes an awareness of mediality, of how art forms, like all forms of human communication, are shaped by their material that we perceive and make sense of. We will briefly introduce some of the fundamental concepts that have played a large role in these discussions. These terms are *paragone, ut pictura poesis, Gesamtkunstwerk* (the total work of art) and medium specificity.

The idea of *paragone* (Italian for 'comparison') originates in Renaissance art theory and relates to a ranking competition among the arts – each form vying to be deemed the best and the most valuable. Famously, painter and inventor Leonardo da Vinci (1452–1519) argued that painting was the highest example of artistic forms. This was refuted by, among others, sculptor, painter and architect Michelangelo (1475–1564), who counter-argued for the primacy of sculpture. The *paragone* debate has been an ongoing discussion in Western cultural history, and in 2010 a German collection of essays, inspired by intermedial studies, reinvigorated the idea of the 'comparative competition' between media types by analysing not only the classical art forms but also TV, advertising, graphic novels and computer games in a framework inspired by the sociology of Pierre Bourdieu (Degner and Wolf 2010). It is therefore possible to see current competition among modern qualified media as a kind of *paragone* debate, for example, seeing film as 'artistic' as opposed to 'popular' television.

Throughout history, discussions of the interrelations between media types have shifted between the tradition of pointing out the benefits of the merging of art forms and the tradition, which warns about such merging. Different terms have been used in different periods, beginning with the Roman writer Horace's (65–8 BC) idea of *ut pictura poesis* (the literal meaning is 'as in painting, so in poetry'), which means that what can be accomplished and admired in painting can be accomplished and admired in literature, too. This was refuted, centuries later, in

German Enlightenment writer G.E. Lessing's (1729–81) essay called 'Laocoon: On the limits of painting and poetry'. Lessing's interrogation inspired some problematic but often repeated dogmas of aesthetic theory concerning the relations between the arts. Lessing's essay offers an interesting discussion of fundamental intermedial insights, namely that the same event has to be represented differently in different media. However, one does not necessarily have to come to the same normative conclusion, namely that literature should deal with and represent time and narrative subjects, whereas painting should stick to spatial, or non-temporal, presentation, for instance, of the landscape. Lessing's treatise has inspired numerous positions that have circled around the idea of medium specificity (see Box 1.2), either as being descriptive formats or as being normative dogma, to the time of writing, across the fields of literature, painting and film.

The struggle of *ut pictura poesis* versus the Laocoon tradition of medium specificity can be traced back and forth through cultural history, and it can be found in academic disciplines and in artistic media types. Richard Wagner's (1813–83) late Romantic concept of a *Gesamtkunstwerk*, a total work of art, is one version of the *ut pictura* tradition, and in many ways the immersive practices of the cinema experience are clear signs of this idea: the darkened movie theatre, with high-quality visual representations and impressive sound systems, very much imitates the dreams of Wagner, who wanted to overwhelm his spectators with the combined powers of orchestral music, performances, poetry and stage props. Even several of the so-called historical avant-garde artists from the beginning of the twentieth century believed that the mixing of art forms was not only possible but necessary to achieve the highest artistic and political/spiritual goals and affect the reader, listener, or spectator in the most efficient way (Bürger 1984). Opposed to this stand the numerous attempts at specifying the different art forms (or media), as well as limiting them to their own formal investigation. A clear example of the medium specificity position is the influential American art critic Clement Greenberg's lifelong engagements with modernist art in the second half of the twentieth century.

Box 1.2 Medium specificity and transmediality

Medium specificity is an influential aesthetic theory that describes the possibilities and limitations of media, which are often called affordances. The concept of medium specificity dates back to German Enlightenment writer G.E. Lessing, who stated that each art form has specific possibilities and limitations that the art forms should not try to transgress. The debate resurfaces from time to time in debates among both artists and critics, often when new media types battle to find stable ground. Elliott (2003) provides a general and historic overview of medium specificity in film versus literature, and Chatman (1980) offers a discussion of film versus literature from a medium specificity perspective. For a discussion of the ideas of medium specificity and visual arts, see W.J.T. Mitchell (2005).

> If medium specificity has to do with creating or upholding borders between media, **transmediality** is a concept that denotes the possibilities of transgressing media borders. Transmediality has to do with the fact that you can, for example, express the notion of 'sorrow' with different basic media types, with an actor's body language, the organized sound of music, or the words of a literary text. Even some structural forms are transmedial – rhythm, for instance. At first glance, rhythm looks like a media-specific phenomenon that is related to the repetition of sounds in music. But rhythm is transmedial in that painting has a rhythm, verse and prose have a rhythm, and so does dance. Narrativity, another transmedial phenomenon, is not specific to literature or to film: narrativity exists in many verbal and non-verbal media types; it is an important aspect of older traditions of painting, for example, but is less significant in sculpture. Newspaper articles as well as popular scientific articles often have a narrative structure.
>
> The relation between medium specificity and transmediality is a very important theme in intermedial studies and it lies at the centre of all analysis of media transformation (see in particular Chapter 9).

As mentioned above, media are connected to values, and these values change over time. In the 1990s, for example, the internet and digital media were often discussed in almost utopian terms as the new hyper-medium that provides unlimited and free democratic access to information. Some thirty years later, we are in fact communicating, learning and working differently, and we are digitally interconnected. What seemed utopian in the 1990s has in a way become true, but so have new power relations that stem from the exploitation of digital data. It is not just communication that is changed by every major media revolution. Just as new forms of communication channels make it possible to question traditional hierarchies and gatekeepers, media revolutions have an impact on social and political stability as well. The use of social media to raise consciousness and gather revolutionary momentum in the Arab Spring during 2010 and 2011 is just one example of this.

Another example of a change in the value judgements related to media is the rise of music within Western aesthetic hierarchies. For centuries, music was ranked lower than visual art and literature because it lacked referential precision and was perceived as suspicious because of its double impact on the listener – it affects both the body (via sounds and rhythms) and the mind (via the order and beauty). Worried thinkers, from Plato (428–348 BCE) to Immanuel Kant (1724–1804), advocated controlling the affective impacts of music.

However, artists in the nineteenth century became increasingly interested in expressing subjective experiences and emotions, and therefore what was considered the lack of referential precision became an asset, and instrumental music rose in the hierarchy of the arts. When modernist writers in the early twentieth century looked for new forms, the structures of art music, the fugue and the sonata form provided alternative models. The idealization of art music as a role model for all arts was, however, seriously disturbed by how the Nazi propaganda drew the very idea of the supremacy of music and the fame of German composers into their racist worldview. So whenever we describe media types, we have to do so in a specific historical context; we cannot simply say what 'the internet' or 'music' 'is'.

A founding idea of intermedial studies is that meaning-making is dependent on technical devices and is formed by earlier cultural forms. This is an important point in Jay Bolter and David Grusin's (1999) *Remediation: Understanding New Media*. This influential book, which clearly works from McLuhan's original ideas, demonstrates that new, digital media work by always nesting earlier forms within them to take one step forward: the computer interface, for example, uses the metaphor 'desktop', and even though literature has been a written form for millennia, we still talk about 'narrators' as if a novel is an oral form.

So, when thinking about media and intermedial relations, it is important to remember the relation between relative structural stability versus historical change, both when it comes to each and every media type and when it comes to the interrelations between media and media aspects. This is what we call contextualized medium specificity: the idea that most media types can be described with a limited number of more or less stable media-specific characteristics but that these characteristics by their very definition change under the pressure of historical contexts.

Media aspects and media modalities

In the first parts of this chapter we have sketched out some of the other academic approaches that are interested in the heterogeneity of media but explore them with a different focus. We have also briefly described some of the historical discussions that, in different ways, have led to our understanding of intermedial studies.

To better understand different intermedial relations, combinations and transformations of media, we now need to describe in more detail the concept of media that we are working with. If we want to address all kinds of intermedial relations, we need a broad and very general framework that explains how all sorts of media work on several levels at the same time. In what follows we present a flexible set of tools that addresses the different levels of mediation and the different ways we interact with media.

In our everyday use of media, we concentrate on what we perceive to be content and tend to ignore the complex interaction of material, sensorial and semiotic processes that not only facilitates but also shapes this content. Actually, we only become aware of mediation in specific cases: when a technical device does not work properly, when it is unfamiliar to us, when we cannot use all our senses or the media product explicitly draws attention to its own mediation. When we want to analyse intermedial relations, we have to consider these processes that are going on underneath the surface, so to speak.

The broad variety of intermedial relations has in the past often been approached by identifying and defining a variety of specific and different forms. Such typologies provide an overview and may be a good first step in approaching a new field. However, if everything can be used as media, how can the typology provide an encompassing overview? And how can we find terminology for the endless variety of intermedial relations? Although typologies and categorizations are built on an order by means of identifying differences, intermedial phenomena are an interplay between differences *made possible* by similarities. Thus, a focus on sorting and categorizing by means of perceptible differences proves to be a difficult method of analysis. The problem is that for each difference on one level, one finds a similarity with another kind. There is no lack of broad concepts of media that stress the ubiquity of mediation in our everyday life and how media concern societal questions (a good case in point is Rust, Monani and Cubitt 2016), but fewer theories offer terminologies that can be used for analysis. While we agree with W.J.T. Mitchell that all media are mixed media, we want to go one step further and ask: how can we deal with this heterogeneity in a specific intermedial analysis? How can we acknowledge that different media have much more in common than we see at first glance but at the same time analyse how basic similarities play out differently in different media types?

When it comes to a theorization that is both precise and relatively flexible, we find that Lars Elleström's terminology is the most helpful (Elleström 2010, 2014, 2021). Elleström tackles the variety and complexity of intermedial relations by focusing on the fundamental characteristics that all media share. In order to analyse intermedial relations, you first need to know what all media have in common. This kind of bottom-up approach provides a flexible framework that addresses how mediation always takes place on different levels and how 'intermediality must be understood as a bridge between media differences that is founded on media similarities' (Elleström 2021, p. 5).

Elleström cross-links the overlapping frameworks of intermedial and multimodal studies, and draws on different traditions that study the mixedness of media and communication (see Box 1.1) by stressing that mediation always involves different aspects and takes place on different levels simultaneously. Thus, with this approach, it becomes possible to not only agree with Mitchell that all media are modally mixed but also to analyse the mixedness of media and how material characteristics, different semiotic processes and their conventions interact in shaping the very communication they facilitate. Therefore, we intend to set out Elleström's model in more detail as it forms the theoretical basis for all the different forms of analyses this book provides.

Media products and the aspects of mediation

We can encounter difficulties when trying to answer the question of what a medium is because we tend to answer the question differently depending on which aspect of mediation we focus on. Regarding 'radio', for instance, we might refer to a technical device (a radio) that receives a particular kind of airwaves of a specific frequency that are used to transmit sounds, but 'radio' can also refer to a broadcasting company, e.g. the BBC. 'Radio' can even designate a specific kind of sound-based content that a broadcasting company produces and transmits to its audience's radios, including particular genres like radio news (as distinct from newspaper or television news) or radio plays. We might also refer to a smartphone application that distributes the content of broadcasting companies (that was previously distributed by radio waves) in the form of digital files. In fact, when we talk about media such as radio, literature and film/cinema, we often do so by *referring to* certain materials but actually *thinking of* them as specific forms of communication that are shaped by cultural conventions.

This tendency to mix up material form with the communicative form they facilitate is not a problem in everyday life and not a problem at all as long as it stays inside disciplinary contexts. However, it becomes a problem when we start to compare different media types, and therefore we need to be more specific concerning which aspect we are thinking of. Are we speaking about *objects* such as books or records; or are we speaking of what they give access to, *configurations* such as text, images or organized sound; or are we referring to the kind of *information* that we make sense of according to the convention of a specific context? We therefore need to clarify different aspects of media and be more precise than in everyday speech.

If we want to talk about media not just on a general level but in terms of the analysis of the various relations that can arise between and within different kinds of media, we have to find a new solution: what we normally call a medium needs to be broken down into three interrelated aspects that are very often confused and conflated. Following Elleström's model, we differentiate between technical media of display and different basic and qualified media types. This allows us to address the physical, perceptual and cognitive aspects of individual media products and how they enable social interaction. These categories are not to be thought of as different groups of media; they are aspects that are part of and are relevant in all forms of mediation.

Media products

Our understanding of different media is based on our experience of how they are used. Our idea about news, social and artistic media consist of our experience of innumerable individual media products – of a multitude of different news articles, messages in group chats, pieces of music, novels or paintings. All of these media products involve different aspects; they use entities that we can physically interact with and display configurations that we can perceive and that we understand as meaningful.

Examples of 'media products' can be a particular news article in *The Guardian*, graffiti art by Banksy on the West Bank Barrier, the computer game *Final Fantasy XV* (Square Enix, 2016) or the latest Facebook status. We access an individual media product with the help of some kind of material object, which we call the technical media of display. These phenomena and objects display constellations of texts, still or moving images, speech or organized sound. These constellations, which we call 'basic media types', work like building blocks and can be used differently in different kinds of media products and in different historical and social contexts. The basic media types of text and images are combined differently in the context of news media to how this is done in children's books or comics.

Taken together, the 'technical media of display' and the way the 'basic media types' are used in a particular context shape our understanding of the third major dimension, 'qualified media types'. Examples of qualified media types could be news, literature, music or visual art. We explain these three aspects of media next: the technical media of display, the basic media types and the qualified media types.

Technical media of display

Technical media of display are the very material bases of mediation: they provide access to the media products. Technical media of display could be clay, paper or stone, or the screens and loudspeakers of electronic communication. Technical media of display are a function of physical objects that sometimes also serve as storage (like books – as opposed to loudspeakers that only display the sound); these objects can also interact with different production tools (like pens, typewriters, keyboards, cameras and microphones), storage devices (like records) or dissemination devices (gramophones and projectors). Their material qualities and the way they function shape what can be communicated.

Sheets of paper provide access to several basic media types, such as text and images. Text and image can be arranged in different ways so that we recognize them as different qualified media types, for instance, poems, scientific articles or graphic novels. The smartphone and computer provide access to innumerable media products and qualified media types. In face-to-face communication, performing arts and music, the presence of the human body functions as a technical medium of display.

It is important to keep in mind that everything in a particular context can be perceived as a technical medium of display: stones in a forest, glasses and a table in a kitchen, or a urinal are not always perceived as technical media of display, but they can acquire that function on a forest path (in a fairy tale), in interaction with other actors' bodies on stage (in a theatrical play) or in the context of the art gallery (as part of an artwork).

While technical media of display are needed to realize media products, they are not in focus in our interaction with media products as long as they are familiar and function well. We perceive and manipulate them, but usually our attention is not focused on these actions but on what they display. We tend to 'look through' the technical media of display as long as communication is functioning.

As a rule of thumb, we notice the technical medium of display when it is broken or when we are unfamiliar with how to manipulate it, such as when we try to make a phone call with a smartphone for the first time or try to read a manga book in the Western reading direction. Some media products self-reflexively draw attention to the presence of its technical device of display, like the Belgian painter René Magritte's (1898–1967) famous painting of a pipe that includes the caption '*Ceci n'est pas une pipe*' ('This is not a pipe'). The painting thus insists on the idea that what we see is not the pipe itself but the depiction of a pipe – and suddenly we are looking at a painting of a pipe. That is probably the reason why the *title* of the painting is *La Trahison des images* (*The Treachery of Images*).

Basic media types

When we are manipulating technical media of display, our attention is focused on certain configurations of sign systems: text or speech, images, organized sound, moving images and gestures. All these basic media types are configurations that in a multimodal analysis can be differentiated into numerous different semiotic modes. These basic media types are not the smallest entities that can provide meaningful information, but they are basic, meaning that they are used and combined in many different kinds of media products, and that is why we refer to them as the building blocks of qualified media types. Obviously, the same basic media types can be combined very differently, such as the text and image in children's books, illustrated novels, comics, advertisements, internet memes and news articles.

Certain technical media of display are particularly well suited to providing access to certain basic media types. Paper or screens are well suited for text or images but less suited to display a basic media type such as organized sound or speech. And while sound waves work perfectly well for basic media types like the organized sound of music and speech, sound waves cannot easily display gestures and facial expressions; these are basic media types of body language that use human bodies as technical media of display.

Qualified media types

We do not automatically understand all kinds of texts, images, organized sounds, gestures etc. Depending on the historical and social context, these basic media types are used and integrated differently and are involved in different forms of meaning-making. This is the aspect that we call the qualified media type.

Text is used differently in a novel, a poem, a news article or an SMS text message, and we look differently at images as art paintings, children's paintings or caricatures. Consequently, we recognize particular qualified media types by the way basic media types are arranged, and we have different expectations of them. Media products can be qualified in more or less detail, depending on which other kinds of media products they are compared with. A general category such as literature, visual art, music and film and can be qualified even more specifically if needed according to the conventions and the context into different genres, or submedia. Novels, short stories, poems, essays are examples of qualified submedia of literature. When we qualify a particular media product as 'art-house cinema' or as 'news reportage' we draw on our previous experience of similar media products. The differences we perceive between different qualified media products are confirmed, challenged or extended with every new media product we interact with, like Alan Moore and Dave Gibbon's graphic novel *Watchmen* (1986–87) challenges the idea that comics cannot tell as complex narratives as text-based novels

These three aspects of media are all present in each media product. The technical media of display gives us access to the basic media types that we understand according to the contexts and conventions of qualified media. There can be no qualified media type that does not consist of basic media; all basic media types need to be displayed for us.

When we use the three aspects of media to explain and understand relations that transgress and challenge media boundaries, these concepts become useful for orientation and differentiation. We might expect a Renaissance poem to be in the form of written text displayed on the pages of a book. However, we might (perhaps often nowadays) also access a particular sonnet by William Shakespeare (1564–1616) as digital text on a screen of a smartphone or watch a YouTube clip of an actor reciting the sonnet. This has an impact on our experience of the sonnet.

In the contemporary digitized media society, the configurations of technical, basic and qualifying media types are no longer as stable as they used to be but involve new combinations and faster changes of media of display that change our understanding of certain qualified media types. Thus, knowledge of the three media aspects makes you aware of the countless processes of combination and transformation, which usually remain unnoticed.

The four modalities of media

The three aspects of media (the technical media of display, the basic media type and the qualified media type) are useful for describing the complex set-up of each and every media product. However, we need to go one step further to find other levels that can help us better understand the workings of media products. This next level is called the modalities of media.

Without ever thinking about it, we interact with each and every media product in very different ways and at the same time. We engage with the following:

- a material object,
- which we perceive with our senses,
- and whose different spatial and temporal characteristics interact with each other,
- and gather that what we perceive with our senses is representing something else, as a sign.

The descriptions in the above list are, respectively, the material, sensorial, spatiotemporal and semiotic modalities of media, according to Elleström.

Being aware of the media modalities helps us to understand what we are actually doing when we communicate and interact with media products: we are interacting with different material objects, we are giving these objects perceptual attention, and we are perceiving signs, but usually we focus only on the sense that we make of these different actions – we jump directly to the 'content'. By looking at the four modalities of media, we can grasp this complexity that we usually tend to overlook, and, exactly as with the three aspects of media types, which cannot be thought of independently from each other, this is also the case with the media modalities: their very definition means that we interact simultaneously with a media product in all four media modalities.

It is a bit like driving a car: you perform movements with your hands and feet, you evaluate what you see, hear and feel, you relate your speed of motion to the movement and positions of other drivers and you interpret all sorts of signs. Once you've learned how to drive, and drive in a familiar area, you do not think about this anymore – you just think about how to get from a to b and perform the necessary actions to get there. In a similar way, we just perform the necessary actions to access a storyworld, to be updated on the latest news and to interact socially with friends and followers. Once we've learned how to manipulate a new technical device, we usually do not think about the complexity of it anymore. However, when we want to compare different kinds of medial engagement, we have to be more aware of what it is we do in different modalities.

The material modality

When we focus on the material modality, we ask how and why do these material objects function as an interface of communication? A page in a book and a screen of an electronic device are different technical media of display. But they are both flat surfaces and thus offer a suitable interface for basic media types such as texts or images. Records and the speech organs of the human body are different technical media of display, but they both produce sound waves and thus offer a suitable interface for basic media types such as speech or the organized sound of music. When we engage with media, we treat material objects and living organisms depending on what kind of interface we consider to be important. Very different material objects such as stones, plasma screens and paper are perceived as interchangeable when we read text or look at images because we primarily focus only on two dimensions of three-dimensional objects and neglect the material quality of the object that provides the surface. When we look at sculptures or engage with architecture all three dimensions as well as the material quality of the objects are perceived as potentially meaningful. In the material modality, we can thus perceive similarities between materially very different devices as long as they provide the same interface. We can also perceive differences in the communicative situations that use the same interface.

The sensorial modality

In the sensorial modality, we are interested in our sensual perception of the material interface that the media product demands of us. Media exist not only materially, as physical objects, but also communicate with us through our five sense organs. In order to 'meet' them, we must be able to perceive them with our senses: to see, hear, feel, smell or taste something. Ultrasonic sounds, for example, although materially present and perceptible to bats and to scientific measuring tools, are unsuitable as a basic media type in human communication, simply because human beings cannot perceive them with their sensorial apparatus.

We sense a particular aspect through one or more sense organs, and then we perceive and process the sensation or sensations in both our brain and body. Experiencing perception through our brain is called cognitive perception, and meaning-making through our body is called embodiment. These processes are deeply interrelated. The embodied reactions to our surroundings that are processed unconsciously or preconsciously are called affects and once we become cognitively aware of these reactions and name them to categorize them, we call them emotions.

Research has shown that sense organs do not operate in isolation from each other: vibrations can be heard and felt, our taste is connected to smell, and multimodal studies show how different kinds of perceptions combine, support and fortify each other. Although we use all our senses when engaging with media products, we usually only focus on some of them regarding what we perceive when we interact with them. We hear the rustle of the pages and feel the weight of a book in our hands and perceive the smell of a new (or old and dusty) book, yet we focus on vision while perceiving the text on the pages. Media products exploit our capacity for cross-modal translations. In the sensorial modality, we construct synaesthetic connections, where the image of ringing bells makes us 'hear' the bells.

If a book is the technical medium of display of a novel, then we need the body to realize this and respond with embodied reactions to the meaning of the words we decode. The importance of the sensorial modality can be experienced when sense organs are temporarily or permanently limited. Many inter-sensorial translations are possible, but they all radically affect communication and consequently the semiotic modality.

The spatiotemporal modality

We perceive all objects in space and time. These two categories are always related, even if we only focus on one of them. If we look at a huge tree, we perceive it as a spatial object, but we might call it an old tree as well, because we realize that its enormous size is the result of a long temporal process. In the same way, we perceive all media products in space and in time. However, media products as such have several different spatiotemporal qualities.

We classify some media types, like images, as primarily spatial objects. We can usually describe the spatial dimensions of these objects in terms of depth, height and length. Although time is involved in producing and perceiving the objects, we would not describe them temporally, as a 'three months' work' or a painting of 'three minutes of watching time'.

We primarily engage with other media types as temporal events, for instance, a piece of music. Here, we can define the event as having a beginning and an end: once it has started, it takes a certain amount of time to finish, be it a four-hour-long opera or a pop song that only last three minutes. But the sound waves of music take up space as well; a rock concert can be heard miles away.

The spatiotemporal qualities of media are important for several reasons. They offer a needed focus on less considered aspects, for instance, the temporal dimensions of spatial objects and the spatial qualities of temporal events. This means that although images are spatial objects in the material modality, we always need time to look at them in the sensorial modality. And although text as a basic media type is as stable as images on the page in the material modality, we engage with text differently as we read one word after another in terms of an ordered sequentially. We perceive the text of a novel as a temporal event. The sensorial time of reading and the virtual time of the represented storyworld interact in different ways. The temporal succession of words on a page communicates the virtual space of a storyworld as well. The perspective of a realistic painting conveys a virtual space that differs from the actual spatial dimensions of the canvas. The spatial qualities of images can be used to represent temporal events to communicate virtual time.

Not all of these spatiotemporal characteristics are essential in every intermedial analysis. However, it is important to keep in mind that intermedial relations tend to exploit the spatial and temporal characteristics of a media product and that they draw on different ways of how space represents time and vice versa.

The semiotic modality

Finally, the reason why we engage with media is not their material, sensorial and spatiotemporal qualities. We engage with media products because they mean something. The material, sensorial and spatiotemporal qualities of media products provide information that we understand to represent something else. Thus, media products employ our ability to make meaning of signs. Media can rely on conventional sign systems such as languages, but also, for instance, body movements in dance that convey meaning which may be difficult to translate into words.

There are different ways to understand how signs work. While Ferdinand de Saussure's (1857–1913) linguistic theory and his concept of the two-sided linguistic sign had a major impact on the development of linguistics and semiotics during the first half of the twentieth century, his language-based model creates difficulties when we want to compare the relations between different kinds of media and compare language to the way images, sounds and other forms of basic media types communicate.

In this book, we draw on the work of the semiotician Charles Sanders Peirce (1839–1914). Peirce differentiates three ways that a sign can relate to what it is supposed to signify: signs can be based on similarity (icons), contiguity (indices) or convention and habits (symbols). We connect the *iconic* signs to an object in the same way that pictures relate to their objects, namely due to their similarity. *Indexical* signs – symptoms, or traces – relate to their objects based on contiguity: they signify that a certain object is or has been present. The *symbolic* signs, for instance, words, form a relation that is based on habit and convention. See Box 1.3 for further explanation.

> **Box 1.3 The three Peircean sign relations briefly exemplified**
>
> In order to refer to a certain species of aquatic birds, you can refer to the bird as a 'duck'. You can also show, or draw, a picture of the bird, and the traces of a duck's footprint in the mud or a feather left on the ground also inform you that ducks were in that place at some point. The *symbolic* signs of the word 'duck' form a relation that is based on habit and the conventions of the English language. We connect the *iconic* signs of a picture of a duck to the actual birds because of their similarity with the object. Footprints or feathers form *indexical* signs of ducks; they are not similar, but they are a sign that ducks have been present. Different signs can thus refer to the same object. And all of the signs involve all three kinds of relations. For instance, a photograph of a duck is an iconic sign and also an indexical sign that ducks were present at the moment the photograph was taken.

Peirce's theory makes us understand that signs are not simply out there, waiting to be discovered and used. Objects can only function as signs if an interpreter attributes significance to them. To reuse an example from above, we may or may not notice a white stone on the ground on a hiking tour, but to Hansel and Gretel trying to find their way home, the stone is an indexical sign, because they relate it to the act of having dropped it there. But that does not mean that all white stones have the conventional meaning 'we came this way'.

Please note that the three kinds of relations – iconic, indexical and symbolic – are present in *all kinds* of signs, even if one of them might be more prominent. Words are not only conventional symbols; they also form iconic and indexical relations to the objects they signify. Many words relate iconically to the objects they refer to. We can hear that in words that refer to sounds, for instance, 'crackle', 'hush' and 'whisper'. The iconic relation is even more prominent in onomatopoeia, that is, sound-imitating words, such as the 'tick tock' of a clock, which at the same time is based on conventions that differ in every language. In Japanese, the sound of the clock is expressed as 'katchin katchin'. When we look at a photograph, we consider the iconic relation it forms with the objects shown in it, but we also consider photographs to be indexical signs that something was present at a certain time and place. Even faked and manipulated photographs draw on the indexical relation between photography and the object, for example, photographs that are deemed to be proof of the existence of UFOs or the sea monster of Loch Ness.

Although many signs are dominated by one kind of relation — the iconic, indexical or symbolic relation — all three kinds of relations are present in all kinds of signs. Intermedial relations often exploit the ambiguity of signs, that is, the possibility of relating in multiple ways to different objects.

By using the four modalities, we can systematically compare and differentiate between what happens in different forms of mediation and intermedial relations. They draw our attention to the fact that we carry out different acts when engaging with media products. We interact with objects; we perceive information with all our senses; we pay attention to certain temporal and spatial relations on material, sensorial and semiotic levels; finally, we understand the sense data as a certain form of signs.

Final comments

As we started to explain when we presented the four modalities, they make it possible to better grasp the different dimensions of mediation and the representation of material presence, sensorial perception, relations in space and time and how we make sense of them. They form the basis of a more grounded analysis of what happens in intermedial interaction when different media types are combined, transformed or represented. The intermedial analysis of the media product can support contextual analyses of meaning-making as well – as exemplified in the following chapters and case studies.

By presenting the three aspects of media products as well as the four modalities in which we interact with them, we have drawn attention to the complex interaction of different activities we carry out to get at what we conceive to be 'content'. The characteristics of technical media of display, of basic and qualified media types and the material, sensorial and spatiotemporal information, as well as different forms of sign relations, provide a kind of 'grammar'. In other words, the three media aspects and the four modalities are part of a toolbox that helps you to more precisely explore the heterogeneity of media products and different forms of interaction between media. You will probably not use all of the tools in every analysis, but you can use the best tools to describe the particular intermedial relations that you are interested in, and they will enable you to analyse how certain media are similar in one media aspect or in one modality but different in another

The introduction chapter has laid out the history, principles and basic terminology used in intermedial studies. The following five chapters will define the modalities of five different qualified media types in more depth.

These chapters can be read in sequence (which would provide a handy overview of central contemporary qualified media types) or in any other order if you have a special interest in one particular media type.

The following chapters will therefore provide you with an insight into several specific qualified media types that you might not be familiar with from 'your own' discipline. When we study intermedial relationships, we typically begin by analysing the media in the same way that we have learned to do in our own field: we are familiar with the material, the processes of production, the historical changes in one, or perhaps two, disciplines, but we are usually much less informed about others.

While all five chapters address the central aspects of media and how we interact with them in the four modalities, each chapter has a slightly different focus on aspects that are important when considering intermedial relationships and invites you to consider aspects other than those which are usually in focus in each discipline's discussions. Also, we conclude each chapter with a schematic overview covering the media and modalities of each specific media type. These diagrams are not meant as a definition but rather as a sort of very brief summary, hinting at the complexity inherent in all media types, when studied closely.

Of course, none of the chapters can provide an encompassing overview: the chapters are meant to give you an introductory overview, and we encourage you to consult the reading references if you want to explore the media type further.

Further reading

Marshall McLuhan's idiosyncratic but highly influential ideas on media from the 1960s can be studied in McLuhan's classic *Understanding Media* (McLuhan 1987).

There are several primers for media and communication studies; among them are the classic introductions in Dennis McQuail's *Mass Communication Theory* (McQuail and Deuze 2020) and John Fiske's *Introduction to Communication Studies* (Fiske and Jenkins 2011).

Several introductions to multimodal studies exist, including Ledin and Machin (2020) and O'Halloran and Smith (2011).

Media studies in its contemporary, philosophically inclined form is nicely covered in the work of W.J.T. Mitchell and Mark B.N. Hansen (Mitchell and Hansen 2010).

The tradition of media archaeology is probably still best introduced with Parikka (2012).

The long history of interart and thus intermedial studies does not exist yet, but Claus Clüver provided a good overview (Clüver 2007).

Irina Rajewsky (2002) and Werner Wolf (1999) offered influential systematizations of the field, whereas Bruhn has suggested an approach to intermedial aspects of narrative literature (Bruhn 2016) and, with Anne Gjelsvik, to cinema (Bruhn and Gjelsvik 2018)

As an entry point into current intermedial research, see Rippl's (2015) *Handbook of Intermediality* and Elleström's (2021) *Beyond Media Borders*.

For the theoretical framework of this book, Lars Elleström's work is important: his revised description of his theoretical model in Elleström (2021) is clarifying, as well as the recent anthology that he co-edited with Salmose (Salmose and Elleström 2020).

References

Bolter, J.D. and Grusin, R. 1999. *Remediation: Understanding new media*, Cambridge, MA; London: MIT Press.

Bruhn, J. 2016. *The intermediality of narrative literature: Medialities matter*. London: Palgrave Macmillan.

Bruhn, J. and Gjelsvik, A. 2018. *Cinema between media: An intermediality approach*. Edinburgh: Edinburgh University Press.

Bürger, P. 1984. *Theory and history of literature, volume 4: Theory of the avant-garde* (M. Shaw, Trans.). Manchester: Manchester University Press.

Chatman, S. 1980. What novels can do that films can't (and vice versa). *Critical Inquiry*, 7(1), pp. 121–140.

Clüver, C. 2007. Intermediality and interart studies. In J. Arvidson, M. Askander, J. Bruhn and H. Führer, eds., *Changing borders: Contemporary positions in intermediality* (pp. 19–38). Lund: Intermedia Studies Press.

Degner, U. and Wolf, N.C. 2010. *Der neue Wettstreit der Künste: Legitimation und Dominanz im Zeichen der Intermedialität*. Bielefeld: Transcript.

Elleström, L. 2010. The modalities of media: A model for understanding intermedial relations. In *Media borders, multimodality and intermediality* (pp. 11–48). New York: Springer.

Elleström, L. 2014. *Media transformation: The transfer of media characteristics among media*. Basingstoke; New York: Palgrave Macmillan.

Elleström, L. 2021. The modalities of media II: An expanded model for understanding intermedial relations. In L. Elleström, ed., *Beyond media borders. Vol. 1. Intermedial relations among multimodal media* (pp. 3–91). Basingstoke; New York: Palgrave Macmillan.

Elliott, K. 2003. *Rethinking the novel/film debate*. Cambridge: Cambridge University Press.

Fiske, J. and Jenkins, H. 2011. *Introduction to communication studies*. London: Routledge.

Ledin, P. and Machin, D. 2020. *Introduction to multimodal analysis*. London: Bloomsbury Academic.

McLuhan, M. 1987. *Understanding media: The extensions of man*. London: Ark.

McQuail, D. and Deuze, M. 2020. *McQuail's media and mass communication theory*. London: SAGE.

Mitchell, W.J. 2005. There are no visual media. *Journal of Visual Culture*, 4(2), pp. 257–266.

Mitchell, W.J.T. and Hansen, M.B.N. 2010. *Critical terms for media studies*. Chicago: The University of Chicago Press.

O'Halloran, K.L. and Smith, B.A. 2011. *Multimodal studies: Exploring issues and domains*. New York: Routledge.

Parikka, J. 2012. *What is media archaeology?* Cambridge: Polity.

Rajewsky, I.O. 2002. *Intermedialität*. Tübingen: Francke.

Rippl, G. 2015. *Handbook of intermediality literature – image – sound – music*. Berlin: de Gruyter.
Rust, S., Monani, S. and Cubitt, S. 2016. *Ecomedia: Key issues*. Abingdon: Routledge.
Salmose, N. and Elleström, L. 2020. *Transmediations: Communication across media borders*. New York: Routledge.
Wolf, W. 1999. *The musicalization of fiction: A study in the theory and history of intermediality*. Amsterdam: Rodopi.

2 Media and modalities – Film

Signe Kjær Jensen and Niklas Salmose

When someone tells you about a film they have just seen, you would probably assume that the film in question is a film with sound that is based on recorded colour images of actors acting out a narrative, complete with synchronized dialogue, sound effects and music. The noun 'film' is ambiguous, however. The Merriam-Webster online dictionary provides eight different uses of the word – ranging from things such as food wrapping to the more relevant material of celluloid used for photographic imprints and film as a specific type of artistic object (Merriam-Webster 2020).

Film in the form of celluloid is defined as a technical device for storage and production: it forms a material basis for storing and displaying the basic media type of moving images that convey semiotic content (mostly narratives) to people. Up until the twenty-first century, when digital film became dominant, movies were produced as imprints on different types of thin strips or plates, which could then be run through a projector to be shown on a big screen. The technical medium of display would be the screen (or display) and loudspeakers: flat surfaces that display the moving images and loudspeakers that produce sound waves (more about the development of technical media of film in Box 2.1). 'Film' also refers to the qualified media type of film art or cinema. The term cinema can refer to a movie theatre, the industry of art and entertainment cinema, and the art of film (cinematography); in this chapter, 'cinema' will primarily refer to film as an art form. These terminological overlaps and ambiguities stem from the interaction of the material, technological, contextual and conventional aspects of the different media types called film, aspects we will map out in this chapter.

In order for a media product to qualify as a film, it needs to live up to certain cultural conventions; besides having a number of unrelated pictures recorded in a coherent order, as in a slide show, there has to be a director and a script (or another sort of plan) behind the composition, and certain communicative and aesthetic parameters need to be considered. If we take the media product of *Casablanca* (1942), the storage medium is the material filmstrip that the movie was imprinted. This works in combination with the projector, the film screen and the loudspeakers to display or realize the film. The basic media types of moving images integrated with sound make us perceive a coherent narrative.

DOI: 10.4324/9781003174288-3

This narrative complies with the conventions of a qualified media type of a Hollywood film of the 1940s.

In this chapter, we will discuss what we actually mean when we say 'film' and how different types of film can be approached using the intermedial perspective presented in this book. We take our point of departure from the cinematic norm, that is, narrative mainstream film, but we will also include, when relevant, examples from artistic or experimental films that play with this norm.

> **Box 2.1 Overview of the development of technical media for displaying film**
>
> Throughout the history of film, different technical media have been developed that has altered the quality of both sounds and images and the possibilities for what content can be displayed. The following is a highly selective historical overview of technical media largely derived from Wells (2002), Enticknap (2005) and Kerins (2010).
>
> The magic lantern (seventeenth century–mid-twentieth century) was a technique in which light was projected through glass plates with paintings or photographs on them. The slides were changed manually or by way of simple mechanics operated by the showman, who sometimes spoke or sang (see Kember 2019).
>
> A phenakistiscope, and a zoetrope, (1833–late 1880s) was used to make successive paintings, made on a disc or inside a drum, spin around, creating the illusion of the paintings moving.
>
> The kinetophone (ca. 1895–early 1900s) moved a strip of film mechanically over a light source in a big box (a kinetoscope) with a peephole and combined this with a phonograph. It was the first machine to display synchronized images with sound.
>
> During the silent film era (1895–late 1920s), the first cinematic film was *La Sortie de l'usine Lumière à Lyon* (Lumière 1995). The film was screened using a silent black and white projection system. Later silent films were typically accompanied by live music.
>
> 'Talkies' (late 1920s–) had synchronized sound (1927–), as in the first American feature film with synchronized sound, *The Jazz Singer* (1927).
>
> Kodak colour film (1935–) modernized colour film with the invention of Kodachrome. In 1937, *Snow White* is released as the first American, fully animated feature film, using both colour and synchronized sound.
>
> Dolby Stereo sound (1976–) introduced four channels of sound and speakers around the room. This replaced mono sound, where one to three speakers in front of the audiences would play the same sound. The system was popularized after the release of *Star Wars* (1977).
>
> In the digital era (1990–), Dolby Digital sound was introduced and *Batman Returns* (1992) was the first film to be screened with Dolby Digital sound.
>
> *Toy Story* (1995) became the first completely computer-animated feature film.

> The first film to be screened using digital film was *Star Wars Episode I: The Phantom Menace* (1999).
> The 3D technique has been in use since the 1950s but had a technical breakthrough with *Avatar* (2009).
> This digital revolution has furthermore significantly changed how we view film, from traditional cinema, television and VHS moving to DVD, Blu-ray and streaming services on TV, computers, mobile phones and home theatres.

Film as an integrated medium

Contemporary film is often considered to be an art form that combines images and a soundtrack or, in intermedial terms, a qualified medium combining the basic media of moving images with several auditory basic media types. In the *material* modality, we interact with moving images on screens and with sound from loudspeakers in theatres and living rooms. This provides a simultaneous audiovisual experience in the *sensorial* modality. In the production process, however, this audiovisual experience is not necessarily produced simultaneously but is a complex combination of two different types of recording technologies: cameras and microphones. And sound is not just sound. When we consider the use of sound in film, we can differentiate between different auditory basic media types: *auditory text*, which provides the resource for monologue and dialogue; non-verbal *sound*, making up the sound effects; and *organized sound* used for music. In fact, moving images, film dialogue, sound effects and film music are highly constructed and conventionalized uses of the resources provided by the basic media of images and different types of sound, uses which work in accordance with aesthetic and communicative conventions of film genres.

To take an example, in the sensorial modality, sound effects are perceived as the 'natural' sound of the objects and bodies shown on screen, and they might, therefore, at first appear to be a basic medium that can be defined by its modalities alone. But in film production, sound effects are *produced* (and not simply *recorded*) separately. The sound of a gunshot, or the metallic sound of a sword drawn from its sheath, depend on aesthetic and communicational conventions (see Theme Ament (2014) and Chapter 9). Even when we compare film music with the qualified medium of music and dialogue with everyday speech, both film music and dialogue have been bent and tailored for filmic needs. In a similar fashion, moving images only become 'film' when they adhere to a number of conventions concerning how to construct an image sequence in terms of lighting, camera perspective and editing. In other words, the closer we look at the use of basic media types of image and sound, the less 'basic' they appear. In the specific context of film, moving images, sound effects, dialogue and film music organize the basic media types of image and sound according to different functions and conventions to the extent that they could even be perceived as qualified submedia.

It is clear that a film is not just a simple combination of sound and images. From a production perspective, film is a complex combination of images with multiple types of produced sound. From a *reception* perspective, however, it makes more sense to talk about an *integration*, rather than a combination, where all of the media types work *together* to create a specific storyworld and an audiovisual narrative (see Chapter 7 for more discussion of combination and integration). The moving images never tell the whole story alone but do so in integration with the auditory media. If, for example, you were to remove all the music from a media product such as the Hitchcock movie *Psycho* (1960), it might still be a film, but it would be a radically different film, perhaps not even classified as horror anymore.

Removing the sound of voices from a film would leave it with a ghostly feel because the actors' lips would move without making any sound. In fact, sound has always been part of the film experience, ever since modern cinema was invented at the beginning of the twentieth century. In silent film, the sound and moving images were combined differently and were less integrated during production, but 'silent' film actually made use of music by having a pianist, orchestra or playback device in the cinema (see, for example, Kalinak 2010), and dialogue was represented by intertitles. Sound could be further implied through indexical relations of characters reacting to sound in the storyworld, which was inaudible to audiences, as in Victor Sjöström's *Körkarlen* (1921), where the main character clearly hears the bells that are visible in the image.

Thus, even though auditory media types and moving images are realized in separate technical media of display, the media types are perceived together and become integrated into our experience of the film. None of the media types of film has an autonomous meaning that can simply be subtracted, and the media types of film are not just loosely combined; rather, all signifying elements are integrated into a holistic understanding of the storyworld.

Filmic media types in the four modalities

Even if the media types of film are deeply integrated, it can be necessary to keep them apart during parts of an analysis, and we will now explore in more detail how they individually draw on different modes in the four modalities. To account for the qualifying aspects of moving images and auditory media types, one needs to take the history of film and the development of filmic genres into consideration, which we will discuss in the last part of the chapter.

Moving images

In the material modality, we interact with a 'moving image' as a 2D projection, which is perceived via vision in the sensory modality. This projection can either be displayed using the technical media of a big screen, as in the cinema, or by using a small screen, such as a laptop or television screen. The type of technical media may not directly change the semiotic content of the moving images, but it still has a very important effect on the viewing experience, thus potentially affecting the interpretation of the semiotic content as well. It can be important to account for this if you are discussing questions concerning sociality and audience reception.

The material mode of the moving-image medium is constant across different technical display media, except in newer, more experimental and artistic types of film, such as the multiscreen film installation version of *Manifesto* (2015) by Julian Rosefeldt (b. 1965), which allows you to walk around among 13 different screens and to freely select the order in which to watch the scenes.[1] Whereas the material mode of the cinematic norm is a flat 2D surface, we will most often perceive the images as having depth nonetheless, thereby adding a virtual space in the spatiotemporal modality. Seen in this way, the innovation of 3D screenings in cinemas is just expanding the virtual space, which we already perceive in any recorded image as having a foreground and a background. Moving images are, of course, also characterized by being temporal, and they are, furthermore, sequentially fixed, as the images change over time in a predetermined and repeatable manner.[2]

The semiotic mode of the moving image is highly iconic[3] – images generally signify something because they look like things we already know – but they also potentially have indexical and symbolic meaning. In classic film theory, which is particularly associated with André Bazin (2018) and Siegfried Kracauer (1960), moving images were highlighted because of their indexical relationship to a pre-filmed reality; what was seen in the images had really happened, even if only in a film studio. However, it has been argued that this indexical reference does not represent reality in itself and that the image is actually highly constructed through camera perspective and post-production editing.

This 'constructedness' of the image has been taken to new levels in the digital era, when films more often than not combine photographic techniques with animation (often just referred to as special effects), for example, with dinosaurs walking around in *Jurassic Park* (1993) or even with something as 'ordinary' as the Wembley Stadium audience in *Bohemian Rhapsody* (2018). In the semiotic modality, the main difference between live-action and animated film lies in how dominant the indexical mode is and thus how we are made to conceive of a film in relation to an external reality. Even though we all know that the images in *Jurassic Park* are highly constructed and mixed with animation, we will still tend to experience the film as recorded, whereas a 'pure' animation film such as *The Good Dinosaur* (2015) doesn't have this indexical link to a pre-filmic reality. Thus, the indexical reference still constitutes an important semiotic mode in film, which has the potential to make depictions of 'reality' more credible.

Finally, the symbolic semiotic mode is present in all images, but it can be used to different degrees. In animation and some live-action films, colour can be used very symbolically, but even in a documentary film, we are likely to see objects or signs that have a symbolic value.

Auditory media types

All auditory media types in film share the material mode of sound waves and the sensory mode of hearing, and they are all temporal and sequentially fixed in the same way as moving images.

Sound tends to be described as non-spatial, but all auditory media can create a virtual space. In film, the space of the storyworld is constructed through the mixing of sound effects. When two characters meet, for example, we might hear the sound of cups being put down on the table right in front of the camera while simultaneously hearing footsteps and small talk further away, creating a space that is a café with a foreground and a background.

As with moving images, the semiotic modes of sound effects are mainly the iconic and indexical modes. When we hear the thump of the coffee cup being put down on the table, the sound is similar, and thus iconic, to the sound we hear when we put our own cup down. We also tend to hear this sound as an index of an actual cup. Sound effects are often created during post-production as Foley sounds or edited library sounds (see Chapter 8). Foley is sound that is recorded specifically for a particular film project in a special studio using props, and library sounds are collections of previously recorded sounds (often Foley created for other projects), which through digital manipulation can be made to fit the film in question. Sound effects are thus not necessarily recorded along with the images and are therefore rarely true indices, but they can still be perceived as though they were.

Music can make meaning via the indexical, iconic and symbolic modes. In the indexical mode, music gains meaning through relations to a particular time, location or social group, a meaning potential that is often used stereotypically in film. At the beginning of *Kung Fu Panda* (2008), for example, highly stereotyped music is used to set the story geographically by using instruments and harmonic schemes that are traditionally associated with East Asian music.

As an icon, music gains meaning via a perceived similarity with non-musical elements, such as the high-pitched 'screeching' violins in *Psycho* being similar to a woman's screams. Particularly for film music, this iconic function is most obvious when music is used as Mickey Mousing, which is a term for music that mimics something in the visuals, for example, when a falling object is joined with a falling melody. Mickey Mousing is so called because it was a standard technique used in short comic Hollywood cartoons of the 1920s–60s. Lastly, music is often considered to be the language of emotions and is regularly used in film to create atmosphere and as a background for understanding characters' feelings. People, at least in Western cultures, tend to hear music as emotionally coloured, and some will also feel that music can alter their own feelings. In this way, music can be used to control the emotional impact of a scene by relying on the conventions of film scoring, thereby highlighting the symbolic mode of music. The indexical, iconic and symbolic modes will most often be present at the same time in film music and can't always be easily separated. Accounting for the semiotic mode of music, just like with all other media is thus a highly analytical and interpretative praxis (see Chapter 4).

Dialogue mostly depends on the symbolic mode of language. We discuss the modalities of text and auditory text in Chapter 3.

Qualifying aspects of cinematic film

Operational qualifying aspects: Different communicative tasks of cinema

Film is an integrated medium but also a qualified medium. Film qualifications can be technical, ideological, aesthetic, political, societal and/or commercial and are referred to as contextual qualifying aspects. Operational qualifying aspects construct 'media types on the ground of claimed or expected communicative tasks' (Elleström 2021, p. 61). In film, these latter functions are entertainment and art (cinema) and commercial, educational, informative, didactic, medical and scientific functions. As we pointed out in the introduction to this chapter, 'film' in everyday speech is most often taken to refer to the qualified medium of cinematic film, but as can be seen from this short list, several other filmic qualified media exist. An educational film is thus based on the same combination of filmic media types as the cinematic film but diverges in its qualifying aspects. While we think it is important to be aware of this diversification of filmic media, we will, in this chapter, continue to focus on the qualified medium of film as art and entertainment, and where nothing else is specified, the term 'film' in the rest of this chapter should be taken to imply the qualified medium of cinematic film. Whether to make a distinction between 'film as entertainment' and 'film as art' is a topic for discussion, but as these qualifying aspects are so thoroughly entangled and the boundary is blurred, we prefer to subsume both categories into cinematic film.

The technical medium of film in relation to its qualifying aspects

All filmic technical media are based on the capacity of the human eye to perceive motion through a series of slightly altered images appearing in rapid succession, which is called 'the persistence of vision'. The setting and experience of seeing these images in succession varies, though, depending on the technical media used to display these images, as different technical media have limitations on mediating certain modes and different opportunities to do so. Hence, the kinetoscope (a technical medium of display; see Box 2.1) did not manage to capture the mode of sound in the sensorial modality of cinema as later technical media constellations did. The subsequent development of sound through Dolby Stereo, Dolby 5.1 Surround Sound and Dolby Digital clearly affected the immersive aspects of cinematic experiences, as did the invention of widescreen formats, such as cinemascope (1953), various 70mm formats and IMAX (1970) and 3D formats, especially in the twenty-first century. And the sensorial modality of cinema was effectively enhanced by the introduction of colour film, especially with the introduction of three-strip Technicolor in 1932, which allowed for more advanced and realistic use of colour than previous motion picture colour techniques. Attempts at creating cinema that also incorporated the sensorial mode of smell, such as Odorama in the early 1980s, which involved scratching sniff cards, have been unsuccessful. Hence, the technical developments of cinema have also played a significant role in qualifying what constitutes 'cinema' today: the success story, for example, of the first full-length feature film in colour, the animated *Snow White and the Seven Dwarfs* (1937), altered the genre of animated film and also influenced how colour was used for fantastic elements for a long time in live-action film. The introduction of CGI (computer-generated images) has both changed the nature of animated film and the potential of live-action film more generally, especially in the science fiction genre: Steven Spielberg, for example, used CGI to create the effect of live dinosaurs in *Jurassic Park* (1993), as mentioned in our discussion of the semiotic mode of moving images.

As the case of CGI technology demonstrates, the limitations on, and potential of, a particular technical medium influence its content. For instance, the earliest films produced using a zoetrope and those made by the pioneer Edward Muybridge (1830–1904) and his zoopraxiscope were very short and repetitive and were not accompanied by any sound at all; therefore, they could not tell a complete story. Although many of these short films were entertaining, they were not narrative and did not lend themselves to dialogue or character and plot development. In fact, early films were mostly produced for educational or scientific purposes, which was why the Lumière brothers developed film in the first place. Hence, the early films were jointly shaped by the limitations of the technical medium, the social context and the practical needs of the inventors of film. Later, film developed further as an art form with each technological innovation, as discussed earlier.

Although the technical advancements in cinema affect the modalities of cinema, the basic structure of these modalities remains fairly intact throughout different cinematic genres even if the emphasis might change. In the semiotic modality, a Hollywood blockbuster and an abstract art video might differ in terms of narrative structure and iconicity (see endnote 4). In the sensorial modality, the Hollywood film would emphasize spectacular sense data (a conventional music score, epic visualizations, widescreen format, and so on). In the spatiotemporal modality, the cognitive output would be different in a 2D film compared with a 3D one. Thus, the progress of technology changes the contexts and practices of dissemination, from Nickelodeons (that offered the first indoor screenings of films in the US for the price of one nickel) to internet streaming, and this, in turn, affects what comes to be considered 'quality' cinema. In summary, the aesthetic, communicative and social conventions that can be stabilized, and which we will delve into next, are also related to the development of technical media.

Cinema and its historical, social and institutional qualifiers

Cinema's historical development also affects the qualifying aspects of film. Cinema developed contextually from the filmic experiments carried out in France and in Brighton, England, in the dying days of the nineteenth century, to the founding works of D.W. Griffith (1875–1948) and Georges Méliès (1861–1938). During these years, film became both a transformed version of highbrow art forms (e.g. theatre, literature, opera) and later a lowbrow entertainment made possible by the mass production of film. However, this transition (which happened during a period of rapid technical development of the medium) also affected the making of films in terms of mise en scène (stage design and arrangement of actors), framing, continuity editing, acting, lighting, the use of a moving camera and a variety of focal lengths.

The earliest narrative films were accused of being 'theatrical' before a standardization of narrative cinema was established through D.W. Griffith's *The Birth of a Nation* (1915) and *Intolerance* (1916). On the other hand, films like those of French magician-turned-film-maker Georges Méliès (*A Trip to the Moon*, 1902) developed in parallel but leaned towards another tradition that is fantastic, surreal, abstract and anti-realist.

In the adolescence of global cinema (1920s), there was a constant debate about the main purpose of the basic and technical media of film, which is related to how film as a medium is qualified. In Germany, film was influenced by expressionist literature, art and theatre, in France by surrealism and the avant-garde, in the Soviet Union by revolutionary politics and psychological experiments, in Scandinavia by literature and notions and representations of nature, and in the US by its commercialization and the myths of the nation (Western genre films).[4]

These discourses are further complicated by some seminal works regarding film theory published before the 1960s, such as Sergei Eisenstein's (1949) essays on film form, later collected in *Film Form: Essays in Film Theory*, theories on film semiotics by Béla Balázs (1884–1949) and Siegfried Kracauer (1889–1966), and the neorealist manifesto 'Some ideas on the cinema' by Cesare Zavattini (1953). This manifesto influenced the works of French film critic André Bazin (2018), a strong advocate for a kind of realistic cinema in which the abolishment of non-diegetic sound and the long take were favoured. Bazin was also, along with Alexandre Astruc (1948), mostly responsible for theorizing that film-makers are auteurs. They believed that a director should be considered to be analogous to a writer and someone who realizes their vision directly in the film medium. The film director as an auteur had a profound impact on all aspects of film-making, including pre- and post-production and screenplays. This notion increased the status of the director as an individual artist, and it also altered the aesthetics of film radically, creating a kind of cinema that was very different to that which existed in Hollywood.

Besides its immediate technical- and history-based aspects, film as a qualified media type has also developed in close proximity to different institutions and social contexts: industrial, political and historical contexts, academic disciplines, corporations and the entertainment industry. To be more specific, within these institutions, we can observe, in relation to film, film criticism, film theory, film education and various tone-setting production organs (such as the Swedish Film Institute or Hollywood). These qualifications are therefore proximate to and co-dependent on the social and political contexts surrounding them. In reality, though, the qualifying aspects are also often interconnected with the operational aspects (expected communicative outcomes). Consider, for example, the concept of body genres in film (horror, melodrama and porn), developed by Linda Williams (1991). The operational qualities found in these genres are linked to how they affect and communicate with the body (fear, sadness, sexual arousal), but at the same time, they are contextually developed through their interrelationship with societal developments such as liberated laws and censorship, politics and gender-related debates.

The qualifying aspects of cinema: Genre

The difference between auteur cinema and Hollywood films is one of categorizations. One way to understand cinema as a qualified medium is to regard it through genre conventions, with each genre as one part of a huge tree diagram illustrating the chronological history of the development of cinema in terms of technical and storytelling conventions. This would include almost all forms of artistic practices within film from the 1910s. Film genres (the French term 'genre' means 'kind', 'category' or 'type') are various forms or identifiable types, categories, classifications or groups of films. Genre categorization can be sorted according to the setting (modern time/historical time, urban/rural, the future, sport, high school), characterization (the use of stock characters and certain stereotypes), subject matter (storyline, themes, plot and structure), audience response (porn, melodrama, horror, art-house cinema), technical aspects (silent cinema, 3D cinema, cinemascope, epic) and an endless hybridization of these categories. We could thus classify cinema as Hollywood film, European art cinema, independent cinema, avant-garde cinema and so on. We may make further qualifications, such as dividing art-house cinema into even more genres, such as horror, road movies or drama. Hence, a horror movie within the art-house genre, such as films by Italian director Dario Argento, would be different from horror films within the Hollywood system, such as *The Lodge* (2020) or *Midsommar* (2019).

As noted in the preceding historical survey, the qualified medium of cinematic film has split into a variety of qualifying and operational subcategories, or genres, with names that stress either their contextual aspects (political cinema, free cinema, Swedish Golden Age, auteur film, Hollywood film, propaganda film) or their operational aspects (pornographic film, expressionist film, montage film, narrative film, art film). As noted earlier, it is hard to distinguish between qualifying and operational aspects: Hollywood film, for example, is not only a categorization of films made in and around Los Angeles, but also of films that are made according to the production standards and storytelling practices of Hollywood mainstream film. When we speak of Hollywood film today, it's not the geographical origin that matters, but rather, the film's aesthetic and narrative qualities; a Swedish film like Mikael Håfström's *Quick* (2019) is often referred to as a Hollywood film because it looks, sounds and tells its story like American mainstream cinema.

38 *Signe Kjær Jensen and Niklas Salmose*

Qualifying aspects of cinema are also useful when we categorize cinema into specific genres: science fiction, action film, drama, horror, splatter films, film noir, soft porn, comedy and so on. What intermediality as a methodology offers here is a more precise analysis of categories, subcategories and genres of film. Although we are always referring to the same four modalities when we discuss film, we can distinguish between different emphases (or even a lack) on certain modes within these modalities, or we may discuss the technical medium involved, or, again, we can refer to how a category is related to particular contexts and define the poetics of its category. All these aspects relate to each other in a complicated web of communication. Defining film as a medium thus allows us to understand its influence as it comes from and acts on other media, such as gaming, radio, music, amusement parks and cinematic novels.

Cinema as an intermedial phenomenon is more complex than the everyday use of the term suggests. The integration of moving images and different auditory media types is qualified through technical and historical factors and a variety of contextual factors and framed by the different conventions of different genres.

Table 2.1 Media and modalities – Film

Media types and modalities	Description
Technical media of display	Screens and loudspeakers **Storage media**: celluloid, VHS, digital **Production process**: basic media types produced partly independently and put together in post-production **Dissemination context**: movie theatres, VHS/DVD via television, DVD/streaming via computers
Basic media types	(Moving) image, auditory text (dialogue), non-verbal sound (sound effects), organised sound (film music)
Qualified media type	**Contextual**: genres; Hollywood film, art film, art video **Operational**: entertainment and art (cinema) and commercial, educational, informative, didactic, medical and scientific functions
Material modality	Flat surfaces and sound waves, light projection, (electronic) screens
Sensorial modality	**Perception**: visual, auditory **Cognition**: implied tactility
Spatiotemporal modality	**Material**: fixed sequentiality of images and audio **Sensorial**: virtual space of images, virtual space created by sound effects and music **Semiotic**: virtual time and space of storyworld
Semiotic modality	**Moving images**: dominantly iconic and indexical (to a lesser degree symbolic, unless it is an art film) **Auditory text**: dominantly symbolic (indexical, e.g. in relation to characters' emotions and social identity) **Sound effects**: iconic and indexical **Music**: iconic, indexical and symbolic

Notes

1 The film also exists in a feature film version.
2 But note that experiments with interactive film, such as *Black Mirror: Bandersnatch* (2018), exist, which break with this convention.
3 Once again, exceptions do exist, primarily when we look to highly abstract and experimental cinema. A lot of experimental animation, such as Viking Eggeling's *Symphonie Diagonale* (1924) and McLaren's *Begone Dull Care* (1949), largely forgo the representative power of the iconic modality in favour of a style that is much closer to that of the expressionist painters. The focus here is on colours, shapes and movement and on visual synchronization with music (animation which aims to illustrate music is also referred to as *visual music*). These types of film still have iconic qualities, of course, but when the visuals are abstract rather than representative, the dominance of the iconic mode tends to be lowered and the symbolic dominance heightened.
4 For more reading on this parallel development, see Bordwell and Thompson (2008).

Further reading

Balázs, B. 1952. *Theory of the film*. London: Denis Dobson.
Bordwell, D. and Thompson, K. 2008. *Film art: An introduction*. New York: McGraw-Hill.
Bordwell, D. and Thompson, K. 2020. *Film history: An introduction*. New York: McGraw-Hill.
Bruhn, J. and Gjelsvik, A. 2018. *Cinema between media: An intermediality approach*. Edinburgh: Edinburgh University Press.
Buhler, J. 2018. *Theories of the soundtrack*. Oxford: Oxford University Press.
Eisenstein, S. and Leyda, J. 1949. *Film form: Essays in film theory*. New York: Harcourt, Brace.
Stam, R. 2000. *Film theory: An introduction*. Malden, MA: Blackwell.

References

Astruc, A. 1948. Du stylo à la caméra et de la caméra au stylo. *L'Écran française*, 30 March.
Bazin, A. 2018. *André Bazin: Selected writings 1943–1958*. T. Barnard (Trans.). Montreal: Caboose.
Bordwell, D. and Thompson, K. 2008. *Film art: An introduction*. New York: McGraw-Hill.
Eisenstein, S. and Leyda, J. 1949. *Film form: Essays in film theory*. New York: Harcourt, Brace.
Elleström, L. 2021. The modalities of media II: An expanded model for understanding intermedial relations. In L. Elleström, ed. *Beyond media borders, volume 1: Intermedial relations among multimodal media* (pp. 3–91). London: Palgrave.
Enticknap, L.D.G. 2005. *Moving image technology: From zoetrope to digital*. New York: Wallflower.
Kalinak, K.M. 2010. *Film music: A very short introduction*. Oxford: Oxford University Press.
Kember, J. 2019. The magic lantern: open medium. *Early Popular Visual Culture*, 17(1), pp. 1–8. doi:10.1080/17460654.2019.1640605
Kerins, M. 2010. *Beyond Dolby (stereo): Cinema in the digital sound age*. Bloomington: Indiana University Press.

Kracauer, S. 1960. *Theory of film: The redemption of physical reality*. New York: Oxford University Press.
Merriam-Webster. 2020. https://www.merriam-webster.com/dictionary/film?src=search-dict-box [Accessed 21 December 2020].
Theme Ament, V. 2014. *The Foley grail: The art of performing sound for film, games, and animation*. Oxford: Taylor & Francis Group.
Wells, P. 2002. *Animation: genre and authorship*. New York: Wallflower.
Williams, L. 1991. Film bodies: Gender, genre, and excess. *Film Quarterly*, 44(4), pp. 2–13.
Wood, M. 2012. *Film: A very short introduction*. Oxford: Oxford University Press.
Zavattini, C. 1953. Some ideas on the cinema. *Sight and Sound*, 23(2), pp. 64–69.

Films referenced

A Trip to the Moon [*Le voyage dans la lune*]. 1902. Directed by Georges Méliès. France: Star-Film.
Avatar. 2009. Directed by James Cameron. USA: Twentieth Century Fox, Dune Entertainment and Lightstorm Entertainment.
Batman Returns. 1992. Directed by Tim Burton. USA; UK: Warner Bros and PolyGram Pictures.
Begone Dull Care. 1949. Directed by Evelyn Lambart and Norman McLaren. Canada: National Film Board of Canada (NFB).
Black Mirror: Bandersnatch. 2018. Directed by David Slade. USA: Netflix.
Bohemian Rhapsody. 2018. Directed by Bryan Singer. UK; USA: Twentieth Century Fox, Regency Enterprise and GK Films.
Casablanca. 1942. Directed by Michael Curtiz. USA: Warner Bros.
Intolerance. 1916 Directed by D.W. Griffith. USA: Triangle Film Corporation and Wark Producing Corporation.
Jurassic Park. 1993. Directed by Steven Spielberg. USA: Universal Pictures and Amblin Entertainment.
Körkarlen. 1921. Directed by Victor Sjöström. Sweden: Svensk Filmindustri.
Kung Fu Panda. 2008. Directed by Mark Osborne and John Stevenson. USA: DreamWorks Animation and Dragon Warrior Media.
Manifesto. 2015. [multiscreen film installation] Directed by Julian Rosefeldt. Australia and Germany.
Midsommar. 2019. Directed by Ari Aster. USA; Sweden: Square Peg and B-Reel Films.
Psycho. 1960. Directed by Alfred Hitchcock. USA: Shamley Productions.
Snow White. 1937. Directed by David Hand. USA: Walt Disney Productions.
Sortie de l'usine Lumière de Lyon. 1895. [short film] Directed by Louis Lumière. France: Lumière.
Star Wars. 1977. Directed by George Lucas. USA: Lucasfilm and Twentieth Century Fox.
Star Wars Episode I: The Phantom Menace. 1999. Directed by George Lucas. USA: Lucasfilm.
Symphonie Diagonale. 1924. [short animated film] Directed by Viking Eggeling. Germany.
The Birth of a Nation. 1915. Directed by D.W. Griffith. USA: David W. Griffith Corp. and Epoch Producing Corporation.
The Good Dinosaur. 2015. Directed by Peter Sohn. USA: Pixar Animation Studios and Walt Disney Pictures.

The Jazz Singer. 1927. Directed by Alan Crosland. USA: Warner Bros.
The Lodge. 2020. Directed by Veronika Franz and Severin Fiala. USA: Hammer Films.
Toy Story. 1995. Directed by John Lasseter. USA: Pixar Animation Studios and Walt Disney Pictures.
Quick. 2019. Directed by Mikael Håfström. Sweden: Brain Academy AB.

3 Media and modalities – Literature

Pedro Atã and Beate Schirrmacher

When we think of literature, we most commonly think of books filled with text, and for a very long time literature has been nearly synonymous with written texts and books, but not with every text in every book. We might think of literature as being novels, short stories or poems. When we speak of literature, we think about text written in a certain way that makes us perceive a strong connection between form and content. What we perceive as literature depends on place and time and the technical devices and media types we have access to.

In this chapter, we will discuss how our understanding of narratives and the experiences communicated in novels, poems, essays and folk tales is formed and shaped by the material objects we interact with and how the basic media types of speech, text and images are integrated differently according to the conventions of different qualified media types. We can approach the question of the mediality of literature from different directions. Different material technologies that are used for writing and reading define and transform literature. This is the technical media of display dimension. We will consider the basic traits and activities that define literature, such as the reading and writing of text and how text and images can be integrated. This is the basic media aspect. Finally, we will also consider how social and cultural settings, norms and institutions construct notions of what is and what is not (considered to be) literature. This is the aspect that concerns literature as a qualified medium. All three aspects are subject to more change and variation than the prototypical image of a shelf filled with books may suggest. Our interaction with them in the four modalities differs depending on whether we read the text of a printed novel, listen to the auditory text of an audiobook, read and decode the graphic narration of comics or listen to a storyteller.

Technical media of display: How to organize flat surfaces

Although the books on a bookshelf are just part of a longer story of writing and reading, the qualified medium of literature is very intimately connected with the book as its technical medium of display. Scrolls, wax and clay tablets and surfaces of stone, as well as books, have in the past provided relatively flat and smooth surfaces that could be marked and used to store and give access to the

DOI: 10.4324/9781003174288-4

basic media type of the written words of texts. Books are a way of organizing larger quantities of flat surfaces, often thin sheets of parchment or paper. But when text could only be copied by hand, the storage and dissemination of text was laborious and expensive. Handwritten books were accessible to a relatively small group of readers and writers, and selected information was written down in order to establish corpora of legal or religious texts; narratives and songs were stored, too, but were meant to be read or performed to an audience. The fact that parchment, sheets made out of animal hide, was not always available in medieval Europe also restricted the information that could be stored and written down. Paper, which had been produced for a long time in China, reached Europe gradually during the Middle Ages; this, along with the technology of the printing press and with movable metal type, changed the reproduction and dissemination of texts. Any new text could be comparatively rapidly set and easily reproduced. The printing press turned books and booklets and single-sheet brochures or chapbooks into mass products: written texts were not for storage only (see Krauß et al. (2020) and Kwakkel (2018)).

Nowadays we not only use sheets of paper but also the screens of electronic media. Literary texts that for a long time have mainly been published in the form of printed books are now frequently published as e-books or audiobooks. The fact that we see these published forms as 'books', though neither of these digital publishing forms uses books as the technical medium of display, is just one of the many examples of how new technical media not only transmediate what is perceived as content but also represent functional aspects of older media types. E-books represent functional aspects of material books in order to achieve a better orientation and navigation in the text.

When we speak of an e-book, we are referring to a specific electronic publishing format for digital text. An e-book is often seen as the digital version of a printed book, which is often correct, for example, when we think about PDF documents, which lock the electronic text into a particular dimension and layout. Other digital text formats, such as e-publications, are not tied to a specific layout but adapt to the scale of the screen of a designated e-reader or any computer or smartphone screen. E-book formats enable new ways of interaction with the text. The fact that digital files are easily searchable is a feature that is specifically appreciated in professional interaction with all kinds of texts. But even when reading fiction, searching the text for keywords can provide new connections between different parts of the book, leading to possible new ways of interacting with a literary narrative and thereby changing the dynamics between memory and text in the reading process (Hall 2013).

The e-book as a publishing format was first developed at the same time as digital media and portable screens. Audiobooks, the recorded reading of a written text, have been distributed via all kinds of audio-storage media such as reel-to-reel tapes, records, cassettes and CDs (Rubery 2011). However, it was the digital formats for compression, such as MP3 files, in combination with portable audio-players and the possibility of internet streaming audio files that have made audiobooks widely and more conveniently accessible. As a consequence, an increasing proportion of the audience of a novel are listeners to instead of readers of literature. Digital and electronic technical media of display do not only update older media types. They provide the basis for a kind of literature that involves digital technology to tell stories and express experiences as well and involves the reader in interactive reading experiences that can be said to be 'born digital' (Hayles 2008).

When we read text, on screens, paper sheets, or stone, we are primarily interacting with a two-dimensional surface and pay less attention to material depth. However, the material aspects of the technical media influence how much text can be stored and moved across temporal and spatial distances. Stone provides storage across time but is less easily transported. Thus, it makes sense that the writing on stone often indicates places of interest or places to remember. It tells stories for different purposes than stories noted on portable surfaces, like the pages of a book. With computers and smartphones, information and even whole libraries of books can be accessed from anywhere.

Another characteristic of how we think about literature and writing is whether we consider reading and writing to be an individual or a collaborative activity. Compared with cinema, for example, writing a poem or a personal essay describing a childhood memory doesn't require a production crew with different kinds of technical skills – this is what we assume, at least. However, children's books and the graphic narration of comics often are the result of teamwork. Digital poetry, for instance, stems from collaborations between writers and programmers. The technical medium of the book requires dedicated technical expertise. There is in fact a whole production crew at a publishing house that turns a manuscript into a published book. Once a manuscript is accepted, the editing process may involve not only proofreading to check the spelling and grammar but also structural changes, choices involving aspects such as the wording of the title, decisions about its visual appearance that concern things like typography and page and cover design, and marketing strategies. Even in the case of self-publishing, which has become much more common on the internet and with easily available software, authors still depend on several other professionals such as designers, marketers, media content producers, retailers and distributors, as well as, of course, the readers – including reviewers, content generators and online communities, which spread the word about new publications (Squires and Ray Murray 2013).

Even if literary works are often discussed as if they are detached from decisions concerning which working material and production style to use, technical possibilities are also important for literature and are not just relevant for cinema or for visual arts. We may not pay very much attention to how typography and page layout influence our meaning-making process (although we might perceive a difference between a first edition and a cheap, everyday edition). But layout and typography always play a certain role in literature, and perhaps in particular in poetry, comics and graphic novels, and children's books.

We often tend to think of writing as something that is not really affected by the *technology* of writing. However, the importance of technical media of display goes beyond 'displaying'. For instance, all kinds of material interfaces that display text mediate between writer and text as well as between writer and reader. Material devices like computers, typewriters and various writing tools shape and organize the role of readers and writers. Interfaces like screens and pages provide the basis for both reading and writing, and for switching between them. Thus, the writer always is the first reader of her text as well as the reader of multiple previous texts. This experience is explored and staged in many postmodern novels. Seen from this perspective, today's digital interfaces only draw our attention to the performative aspect of material interfaces in general, that not only dsiply but engage in interaction (Drucker 2013).

However, digital media change the way we write and think about writing. The rewriting and reworking of a manuscript written by hand or on a typewriter is a different process from editing a digital text using 'delete', 'copy' and 'paste'. Of course, you can consciously work with different drafts using the computer, but digital writing does not force you to rewrite each draft from beginning to end to the same extent as previous writing techniques. The fact that you can easily edit digital words also affects their authority. Text is no longer carved into stone and no longer unchangeable when printed; it has become much more flexible and changeable.

Basic media types: Text, speech, images

The printed book is closely connected to our idea of literature, and the relation is so conventionalized that it has become 'invisible' for us. The printed book has long been central for the whole network of organizing, storing and disseminating information. The basic media type of text has been used even longer to both store and transfer thoughts, memories, narratives and experiences on flat surfaces. Until the emergence of auditory and audiovisual recording techniques, writing as a notational system to record the transitory sound waves of speech was for a long time the main option to store and disseminate information across time and space (Kittler 1999). The written words of a text can no longer rely on a multimodal context of face-to-face communication, and therefore we use language differently when writing and speaking. On pages and screens, the written words of a text are integrated into other multimodal contexts on pages and interact, for instance, with images, and the spatial information of layout.

In audiobooks, however, the basic media type of text is not perceived visually on a page but acoustically via electronic sound waves. This difference changes the affordances of the reading experience, for example, listening to an audiobook enables reading while moving through space, allow for auditory forms of immersion, and benefits readers who like to learn by listening (see Have and Stougaard Pedersen (2016) and Engberg et al. (2021)). In spite of the changes in the material and sensorial modality, the basic medium of audiobooks is still text (not speech): the voice actor reads a text that has been written. We can therefore speak of auditory text.

Listening to the auditory text of an audiobook is a different experience from listening to a skilled storyteller. Before writing and reading were widespread competences, narratives were communicated via the basic media type of speech, performed in front of an audience and stored in human memory. Using spoken words to share stories and experiences, the technical media of display are the body and voice of the performer. In the embodied context of speech, the words interact with, for instance, intonation, rhythm and gestures. Professional performers can store long speeches, poems and narratives in their memory using different kinds of mnemotechnics. When using the basic media type of speech, the narratives, experiences and dramatic conflicts worthy of being passed on have to be structured in a way that suits human memory. Repetitive structures of rhythm (verse) and sound (rhyme) formulas help people to tell good stories and help listeners to be able to remember them. The verses of a poem or a song are always easier to remember as compared to paragraphs of prose (Ong 2002).

What do we do when we read text? In the *material modality*, we engage with a stable object. As printed text is stable on the page, we have to move our eyes and our head or adjust the position of the book as we read. All this physical action brings a muscular, embodied component to the act of reading. When we write and read digital texts, the text moves as well. Recent research has investigated whether this muscular action influences how people remember, recall and pay attention to written text (see Baron (2015) and Mangen (2016)). In the *sensorial modality*, we primarily perceive text visually. However, certain types of writing technologies, like carving or using individual pieces of metal type in a printing press, can be experienced via touch as well. The written language of Braille, which was designed for people who are blind or visually impaired, is based on this kind of tactile information. Even if the text on pages in a book is primarily experienced visually, sound either explicitly or cognitively plays an important part in reading. When we read, we utter sounds, either explicitly or quietly within our brain or body. Even the silent reading of words continues to trigger the auditory imagery of the sound of spoken words in what is called silent speech or subvocalization (Smith et al. 1992). Reading digital literature, on the other hand, may involve a multisensory reading experience that involves visually perceived text, auditory text, sounds, and moving images (Engberg et al. 2021)

Box 3.1 Embodied reading

The multisensory reading experience of digital literature draws attention to the fact that even reading a book engages more than our eyes and draws attention to the dimensions of embodiment. The pages of books and screens of e-books also involve different tactile and other sensorial impressions. In the material modality, we touch the book and feel the surfaces of the pages, hear the rustle and perceive the smell of an old (or new) book. Reading a printed book requires the physical action of flipping the pages.

> When reading an e-book on a touchscreen, the swiping imitates the flipping of paper pages. Or, in the case of literary apps, touch gestures of different kinds (panning, tapping, rotating, pinching, dragging and dropping) may be used to not only flip through metaphorical pages, but to navigate through text segments and through a variety of other media such as images, sounds, or moving images according to widely different interactive structures which may or may not resemble pages of linear texts.
>
> The printed book weighs something and takes up space. When we read a printed book, we notice how the progress of our reading transfers weight from our right hand to our left hand (in the West). The spatial dimensions of a printed book already provide temporal and organizational information. When we look at a novel of 900 pages, we infer from the spatial extensions the amount of time it will take to read it. E-books, and in fact all digital documents, therefore need other markers that will help us to orient our reading and navigate whether we are at the beginning, the middle or the end of the text.
>
> While we may perceive reading as a primarily visual activity, learning how to read highlights an activity that involves the body: we may trace lines with a finger or move our lips while reading aloud. Reading text also evokes haptic sensations through certain lip and tongue movements, which might have consequences for the spatial perception of certain sounds (Ramachandran and Hubbard 2001, p. 10). While the reading of a word thus closely connects us with the experience of its sound, other sensational feelings linked to smell, taste and touch are not immediately linked to the reading of words. Instead, these sensorial modalities are represented in the semiotic modality by words that represent smell, taste and touch. This process exploits our cross-modal capacities and resembles the sense of tactility that viewing a statue without touching it still evokes.

Although words are stable on printed pages, the reading of texts, specifically of prose, is perceived as more of a temporal event in the *spatiotemporal modality*. We read one word after the other in a fixed sequentiality. The reading directions differ with different alphabets, but almost every text has a fixed linear sequentiality. As readers, we are more or less in control of the temporal sequentiality of the text; we can read as fast or slow as we want to or can. We can choose to stop in the middle of a sentence or at the end of a chapter. Here, the sequentiality of text behaves differently from the temporality of the performance of film, music or theatre that is temporally fixed already in the material modality. The linear sequentiality of the text is not only present in our reading, however. Whenever we write something, we have to translate a multidimensional web of ideas into a linear stream of information. The syntax of languages allows them to nest hierarchical structures into sequential texts. The word 'text', which has the same root as 'textile', derives from the Latin *textere*, 'to weave', and points to this property of reading and writing as an interweaving line. Thus, whenever we meet words, we relate them to the context of other written words. This, in fact, is what is defined as 'intertextuality', one of the basic concepts of modern literary theory and cultural studies.

Literary works can also creatively experiment with or even break with the linear sequentiality of the text. Qualified media types such as poetry or comics exploit the more spatial relations and visual perception of text, the words and letters on a page, and the choices of layout and typography such as contrast, shapes, proportions, visual intervals and colour. An interesting example is concrete poetry, a neo-avant-garde literary movement which was started in the 1950s by the Brazilian poets Augusto de Campos (b. 1931), Haroldo de Campos (1929–2003) and Décio Pignatari (1927–2012), the Bolivian-Swiss poet Eugen Gomringer (b. 1925), and the Swedish artist Öyvind Fahlström (1929–76). Concrete poems can break away from textual syntax and instead adopt a two-dimensional syntax using the flatness of the page. Reading these poems can be similar to reading graphs and diagrams (such as Décio Pignatari's 1956 *Semi di Zucca*), and perceiving them visually can be similar to perceiving geometric abstract paintings (such as Augusto de Campos's 1972 *Viva Vaia*). Breaking away from syntax also changes how words convey meanings. Considering words in themselves sometimes makes them sound and appear strange. Some concrete poems create this effect – they merely suggest vague possibilities of association between the meaning of words, their appearance and their sound (such as Eugen Gomringer's 1953 'Untitled poem' ['*Silencio*']). They illustrate how the basic medium of text can in itself be a vast domain for creative exploration and not just a tool to convey structured thoughts and messages. Similar to how digital literature involves digital technology, code and algorithms, concrete poetry involves the materiality of the book, and the visual and auditory basic media types in the sensorial modality.

When reading text, we do not usually pay attention to all the aspects we have discussed above. We very seldom pay attention to the fact that we interact with words on paper (or screens) unless a specific text self-referentially draws attention to the existence of words on a page. Usually we cognitively interact with what they represent, namely the storyworlds, and characters with emotions and experiences. In the *semiotic modality*, written language is primarily symbolical, representing objects by means of conventions. When using words, both the writer and the reader primarily connect the words to their objects by habit. But literary language may also draw attention to the iconicity of words, which happens in different ways in poetry, in comics and in the representation of speech in dialogue. The choice of words can have onomatopoetic qualities. In written dialogue, the spelling of words can be in iconic relation to a specific pronunciation. Comics often highlight or create iconic relations between the sound and shape of words and their meanings: If you write a dialogue IN ALL CAPS to indicate that someone is shouting, the size of the letter forms an iconic relation to the loudness of the voice that the letters represent.

When we not only consider words, but text, indexical relations are important as well. Indices are crucial for the interweaving of a text. Many words in a text merely indicate an idea that has been presented previously. All kinds of pronouns, words such as 'they', 'it' and 'this', indexically point towards the noun they replace. Another kind of indexicality weaves together the text itself with the world around it, such as the signature of an author, the handwritten text of a manuscript, or the handwritten comments of a previous reader in the margins. They point to a presence of a person and the movement of her hand.

On the flat surface of the page, texts are often combined with images. Images on a cover of a book, illustrations and photographs in novels, travelogues or in artistic literary magazines are part of the reading experience even if they have not been chosen by the author of the text. Text and static images have a lot in common in the material and sensorial modalities: they appear on flat surfaces, are perceived visually and are primarily spatial in the material modality. They are most easily integrated when writing and drawing by hand, as seen in comics or in the illuminated letters of medieval manuscripts. In printed texts, the technology of printing decides how closely text and image can be combined. In qualified media types like children's literature and comics, images are not only illustrations for a text but an integrated part of a narrative that is told by the text and the images (see Nikolajeva and Scott (2001) and Kukkonen (2013)).

Although text and images integrate closely on the page, we engage with them differently in the spatiotemporal and semiotic modality. We understand images primarily as iconic and as representing their objects through similarity. Singular illustrations are not arranged in a temporal sequentiality like text – yet the panels of comic books are. The images in comics also illustrate how images are not only iconic but involve a high degree of convention. The conventions for expressing emotions such as anger, sadness and joy differ between Western and Asian comics, for instance (see also Chapter 8).

Qualifying aspects

Technical media influence qualified media types

The use of technical media and basic media types, whether we use text or speech, publish a printed book or share texts in social media, shapes our understanding of what kind of stories can be told and which kind of experiences and memories and feelings can be expressed. Therefore, when we say we have read a good book lately or discuss texts in a literary seminar, we refer to the technical and basic media types, but we appreciate and discuss narratives, thoughts, ideas and experiences that are, for instance, disseminated as books and that are constructed and expressed in the linearity of the text.

Earlier in history, when it was not as easy for most people to choose to read and write as it is today, narratives and experiences were shared via oral storytelling in the form of epics, folk tales, myths and legends. Some of them have been transcribed at some stage. The first works in any literary tradition tend to be epic poems that presumably have long been part of an oral tradition before they were written down, such as the epic of *Gilgamesh* (ca. 2100 BC) or the *Mahābhārata* from Ancient India (the oldest parts are from 400 BC). And even after they were written down, these poems were composed to be shared, sung and performed; not only the words but the orality and the gestures of the storyteller were important. The co-presence of the storyteller and the audience allowed for interaction, feedback and improvisation (Ong 2002). These aspects are easily forgotten if you read transcriptions of oral storytelling, such as the folk tales that were collected in Europe during the nineteenth century, and compare them with the eloquence and style of written narrative prose. And in fact the term oral literature is self-contradictory, as the very term literature refers to the use of *letters*. The term 'orature', coined by the Ugandan linguist Pio Zirimu (d. 1977) to refer to the African non-written tradition, captures the mediality aspects better (Thiong'o 1998).

The sharing of spoken narratives does not only belong to the past. Storytelling is a fundamental human activity that not only engages literary scholars but also anthropologists, psychologists, linguists and historians (Anderson 2010). In informal contexts, we tell stories about our lives, crack jokes and share urban legends. Telling stories and appealing lyrically to an audience is something that people do in stand-up comedy shows and spoken poetry, or during professional storytelling. These are all contemporary qualified media types of oral traditions with its own social contexts, conventions, festivals and prizes.

The novel and the printing revolution

The printing press enabled mass reproduction and distribution of books and changed what kind of narrative, argumentative and poetic texts could be conceived and distributed to an increasing audience of readers. Written text that is reproduced and distributed to be read instead of being spoken orally enables another kind of narration. Written narratives are not restricted by the frailty of human memory, but they cannot rely on the multimodal context of the co-presence of oral performance. At the same time, a change in the material and sensorial modality meant that narratives distributed on surfaces could be perceived visually as well as orally, and authors were very quick to exploit the new possibilities of this.

The narrative prose and the novel as qualified media types are deeply dependent on printed texts being distributed as books. Early modern prose is full of digressions, detail and long enumerations that indulge in the possibility of telling a story that does not need to be remembered by heart. The French Renaissance writer Francois Rabelais' (ca. 1495–1553) grotesque and satirical stories of the giants *Gargantua and Pantagruel* (1532–64) are full of such examples, e.g. when a character asks the same question in many different languages, or when the foods offered at a feast are enumerated in what seems like an almost endless list. Baroque poetry enjoyed exploiting the visual aspects of texts by making the words on the page form an iconic relation to what the words represent; for instance, the 1686 poem '*Ein Sanduhr*' ('An Hourglass') by the baroque poet Theodor Kornfeld (1636–98) is a poem about the mortality of life that is arranged in the shape of an hourglass. This kind of poetry depends on the audience of the poem being readers rather than listeners.

On the other hand, the context of reading a text is different to the multimodal context of speech and lacks the interactivity between narrator and audience in the co-presence of performance. Early modern narrative prose was clearly aware of moving the situation of oral storytelling into a new medium. In prefaces and other forms of direct addresses to the reader, writers reached out to their audience across time and space. These prefaces to a 'Dear reader!' might appear old-fashioned conventions to us, but they were an attempt to bridge the gap between narrator and audience that came with the distribution of books and the reading of texts. Rhyme and a regular metre, characteristics of the qualified media type of the oral tradition, turned into genre conventions. High-status genres such as tragedy and poetry or the epic continued to be qualified by a regular metre for a long time. Narrative prose, however, which qualifies as the media type of the novel – today the bestselling and most widespread literary form – did not, for a long time, possess the high status it has today. In the early nineteenth century, novel-reading was considered to have the power to damage readers' character, just as reading comics or playing computer games were viewed by later generations.

Literature inherits forms of expression that are older than writing or printing. Currently, digital technologies have been and continue to reshape the qualified medium of literature, including some very basic assumptions about how literature is created and communicated. Digital poetry can be composed with the help of algorithms, which challenges the assumption that a poem is constructed so as to expresses a poet's thoughts and feelings. Also, when digital technology allows for new technical media of display beyond the printed book, changes occur in our use and understanding of the basic media type of text. And it changes the conditions for how text, sound and images can be combined. Digital technology allows new forms of reading, for example, by allowing readers an interactive experience with narratives, such as the hyperlink novels in the 1990s. Different forms of what is called twitterature engage with the character restriction of the microblog as a creative challenge. The microblog disseminates, for instance, short poems, very short stories that fit into one single tweet, or entire novels, disseminated in a succession of tweets. Reading twitter novels or fan fiction together with the comments of thousands of other fellow readers turns the reading experience into a socially shared phenomenon.

In sum, it is not only written words that tell stories and express poetic experience. We meet audiovisual complex storytelling in films and television shows. Narratives and poetic language develop interactively in computer games and in many other contemporary media types. All of these expand our understanding of what literature is. Writers (or, more broadly, artists working with literature as one of their preferred media) are constantly experimenting with new and alternative ways to use words, spoken or written, in combination with other basic media types to mediate experiences, tell stories and promote forms of reading interaction.

Social context and conventions

Let us not forget that simply talking about basic media such as written text and technical media of display such as the book still don't allow us to differentiate between literary and non-literary media products. It is, rather, social and cultural settings, norms and institutions that construct notions of what is and what is not (considered to be) literature. In contemporary Western settings, we probably think of novels, short stories, poetry, perhaps travel writing, possibly essays: texts involving characters, feelings, ideas, conflicts written by professional authors and published by publishing houses, sold in bookshops, book fairs or online, found in libraries, discussed in reading circles, read individually or in book-reading events. Literature is not only text and objects; it involves social interaction and economics as well. Books need to find their readers or customers so that professional writers can make a living. This market for literature qualifies the medium of literature as well. We should be careful not to forget that literature in the past, present and future is a historically constructed notion that is shaped by social institutions and power constellations that decide what kind of literary texts are stored, published and spread.

It is not only context and convention but also how we use a text that defines what we call literature. Audiobooks not only transform the reader into a listener but mean that the listener can combine listening to literature with other activities, for instance, commuting, running or doing housework. Therefore, having access to audiobooks means that you do not have to make time to read and do anything else. These changes in the material and sensorial modalities make literature more accessible. From being a by-product of book-publishing for specific target groups, the audiobook has changed into an option for a much broader audience. The rise of audiobooks thus includes a shift in reading practices that challenge traditional hierarchies (see Have and Stougaard Pedersen (2016) and Engberg et al. (2021)).

The fact that publishing houses issue guidelines on how to write a text that is suitable for the audiobook format (recommending a clear and chronological storyline, told from one perspective) does not necessarily mean that the audiobook as a literary media type is destined to mark the end of complex, rich, literary storytelling: instead, it reflects changes in the operational qualifying aspects of literature, that is, the contexts in which we use literature are changing. A parallel development has been clear in certain mainstream crime and thriller genres, where novels have clearly been designed to be able to be made into action films or thrillers.

We must also acknowledge that the auditory perception of written text, which some literary critics think leads to a reduction in complexity, can accomplish the very opposite. The performance of the voice actor can highlight the auditory experience of words, rhythm and voices in a way that can also make complex literary texts more accessible. Thus, different technical media of display seldom mark 'the death' of a specific kind of qualified medium; instead, when we look at literature as a qualified media type in the digital age, we can see how new technical media are slowly changing the qualifying aspects of literature.

Therefore, digital technology not only changes how we access written narratives and what they look like, but also influences our understanding of what literature is and can be as the context, the conventions and the uses of written literature change: we demonstrated this earlier concerning both the searchable e-book and the new affordances of an audiobook. In the same way that the printing press allowed for new literature-related possibilities in the early modern epoch, digital media in the twenty-first century allow different kinds of often (but not always) more interactive, collaborative forms of literature.

Table 3.1 Media and modalities – Literature

Media types and modalities	Description
Technical media type	Handwritten or printed books, computers, e-readers, smartphones, computers performance
Basic media type	Text, image **Audiobooks**: auditory text, organized sound, sound effects **Oral literature**: speech, orality and gesture **Digital literature**: text, auditory text, organized sound, sound and haptic effects
Qualified media type	Text, auditory text or speech convey narratives, emotions and experiences (sometimes together with images or organized sound) **Genres**: Prose narratives, epic poetry, poetry, concrete poetry, drama, oral narratives (folk tales, legends), digital literature (digital poetry, twitterature, literary apps), text and image narratives (children's books, comics)
Material modality	Flat surfaces of pages (or screens) **Storytelling**: body and speech organs of performers **Digital literature**: screens, loudspeakers
Sensorial modality	**Text-based**: primarily visual, embodied **Performance-based**: auditory, co-presence **Digital literature**: visual, auditory, tactile (multisensory reading)
Spatiotemporal modality	**Material**: spatial object of a book, reading time **Sensorial**: fixed sequentiality of a text Loose sequentiality of images Spatial relations of text and images on the page **Semiotic**: virtual time and space of the storyworld
Semiotic modality	**Text**: dominantly symbolic (increased iconicity in, e.g. poetry or comics, indexical in manuscripts, autographs and comics to act of writing **Image**: dominantly iconic (increased symbolicity in, e.g. comics) **Speech**: dominantly symbolic, iconic/indexical in relation to the expression of emotions

Further reading

Emerson, L. 2014. *Reading writing interfaces: From the digital to the bookbound*. Minneapolis: University of Minnesota Press.
Have, I. and Stougaard Pedersen, B. 2016. *Digital audiobooks: New media, users, and experiences*. New York: Routledge.
Hayles, N. K. 2008. *Electronic literature: New horizons for the literary*. Notre Dame: University of Notre Dame Press.
Kukkonen, K. 2013. *Studying comics and graphic novels*. Somerset: Wiley.
Kwakkel, E. 2018. *Books before print*. Amsterdam: Amsterdam University Press.
Nikolajeva, M. and Scott, C. 2001. *How picturebooks work*. London: Routledge.
Ong, W.J. 2002. *Orality and literacy: the technologizing of the word*. London: Routledge.
Rubery, M. ed. 2011. *Audiobooks, literature, and sound studies*. [e-book] New York: Routledge.

References

Anderson, K. 2010. Storytelling. In H.J. Birx, ed., *21st century anthropology: A reference handbook* (pp. 277–286). London: SAGE. doi:10.4135/9781412979283.n28
Baron, N.S. 2015. *Words onscreen: The fate of reading in a digital world*. Oxford: Oxford University Press.
Drucker, J. 2013. Performative materiality and theoretical approaches to interface. *DHQ: Digital Humanities Quarterly*, 7(1). http://digitalhumanities.org/dhq/vol/7/1/000143/000143.html [Accessed 10 April 2021]
Engberg, M., Have, I., Quist Henkel, A., Mygind, S., Stougaard Pedersen, B. and Bundgaard Svendsen, H. 2021. To move, to touch, to listen. Multisensory aspects of the digital reading condition. *Poetics Today*, forthcoming.
Hall, F. 2013. *The business of digital publishing. An introduction to the digital book and journal industries*. New York: Routledge.
Have, I. and Stougaard Pedersen, B. 2016. *Digital audiobooks: New media, users, and experiences*. New York: Routledge.
Hayles, N.K. 2008. *Electronic literature: New horizons for the literary*. Notre Dame: University of Notre Dame Press.
Kittler, F.A. 1999. *Gramophone, film, typewriter*. Stanford: Stanford University Press.
Krauß, A., Leipziger, J. and Schücking-Jungblut, F. 2020. *Material aspects of reading in ancient and medieval cultures: Materiality, presence and performance*. [e-book] Berlin; Boston: de Gruyter. doi:10.1515/9783110639247
Kukkonen, K. 2013. *Studying comics and graphic novels*. Somerset: Wiley.
Kwakkel, E. 2018. *Books before print*. Amsterdam: Amsterdam University Press.
Ong, W.J. 2002. *Orality and literacy: The technologizing of the word*. London: Routledge.
Mangen, A. 2016. What hands may tell us about reading and writing. *Educational Theory*, 66(4), pp. 457–477. doi:10.1111/edth.12183.
Nikolajeva, M. and Scott, C. 2001. *How picturebooks work*. London: Routledge.
Ramachandran, V.S. and Hubbard, E.M. 2001. Synaesthesia: A window into perception, thought and language. *Journal of Consciousness Studies*, 8(12), pp. 3–34. https://philpapers.org/rec/RAMSA-5 [Accessed 1 December 2020].
Rubery, M., ed. 2011. *Audiobooks, literature, and sound studies*. [e-book] New York: Routledge.

Smith, J.D., Reisberg, D. and Wilson, M. 1992. Subvocalization and auditory imagery: Interactions between inner voice and inner ear. In D. Reisberg, ed., *Auditory imagery* (pp. 95–119). Hillsdale: Lawrence Erlbaum.

Squires, C. and Ray Murray, P. 2013. The digital publishing communications circuit. *Book*, 3(1), pp. 3–24.

Thiong'o, N.W. 1998. Oral power and Europhone glory: Orature, literature, and stolen legacies. *Penpoints, gunpoints, and dreams: Towards a critical theory of the arts and the state in Africa* (pp. 103–128). Oxford: Clarendon Press.

4 Media and modalities – Music

Signe Kjær Jensen and Martin Knust

There are different ways to experience music; You can sing or play an instrument, you can go to concerts or listen to the radio, you can play a record, listen to a CD or stream music. You experience music in different ways, using different devices and senses. Though most people in the West might agree that music is a sounding phenomenon that involves auditory experience, both the technical media of display and the conventions that qualify music in different contexts shift culturally and historically. For a long time, music could only be experienced as a live performance (if you were not able to read sheet music). Most of the music you hear today is probably not experienced as a live performance but is played back to you from records, CDs or MP3 files, broadcast on the radio or accessed via digital streaming platforms.

While music involves auditory experiences, it involves the other senses as well. You can read music just like you read text. The German composer Ludwig van Beethoven (1770–1827) famously kept *writing* music using pen and paper after he had gone deaf. The Scottish multi-percussionist Evelyn Glennie (b. 1965), who has been deaf since the age of 12, performs barefoot on stage to better *feel* the music. While the Western conception of music focuses on music as a sounding phenomenon, other concepts found in other cultures may include dance as well.

How music sounds, how we listen to it, what we use music for and which ideas are connected to it depend on historical, social, cultural and generic dimensions. Just compare the music style and social circumstances of background music played in hotel lobbies or elevators (piped music) with the trance experience induced through the religious–animistic music of the Gnawa people in the Northern Sahara, or the casual singing of a children's counting rhyme with the meticulous and exhausting work of classical musicians in a studio.

In this chapter, we will discuss the characteristics and communicative conventions that qualify Western art music, popular music and folk music. Despite major differences in the traditions of these qualified media types of music and the emphasis they put on musical notation and performance, they all share certain characteristics that relate to technical media of display and their basic media types.

DOI: 10.4324/9781003174288-5

Technical media of display in music

Music can be heard, but it can also be read. In this respect, it is not so unlike verbal language. We can listen to music that is being performed or to recordings as a sounding phenomenon. We can read sheet music as a written, visual phenomenon like text. Contrary to the case of literature, most of us listen to music more than we read music. Not as many people are able to read sheet music as fluently as most of us would read text in a familiar language. When we listen to sounding music, the technical media of display are sound waves that are realized via instruments and singers in a live performance or via electric speakers (in combination with different storage media such as records, LPs, tapes, CDs, computers or smartphones).

Like language, music can be written down, read and stored. Writing also means storing information. In the Western context, musical notation was used to store music long before the invention of audio recording. The type of notation in use today can be traced back to systems from the ninth century and it was part of the typographical discourse network (*Aufschreibesystem*) Friedrich Kittler (1986, p. 11) has described. Other cultures have developed notational systems that are even older (Bent et al. 2021). Written music (realized using, for example, paper and ink) exists in most musical cultures in different variations. The technical medium of display is the flat surface of the paper sheets, pages or screens. For people who are trained in reading written music, it can evoke a virtual musical experience. The visual perception of reading signs on the paper can evoke a cross-modal translation and conjure up the auditory imagery of sounds. This is similar to the way in which we silently read a written word and cognitively evoke the auditory imagery of speech. Because music can be conjured up cognitively from a written representation, music is sometimes thought of as an immaterial medium consisting of an *idea* rather than a material phenomenon that we can touch and feel or even hear (Cook 1998, pp. 63–71).

Yet, for most people, music is something that is listened to, and no matter how we listen to music, music needs to be performed to be heard, which often involves human bodies creating sound waves or interacting with instruments to produce organized sounds of music. In this chapter, we will draw attention to the material and medial aspects of music. The way we interact with music in the different modalities differs depending on whether we think of music as sounding or written, but our main focus will be on sounding music.

Basic media types of sounding music

Music is based on the basic medium of *organized sound*. When sound is organized in accordance with certain cultural conventions, the sound turns into the qualified medium of music. Organized sound is often combined with speech in vocal music, i.e. songs. Some people would argue that most vocal music constitutes a *combined* medium that adds the basic medium of auditory text, or even the qualified medium of poetry, to the music in the form of lyrics. And it may look like that if you consider a piece of written vocal music that uses two notational systems, text for the lyrics and musical notation. The use of two notational systems suggests a combination of two qualified media. In the semiotic modality, two different ways of meaning-making are simultaneously present in vocal music. However, even though it can be helpful from an analytical perspective to distinguish between the meaning potential of the words in a song and the construction of the musical accompaniment, one should be aware that in the material and sensorial modalities, the two media are deeply integrated in terms of the way we perceive them both as sound waves, and in praxis, they can't be completely separated. Words sung in a language we understand will especially shape how we hear the music. And the music will shape how the words are realized and how they are heard, most notably by replacing the natural intonation of spoken language with a forced musical melody and rhythm. Language is in itself highly musical, even if we don't often think about it, and music of different styles can stay close to spoken language's natural musicality (Billie Eilish often does this) or make a point of diverging (think of arias in classical opera, or Mariah Carey). Similarly, the sound of a singular vowel will affect the timbre of the sung melody – singing an 'uhh' and an 'ohh' on the same pitch will, for example, have very different musical qualities, and people who are trained as singers will know that some vowels are easier to sing than others in different registers. The deep integration of words and organized sound can also be seen in the fact that the boundaries between speaking, reciting and singing are anything but constant over time and culture.

Auditory text and organized sound also share a range of characteristics in terms of their modalities, reinforcing this strong integration. Both the words and the music in a performed song are auditory; in the material modality both media consist of *sound waves*, which we hear in the *sensorial modality*. Sometimes we can even feel the music through the pressure of the soundwaves on our bodies (like the high-volume base sounds in a rock concert). When it comes to the *spatiotemporal modality*, the words and the music of a song also have a lot in common. Both of them are perceived as *temporal* and have the potential for fixed sequentiality in the case of a recording (that is, the *sequentiality*, or the *unfolding*, of words and music is *predetermined*, thus *fixed*), non-fixed sequentiality in the case of improvised performance, and a 'regular' performance of a poem or piece of music that exists in written form would have partially fixed sequentiality – as a performance is highly dependent on the written form, there is a level of fixation, but performances can never be repeated in exactly the same way, making the fixation only partial. Furthermore, both media have the potential for an *implied virtual space and time*. A poem or a lyric that tells a story will create a virtual space and time of that storyworld. The sound volume of music is also often spatially perceived; low sounds can be perceived as coming from far away and an increase in volume as something approaching within a virtual space. This virtual space differs depending on the *actual* space the music is played in, and how different instruments, singers or electronic speakers are placed in relation to each other in that space (think of how your voice sounds in a church compared to out in free nature, or how the sound of your favourite band differs depending on whether you are listening to it in your living room or in a concert). Most Western music, except ambient music and maybe also some types of modal jazz and similar styles, is additionally based on a development, which implies *a virtual time* in the same way as a narrative. Music even has a *cognitive space*. In many cultures, including the Western ones, musical pitches are described as being high or low, meaning that melodies are also described as moving up and down. This way of describing music implies that we are creating a *cognitive* space in which to understand music.

The semiotic modality of sounding music

Where auditive text and organized sound really differ in terms of modalities is in the semiotic modality. Most text is dominated by the symbolic modality, although lyrics can also have an important iconic function when words are used for their auditory qualities and not only for their symbolic meaning (as with onomatopoeia). The meaning of words in a song interacts with music, performance and context; they are words that are 'meant to be sounded' (Eckstein 2010, p. 10). Especially in relation to the lyrics of pop songs, it is clear how music can provide meaning to otherwise incoherent or even meaningless lyrics (Frith 1996). Musical meaning can be more difficult to talk about. There is no consensus about denotative meaning in music, including the question of whether there is such a thing at all. Music gains meaning through the connotations (including emotional connotations) and metaphors we associate with different sounds and movements, and the feelings that are invoked in us when we listen. How we react to music not only depends on the cultural context but also on the physiology of hearing. The sound waves of music physiologically affect us. Although music is culturally understood as organized sound, the responses of the mind and body to music can be in tension with each other, and we can enjoy music that on a physiological level is perceived as stressful. The meaning of music is not only about aesthetics or how we make meaning out of it however, but also and at the same time about the power of sound in social interactions (Johnson and Cloonan 2008). There are many theories and discussions concerning the meaning potential of sounding music, some more relevant to specific genres than others.

The very question of whether the potential of musical meaning is even worthy of scholarly attention has been much debated in musicology, specifically in relation to the concept of *absolute music* (Dahlhaus 1989). The idea that music does not and cannot express anything but has to be seen as 'sonically moving forms' was championed by the influential music aesthetician Eduard Hanslick (1825–1904) in relation to Western art music (Hanslick 1922, p. 23). According to him, music can be linked to certain feelings by convention but can never represent them.

Traditionally, what many people think of when they think of musical analysis is structural or harmonic analysis, that is, looking at how the music is composed and organized and often using sheet music or other graphical representations to help with this. This is an approach that doesn't necessarily imply any meaning in the music. Meaning is put aside in favour of structural qualities. Different musical genres have conventions for how to organize musical development and harmony, which have developed from one musical period to the next. For instance, a typical chord progression in Western art music from around 1600 until 1900 was to use a chord with a minor seventh (e.g. G7) to lead 'back' to the tonal centre (here the chord C). The minor seventh in this tradition is assumed to create a feeling of tension – a strive to come 'home' to the tonal centre. In blues or jazz, however, this tension towards 'home' is per convention not resolved, and a chord with a minor seventh can stand on its own. Looking at structural or harmonic properties provides an objective way of describing music in relation to different genres or forms and thereby of placing a piece of music in a historical and cultural context.

The study of the potential of musical meaning can be approached from different theoretical positions that focus on expression, arousal or the referential meaning.

Music can be studied for its potential to express or represent emotions: we can describe music as sounding sad or happy. A scholar who is often highlighted in relation to this is the philosopher Susanne Langer. She believes that we understand musical forms as signs of certain emotions because there is a similarity between those forms and our emotions:

> Because the forms of human feeling are much more congruent with musical forms than with the forms of language, music can *reveal* the nature of feelings with a detail and truth that language cannot approach.
> (Langer 1954, p. 191)

Langer describes music as a 'symbol' of emotions, but it is important to note here that she does not define 'symbol' as a sign based on habit and convention. Indeed, Langer's comments that the musical form is 'congruent' with the forms of emotions describe a relation between music and emotion that is based on similarity, which is in line with how we discuss iconic sign relations in this book (Elleström 2021, pp. 50–1). Music might also be considered to signify emotionally through a *symbolic* mode, however, if the recognition of a particular emotional content is highly tied to the use of conventions. Sometimes we might, for example, refer to a slow movement in a string quartet as romantic because we associate this type of music with its use in romantic scenes in a film more than we recognize the timbre and dynamic qualities of the music as romantic. There are thus no either/or solutions to which semiotic mode is dominant; instead, it is a matter of analytical focus.

There are empirical studies that show how different groups of listeners understand certain musical structures as associated with emotional meaning, which indicate certain shared meaning-making patterns among people with similar sociocultural backgrounds (see Jensen (2021) and Gabrielsson & Lindström (2010)). Some scholars have argued that even structural and harmonic conventions of 'absolute' music have become embedded with meaning through listeners' familiarity with these conventions:

> Embodied musical meaning is, in short, a product of expectation. If, on the basis of past experience, a present stimulus leads us to expect a more or less definite consequent musical event, then that stimulus has meaning.
>
> (Meyer 1956, p. 35).

What this means is that familiarity with musical structures can make these structures meaningful, as they make it possible for us to predict the musical development and to place the music within a certain style. Following this line of thinking, musical structures can arouse emotion in a listener by delaying or discarding a conventional resolution (cf. Meyer 1956). There are other ideas about how music can arouse emotion, but the important point in the context of this book is not exactly how this process happens, but that it happens at all. The idea in arousal theories is not that music is 'like' emotions but that musical patterns can have different affective effects on the listener. The music is associated here with an *indexical* mode; rather than gaining meaning through a similarity, it gains meaning through a causal effect on our own bodies and emotional state. Emotional expression and the arousal of emotion are not mutually exclusive in a piece of music. The distinction can be important to keep in mind when analyzing musical meaning, however.

Music can also be studied for what we might call its referential meaning potential, that is, the way that it gains meaning through associations with things other than emotions, such as when rap music is associated with urban American culture, but also when a falling melodic line is associated with an object falling, or a cymbal is used to connote thunder through an auditive similarity.

When music is studied for its referential potential, it gains meaning as an *index* of a social, cultural, historical or geographical context, or it gains meaning as an *icon* by perceiving a similarity with other sounds or movements (such as thunder or objects falling, see Tagg 2012). One should keep in mind that the metaphors and associations we use to understand music change considerably from culture to culture, thereby possibly changing the meaning heard in the same kind of music. Think, for example, of the beginning of the theme song to *The Simpsons* (1989–). The tonal distance between the notes sung on the opening lyrics 'The Simp–' constitute an interval called a tritone. In Western art music, this interval has historically had changing significations due to its dissonant character, going as far as to associate it with the devil and evilness, particularly during the Middle Ages and in the Renaissance, but Romantic composers also used these associations deliberately (Drabkin 2001). In the contemporary *The Simpsons*, the significance has shifted, and we would argue that this 'strangeness' of the dissonant interval is here used to provide a quirky and rather unique identity to the series, setting the tone for the show.

Qualifying aspects of music

The conventions and the use of art music, popular music and folk music clearly differ from each other. They imply different communication chains of music distribution and hence produce different materialities of music.

Art music is a concept of music that in a Western context has been very dominant throughout history. Art music is listened to in concerts and recitals by a silents seated audience following specific conventions. There are concert halls designed for its performance. The sounding music that is performed and the written sheet music both play an important part in this qualified media type of music.

The tradition of art music has a lineage that stretches back into Greek antiquity when 'music' as such was first defined by the Greek philosopher Pythagoras (ca. 570–ca. 495 BCE). However, in the context of Greek antiquity, the term *mousiké* was a much broader concept than what we call music today. *Mousiké* originally referred to works or products of all or any of the nine Muses and thus could refer to what we today differentiate as music, poetry and dance and only gradually came to refer to organized sound in particular.

Different ideas have been connected with different aspects of music. For a long time, music in a Western context has been regarded as a sister discipline to mathematics and astronomy. This is crucial for understanding the high esteem that music had among certain philosophers and theologians. Music until the baroque period was seen as something that modern people might call applied physics, and it was part of the mathematical disciplines in the seven medieval liberal arts. During antiquity and until early modernity (Kircher 1650), harmonies – that is, the synchronous combination of different tones – were seen to be analogous to the order of the cosmos and the human body, proving that macrocosms and microcosms followed the same rules. Since Pythagoras, the Western tonal system has had seven tones, which are analogous to the seven planets that, according to ancient and medieval belief, surround the earth. Even though heliocentrism became the norm in early modernity, this explains why composers like the leading modernist Karlheinz Stockhausen (1928–2007) regarded their music as mirroring the order of the cosmos by employing advanced mathematics. This way of thinking explains the significant structural complexity of Western music in terms of harmony and pitch order (but not in terms of rhythm). It also explains why the first atonal compositions written at the dawn of WWI were met with hysterical scepticism as they were seen as causing anarchy in society and politics.

Throughout history, there has also been a sceptical response to actual sounding music. Music has been perceived as highly suspicious because of its double impact on body and mind, and philosophers and churchmen called for its affective impact to be controlled. The idea that music has a direct influence on morals was first formulated by Plato (428–348 BCE) and has survived to this day. Certain music styles, for instance, are thought to have a negative impact on youngsters. The Parents Music Resource Center (PMRC) was founded in

1985 in the US and introduced censorship for music through the Parental Advisory stickers, which are still in use.

In art music, there is a clear division into production, performance and reception carried out by the composer, the interpreter/performer and the listener. The prominent role of the composer as a mediator between the cosmic laws of harmony and the actual sounding music became defined explicitly in the early 1800s. Ever since, composers have been seen as geniuses who are capable of defining 'the laws of music for eternity', as the composer Jean Sibelius (1865–1957) put it (entry in his diary dated 7 May 1918 in Dahlström (Fabian 2005, p. 274)). Normally, the first act would consist of the composer delivering a written score, which in traditional musicology and aesthetics is regarded as 'the actual musical work'. Experienced musicians can read those scores and imagine the sound of the music when it is played by an orchestra. This is an important but, of course, also somewhat esoteric materiality of music as auditory imagery.

The second act occurs when the interpreter enters the stage. The interpreter's role in art music is normally to execute the score and thus execute the ideas of the composer as accurately as possible. The visual signs of the score are transformed during performance into the movements of limbs that the performer carries out to produce the physical sound waves of sounding music – either by playing an instrument or using the body as an instrument when singing. Interpreters are thus *in between* the visual and the auditory media types of music, mediating the written score into sound. This division between the composer and the interpreter/musician, the division between music as compositional idea and music as sounding phenomenon, ties back to the complicated question of how to define music in terms of idea and materiality, which we already touched upon at the beginning of this chapter. Is music that is never played or sounding at all even 'real' music? To many jazz musicians, who tend to rely on performance and improvisation more than on notation, the answer might be no. But in the Western art tradition, it would be more common to think of non-sounding music as the highest level of musical purity. Take, for instance, the speculative music that was part of the quadrivium – the standard curriculum for any students in medieval Europe. Or the last compositions of Johann Sebastian Bach (1685–1750), *Das musikalische Opfer* and *Die Kunst der Fuge*, which are highly complex compositions that were not intended to be played by a certain instrument but to be 'music as such' and more related to mathematics and religion.

Finally, the listener receives sound waves produced by the interpreter. The listener responds physically to the sounds (or noises) and at the same time responds to them in the semiotic modality and transforms them into some form of subjective meaning. In this process, all kinds of cognitive, emotional, affective and physiological effects overlap, and there is still no encompassing model for explaining how exactly this process of musical meaning-making works, although the different approaches to musical meaning just presented highlight different aspects. That it works very well is proven by the fact that musical fan cultures, which go well back into the eighteenth century, turn listening to music into some kind of religious act and that certain fans find the meaning of their lives in music (cf. Kjellander 2013).

In art music, the three instances of creating, producing and receiving a musical media product are neatly distinguishable. They are not in popular and folk music. In popular music, the composer – or arranger – can often be the interpreter as well, and written scores are normally not employed during the production process. Instead, the musicians will create their works more or less by improvising, which means by playing freely on their instrument to gather ideas for the future piece. The creation of a media product in commercial popular music may be even more detailed than it is in art music. The production of a mainstream pop song may include many more steps, such as those involving arrangement and lyrics specialists. As much of popular music is produced in studios, it involves the work of sound engineers, technicians and music producers.

What is more important, however, for the reception of popular music is that it is nowadays practically always electronically mediated. The development of popular music in the twentieth century is closely connected to the invention of gramophones, the radio and other technical devices that have shaped popular music to a large extent. The vinyl 'single' – still in use as a term – defined the length of a pop song. Recording devices had an impact on the sound of voices. In the era of cylinder recordings, singers needed much more effort in order to be audible. A microphone allows the singer to whisper and still be audible.

Popular music is a commercial system that is based on the idea of producing many copies of a recording and/or broadcasting music to a mass audience. Music that can be considered 'popular' existed even before the twentieth century; take, for instance, the entertainment music like dances and waltzes in the nineteenth century. Before recording, sheet music was the distribution device.

In popular music, there is no original score like in art music, nor can we easily distinguish a piece of work in popular music. Instead of an original score that is correctly executed during a performance, a piece of popular music exists in multiple versions. There is the master tape that is produced by singing and playing a piece successively in time on different tracks in the studio, and there are the uncountable copies on records, CDs, tapes and digital files. As the technical media of pop music stores sounding music (and not written music, such as the score), does this mean that the piece of popular music only exists in the moment of its performance, when it is listened to and played, on radio and in concert?

At the same time, the music industry claims it is producing musical works that are protected by the copyright against unlawful copying. But when does this unlawful copying occur? When playing a record to a large group of people, or when singing a famous pop song in the shower? The answer is maybe not as clear as copyright rules suggest. The question of what a musical work is has become even more difficult to answer after the act of digitalization. Music was turned into binary codes first on CD and then as an MP3 file and finally into a stream of digital signals when distributing it over the internet. The materiality of recorded digital music is thus fundamentally different from recorded analogue music. Analogue recording techniques mechanically transform sound waves using a needle sitting in groves in a soft medium like wax, rotating discs or patterns of magnetic material on a tape. When playing a recording, the same process is reversed. Digital music transforms sound waves into binary code and chunks the sound into discrete units, similar to the way how analogue film chunks moving images into discrete units of 24 images per second. Recorded analogue music does not record discrete units. Thus, although gramophone and film both developed at the same time, their recording techniques are completely different (Kittler 1986).

Folk music blurs the lines between musician and listener entirely. Folk music does not operate with an entirely passive listener like in a classical concert. Folk music is thought to have a collective origin and, therefore, traditionally was not created by one person, such as a composer. Like the ancient Greek *mousiké*, it unites sound, body movements and often also language when the performer sings. It can be written down, but, more importantly, it is often handed down and passed on between musicians by playing it. Performances of folk music, such as that played to the Swedish dance around the maypole, or a jam in a Scottish pub, exhibit foremost the social aspect of music-making. Often, a musical work cannot be identified.

The different contexts and conventions of art, folk and popular music consequently generate different forms of reception as well. Not only are different types of behaviour expected, whether the audience is silently seated or allowed to spontaneously respond with clapping, shouting and dancing. In different musical contexts, different forms of meaning-making are conventionally employed and expected. For instance, a classical symphonic concert that mostly presents instrumental music is based on the idea that the music should be at the centre of the perception of the listener with no distractions. When music is understood as absolute music, as 'sounding moving forms' in the sense of Eduard Hanslick, it appears to be structured exclusively according to musical laws. Listening to music in this tradition resembles the study of ornaments. Hanslick's abstract concept of music reception had a fundamental impact on the modernistic turn of music in the 1910s, which fundamentally shaped art music all over the world for decades to come.

When we look at film music and music theatre and other qualified media that integrate music instead, music is employed to a much greater extent as a device of expression and received as a 'language of emotion'. This receptive strategy is today by far the most popular of the two. It dates back to the late Renaissance era and was most influentially shaped during the Romantic era in the early nineteenth century. When talking about the integration and combination of music with other qualified media, the ability of music to communicate specific emotions is by many seen as the most natural function of music. However, this perspective may be an exclusively Western way of receiving music, and it cannot be taken for granted in non-European music cultures. Stressing a connection between music and emotions tends to overlook how this connection depends on context and conventions.

We still don't know much about what the impact of certain musical structures on the human psyche looks like and how receptive concepts and strategies are to being passed from one generation to another. What is known is that newborn infants already have different musical preferences and use their voices differently depending on which culture they are born into (Webb et al. 2015). This lack of knowledge is intriguing given the fact that music can be analysed with mathematical precision like no other art form.

Table 4.1 Media and modalities – Music

Media types and modalities	Description
Technical devices and media of display	Bodies, instruments producing sound waves **Production**: live performance, studio recordings, sheet music **Dissemination**: sheet music, live performance, auditory storage media (records, etc.) and loudspeakers, streaming platforms
Basic media types	Organized sound Verbal sound and auditory text (vocal music) Body language (live performance)
Qualified media type	Sound qualifies as music when organized following genre conventions /aesthetic expectations. Genres include art music, folk music, popular music Genre conventions: • in art music tied to the role of sheet music, the concert hall, and certain compositional rules • in folk music tied to performance and authenticity of the performer • in popular music, many genres include electronic recording and manipulation
Material modality	Sound waves print on paper (sheet music) Moving bodies or objects
Sensorial modality	Auditory, visual, tactile, (implied) tactility
Spatiotemporal modality	**Material**: fixed sequential time and spatial range of sound **Sensorial**: Experience of space designed by sound. Experience of time ordered by sound (slow, fast) **Semiotic**: virtual time for music that is perceived to have a (narrative) development (like songs, programme music) Virtual space: low volume sounds perceived as far away in a virtual space. Crescendo = approaching
Semiotic modality	Symbolical Iconic Indexical

Further reading

Absolute music

Hanslick, E. 1922. *Vom Musikalisch-Schönen*. Leipzig: Breitkopf & Härtel. https://www.gutenberg.org/files/26949/26949-h/26949-h.htm

Hanslick, E. 2008. The beautiful in music. In S.M. Cahn and A. Meskin, eds., *Aesthetics: A comprehensive anthology* (pp. 217–221). Oxford: Blackwell Publishing.

Music and emotion

Juslin, P.N. and Sloboda, J.A. 2010. *Handbook of music and emotion: Theory, research, and applications. Series in affective science*. Oxford, New York: Oxford University Press.

Langer, S.K. 1954. *Philosophy in a new key: A study in the symbolism of reason, rite, and art.* New York: The New American Library.

Meyer, L.B. 1956. *Emotion and meaning in music*. Chicago: University of Chicago Press.

Music, 'referential' meaning and interpretative approaches

Cohen, A.J. 2015. Congruence-association model and experiments in film music: Toward interdisciplinary collaboration. *Music and the Moving Image*, 8(2), pp. 5–24. doi:10.5406/musimoviimag.8.2.0005

Cook, N. 1998. *Analysing musical multimedia*. Oxford: Oxford University Press.

Cooke, D. 1959. *The language of music*. Oxford: Oxford University Press.

Klein, M.L. and Reyland, N.W. eds. 2013. *Music and narrative since 1900*. Bloomington: Indiana University Press.

Kramer, L. 2001. *Musical meaning: Toward a critical history*. Berkeley: University of California Press.

Machin, D. 2010. *Analysing popular music: Image, sound, and text*. Los Angeles: SAGE.

Music semiotics

Agawu, K. 2014. *Music as discourse: Semiotic adventures in romantic music*. Cary: Oxford University Press.

Nattiez, J.J. 1990. *Music and discourse: Toward a semiology of music*. Princeton: Princeton University Press.

Tagg, P. 2012. *Music's meaning: A modern musicology for non-musos*. New York: The Mass Media Music Scholars' Press.

Tarasti, E. 2002. *Signs of music: A guide to musical semiotics*. Berlin: de Gruyter.

Structure in classical music

Caplin, W.E. 2013. *Analyzing classical form: An approach for the classroom*. New York: Oxford University Press.

Cook, N. 1994. *A guide to musical analysis*. Oxford: Oxford University Press.

Pankhurst, T. 2008. *SchenkerGUIDE. A brief handbook and website for Schenkerian analysis*. New York: Routledge. doi:10.4324/9780203928882

References

Bent, I., Hughes, D., Provine, R., Rastall, R., Kilmer, A., Hiley, D., Szendrei, J., Payne, T., Bent, M. and Chew, G. (2001). Notation. *Grove Music Online*. https://www-oxfordmusiconline-com [Accessed 27 January 2021].

Cook, N. 1998. *Music: A very short introduction*. Oxford: Oxford University Press.

Dahlhaus, C. 1989. *The idea of absolute music*. Chicago: Univ. of Chicago Press.

Drabkin, W. 2001. Tritone. *Grove Music Online*. https://www.oxfordmusiconline.com/grovemusic/ [Accessed 27 January 2021].

Eckstein, L. 2010. *Reading song lyrics*. Amsterdam: Brill.

Elleström, L. 2021. The modalities of media II: An expanded model for understanding intermedial relations. In L. Elleström, ed., *Beyond media borders. Vol.1. Intermedial relations among multimodal media* (pp. 3–91). Basingstoke; New York: Palgrave Macmillan.

Fabian, D. 2005. *Jean Sibelius dagbok 1909–1944*. Helsinki; Stockholm: Society of Swedish Literature in Finland and Atlantis.

Frith, S. 1996. *Performing rites: Evaluating popular music*. Oxford: Oxford University Press.

Gabrielsson, A. and Lindström, E. 2010. The role of structure in the musical expression of emotions. In *Handbook of music and emotion: Theory, research, applications* (pp. 367–400). Oxford: Oxford University Press.

Hanslick, E. 1922. *Vom Musikalisch-Schönen*. Leipzig: Breitkopf & Härtel. https://www.gutenberg.org/files/26949/26949-h/26949-h.htm

Jensen, S.K. 2021. *Musicalised Characters: A study of music, multimodality, and the empiric child perspective on mainstream animation*, PhD thesis. Växjö: Linnaeus University Press

Johnson, B. and Cloonan, M. 2008. *Dark side of the tune: Popular music and violence*. Aldershot: Ashgate.

Kircher, A. 1650. *Musurgia universalis*. Rome: Francesco Corbeletti.

Kittler, F. 1986. *Gramophone, film, typewriter*. Berlin: Brinkmann & Bose.

Kjellander, E. 2013. *Jag och mitt fanskap: Vad musik kan göra för människor*. Örebro: Örebro University.

Langer, S.K. 1954. *Philosophy in a new key: A study in the symbolism of reason, rite, and art*. New York: The New American Library.

Meyer, L.B. 1956. *Emotion and meaning in music*. Chicago: University of Chicago Press.

Tagg, P. 2012. *Music's meaning: A modern musicology for non-musos*. New York: The Mass Media Music Scholars' Press

Webb, A.R., Heller, H.T., Benson, C.B. and Lahav, A. 2015. Mother's voice and heartbeat sounds elicit auditory plasticity in the human brain before full gestation. Proceedings of the National Academy of Sciences of the United States of America, 112(10) (March 2015), pp. 3152–3157.

5 Media and modalities – Computer games

Péter Kristóf Makai

Computers are the default mode of creating and accessing all kinds of commercial media products today. Computer-assisted design and video-editing programs, digital distribution platforms for film, books and games, and news media are all thoroughly digital. This is because semiotic meaning can be easily broken down into digital bits, as a series of differences in electrical voltage or current pulse represented by 1s and 0s. Meaning is stored in the brain in a similar format, as neurons firing or not firing, processed at breakneck speed.

Intermedial scholars study how meaning travels from person to person, from one brain to another, as humans create signs using different basic media types such as bodies, text, images or computer code. With the help of the microprocessor of a computer these are transformed into other basic media types, such as moving images, text and sound effects that we can interact with more easily via our senses. We access a lot of different qualified media through computers today. Video games are simply the medium of entertainment most associated with the microprocessor.

This chapter discusses video games, also known as computer or digital games, as a distinct form of meaning-making (Egenfeldt-Nielsen et al. 2013). The primary focus of the chapter is the single-player game, but we will touch upon multiplayer games as well. For the purposes of this chapter, we treat video games as a qualified media type, defined in its prototypical format as a piece of entertainment software that is run on specific hardware, operated by user(s) via a technological interface, who exercise agency in a digitally realized virtual environment created by game designer(s) to influence the internal state of that environment in order to derive enjoyment from their actions at little to no risk to themselves. Because of their extreme diversity in form and content, as well as the ease with which they combine with and transform other media types, some scholars consider video games as a set of different media types (see Ruggill and McAllister (2011) and Jørgensen (2020)). There is merit in this approach, since computer games are multimodal integrations that include elements of other media to create memorable experiences. Indeed, our definition is primarily meant to separate computer games from board games (which are designed to be physically manipulated, played on a tabletop in the primary world of our experience, rather than a virtual world), role-playing games (a

DOI: 10.4324/9781003174288-6

collaborative storytelling format, often with elaborate rule systems and elements of randomness, whose virtual worlds are not required to be physically or digitally realized at all) and gambling (games of chance played for the express purpose of gaining extrinsic monetary rewards). Computers, being promiscuous mediators of other media, can obviously implement analogue games, hybridize with them (Booth 2016) and serve as useful accessories and companions to tabletop play, but in these cases the role of the digital device is auxiliary, or at a degree removed from the originally designed experience.

With these caveats in place, we can now begin exploring digital games as a medium with complex capacities for engaging its users and enriching their lives with fun, challenges, success, narratives and even real-life knowledge. We explore the production process of games, accounting for how other media leave their mark on the creation of new games, followed by a survey of the basic media types and their role in generating meaning in games. The qualifying aspects of computer games shed light on how different service models, development stages, player modes and platforms affect their form and reception. The chapter then closes with how the four media modalities can be apprehended in video games, and what each contributes to the joys of gaming.

Video games harness the participatory and procedural capabilities of computing to make the player experience places, processes and emotional transformation (Murray 2017, pp. 68–170). Unlike other media, games can both represent and simulate (see Juul (2005, pp. 170–7) and Karhulahti (2015)). Representations of the material objects of thought, like a particular artwork, such as a sculpture, novel or film, exist as one, shared thing, with a form and content that will be the same for everyone even if we experience them differently. Simulations, however, are variable and dynamic entities that showcase how a system works. They are models that give players agency to create meaningful changes to their storyworlds, functioning as systems of storytelling that are capable of simulating processes with different outcomes each time they are played (Koenitz et al. 2020). A game that simulates how a virus spreads (as in the game *Plague, Inc.* 2012) has built-in principles that can be brought to life by you, the player, and the artwork will change according to your input. Similarly, in games that have stories, the story might change considerably based on the choices you make (Ryan 2001, pp. 242–70). Therefore, you can have a radically different mental representation of the game's simulated world than that of other players.

Typically, games have represented play areas that circumscribe the domain in which the player can take action and to which a game's rules apply. A simple tile-matching game, like *Bejeweled* (2001), 'fits' on a single, discrete screen displaying an abstract plane of jewels and everything else the player needs to know or can act upon. Meanwhile, other games create a sense of 'worldness' (Klastrup 2009), in other words, spatially organized constructs that adhere to some governing logic that makes the space intelligible, discoverable and navigable. *Grand Theft Auto V* (2015), for example, is set in the fictional American state of San Andreas, representing a geography and a built environment that is similar to California.

Because games are a qualified media type that is capable of both the representation and simulation of other media, they have the potential to tell stories, but not all games do (Thabet 2014). *Bejeweled* (2001) doesn't tell a story, as you only have to switch the position of adjacent jewels to play. On the other hand, *Grand Theft Auto V* (2015) has complex narratives that are told and played from multiple viewpoints. The early history of video game scholarship debated the role of narrative in making sense of games, and while games are unique among media in their need for the player's interaction every step of the way, players also re-enact stories via their in-game performance (see Frasca (2013) and Holmes (2013)). As computer games are simulations, we treat them differently from the way we engage with other kinds of media products. All media products have to be manipulated in the material and sensorial modality. A novel needs to be read and a film must be watched to engage with their respective storyworlds. In computer games, the player's agency changes how the semiotically encoded storyworld unfolds, and players can influence the rules of the storyworld as well.

When we talk about 'a game' and its properties, we may be meaning any one of three interrelated aspects of games: the game as a rule-based design (a system), the actual behaviour of the game system when it is being operated (a process), or the experience of playing a session of a particular game (a product) (Koenitz 2010). The system describes what is possible within the simulated world of the game, the process actuates a subset of these possibilities which may interact with one another, and the final product is the mental construct of lived experience unique to the individuals participating in the process. This tripartite model has also been called the Mechanics–Dynamics–Aesthetics (Hunicke et al. 2004), or the Design–Dynamics–Experience model (Walk et al. 2017). To illustrate with a quick example, making this distinction can be useful when talking about LGBT+ issues in a life simulator, such as *The Sims* (2000). Although gay marriage was not implemented within the game system of the original Maxis title (2000), the actual Sims characters are functionally bisexual when the game runs (they can woo and romance both male and female Sims), and indeed some players chose to enact same-sex relationships in their own households even in the original game, producing an LGBT+ experience inside *The Sims* that was programmed into later instalments.

The notion of mechanics is central to understanding games as systems influenced by player action. Mechanics are designed by game developers to translate the players' intended actions into consequences that change the state of the game world. Thus, mechanics are actual, effective procedures put in place to generate played meaning. In a computer role-playing game, for example, the clothes the characters wear might be purely cosmetic (i.e. it might not help or hinder the player from achieving any goals), but in other cases they might give them new abilities. Note that even though cosmetic outfits do not create any gameplay advantages on the level of mechanics, they might influence the players' experience deeply.

Within game studies, useful introductions to game interpretation already exist, covering widely different aspects of the gaming experience (Jones (2008), Egenfeldt-Nielsen et al. (2013) and Upton (2015)). Game analysis covers the aesthetics of visuals, music, sound and haptics as well as user interface design, the mechanics of gameplay and the narrative details of interactive storytelling. The main insight provided by intermediality theory is that acts of communication can use several different modalities and media to convey a message or tell a story. This insight can be applied to any medium, including video games.

Video games offer players the pleasures of toying with all other technical, basic and qualified media types within the confines of their virtual realms. We might perceive them as 'immaterial' because most games simulate the material modality of our primary world to make believable facsimiles. For example, when you play the historical action-adventure game *Assassin's Creed: Odyssey* (2018), you experience the simulated world of Ancient Greece and the historical event of the Peloponnesian wars. You have paid for the software online, downloaded it via the digital distribution platform Steam and run it on your PC, but the digital artefact, the game, is influenced by artistic and scientific writings on Greece. Maps, architectural models and other media products all contribute to the experience. In the game, your character, Alexios or Kassandra, gets access to an immersive collage of other media types that are woven together to create a sense of worldness. They can attend theatrical performances, see and climb a model of the Acropolis where the Parthenon is, wear period-accurate armour and listen to sea shanties performed in Ancient Greek. Over the course of the game, you meet representations of historical figures such as the philosopher Socrates (ca. 470–399 BCE), the general Cleon (d. 422 BCE) or the writer and historian Herodotus (ca. 484–ca. 425 BCE), fight simulated naval battles and travel to every major island of the Greek archipelago in order to experience a story designed to bring the ancient world to life. Thus, even a mostly 'immaterial' medium, a digital game, is thoroughly affected by a wealth of other media that bring a piece of Ancient Greece to the contemporary world.

The technical medium of display

The computer is a technical medium, perhaps the most obviously technical medium in our lives today. It is a medium that not only puts on display different kinds of qualified media but helps to realize them by computing calculations that need to be performed so that the computer screen, loudspeakers and controllers can function as technical media of display. Computer games require expensive machinery to design, run, display and interact with. Very schematically, we talk about hardware (devices that run on electricity), operating systems (programs that define what can happen once the machine is turned on and how we can interact with it), middleware (programs such as drivers and engines that define how code is presented to the user) and software components (pieces of code that are executed to perform a service to the user); all of these aspects work together to deliver an experience. The part of the media product that users buy is the software (and sometimes the controllers), the digital code that has to be run on hardware with operating systems. They can be purchased in various physical data storage formats, but the disc is not necessarily the only means of storage and dissemination.

We use digital media that are based on binary code to access all kinds of qualified media. But while we primarily focus on the screens and loudspeakers of computers to read e-books, watch films and read news, computer games involve the use of manipulation devices to a greater extent than other media. Controllers come in all shapes and sizes, but most make use of the most agile part of the human body, the hand. Controllers are mostly proprietary, which binds consumers to particular companies. Some games, such as those developed for use with the Nintendo Wii (Jones and Thiruvathukal 2012) or Microsoft Kinect, also involve the whole of your body, so you have to physically jump or slash with your hand rather than just press a button.

Production process: Game design and programming

Crucially, in computer games, the experience is designed to make the player feel certain emotions to entertain them. Although players look for 'fun' in games, playing a digital game can involve frustration (Melhárt 2018), failure (Juul 2013), grief (Chittaro and Sioni 2018) and even boredom (Buday et al. 2012) for various aesthetic reasons. An intermedial understanding of computer games must start from an awareness that various media are employed in making the game experience meaningful to the player.

Game design can be the work of a single person or a vast collaborative studio. A game such as *Stardew Valley* (2016), for example, is the creation of one man, Eric Barone, who came up with the idea of the game, wrote its code, drew its visual assets, composed its music and wrote its dialogue on his own. In contrast, *Assassin's Creed: Odyssey* was made by literally thousands of people, spread across the globe from Montréal to Bucharest, Pune, Kiev and Shanghai; hundreds of coders, designers, voice actors, quality assurance personnel and even its own historians were hired. The end credits run for over thirty minutes. Yet both games can produce similar feelings in players: moments of tenderness in response to a love relationship being represented, moments of tedium as the player does repetitive tasks and moments of excitement as the player unlocks new gameplay features or explores a new storyline. How those experiences are achieved can be studied by paying attention to the cumulative effects of different modalities of media on what is expressed in the program.

Researchers should always be mindful that a digital game is not a fixed media product in the same way as a novel or a film is. It is often said that a game is never finished; designers just stop iterating on a product. Because games are a product of development, the media product changes even past its release. Prior to release, they are often opened up to the playing public for a reduced price to gain insight into ordinary players' interactions with the game and to secure continued funding for development. After release, a game often receives patches and additional content, such as expansion packs and downloadable content to extend the core media product.

Players, of course, not only vote with their wallets, but they can also be quite vocal in giving feedback when they find some aspects of a program particularly satisfying or frustrating. Such feedback influences the finished product in a myriad of subtle ways. More importantly, some players are technically adept enough to create modifications (mods) for existing entertainment software, which might alter the appearance or behaviour of the program to redress what the modder(s) felt lacking in the original. These, in turn, might even be re-incorporated into the published games at a later date, an issue that is contentious in the industry, because the unpaid labour of players can then be capitalized upon by canny developers.

Basic media types

If the computing machine (including consoles, smartphones, coin-operated arcade machines and online servers, among others) is the technical medium for delivering the experience, then *code* is its *basic medium* in the production of computer games. Digital code is infinitely reproducible data that suffers no loss of information through copying, unlike analogue data. Digital code is written in a *programming language* that describes how the human conventions of programming define computer behaviour. Code in a programming language must be translated into lower-level code through the use of a *compiler*, either into a code that is written for particular processors (called an assembly language) or directly into *machine code* (which is what the processing unit 'understands'). These levels are not usually studied in humanities research of computer games (but see Jerz 2007, who does study them). This is because these levels are not directly accessible to the player and the aesthetic experience they have. Nonetheless, all these levels of communication serve as the precondition for experiencing the media product, and their artificiality is often exposed when malfunctions happen. Video games often behave in ways that were not intended by its developers: software bugs, exploits and related phenomena are part and parcel of the gaming experience precisely because its basic medium, code, defines principles of simulation rather than working as a mere representation.

The basic media type of code is processed into other basic media types that the player accesses via the user interface, such as moving images, sound waves and text, which the player interprets as the qualified submedia types of the soundtrack, dialogue, cut-scene, introductory cinematic, and so on (see Chapter 2). These basic media types are integrated and provide the simulation of the game world, mediate narrative events, instruct players on how to interact with the game, establish mood and tone, and reward the players aesthetically for achieving game goals.

Games challenge their players to varying degrees: a game's difficulty often makes it memorable. Challenges may be related to navigation, speed, collecting objects, conflict, dialogue, the use of logic, tactical decisions and following a strategy. The challenges are often presented multimodally and require thinking across modalities. Puzzles in games like *The Witness* (2016), for example, notoriously depend on the manipulation of perspective for the solution of their puzzles. On the other hand, some games such as *Crypt of the NecroDancer* (2015) rely on the seamless integration of music into their challenges by forcing the player to push control buttons in sync with the game's soundtrack.

Performing tasks and spending time in the material modality (see Table 5.1) in the simulated game world is an important part of the experience of a video game. In order to analyse a video game, one must engage with it extensively to

Table 5.1 Media and modalities – Computer games

Media types and modalities	Description
Technical devices and media of display	Computing machines (including consoles, smartphones, coin-operated arcade machines and online servers) **Production**: programming code, engines, authoring tools **Dissemination**: arcade cabinets (1970s), home computers (1977–, console computers), mobile devices, VR and AR equipment
Basic media types	Programming code (Moving) image, (auditory) text (voiceover dialogue), non-verbal sound (sound effects), organized sound (game soundtrack)
Qualified media type	An entertainment software to exercise agency in a digitally realized virtual environment Technical development's effect on interaction and simulation **Contexts**: transmedia context, social interaction around games **User coordination models**: single-player, multiplayer, offline, mobile **Genres**: adventure game, first-person shooter, real-time strategy, business simulation, etc. **Intended reception**: entertainment, educational, or serious games **Main mechanics and interactions**: e.g. navigation, puzzles, collection, combat, dialogue and ethical choices
Material modality	Flat surfaces of screens, sound waves and loudspeakers, interface objects (controllers)
Sensorial modality	Perception: auditory, visual, tactile Cognition: interpretation of game state, prediction of future game states, practical know-how of control
Spatiotemporal modality	**Material**: length of play. The space needed for computer and equipment **Sensorial**: the sequentiality of the simulated events **Semiotic**: the simulated space of the game world, the virtual time of a narrative
Semiotic modality	**Image**: iconic and symbolic (when used to explain manipulation of the computer and interaction in the game) **(Auditory) text**: dominantly symbolic (also used to explain the rules of the game, indexical, e.g. in relation to characters' emotions and social identity) **Moving images**: dominantly iconic and indexical **Sound effects**: iconic and indexical **Organized sound**: dominantly iconic and indexical but symbolic as well Basic and qualified media types within the game world are often interpreted as indexical (in relation to solving the tasks)

make well-supported statements about its behaviour and contents. Because games challenge players and reward them with gameplay and story progress, they require significant time commitment and effort on the part of players to experience the game in full: they can be quite hard and failure is always an option. Unlike when engaging with other media, players can get stuck and will fail to see the unfolding of narrative arcs or the growing complexity of gameplay if they give up in frustration or boredom. Games bring in new mechanics, flesh out their stories and crank up the challenge as players progress, which adds layers of complexity that are essential to the enjoyment and critical assessment of the media product. The increased depth of understanding is integrated into the temporality of playing the game.

Qualifying aspects of computer games

What kind of experience we get out of the qualified media type of a computer game depends upon a bewilderingly wide array of cultural contexts. They range from the economic realities of how to make a successful commercial game under capitalism to audience expectations about the game experiences they are in the market for. Scholars might include the decisions about which groups are targeted as the core audience of a media product in their analysis, or the cultural background of various player cohorts. More technically minded interpretation may consider the hardware and software environments available for new designs. Sociocultural studies can highlight the historical contingencies of the evolution of gameplay genres, the media products in other qualified media, and many more. Intermedial scholars of computer games are advised to always consider the relevant social, historical and cultural forces that shape the media product under scrutiny.

> **Box 5.1 Interpretative frameworks for making sense of games**
>
> Since their inception, video games have been analysed from a variety of disciplines and each read games on their own terms. Game studies scholars with a literary background are prone to analyse **games as texts** authored by the designer, with characters, narratives, and the player as an interpreter that 'reads' the game. Scholars with a focus on design or architecture might treat **games as worlds**, paying close attention to how the spatial arrangements of the game's areas, the player's access to them, the background story, and other elements fuse together to create a game world. Scholars who sought to vindicate the uniqueness of computer games and their irreconcilability with other media (a stance that intermedial theories of games should always question) point towards **games as simulations**, highlighting their capabilities of representing complex, rule-based systems, and argue that simulations produce less fixed aesthetic products than the representations produced by traditional art. Scholars informed by the methods and theories of cultural studies tend to interpret **games as cultural artefacts**,

> which encode and challenge particular cultural conventions and social identities; these scholars often work on issues such as class, race, religion, gender, sexuality, disability as represented by games and experienced by players (based on Jørgensen 2020, pp. 67–102).

There would be no games without people to play them. Many of the controversies surrounding computer games stem from what players do when gaming, or what effect games have on their players. Different player groups interact with games differently. Single-player games, especially those with a strong narrative thread, tend to constrain player's actions more than multiplayer games, which thrive on player-to-player interaction. Multiplayer games come both in game modes that emphasize cooperation against computer-controlled opponents and in modes that pit players against each other in competitive settings. Several of the most popular multiplayer titles, such as *Counter-Strike* (1999), *League of Legends* (2009) or *Fortnite* (2017), thrive on player conflict and high-level team tactics. This last point highlights another important aspect of multiplayer games: that they also provide a venue for connecting players, enabling them to socialize through games as a media platform, building communities and challenging others to display gaming proficiency. Similarly, massively multiplayer online games also create game mechanics to foster the reliance of players on each other to defeat enemies and other players' teams in combat. Because their representations in games (often called their 'avatars') allow gamers to trade equipment, display their in-game wealth in the form of wearable items and general appearance, there are entire player-run economies, as well as leaderboards, to relate players' performances against each other.

It is precisely because of the competitiveness of these multiplayer games that players who are too emotionally invested in their in-game success at the cost of others' tend to exhibit behaviour that can be characterized as hostile or toxic (see Condis (2018) and Salter and Blodgett (2017, pp. 73–99)), making these venues unpleasant places for players with an expectation of fairness, good sportsmanship, equal treatment and more of a live-and-let-live mentality.

Video games as media products are diverse enough on their own that making general statements about the medium is close to impossible. Single-player, multiplayer and massively multiplayer games elicit very different expectations and provide very different experiences. For example, single-player games can weave complex, dramatic stories with a definite closure; multiplayer games offer a tougher challenge by pitting the player against other humans rather than AI-controlled opponents; Massively Multiplayer Online games are played across the globe in persistent game worlds that evolve and a working market economy that booms and goes bust as time goes on. Many games offer both single-player and multiplayer options, and a lot of content in MMOs can be accessed as a single player.

Offline games have a different business model to online games and software-as-a-service games, which affects the available content and gameplay experience. Notably, offline games are purchased for a flat fee in a game shop or a digital distribution platform, and the player can experience the core content without being connected to the internet. Online games use the internet to enhance the single-player experience, by providing additional purchasable content, connecting players, for example, into collaborative teams that compete against others, or by offering an online trading system that forms an in-game market economy. Software-as-a-service games are purchased as a subscription for a defined period of time, which opens up a play experience that can be expanded by paying additional sums.

Mobile games have a different look, feel, control scheme and target audience from console and PC games. This is due to the technical limitations of the hardware and the conditions of the play environment. So-called 'casual games' (Juul 2012) also cater to a different demographic from core gaming audiences, which means that the entire design philosophy changes, especially with regard to the level of difficulty, accessibility, subject material and methods for encouraging player engagement. Casual titles are meant to be learned easily, not to require long play sessions and are designed to tone down challenges in favour of providing a light-hearted atmosphere. The distinction between titles intended for core gaming audiences and casual players are often insidiously couched in gendered terms, with repercussions to which groups of players are considered 'real' gamers and have the 'rightful' access to the cultural capital associated with gaming (Shaw 2012). Major developers can bring vast open worlds with photorealistic graphics to life, by designing a narrative that spans hundred hours of gameplay, complete with orchestral music and Hollywood voice actors, but they are beholden to shareholders and the profit motive, which entails making risk-averse business decisions. Indie developers, on the contrary, can afford to experiment with radical new game mechanics and unusual visual aesthetics (Juul 2019), but they are much more likely to pursue game design as a hobby rather than a full-time job, and the markets can be fickle with praise and in terms of success. Independent game development is not necessarily synonymous with the 'indie style' of games being produced; indeed, many independent games are produced professionally, and cannot be easily subsumed under 'indie game' aesthetics (Garda and Grabarczyk 2016).

As for the **intermedial** context of a given media product, it has to be noted that the video game medium is especially receptive to (and generative of) intermedial influences. This capacity undoubtedly owes much to the digital materiality of the medium, its protean capacity to remediate other media types, as well as the sensorially stimulating, viscerally emotional experiences it generates and corporeally involving performances it requires of its players. Many videogames capitalize on the intellectual properties of other media: they are especially keen to adapt sports, board games, films, comic books and novels. In turn, games create new franchises that often make it to the silver screen, the pages of graphic novels, licensed novelizations, not to mention the ubiquitous merchandizing products that exploit the deep desire of players to possess some tangible and material extension of the virtual worlds they have experiences in. Games themselves are media that have affected the aesthetics of other media, from the emergence of the literary role-playing or 'LitRPG' genre of novels to the game-like presentation of certain films (Navarro-Remesal 2019), such as Ilya Naishuller's *Hardcore Henry* (2015), Tom Tykwer's *Run, Lola Run*, Christopher Nolan's *Inception*, and others.

Box 5.2 The paratexts of computer games

The challenges posed by gameplay have led to the burgeoning industry of gaming paratexts, secondary media products that spring up around an original work of art to explain, configure, contextualize or extend the media product, or to make it available for critical scrutiny. They can be as simple as a soundtrack released as a CD or as complex as a Wiki-style knowledge base with 100,000 pages.

Game-specific paratexts include but are not limited to the following: 1) the game manual, usually a printed supplement, explaining in greater detail how to operate the program, 2) technical support media, such as online customer support or – formerly – phone-in services, where users can contact the company if there is a technical malfunction or to request a refund and 3) official communities, such as developer-operated online forums, where players can meet for in-depth discussions of games, or online voiceover protocol services for communicating while gaming.

Additionally, users and third-party service providers create their own paratexts as a labour of love or for profit: two game-specific forms of paratexts are 1) walkthroughs and guides, ranging from detailed step-by-step descriptions of how to complete a game (for more story-driven and linear games) to strategic tips and tricks (for more open-ended, abstract or simulation-based games) that help mitigate the challenge factor of the game, and 2) game retellings (see Eladhari (2018) and Sych (2020)), which narrow the many potential stories of games into one experience. They can take the form of recorded play sessions, ranging from text-based after-action reports of strategy games to 'Let's Play!'-style captioned screenshot narratives and video recordings, which add the unique voice and personality of the commentator to a playthrough. These are all valid targets of (inter)medial research, but their secondary status and the problem of the sheer volume in which they are produced present unique methodological challenges to scholarship.

Gaming experience in the four modalities

Digital games make use of all available media modalities to create a gaming experience. How those experiences are achieved can be studied by analysing the cumulative effects of different modalities of media on what is expressed in the program. The discussion in this section is based on Lars Elleström's typology of media modalities (for an even more nuanced and medium-specific approach, see the ludophile intermedial framework of Jørgensen 2020, pp. 174–84).

Most video games use multiple *material* interfaces, one of which is almost always a screen (some experimental, non-commercial games have tried to forgo them, with limited success). But in order to express your agency within the game, you manipulate certain objects. First, not all games are equally material, but they would not exist if they did not at one point become physical objects. Even though video games are written in code, the machines that run them must be purchased. Storage media that deliver the code, such as magnetic or optical discs, are easy to copy, but suffer from data loss over time, known as 'disc rot', making the preservation of games more problematic than, say, books. Games also involve your body and prompt you to perform certain operations on the machine to influence the game state. Historically, games first appeared for mass consumption in video arcades, where large cabinets were installed. Arcade games usually require you to stand up next to a cabinet, while most PC and console games are played sitting down. Usually, there is some physical interface that translates your actions. Some are more abstract or symbolic, such as joysticks and buttons, while others are more iconic in the Peircean sense, like toy guns, steering wheels and even motorbikes that you can ride. A significant element of gaming's attractiveness is its *sensorial* appeal, whether we are referring to its eye-pleasing visuals, haunting soundscapes or the shock of the controller as it vibrates. The very name 'video games', which was coined in the 1970s, suggests that the display of visual elements (*video* means 'I see' in Latin) in the virtual space provides its main allure when compared to their main competitor in the arcades: pinball machines.

Accordingly, the discussion about what machines can or cannot display became the chief domain of competition between the designers of different games and platforms – a race that continues today. However, as Torben Grodal (2003) notes in the title of his influential article, video games are 'stories for eyes, ears and muscles' at the same time. Interaction with and within the game world is not only facilitated via vision but via other senses as well. Audio cues provide important feedback to the player, affirming that the action they took had an effect in the game world; dialogue lines might be read by recognized voice actors; an original soundtrack sets the mood for scenes and can become memorable in its own right (which is the reason why soundtracks are sold separately, as is the case with feature films); licensed songs bring their previous associations with them to new gaming contexts. Some games also incorporate elements of haptic (touch-based) controls and gameplay. Gestural control is how you interact with touchscreens and Microsoft's Kinect games, and they can mimic in-game motions, such as slicing, jumping or beckoning; modern steering wheels give players so-called 'force feedback' by using motors in the wheel to simulate the real forces experienced by drivers, while some controllers can vibrate to indicate something spooky or hidden in the game world. A few games have even made use of our sense of smell, as they distribute 'scratch and sniff' cards, which players use to progress through the game or to immerse themselves into the game world (Montfort 2003, p. 159).

Games take *time and place* both literally and figuratively (see Aarseth (2007), Borries et al. (2007) and Zagal and Mateas (2010)). The spatiotemporal modality accounts for the real place and time where and when gaming happens, on the one hand, and the place and time of the game worlds being simulated, on the other. The discrepancy between the simulated time and the experienced time of games in the real world is a fruitful avenue for inquiry. The amount of time people spend video gaming, especially excessive game usage, has been a constant source of consternation in news articles. Early arcade games had play sessions that lasted minutes, similar to some of today's mobile games, while modern open-world games regularly last for between 40 and 60 hours, and online games offer content into which players can sink hundreds of hours. Historically, places where video games were played prior to the home computer revolution, such as video arcades, were thought to be dens of iniquity and listlessness, little better than casinos. With the advent of home computers, people started incorporating dedicated play spaces into their living rooms; and today, motion-controlled and VR consoles require extensive floor space for freedom of movement. Portable and handheld gaming devices (like Game Boy, a cultural icon of the 1990s) brought gaming out into the open, and once smartphones became widespread, location-based gaming gave rise to the whole genre of 'alternate reality games' or ARGs, such as *Harry Potter: Wizards Unite* (2019), which use the location services of phones to extend play into the world at large. Video games, being simulations, can theoretically represent any known real-world location in any time period, as well as literally any range of fictional scenarios, that is, worlds with different physical and behavioural attributes. Nonetheless, the simulationist aspect of the media type offers a fertile ground for adapting games' plots and settings from the tropes of popular franchises and fictional genres: Tolkienian fantasy, military science fiction, horror, swashbuckling adventure, historical and modern warfare, and contemporary sports are perennial favourites. Do note that these are genres based on the spatiotemporal location and the aesthetic presentation of a game's storyworld, not the genre of a game itself. As part of the representational discourse of games, they do not affect the interactional schemata of the games. Video game genres are defined by what sort of challenge they pose to the player, what kind of actions or skills are needed to perform within the game, and which aspects of the world are simulated. In fact, one could argue that video games are so diverse that what the industry calls different genres mean different qualified media types in our terminology. For the purposes of this introduction to the intermediality of computer games, it is more instructive to consider what unites these various forms under one banner.

Finally, digital games are deeply *semiotic* by nature; they depend on the processing and interpretation of signs on several levels. Code is nothing but a series of signs, as anyone who programs or has seen *The Matrix* (1999) will tell you. The game world the player perceives and the interactions the player can perform are the results of two kinds of sign interpretations: the machine interprets the signs from the user interface, and the player interprets the state of the machine and the player action that is required to perform adequately. The graphical user interface is a set of intermediate signs that facilitate the manipulation of the game world. All computer programs rely heavily on the use of visual icons. Iconic representations are used in interfaces to give visual hints about what a particular portion of the screen does, that is, how it changes the computer's operations when it is interacted with. Iconic/symbolical sounds give feedback about whether an operational action was carried out successfully or not. Finally, when interacting within the game world, the player also interprets the information gained from iconic images and symbolic signs of written or spoken language indexically as traces of what happened or hints about how to proceed and what kind of action to take. This kind of indexical information can come in all forms of basic and qualified media types: gamers activate recorded audio dialogues, see hand-drawn and scanned artwork or digitized filmstrips or follow tutorial arrows pointing to the user interface or the next game goal. And last but not least, symbolic interaction with signs occurs whenever players read or click on text, listen to dialogue, learn the conventions of game genres and come to expect them in the next game of the same sort, or when they decipher codes in certain games (see Chapter 17)

Further reading

Arjoranta, J. 2016. Game definitions: A Wittgensteinian approach. *Game Studies: The International Journal of Computer Game Research*, 14. https://jyx.jyu.fi/handle/123456789/50880?locale-attribute=en [Accessed 3 December 2020]

Arsenault, D. 2009. Video game genre, evolution and innovation. *Eludamos. Journal for Computer Game Culture*, 3(2), pp. 149–176. http://www.eludamos.org/index.php/eludamos/article/view/vol3no2-3/125 [Accessed 3 December 2020].

Bogost, I. 2007. *Persuasive games: The expressive power of videogames*. [e-book] Cambridge, MA; London: MIT Press. https://books.google.se/books?id=L-2FSAAACAAJ [Accessed 3 December 2020].

Bogost, I. 2008. *Unit operations: An approach to videogame criticism*. Cambridge, MA: MIT Press.

Consalvo, M. and Dutton, N. 2006. Game analysis: Developing a methodological toolkit for the qualitative study of games. *Game Studies* 6(1). Available at http://gamestudies.org/06010601/articles/consalvo_dutton [Accessed 3 December 2020].

Dyer-Witheford, N. and De Peuter, G. 2009. *Games of empire: Global capitalism and video games*. Minneapolis, MN: University of Minnesota Press.

Fassone, R., Giordano, F. and Girina, I. 2015. Re-framing video games in the light of cinema. *G|A|M|E Games as Art, Media, Entertainment*, 1(4). https://www.gamejournal.it/4_giordano_girina_fassone/ [Accessed 3 December 2020].

Grau, O. 2003. *Virtual art: From illusion to immersion*. Cambridge, MA; London: MIT Press.

Henthorne, T. 2003. Cyber-utopias: The politics and ideology of computer games. *Studies in Popular Culture*, 25(3), pp. 63–76.

Laurel, B. 2013. *Computers as theatre*. 2nd ed. Menlo Park: Addison Wesley Professional.

Maher, J. 2012. *The future was here: The Commodore Amiga*. Cambridge, MA: MIT Press.

Montfort, N. and Bogost, I. 2008. *Racing the beam: The Atari Video Computer System*. Cambridge, MA: MIT Press.

Myers, D. 2009. The video game aesthetic: Play as form. In B. Perron and M.J.P. Wolf, eds., *The video game theory reader* 2 (pp. 45–63). New York; London: Routledge.

References

Aarseth, E. 2007. Allegories of space: The question of spatiality in computer games. In F. von Borries, S.P. Walz and M. Böttger, eds., *Space time play: Computer games, architecture and urbanism: The next level* (pp. 44–47). Berlin: Birkhäuser.

Booth, Paul. 2016. Board, game, and media: Interactive board games as multimedia convergence. *Convergence* 22(6), pp. 647–660. doi:10.1177/1354856514561828

Borries, F., Walz, S.P. and Böttger, M. 2007. *Space time play: Computer games, architecture and urbanism: The next level*. Berlin: Birkhäuser.

Buday, R., Baranowski, T. and Thompson, D. 2012. Fun and games and boredom. *Games for Health Journal*, 1(4), pp. 257–261. doi:10.1089/g4h.2012.0026

Chittaro, L. and Sioni, R. 2018. Existential video games: Proposal and evaluation of an interactive reflection about death. *Entertainment Computing*, 26, pp. 59–77. doi:10.1016/j.entcom.2018.01.004

Condis, Megan. 2018. *Gaming masculinity: Trolls, fake geeks, and the gendered battle for online culture*. Iowa City: University of Iowa Press.

Egenfeldt-Nielsen, S., Smith, J.H. and Tosca, S.P. 2013. *Understanding video games: The essential introduction* [e-book]. Hoboken: Taylor & Francis. http://public.eblib.com/choice/publicfullrecord.aspx?p=1181119 [Accessed 3 December 2020].

Eladhari, M.P. 2018. Re-tellings: The fourth layer of narrative as an instrument for critique BT – interactive storytelling. In R. Rouse, H. Koenitz and M. Haahr, eds., Interactive Storytelling 12th International Conference on Interactive Digital Storytelling, ICIDS 2019, Little Cottonwood Canyon, UT, USA, November 19–22, 2019 (pp. 65–78). Cham: Springer International.

Frasca, G. 2013. Simulation versus narrative: Introduction to ludology. In M.J.P. Wolf and B. Perron, eds., *The video game theory reader* (pp. 221–235). New York: Taylor & Francis. doi:10.4324/9780203700457

Garda, Maria B. and Paweł Grabarczyk. 2016. Is every indie game independent? Towards the concept of independent game. *Game Studies* 16(1). http://gamestudies.org/1601/articles/gardagrabarczyk

Grodal, T. 2003. Stories for eye, ear, and muscles: Video games, media, and embodied experiences. In M.J.P. Wolf and B. Perron, eds., *The video game theory reader* (pp. 129–155). New York: Taylor and Francis. doi:10.4324/9780203700457

Hardcore Henry. 2015. Directed by Ilya Naishuller. Beijing: Huayi Brothers Pictures.

Holmes, D. 2013. *A mind forever voyaging: A history of storytelling in video games*. San Bernardino, CA: CreateSpace Independent Publishing Platform.

Hunicke, Robin, Robin Hunicke, Marc Leblanc and Robert Zubek. 2004. *MDA: A formal approach to game design and game research*. Proceedings of the Challenges in Games AI Workshop, Nineteenth National Conference of Artificial Intelligence, 1–5. https://citeseerx.ist.psu.edu/viewdoc/summary?doi=10.1.1.79.4561

Jerz, D.G. 2007. Somewhere nearby is a colossal cave: Examining Will Crowther's original 'Adventure' in code and in Kentucky. *Digital Humanities Quarterly*, 1(2). http://digitalhumanities.org//dhq/vol/1/2/000009/000009.html

Jones, S.E. 2008. *The meaning of video games: Gaming and textual strategies*. New York, London: Routledge.
Jones, S.E. and Thiruvathukal, G.K. 2012. *Codename revolution: The Nintendo Wii platform*. Cambridge, MA: MIT Press.
Jørgensen, Ida Kathrine Hammeleff. 2020. Games as Representational Artifacts: A Media-Centered Analytical Approach to Representation in Games. *IT-Universitetet i København*. https://pure.itu.dk/portal/en/publications/games-as-representational-artifacts(046bb469-1582-404b-8f3c-62de5836d3f5).html
Juul, J. 2005. *Half-real: Video games between real rules and fictional worlds*. Cambridge, MA; London: MIT Press.
Juul, J. 2012. *A casual revolution: Reinventing video games and their players*. Cambridge, MA: MIT Press.
Juul, J. 2013. *The art of failure: An essay on the pain of playing video games*. Cambridge, MA: MIT Press.
Juul, J. 2019. *Handmade pixels: Independent video games and the quest for authenticity*. Cambridge, MA: MIT Press.
Karhulahti, V-M. 2015. Do videogames simulate? Virtuality and imitation in the philosophy of simulation. *Simulation & Gaming*, 46 (December), pp. 838–856. doi:10.1177/1046878115616219
Klastrup, Lisbeth. 2009. The worldness of EverQuest: Exploring a 21st century fiction. *Game Studies* 9(1). http://gamestudies.org/0901/articles/klastrup
Koenitz, Hartmut. 2010. Towards a theoretical framework for interactive digital narrative. In Ruth Aylett, Mei Yii Lim, Sandy Louchart, Paolo Petta and Mark Riedl, eds., Interactive Storytelling Third Joint Conference on Interactive Digital Storytelling, ICIDS 2010, Edinburgh, UK, November 1–3, 2010 (pp. 176–185). Berlin, Heidelberg: Springer.
Koenitz, H., Eladhari, M.P., Louchart, S. and Nack F. 2020. INDCOR white paper 1: A shared vocabulary for IDN (Interactive Digital Narratives), October [online]. http://arxiv.org/abs/2010.10135 [Accessed 3 December 2020].
The Matrix. 1999. Directed by Lana Wachowski and Lilly Wachowski. USA: Warner Bros. Pictures.
Melhárt, D. 2018. Towards a comprehensive model of mediating frustration in videogames. *Game Studies*, 18(1). http://gamestudies.org/1801/articles/david_melhart [Accessed 3 December 2020].
Montfort, N. 2003. *Twisty little passages: An approach to interactive fiction*. Cambridge, MA: MIT Press.
Murray, J.H. 2017. *Hamlet on the holodeck: The future of narrative in cyberspace*. Cambridge, MA: MIT Press.
Navarro-Remesal, Víctor. 2019. *Cine ludens: 50 diálogos entre el juego y el cine*. Barcelona: Editorial UOC.
Ruggill, Judd Ethan and Ken S. McAllister. 2011. *Gaming matters: Art, science, magic, and the computer game medium*. Tuscaloosa: The University of Alabama Press.
Ryan, M.-L. 2001. *Narrative as virtual reality*. Baltimore, MD: Johns Hopkins University Press.
Salter, Anastasia and Bridget Blodgett. 2017. *Toxic geek masculinity in media: Sexism, trolling, and identity policing*. Cham: Palgrave Macmillan. http://public.eblib.com/choice/publicfullrecord.aspx?p=5143375

Shaw, Adrienne. 2012. Do you identify as a gamer? Gender, race, sexuality, and gamer identity. *New Media & Society* 14(1) (February 2012), pp. 28–44. doi:10.1177/1461444811410394

Sych, S. 2020. When the fourth layer meets the fourth wall: the case for critical game retellings BT – interactive storytelling. In A-G. Bosser, D.E. Millard and C. Hargood, eds., Interactive Storytelling. 13th International Conference on Interactive Digital Storytelling, ICIDS 2020, Bournemouth, UK, November 3–6, 2020 (pp. 203–211). Cham: Springer International.

Thabet, T. 2014. *Video game narrative and criticism: Playing the story*. London: Palgrave Macmillan.

Upton, B. 2015. *The aesthetic of play*. Cambridge, MA: MIT Press.

Walk, Wolfgang, Daniel Görlich, and Mark Barrett. 2017. Design, dynamics, experience (DDE): An advancement of the MDA framework for game design. In *Game dynamics* (pp. 27–45). Cham: Springer International Publishing. doi:10.1007/978-3-319-53088-8_3

Zagal, J.P. and Mateas, M. 2010. Time in video games: A survey and analysis. *Simulation & Gaming*, 41(6), pp. 844–868. doi:10.1177/1046878110375594

Games cited

Assassin's Creed: Odyssey. 2018. PC. Ubisoft.
Bejeweled. 2001. PopCap. iOS, Windows, macOS, etc. PopCap/Electronic Arts.
Counter-Strike. 1999. Minh Lee and Jess Cliffe. Valve/Sierra Studios.
Crypt of the NecroDancer. 2015. Windows, OSX, Linux, PlayStation, etc. Music composed by Danny Baranowsky. Brace Yourself Games.
Fortnite. 2017. Epic Games. Windows, macOS, PlayStation5, Xbox, etc. Epic Games/Warner Bros.
Grand Theft Auto V. 2015. PC, Xbox, PlayStation 3 & 4. Rockstar Games.
Harry Potter: Wizards Unite. 2019. Android, iOS. Niantic.
League of Legends. 2009. Riot Games. Windows, macOS. Riot Games/Tencent.
Plague, Inc. 2012. iOS, Android, Windows Phone. Ndemic.
The Sims. 2000. Maxis. PC, macOS. EA Games.
Stardew Valley. 2016. Windows, macOS, PlayStation 4, etc. ConcernedApe/Chucklefish.
The Witness. 2016. Thekla Inc. Windows, macOS, PlayStation 4, etc. Thekla Inc.

6 Media and modalities – News media

Kristoffer Holt and Beate Schirrmacher

As we were writing this chapter, the 2020 election campaign in the US was entering its last week before the elections. There are probably few more news-intensive events in the world than the American presidential elections. The smallest and, in other settings, seemingly irrelevant details of a candidate's behaviour and appearance (a slip of the tongue, the way that they laugh or their temporary memory losses) are immediately picked up by cameras and microphones and publicized across news networks and commented on and shared throughout social media networks in a matter of seconds and minutes, possibly affecting people's attitudes towards particular politicians and parties (directly or indirectly).

The circulation of news is a prerequisite for any modern democratic society and is typically expected to serve the purpose of scrutinizing those in power, expose abuse and corruption while at the same time informing citizens about important events, risks and developments (Aalberg and Curran 2013). How news is produced and received has been studied quite extensively, and the effects of news consumption have constituted a long-standing issue in communication scholarship (see, for example, Ells (2018) and Harcup and O'Neill (2016)). The way news is mediated is fundamental to our understanding of the meaning of news in our societies and cultures (see Zelizer (2017) and Bennett (2016)). Lacey and Rosenstiehl (2015) proposed a definition that is both representative of scholarly perspectives and summative of the components and use of news: 'Journalism is the serial presentation of information and conversation about public events, trends and issues distributed through various media with the primary purpose of informing, entertaining and connecting citizens in communities' (p. 5). In everyday speech news media are '*the* media'. News media highlight in a nearly paradigmatic way how our idea of any media depends on the ways they are produced and disseminated. News looks and sounds very different depending on whether we read newspapers, listen to the radio, watch the evening news or check our social media feed. What do all these different media products have in common? And does it matter whether we read our news on paper or whether we scroll the latest headlines on our smartphone? What happens when we share news on social media?

DOI: 10.4324/9781003174288-7

An intermedial perspective allows us to point out how these questions are interconnected. We will explore the role of mass media as technical media of display. We draw attention to how basic media types such as text, still or moving images or auditory media types are integrated into a characteristic mode of presentation. Taken together, these characteristics form the conventions that qualify our perception of news.

What is news?

News has been a crucial aspect of human life for as long as we have organized ourselves in societal structures. Up-to-date knowledge about available resources, prices and army sizes have determined fates throughout history (Barnhurst and Nerone 2002). Narrations of recent battles, discoveries, royal marriages, power struggles and intrigues have always attracted attention – as much around the tribal fires of long ago as they do today, even though we can now access news via screens or headphones. Throughout human history, pieces of news have thus always been – in some form or other – commodities with a specific value. And being able to share relevant news has always been connected with status – even long before the invention of social media. In today's hybrid media landscape (Chadwick 2013), however, defining what is 'news' is trickier, from a scholarly perspective, than it used to be when most of the news was primarily distributed by powerful, authorized mass media with massive reach. Social media have become crucial not only for the dissemination and sharing of news, but also as a tool for research into current topics and a way of reaching out to people for interviews. It is not only professional journalists who disseminate news via digital media; bloggers and Facebook users do so as well, as do various alternative media, which challenges the previously privileged position of legacy news providers (Hendrickx 2020).

In a traditional journalistic sense, news is often defined in terms of newsworthiness: news tells stories about current events, about people, things and events that are deemed important (for example, in terms of political implications), novel, unusual or peculiar and that have some element that is of interest to humans. But the concept of news is also shaped in a heuristic way by the technical media of display: news is what pops up in newspapers or news broadcasts on a daily basis. News is what you read on folded paper, news is a text with a bold headline, and news is what you hear and watch at a particular time of day. News is formed by the technical media that display them and involves a particular use of basic media types. But looking at the issue like this quickly leads to the realization that defining news according to its external appearance is a 'primitive construct' (Shoemaker 2006, p. 105). And what ends up as links to pieces of news (often with comments that frame them) in your Twitter feed is the result of a complex web of decisions, production processes, algorithms and editorial value judgements. For an event to become news, it has to be selected and edited. Also, the value of news as a commodity, like that of currency, depends on what people are willing to pay for it.

The intrinsic quality of novelty

What is a piece of news and why does it exist? The definition of news has shifted historically and so have the shapes and formats in which it is delivered to users. The most obvious constitutive element of news as an object is the intrinsic promise of the novelty and freshness it offers to anyone who is longing to consume it. News is like water that is drawn from a sparkling river and served cold in a glass to the thirsty. In order to qualify as 'news', it has to be retrieved from the never-ending stream of fresh events that flows through the world of humans and that is packaged and served to users who have not yet tasted these specific drops of water – even if they come from a river that everyone has drunk from before. As soon as it has been tasted, it loses value as rapidly as it loses its freshness/novelty, like a bottle of sparkling water that soon gets stale after it has been opened. And like the water in a bottle that is sold at the airport, news has a best-before date. News items are sought out and collected, quality controlled, packaged, branded, transported, distributed and sold to serve the fundamental needs of the masses – to be consumed before the expiry date. News exists on the assumption that 'there is more where this came from'. Its consumption, like rituals and habits, makes sense because of the repetition of this action (Carey 2008). In other words, its raison d'être and general appeal lie, paradoxically, in its intrinsic transience coupled with the promise of there being more tomorrow. Thus, it is important to acknowledge that news is not always sensational or shocking. Routines of production and consumption coupled with expectations of a steady flow of reporting generate many stories that are more or less predictable.

What distinguishes news qua news from mere bits of information is precisely this: the way in which it reaches people and the package in which it comes. In a sense, when we think of news, 'the medium is the message', as Marshall McLuhan (McLuhan and Fiore 1967) famously put it. Information is (and has always been, to some extent) readily available in vast amounts, but this is the case today more than ever before. A set of statistics, however, obtained through some database and automatically imported into a field in a spreadsheet, is not necessarily a piece of news (Clerwall 2014). It can become news the minute it is actively retrieved by journalists, processed editorially and placed within the context of a narrative of an article or a feature in which it sheds light on some aspect of existence that is novel and that makes sense. An event becomes news as it is told as a news story. Ideally, news not only should inform us of what happened but provide some kind of context and understanding of why this particular event matters. When a stock price drops, it makes a splash in some database that is monitored by traders, and that might inform the trader's immediate buying behaviour. To put the event into context, the journalist writes a story based on research and observation and disseminates that story to a large audience. One of the qualifying traits of news, in other words, is its close affinity with the narrative form (see Elleström 2019) as well as with distribution. An often-used synonym for 'news' is indeed 'story'. The function of the story is to inform about an event. To fulfil this task as smoothly as possible, a news story follows well-defined patterns and pre-defined formats.

The technical media of display: News and the mass media

News consists of stories about recent events that are distributed by mass media like newspapers, radio, television and via the internet (along with the old-fashioned mass medium of gossip). There is a very close connection between news and the newspaper as a technical medium of display that was invented to spread news and that is primarily dedicated to spreading news, even if other qualified media types are disseminated as well. Each of these mass media has a specific history of its own. They not only shape the conception of news, but have a particular impact on society and on the public debate. The invention of newspapers helped to establish what we call the public sphere and public debate (Conboy 2004). The internet and rise of social media have radically changed the terms of public discourse.

The technology and business model of mass media include spreading and reaching as many as possible and leads to standardized production processes and story patterns. Whatever is spread via mass media has to comply with the 'media logic' (Altheide 2015). News always exists in a plural form; it reaches its audience in compilations. A media product such as one issue of a newspaper or a particular news programme always consists of different minor media products. A newspaper or news programme will involve different genres of news of different sizes and styles; short reports and longer features, editorials and commentaries, different topics like politics, sports or culture. In newspapers, on the radio and television, news is integrated into larger conglomerates of different media types (Kolodzy 2006).

Thus the news media and their technical media of display form complex networks of relationships on different levels: the production process of news is based on networks and collaborations (Barnhurst and Nerone 2002). News connects different audiences that are addressed differently on different levels, as citizens and consumers. Journalists as professional producers of news always are in dialogue with different audiences.

News and the four modalities

Depending on the technical medium of display, different basic media types are multimodally integrated. Text and images appear on the pages of printed newspapers; auditory text, speech, sound effects and music are used in radio; and moving images, sound effects, auditory text, speech and music are used in television. Historically, different media outlets used different basic media types depending on their technical media of display. In digital communication, there is a convergence of printed, audio and television news, and all kinds of news outlets use text and/or images, videos and new digital forms of news updates.

The basic media types interact closely but are often separately produced in different departments or at different stages of the standardized production process. Separately produced elements are connected by additional elements. Headlines and captions, for instance, connect body text and news photographs.

The quality of news as stories of recent events also influences how audiences interact with the basic media types of news media in the four modalities. In the *material* modality, we interact with surfaces (like screens or pages) when we read a newspaper, we interact with a screen and sound waves from loudspeakers when we watch the TV news, and we interact with sound waves from loudspeakers when we listen to the radio. This means that news uses the same interfaces as many other qualified media types. Contrary to what happens with a novel, a scientific article or a Hollywood movie, the printed pages that display news are repeatedly replaced in daily issues, the screens of news sites are continually updated, and on television and the radio there are several news bulletins a day at certain times.

In the *sensorial* modality, news is therefore constructed to draw our sensory attention to the latest issue/update/developments. Basic media types such as text, images and auditory media types are used to draw attention to the news, for example, the large fonts used for headlines, the jingle that is often played just before radio and TV news, the old-fashioned call of the newspaper sellers in the street and the push notification that makes your smartphone vibrate. Certain media products such as posters and breaking-news banners are designed purely to draw attention to the latest news.

In the *spatiotemporal* modality, we perceive news items as temporal events and developments. But this temporality is not the same as the unfolding that takes place in an ephemeral live theatre performance or in a music performance. News programmes, although temporal events, consist of media products that are produced, archived and often repeated. Similar to the way in which we perceive the sequentiality of texts as temporal because we read one word after the other, one article after the other follows up on the same event. Each individual piece of news is thus part of an unfolding event of news development. This sequential order of pieces of news used to be strictly chronological. In digital media, the position of individual pieces of news in the chronology of news development or their position in the hierarchy of a newspaper or news programme is not stable anymore. Individual news stories are linked and shared on social media. 'Old' news appears as a reading suggestion related to the latest developments (Carlson 2017, pp. 60–6). Another temporal aspect of news not only covers the present and the recent past but the possible future. News not only tells what has recently happened but often involves different scenarios of what might happen as a possible result of the present events. Regarding the spatial characteristics of news, it is clear that news often reports in the material modality from a particular place. The journalist reports from a place where the audience is not, something that Jay Rosen (2013) expresses as the condition of 'awayness'. This condition not only applies to foreign correspondents but expresses the asymmetric relation that the journalist was present at a particular event while most of the audience was not. On the page of the newspaper, spatial relations equal the importance of the event. On television and radio, the amount of time dedicated to reporting an event equals the importance of an event. On the internet, hyperlinks to other articles create a spatiotemporal network.

In the *semiotic modality*, the factual truth claim of news plays an important role. The news tells stories to provide information about an event. In the news, the cohesion of narrative patterns is used to put the particular event into a meaningful context (Carlson 2017, p. 54). This has effects on the visual and auditory form of news. In the factual mode of storytelling, language both in text and in speech is primarily used in accordance with its conventional meaning, as journalism generally strives to take an objective stance. Still, the iconic relations in language can be perceived in the use of metaphors that effectively frame the current event. The truth claim of a factual narrative also highlights the indexical function of written or recorded quotes of sources that are integrated into journalists' reports and the indexical function of photographs and moving images taken at the site of events. Archival or stock images and sounds that are not taken on the site of events illustrate and relate iconically to the event. However, like the verbal imagery of metaphors, stock and archival images frame the event to some extent, and so does music when it is added to the soundtrack.

Qualifying aspects: Turning events into news

So far, we have identified the intrinsic quality (and promise) of novelty and how it is supported by the rapid distribution of mass media as technical media of display. We have also explored how the basic media types combine and integrate to tell the news as a story using standardized narrative patterns.

However, news is also defined by its context. News is socially constructed and shaped by the expectations of both newsrooms and audiences. As we mentioned earlier, news is not only qualified by communicating actual recent events; actual events are turned into news by way of several processes: they have to be identified as news, told as news stories and perceived as news by an audience, and all of this must be done according to certain conventions. News, along with money, is one of the most obviously socially constructed things in society. Hacking (1999) defines social constructions as things that are put together in a certain way and are therefore perceived in a certain way because of the choices made during the construction and the collective attribution of value by certain groups. The point here, of course, is that the object itself might have been constructed and perceived differently if other choices had been made during the construction (Berkowitz and Liu 2014). This observation is especially obvious in relation to news. The choices made during the construction of the media product have a direct impact on our understanding of reality. In the following, we explore these qualifying processes that turn events into news: recent events are selected as relevant, newsworthy. They are presented in the form of a story. These stories convey certain truth claims. They are written to be spread. In this final part of the chapter, we explore these qualifying aspects of news and discuss how the way they are produced and used characterizes what news is.

First, the content of news is not only defined by the criterion of novelty. Not all new events become news. There is a tough selection process that determines what becomes news; this is based on criteria that are called news values, such as geographical proximity, cultural affinity and degree of spectacularity or danger/risk (McIntyre 2016). This process is determined by an editorial logic, which follows traditions and ways of working within the journalistic profession, resulting in a specific set of topics that typically become news. In newspapers, this becomes manifest and visible through the different sections in the paper, of course (i.e. 'Sports', 'Politics', 'Culture' etc.). Likewise, similar labels operate in radio and TV as an established typology of news in various media forms. Within this typology, various selection processes operate to sift the infinite flow of possibly newsworthy events into actually reported and commented-on events. Most of them follow routines and predictable cycles. Elections, 'the beat' of reporters in Washington, the announcement of the Nobel prize or the Oscars, the Olympics are highly anticipated recurring media events. Other events, such as terror attacks, wars, financial crises and pandemics, suddenly appear on the horizon and can occupy and dominate the news for longer or shorter periods of time (Edson, Tandoc and Duffy 2019).

The way in which the news tells stories about current events matters. Although we are focusing on becoming informed about the latest events when we are reading news, at the same time we are reading a story, a standardized narrative, that helps both the journalist to produce news reports fast and the audience to put the new event into the context of previous events. The story of the same event can be told differently. Lippmann (1922) pointed out that in modern mass society, news interferes with people's perception of reality to a great extent. The reality does not matter as much as what people think reality is like. When decisions have to be made, it is the 'pictures in our heads' that will be our deciding factors. Therefore, how news stories are told has implications. And referring again to the presidential election campaigns in the USA, these points can be readily demonstrated by simply flipping between the Fox News and CNN channels. Depending on which channel you watch, you are presented with substantially different accounts of the same events. Donald Trump's (b. 1946) campaign rally in North Carolina was described in terms of crowd size and enthusiasm, which were illustrated by footage (Fox News), or as the probable cause of two new registered cases of COVID-19 (CNN). Stories are never only about events. Stories connect events into causal chains that provide meaningful cohesion. Stories, novels, biographies, news and myths always make us understand how the world functions. Thus, news stories do not just provide information about an event. They tell us about the event by putting it into a narrative context. News stories always include framings and insinuations about what is important or problematic, who is culpable and what should have been done about problem x, y and z (Scheufele and Iyengar 2012). Culturally, therefore, the reception and interpretation of news will always involve the inspection of the piece through the lens of asking, 'Do I agree with the way the story is being told, or not?' This is a huge part of what makes news endlessly fascinating to so many.

There is a certain claim of epistemic superiority attached to news compared to other stories about recent events, told, for instance, by a friend on social media. News is a particular form of knowledge production that is based on current events (Carlson 2017, p. 40). In the mass communication era, journalism is the primary source of this kind of knowledge and is reinforced by the halo of 'truthiness' (Zelizer 2009). In other words, truthiness is the quality that makes it possible, for example, in a satire of news, to imitate news humorously – if there is no truthiness in real news, the apparently false assertions often made in satirical news would not make sense (Littau and Stewart 2015). Although the story of the event is constructed, a news story claims to be truthful in relation to the event. Matt Carlson (2017) describes journalistic authority as relational. It is based on the claim that a journalist follows professional practice, on a relevant evaluation process in the newsrooms. Having the authority to tell truthful accounts of recent events is also reiterated by complying with the usual visual and narrative patterns of news. Using the visual and auditory form of news reports gives rise to a truth claim concerning objectivity and truthful narration.

Today, in 2020, other sources compete with news for the attention of audiences, and they make similar truth claims and also draw on the visual and auditory form of news media to gain authority. The institutions that have traditionally produced news commodities throughout the centuries (legacy newspapers, large private and public service TV broadcasters and the major radio stations) have often sold their products with an attached promise of trustworthiness. The news and views disseminated through these channels were considered to be the backbone of modern democracy for a long time – the sine qua non for informed public debate – and the major players still enjoy today, to a certain degree, the privileged position of setting agendas about what is considered important and setting standards about what is to be trusted (McCombs and Shaw 1972). The trustworthiness of news was always linked to a certain journalistic methodology concerning verification: checking the story, listening to both sides, fairness and objectivity. Such truth claims are closely related to ideals of modernity, of course, and are good examples of how a journalistic construal of news goes hand in hand with a modern construal of society at large (Conboy 2004).

While the success of such enterprises bears testimony to the fact that, for the most part, people have been willing to pay for news supplied by these actors, the legitimacy of news providers has always been questioned. Media critics have always pointed out the flaws of news organizations and challenged their integrity (Holt and von Krogh 2010). Today, leaving aside the entertainment industry, stories containing accounts of current events in the form of narratives can be obtained through a plethora of alternative channels, the content of which is produced by actors other than the established news providers, whose aims differ from those of the established news outlets (Holt et al. 2019). The distinctive feature of news as a trustworthy source of orientation in society is therefore increasingly being problematized. In recent years, the flawed and problematic notion of 'fake news' epitomizes a seemingly sudden large-scale realization that not all news can be trusted to tell accurate stories about current events. Of course, it is fake news that fake news is something new; it has always been a current in the stream of news, but today it highlights, perhaps more acutely than ever before, the epistemic dimension of news. This fourth attribute of news is therefore increasingly considered to be in play at the moment, as modern truth claims are increasingly challenged in postmodern times. Also, when more and more of the distribution runs through social media platforms, which are controlled by Big Tech companies, like Google, and non-proprietary platforms, the 'epistemic claims of news journalism and the practices of justifications' (Ekström and Westlund 2019) are increasingly challenged. This is indicative of a more complicated task for news providers: they need to justify their truth claims in relation to changing audience behaviour and in competition with other actors and other platforms.

News needs to be spread reasonably quickly or it becomes yesterday's news. News items should be considered as commodities that consist of novelty, packaged as stories, whose meaning and relevance is socially constructed but still carries specific epistemic qualities for which it is valued. This narrows down what news supposedly is. The question of how it is disseminated is another issue. The technical media of display and their dissemination not only form our understanding of what news looks (or sounds) like but how and when news is received. The distribution of news follows fashions in modern society. Many people still read their morning paper along with their first cup of coffee in the morning. Commuters can tune in to the morning briefing on the radio while they drive to work or can listen through headphones on the subway. Others can wait until they have a less busy few minutes during the day to browse the webpages of their trusted newspapers. Often, we have already been alerted to important news through our social media networks, and those who pay more attention to what is going on inform the rest of us by sharing links to news about recent developments. In any case, our news consumption is always tied to specific technologies that facilitate certain reception activities. These activities in themselves, through repetition, develop a ritual function: the form of news and the ritual of reading/scrolling/listening to news promises an overview about recent events (Carlson 2017, pp. 69–73).

The printing press, the radio, the TV, the internet: each technology has introduced new implications for the understanding of news. Printed newspapers narrowed the time slots between news updates and turned news into something that can be expected on a daily basis. The order of news on the pages of newspapers also increasingly implied a structured presentation of the daily news in a hierarchical order, like a kind of social map (Barnhurst and Nerone 2002). When the radio entered households and workplaces (and eventually cars) in the early twentieth century, news became something that could be switched on or off. It also shortened the time it took for news to circulate because there were updates every hour or every half hour. The difference between reading and listening implied a shift in the ritual of imbibing news content. While the same type of stories generally became news, radio changed expectations regarding the level of attention being given by the listener, the mode of perception and the timings for interacting with news. Radio news enabled live reports to be broadcast from the site of events, so sources were not only quoted in written words but were heard via their voices.

The moving images of television offered an even more engaging form of news consumption and brought new qualities to it. Live broadcasting, for example, of events such as the heavyweight boxing world championships, coronations and fiction readings and plays allowed a sense of immediacy that had never been possible before (Enli 2015). The introduction of the worldwide web in the 1990s completely changed many aspects of news: the time frame of the daily news cycle went from morning and evening news to news 24/7 coverage. News is updated and replaced continuously. Hyperlinks opened up the news as never-ending text. The network of news, that is, how news items relate to each other, became more visible. From being finite and linear accounts of events with a limited context, news could include links to an infinite amount of contextual information, allowing for higher levels of transparency and further reading than before (Karlsson and Holt 2016). Interactivity and participation were enabled in ways that would have been unfathomable just a few years earlier, and the possibility of commenting on, sharing and eventually liking and retweeting news has transformed the way people interact with news and has also allowed for a new transparency in the measurement of what people deem relevant. The number of interactions with pieces of news published online is now a standard by which salience is measured, and the tools that are used for doing so are increasingly sophisticated and increasingly informing editorial decision-making.

News is always receptively negotiated; that is, it is always actively received by specific audiences in specific contexts at specific times (Fletcher and Nielsen 2017). At all times in history, news has been exchanged when people meet, for instance, in the marketplace, in a pub or at family reunions – the exchange of information is a social activity (Marshall 2017). In the news distribution system of mass media communication, one aspect has been emphasized in the reception of news: how it reaches end-users through other influential actors. When we look at pre-digital newspapers, television and radio news, the distribution and communication of news looks like a one-way communication. What Katz (1957) called the 'two-step flow of communication' (the continuous remediation and consequent influence on the reception of political news stories through influential voices such as pastors, village mayors or other 'opinion leaders') is made visible in 2020, the time of writing, by the circulation of news through social media. People nowadays do not always encounter news items directly through newspapers, the radio or TV stations; they might access news via links shared on social media by friends and other influential people they follow (Singer 2014). Even before news was publicly distributed by the mass media, politicians and business owners had a network of correspondents who told them about local news by letter (Droste 2018). In these networks, the sharing of news involved social status and power. The potential to share news and interact with news digitally highlights the social (and even sociopolitical) aspects of sharing news.

In sum, the ontological features of news cannot really be separated from its chains of distribution. Our understanding of news is shaped by the technology used to communicate it, by social contexts and conventions and by the way we share and consume news as a habit. The technology with which news is disseminated inevitably alters our perception of, interaction with and valuation of the salience of news. In this respect, digital media have once again changed and redefined what news is. Digital news has often been distinguished from more analogue forms of news along the lines of interactivity, immediacy, hypertextuality and multimodality. These indicate areas where news that can be accessed via the internet adds something new in comparison to older forms. Interactivity signals user participation and active interaction with news that is made possible by the online format. The immediacy of online news relates to the speed of publication online. Hypertextuality signifies the new possibility of linking to other texts. Multimodality indicates the use of various modes combined (Karlsson and Holt 2016). The mediation of news is currently in a stage of renegotiation in terms of materiality, modality and contextuality. This process of renegotiation is to some extent also indicative of a destabilization of long-held common construals of what news is, where it comes from and how it reaches its audience.

Table 6.1 Media and modalities – News media

Media types and modalities	Description
Technical media of display	**Mass media**: newspapers, radio and television sets, computers, e-reader, tablets, smartphones **Production process**: selection, standardized production, compilation **Dissemination**: in regular issues/broadcasts/updates, in conglomerates with other media types, through social networks
Basic media types	**Printed newspaper**: text (headlines, captions, body text, lead, byline) and image (photographs, illustrations), text + image: infographics **Radio**: sound (auditive text, speech, jingles, music) **TV**: image (still and moving), sound (auditive text, speech, jingles, music) **Internet**: convergence of all/some basic media types
Qualifying media type	Stories about current events based on research and observation, selected and edited according to news values **Genres**: editorials, reports, features **Operational**: shared and consumed according to regular/ritual habits

Media types and modalities	Description
Material modality	**Newspaper**: Flat surfaces (pages and screens) **Radio**: electronic sound waves **Television:** surfaces (screens), electronic sound waves **Internet**: surfaces of screens, electronic sound waves, and interactive tools (keyboard, mouse, touchscreen)
Sensorial modality	**Newspaper**: dominantly visual **Radio**: auditory **Television**: audiovisual **Internet**: audiovisual and tactile Designed to attract attention and evoke an emotional response
Spatiotemporal modality	**Material**: recentness and 'awayness' **Semiotic**: extrapolation from current events to future events (virtual time and space)
Semiotic modality	**Text and auditory text**: dominantly symbolic, but iconic use of metaphors as frames, indexical in quotes **Images**: indexical (photographs, footage from site), iconic (illustrations, archival images) **Infographics**: dominantly symbolic **Sound**: indexical and symbolic

References

Aalberg, T. & Curran, J. eds. 2013. *How media inform democracy: A comparative approach.* New York: Routledge.

Altheide, D.L. (2015). Media logic. *The international encyclopedia of political communication,* 1–6. Oxford: Wiley Online Library. doi:10.1002/9781118541555

Barnhurst, K.G. and Nerone, J. 2002. *The form of news: A history.* New York: Guilford Press.

Bell, A. 1991. *The language of news media.* Oxford: Wiley-Blackwell.

Bennett, W.L. 2016. *News: The politics of illusion.* University of Chicago Press.

Berkowitz, D.A. and Liu, Z. 2014. The social-cultural construction of news. In Robert S. Fortner and P.M. Fackler, eds., *The handbook of media and mass communication theory* (pp. 301–313). Oxford: Wiley Online Library.

Carey, J.W. 2008. *Communication as culture, revised edition: Essays on media and society.* London: Routledge.

Carlson, M. 2017. *Journalistic authority: Legitimating news in the digital era.* New York: Columbia University Press.

Chadwick, A. 2013. *The hybrid media system: Politics and power.* Oxford: Oxford University Press.

Clerwall, C. 2014. Enter the robot journalist. *Journalism Practice,* 8(5), pp. 519–531. doi:10.1080/17512786.2014.883116

Conboy, M. 2004. *Journalism: A critical history.* London: SAGE.

Droste, H. 2018. *Das Geschäft mit Nachrichten: Ein barocker Markt für soziale Ressourcen.* Bremen: Edition lumière.

Edson C., Tandoc, J. and Duffy, A. 2019. Routines in journalism. In *Oxford research encyclopedia of communication.* London: Oxford University Press.

Ekström, M. and Westlund, O. 2019. The dislocation of news journalism: a conceptual framework for the study of epistemologies of digital journalism. *Media and Communication*. doi:10.17645/mac.v7i1.1763

Ellestöm, L. 2019. Narration in qualified media types. In L. Ellestöm, ed., *Transmedial narration: Narratives and stories in different media* (pp. 115–135). Cham: Springer International.

Ells, K. (2018). Breaking 'news': Majority can't define mass communication. *Journalism & Mass Communication Educator*, 74(1), pp. 92–101. doi:10.1177/1077695818756738

Enli, G. 2015. *Mediated authenticity: How the media constructs reality.* New York: Peter Lang.

Fletcher, R. and Nielsen, R.K. 2017. Are news audiences increasingly fragmented? A cross-national comparative analysis of cross-platform news audience fragmentation and duplication. *Journal of Communication*, 67(4), pp. 476–498.

Hacking, I. 1999. *The social construction of what?* Cambridge, MA: Harvard University Press.

Harcup, T. and O'Neill, D. (2016). What is news? *Journalism Studies*, 18(12), pp. 1470–1488. doi:10.1080/1461670x.2016.1150193

Hendrickx, J. 2020. Trying to survive while eroding news diversity: Legacy news media's catch-22. *Journalism Studies*, 21(5), pp. 598–614.

Holt, K. and von Krogh, T.R. 2010. The citizen as media critic in periods of media change. *Observatorio (OBS*)*, 4(4). doi:10.15847/obsOBS442010432

Holt, K., Ustad Figenschou, T. and Frischlich, L. 2019. Key dimensions of alternative news media. *Digital Journalism*, 7(7), pp. 860–869. doi:10.1080/21670811.2019.1625715

Karlsson, M. and Holt, K. 2016. Journalism on the web. In J.F. Nussbaum, ed., *Oxford research encyclopedia of communication.* Oxford: Oxford University Press.

Katz, E. 1957. The two-step flow of communication: an up-to-date report on an hypothesis. *Public Opinion Quarterly*, 21(1), pp. 61–78.

Kolodzy, J. 2006. *Convergence journalism: Writing and reporting across the news media.* London: Rowman & Littlefield.

Lacy, S. and Rosenstiel, T. 2015. *Defining and measuring quality journalism.* New Brunswick, NJ: Rutgers School of Communication and Information. https://www.issuelab.org/resources/31212/31212.pdf [Accessed 1 February 2021].

Lippmann, W. 2010 [1922]. *Public opinion.* LaVergne: Greenbook Publications

Littau, J. and Stewart, D.R.C. 2015. 'Truthiness' and second-level agenda setting. *Electronic News*, 9(2), pp. 122–136. doi:10.1177/1931243115581416

Marshall, J.P. 2017. Disinformation society, communication and cosmopolitan democracy. *Cosmopolitan Civil Societies: An Interdisciplinary Journal* 9(2), pp. 1–24. DOI: https://doi.org/10.5130/ccs.v9i2.5477 [Accessed 7 January 2021].

McCombs, M.E. and Shaw, D.L. 1972. The agenda-setting function of mass media. *Public Opinion Quarterly*, 36(2), pp. 176–187.

McIntyre, K. 2016. What makes 'good' news newsworthy? *Communication Research Reports*, 33(3), pp. 223–230.

McLuhan, M. and Fiore, Q. 1967. *The medium is the massage.* New York: Random House.

Rosen, J. 2013. The 'awayness' problem. *Columbia Journalism Review*, 3 September. https://archives.cjr.org/cover_story/the_awayness_problem.php [Accessed 21 December 2020].

Scheufele, D.A. and Iyengar, S. 2012. The state of framing research: a call for new directions. In *The Oxford handbook of political communication theories* (pp. 1–26). New York: Oxford University Press.

Shoemaker, P.J. 2006. News and newsworthiness: A commentary. *Communications*, 31(1), pp. 105–111.

Singer, J.B. 2014. User-generated visibility: Secondary gatekeeping in a shared media space. *New Media & Society*, 16(1), pp. 55–73. doi:10.1177/1461444813477833

Stephens, M. 2007. *A history of news*. 3rd ed. Oxford: Oxford University Press.

Zelizer, B. 2009. *The changing faces of journalism: Tabloidization, technology and truthiness*. London: Routledge.

Zelizer, B. 2017. *What journalism could be*. London: John Wiley & Sons.

Part II
Intermedial analysis: The three fundamental intermedial relations

7 Media combination, transmediation and media representation

Jørgen Bruhn and Beate Schirrmacher

In Part I, we demonstrated and exemplified different types of interactions and how technical media of display relate to basic and qualified media types. We also discussed how the functions of different media types are qualified by historical and social contexts. In Part II, we explore the intermedial combinations and different forms of transformations. We present analytical models and case studies from a variety of different qualified media types in different historical settings.

The same media product can always be approached from different perspectives. A synchronic perspective explores the interaction of different basic or qualified media types – we call this the **media combination** perspective. We can even explore the diachronic aspect – we call this the perspective of **media transformation**. Here, we can either explore the transfer of ideas or narratives across media (**transmediation**), or the **media representation** of one media type or product in another (Ellestrøm 2014).

Discussing the **media combination** means being interested in the combination and integration of media types in particular media products of qualified media types. Media combination and integration do not refer to two different sorts of media products but express a different analytical focus. The different basic media types can be produced separately and combined in the production process. To the audience of a live-action film, for instance, the moving images, sound effects, music and speech can be analytically divided into basic media, but are experienced as a unity because they are deeply integrated into the sensorial modality (see Chapter 2). When we approach media combinations with the four modalities, we can see how the material and sensorial integration of basic qualified media types enables intricate combinations of different forms of meaning-making that support and interact with each other.

We can explore the combination and integration of different modes in the different modalities of one particular media product and any qualified media type. Different basic media types can share the same material interface, for instance pages and screens when we think of the combination of text and image, or sound waves when we think of the lyrics and melody in a pop song. Other qualified media types combine different material interfaces, like screens and loudspeakers in film, which provide an integrated audiovisual experience.

DOI: 10.4324/9781003174288-9

The material space of the theatre stage allows for all kinds of basic and qualified media to be combined in a performance.

In the combination dimension, intermedial and multimodal approaches overlap. A multimodal analysis provides the tools to analyse the synchronic integration not only between but *within* basic media types, like text, image and organized sound, and involves an even more fine-grained analysis, understanding, for instance, how the typography, colour, layout of a text is part of the meaning-making of a text.

The broad term **media transformation** refers to all kinds of processes in which the form or content of one media type is reconstructed and thus transformed by another media type, for instance, a certain narrative (say, the plot of a book) or a set of ideas (say, the hypothesis of a scientific article) or the visual aesthetics of an oil painting that is reused in a commercial ad. All media transformation relies on two interrelated aspects: transmediation and media representation.

Transmediation reconstructs meaning that was previously mediated by another media type; a film adaptation, for example, may mediate the same story as a novel. When we analyse transmediations, we focus on a diachronic process and we explore the relation between a *source media product* and a *target media product* and analysing what is transferred and what is transformed. We often speak of transmediations as if they were a transfer of the media product, how a 'novel is turned into a film'. But strictly speaking, it is not the source media product that is transformed. Instead, it is the ideas, narratives and concepts previously communicated in the source media product that are reproduced or reconstructed in the target media product. Therefore, in the process of transmediation, narratives and ideas can only be transferred across media by being transformed. The analysis of transmediation investigates the interplay between medium specificity and transmediality, asking how transmedial concepts and structures of a source media product are reconstructed in the target media products in a media-specific way.

When exploring **media representation**, we analyse how one medium represents the characteristics of another medium, such as when a poem describes a painting not only by way of representing the image or the depicted scene but also offers a depiction of the painting as an object. Media products constantly refer to and represent other media products or media types or specific technical media of display. By representing other technical devices and basic media types, a media product like a video game also refers to the contexts and conventions of the represented media types. Therefore, media representation is sometimes discussed as an intermedial reference. By representing other media, media products almost by necessity draw on the history and content connected with the represented media. We can explore media representation in the storyworld, and we can also explore how the presentation of a narrative appears to represent structural patterns that are in fact transmedial but that we associate with certain specific media types. A literary text which focuses on visual and aural perception and frequently changes point of view is perceived as having filmic traits. A feature film that does not tell a linear story and instead appears to repeat and vary a single theme may seem 'musically structured' to the audience.

Transmediation and media representation are like two sides of the same coin. You cannot have one without the other. A film can transmediate the plot of a novel without drawing much attention to its source – but it is forced to include a minimum of media representation, directly or indirectly, such as a comment that the film is 'based on the novel of …' Also, it is difficult, perhaps even impossible, to represent other media types without representing narratives, ideas and thoughts that are usually communicated via that particular kind of media type.

Combination, transmediation and media representation may look like three independent categories typical for different media types, but that is not the case: combination, transmediation and media representation are analytical approaches, and thus two or even three of them can be used to explore the very same media product. A film, for example, can be analysed from the perspective of combination: how moving images and auditory media types integrate. A film can be analysed as transmediation if we analyse the adaptation process that turns a novel into film. You can also study the role of different kinds of media that are represented in a film. And no matter which aspect you choose to focus on, you should at least consider how aspects of the other two support your analysis.

References

Elleström, L. 2014. *Media transformation: The transfer of media characteristics among media*. London: Palgrave Macmillan.

8 Intermedial combinations

Mats Arvidson, Mikael Askander, Lea Wierød Borčak, Signe Kjær Jensen and Nafiseh Mousavi

Media products of all sorts form a complex web of different relationships. Media products involve transformations, integrations and combinations as well as transmedial aspects. When we look at media combinations in this chapter, all these different aspects are brought into play. Media combinations of different basic media types are always, literally, intermedial combinations that involve intermedial relations between different forms of communication.

This chapter deals with different kinds of combinations of technical, basic and qualified media types in comics, films, radio drama, songs/singing and music videos. Some of them are more obvious in this aspect. The music video, for instance, integrates sound, words and (moving) images. The pages of comics display text and image, and these two basic media types communicate differently in the semiotic modality. In radio dramas or songs, the combination aspect is not as visually apparent. Still, the soundwaves of a song or a radio drama firmly integrate several auditory media types.

With specific examples, we discuss how to understand the different intermedial aspects at play whenever different media types are brought together in a particular media product. Different perspectives are possible. Should one focus on the combination of different forms of meaning-making, or instead stress how deeply integrated these different media types are? Should one approach a song as the combination of different qualified media (poetry and music), or focus on the close integration of different auditory media types (words and organized sound)? When we approach media combinations with the four modalities, we can focus on both. When words, (moving) images, and organized sounds are brought together in media products, such as comics, songs and music videos, they form an integrated whole. We can focus on how different basic media types in the material and sensorial modality are firmly integrated. We can then explore how these integrations on pages, in soundwaves, on stages or in the studio enable an intricate combination of different forms of meaning-making that support and interact with each other in the spatiotemporal and semiotic modality.

First, we will take a look at how words and images on pages convey a graphic narrative in comics. Then we will highlight the importance of sound effects in the complex combination of moving images and auditory media types

DOI: 10.4324/9781003174288-10

in film. We then explore how different auditory basic and qualified media types together create a complex auditory narrative in radio drama, using the specific example of *The Unforgiven* (2018). We will also discuss how word and music combine on different levels in art and pop songs. The chapter will end with a few reflections on the audiovisual combinations of basic and qualified media types at work in music videos.

Words and images on the go: Intermedial meaning-making on the comics page

As 'a medium that communicates through images, words, and sequence' (Kukkonen 2013b, p. 4) or 'intermedial narratives based on words and images' (Rippl and Etter 2013, p. 191), 'comics' or 'graphic narratives' are qualified media that conventionally tell stories through an interaction between words and images on the page. The term comics is a general term that refers to a wide range of media such as comic strips, comic books and graphic novels, which differ regarding institutional conditions of publication and reception that are part of their qualified media aspects. The description 'graphic narrative' is being used more and more, especially in the research on comics, to be able to equally account for fiction and non-fiction comics and to emphasize the narrative work being done. Comics were initially tied to printed material and framed within other qualified media such as newspapers and magazines or published autonomously as books. Since the 1990s, the internet has been a popular canvas for the digitalized production and distribution of comics in different forms, widely known as webcomics. Professional or amateur comic artists have been able to create brief or lengthy graphic narratives in various hand-drawn or computer-generated formats and publish them in personal blogs or more institutionalized platforms such as Webtoons. This, in other words, is a clear example of how the development of the technical media of display affects the production and dissemination of qualified media types.

The integration of text and image in comics has indeed been a touchstone for first dismissing and then embracing comics as an object of study. The enmeshed use of images was initially used as a pretext to dismiss comics because they were not considered to be a serious medium and were thought to be unable to do anything beyond entertaining teenagers. This dismissive attitude may also have been a symptom of the difficulties comics posed to the disciplines of visual art and literature because both were unable to acknowledge and address the 'very adoption of pictorial information as narrative resource' (Bateman 2014, p. 91). It was with the publication of ground-breaking graphic narratives such as Art Spiegelman's *Maus* (published serially between 1980 and 1991; Spiegelman 1991) that the potential of the medium was brought into sight.

The graphic narrative is now a popular case study for both intermedial and multimodal studies due to its explicit foregrounding of the interaction between text and image. It is quite difficult to draw a clear line between multimodal and intermedial approaches to comics as they have a lot in common. The relation between various semiotic modes in comics has been studied by scholars who situate themselves in the linguistic and multimodal directions (see Groensteen (2007), Cohn et al. (2012) and Bateman and Wildfeuer (2014)). Scholars working in literary studies, narratology and comics studies (see Chute (2008), Kukkonen (2013a, 2013b) and Stein (2015)) have also profited from using the terminology and analytical tools of intermediality and multimodality to discuss political, social and cognitive aspects of perceiving and interpreting comics.

Although words/texts and images are the basic defining elements of comics, they immediately lose their transparency when confronted on the comics page and the demarcating borders between the two, as agents of 'telling' (by words) and 'showing' (by images), start to blur. A comics page conventionally consists of basic media types of text and image framed within further non-linguistic elements such as colours, lines, panels, gutters, captions and speech balloons, which can as well be thought of as part of the 'image' element. Graphic narratives can also be wordless, as, for instance, is *The Arrival* by Shaun Tan (2007), which tells the story of a migration through a sequence of images unaccompanied by text, but wordless graphic narratives are not that common. Whether or not graphic narratives include text, all of their elements overlap at the material and sensorial levels as they are materialized altogether on the flat surface of a page, in print or digital, and are mainly perceived through the visual sense. When text and image are combined, they are closely integrated on the page in the material modality and we perceive them both visually in the sensorial modality. As will be explained in the rest of the chapter, it is mainly in the spatiotemporal and semiotic modalities that the differences between various interacting modes emerge. Before moving forward, however, it would be useful if you had a look at the technical terms in Box 8.1.

Box 8.1 Comics terms explained

Panel: an image on the page representing a single moment of action. One comics page might contain one or several panels that are separated from each other.
Gutter: the space between the panels.
Caption: words in a separate box that accompany the panels.
Speech balloons/bubbles: balloon-shaped images containing characters' dialogues that are connected to the character with a 'pointer'. **Thought balloons**, which usually look like clouds, contain characters' thoughts.
Sound-effect: words that simulate sounds and usually exist outside the captions or speech balloons.

Before delving deeper into these interactions, it is important to think about the process of 'meaning multiplication', which happens in the intermedial event that occurs when various semiotic modes join together. As John Bateman

(2014) defines it, meaning multiplication refers to new meanings that emerge from the interaction between different semiotic modes:

> Under the right conditions, the value of a combination of different modes of meaning can be worth more than the information (whatever that might be) that we get from the modes when used alone. In other words, text 'multiplied by' images is more than text simply occurring with or alongside images.
>
> (Bateman 2014, p. 6)

Meaning multiplication is of course not exclusive to word–image interactions in comics and is a principle that applies to all sorts of media combinations. In the specific case of comics, scholars have attempted to categorize different types of interaction between words and images, which create different added values in the process of meaning-making. Based on the level of integration or separation between the modes, or the dominance of one over the other, comics' styles are categorized as picture-specific (where pictures dominate and there are not many or even no words) or word-specific (where pictures are mostly additive or illustrative) or as having other integrated styles where the pictures and words have almost equal weight in the narrative and alternate to advance the story or mutually engage in doing so.

Often, as mentioned above, it is not easy to separate the basic media types of text and image and evaluate their weight as they merge together on the page and semiotically interact in a way that means we can say that words become images and images become words. In semiotic terms, that is, in terms of readers being conventionally used to words performing the symbolic function and images being mostly iconic and maybe to a lesser extent indexical on the comics page, these functions radically merge. Visual aspects of words become important through strategic usage of typography, and images, through their sequential repetition, convey meanings and narratives *just like* words. The semiotic interplay can go even further and summon sound through visual perception, such as by using bold characters in a speech balloon to imply that the words are being pronounced louder than the rest, or using sound effects and onomatopoeic images or words to represent the sound of a creaking door or a grumpy dog.

Let's take a look at a few examples. 'Space' (http://www.lunarbaboon.com/comics/space-1.html) is one of a series of single-paged webcomics picturing a character called 'Lunarbaboon', who is a half-man/half-monkey, and his daily life (Grady 2020). *Lunarbaboon* (http://www.lunarbaboon.com) comics are created by Christopher Grady (2012–) present) and they are published 2–3 times a week on a blog of the same name, and also on other webcomics platforms. The short graphic narratives, resembling flash fiction (extremely brief stories of no longer than a few paragraphs) have a minimal and readily graspable style and use a minimum yet clever mixture of semiotic modes. In Space, like other *Lunarbaboon* comics, you can see how the non-demarcated use of dialogue within the images and the style of the handwritten words capture the casual and ordinary elements of a father–daughter interaction over a day.

One interesting aspect of comics with which 'Space', (http://www.lunarbaboon.com/comics/space-1.html) plays is how temporality is constructed through spatial elements. Indeed, comics are a qualified media type that spatializes temporality, or, as Hillary Chute puts it, '[c]omics might be defined as a hybrid word-and-image form in which two narrative tracks, one verbal and one visual, register temporality spatially' (Chute 2008, p. 452). This representation of time and the implication of advancement in time is to a great extent performed by gutters. As Daniel Stein (2015) explains,

> This spatiotemporal construction – the representation of time through the techniques of panel design and sequencing – enlists readers to invest the gutters with meaning: to provide the links between panels by way of imagining what must have happened between one scene and the next.
>
> (Stein 2015, p. 424)

You can see that in the *Lunarbaboon* example, the gutter is foregrounded and played with to make the reader/viewer jump between temporal spots and become self-aware of the concept of time and its limitedness. The narrative is indeed told through panels 1, 2 and 4 and we are guided to jump over the third panel by the characters' hands. If we follow the pointing finger of one of the characters, this would mean that we would view the end of the narrative first (in the fourth panel) before looking at the third panel to glimpse several moments of the day in sub-panels. A diversified set of temporal concepts such as speed, a moment, past and present are represented like this through spatial elements and in the minimal and brief interaction between different semiotic modes.

Navigating through graphic narratives is not always an easy job and is called 'decoding' by scholars and artists. 'Reading' is obviously not enough because different types of signs with different dynamics of interpretation combine and merge and the mind has to be ready to make decisions and shift at any moment. To interact with comics, it is necessary to adopt a certain level of 'intermedial literacy' and be aware of the relations between modes to understand the intermedial relations.

Depending on the complexity of the relation between the words and images, different degrees of 'narrativization' efforts are needed to comprehend comics. Comics, with their complex engagement of semiotic modes, have been considered to work in some ways like films, but one of the main differences between the two media types is that in comics the narrative movement needs to be fuelled by the perceiver's mind. The perceiver has to move over the empty spaces of gutters while filling them with meanings and advancing the narrative. This process gets even more complicated when frames and borders are played with on the comics page.

In Figure 8.1, taken from *Fun Home, a Family Tragicomic* by Alison Bechdel (2007), you can see a sophisticated engagement with the medium via multiple layers of intermedial relations. As one of the most critically acclaimed and widely known graphic novels, *Fun Home* is distinguished by its complex

Intermedial combinations 111

Figure 8.1 Fun Home (Bechdel 2007, p. 120).

autobiographical and contemplative wordy narrative and realistic style of drawing, which negotiates authenticity by representing and mixing different media. In the panel you can see a moment of 'remembering' which is happening through media representation, which is presented twice, one in the bottom panel and one in a more focused way in the top panel, as the narrator is looking at her father's photos and thinking about them. Although the words and images are quite neatly distinguished on the page, they create a complicated decoding moment, forcing the reader/viewer to pause, just like the narrator is doing, to get closer to or further from the object that is within view and to move between the images and their descriptions which are themselves, to some extent, transmediations of the images into textual descriptions.

Furthermore, the very act of mediation is foregrounded in the narrative and in the caption: the photos are viewed and read as incomplete 'translations' of what they have captured. This neatly shows the multiple layers of transmediation that are further intensified via the autobiographical agenda of the book: drawn photos on the page are suggested as representations of actual photos; those photos in turn are transmediations of actual moments and are parts of a whole that are being transmediated to ekphrastic texts and that is being commented upon on the comics page. What seems to be a media combination at first sight is actually made up of diversified sets of intermedial relations, including both media transformation and media representation.

Both of the examples discussed here have been recreated in new forms. *Lunarbaboon* was remediated as a book in 2017 and *Fun Home* was adapted to become a musical by Lisa Kron and Jeanine Tesori in 2013 and had widespread success. The medium of comics has proved to be popular for adaptations. It is now very common to see comics adapted to become feature films and TV series, especially in the case of pop-culture media products, such as *The Avengers*, *Batman* and *Wonder Woman*; it is as if comics invite adaptation – that the medium of film is asked for to fill the gaps in the gutters, so to speak.

Understanding filmic sound design. Or how raindrops can become a qualified medium

Sound film is frequently brought up as being an example of a medium that consists of intermedial combinations, because it so clearly depends on combining sound and image – two distinct basic media types. Yet it should be noted that when we watch a film, sound and image are *always* experienced together, and the potential for different meanings are interwoven to such a degree that the film should be considered more of an integrated medium than a combination (see Chapter 2). A great example of this is *sound effects*, which can be considered to be a qualified submedium in itself. Sound effects, as we will show in this section, contribute significantly to our understanding of a film, even when we don't think about sound consciously. As we will show, the images and the sound of, for example, a door slamming will often be *produced* independently of each other and then *combined* in post-production, but that doesn't mean that we *experience* the door slamming in a film as a combination. We know from real life that a door slamming will cause a sound, and therefore the intuitive way for us to experience this event in a film would be to experience the sound and the image as an inseparable unit. There is, therefore, an analytical difference in whether a film is studied from the point of production or from the point of audience reception.

Keeping this integration and co-dependence of the medial forms in mind, it can still be useful from an analytical perspective to try and map out the different constituting media types of a film; that is, to look at how they are individually 'composed' and how they are combined to form an integrated audiovisual experience. In this section, we delve into the importance of sound effects for creating an audiovisual narrative. We first present a few key terms and functions of sound effects, which are then put to use in an analysis of a brief segment from the animated film *My Neighbor Totoro* (1988). Lastly, we present a short discussion on how to understand sound effects as a qualified medium in itself, which shows how we can think about the contextual and operational qualifying aspects of this particular medium.

What are sound effects?

Sound effects refer to all sounds in a film that cannot be classified as either speech or music, but the divide between sound effects and music is becoming more and more blurred, with sound and music often working closely together, or sound effects taking over the role of music altogether (cf. Kulezic-Wilson 2020). An example of the first instance can be seen in the intro sequence to *Corpse Bride* (2005), where 'mundane' sounds of a pen scratching and the noises of cutting a fish and sliding it off a counter are used both as a supplement and a contrast to the tune being played on the piano. Another example can also be found in the intro to *Atonement* (2007), where the tapping noises of someone using an old typewriter continue long after the writing is done and are integrated as a percussion element into the music that follows. Sound effects that are used 'in place' of music can be seen in *The Birds* (1963) in the scene where the schoolchildren and Melanie are fleeing from the school. A scene like this would conventionally be underscored with music to emphasize the terror and drama, but in *The Birds*, the sounds are electronically created sound effects that mimic the flapping and shrieking of birds, which combine with the children's screams to create the panicked atmosphere (cf. Wierzbicki 2008). These examples aside, the primary function of sound effects is to provide the sounds that objects, interactions and environments make in a film, such as slamming doors, blowing wind and footsteps on gravel.

Just like the electronic sounds in *The Birds*, most sound effects in contemporary mainstream film will be produced either as 'Foley sounds' or as 'library sounds', i.e. pre-recorded Foley or midi sounds stored in a digital library for later use. Foley sounds are effects that are performed by special Foley artists in a studio, where they use their own bodies and props to create sounds that can replace or enhance selected sounds from the production track (audio recordings taken simultaneously with the visual recordings), such as the noises of footsteps or horses galloping (the classic example is to mimic this sound using coconut shells). Very often, the sound that is recorded while filming is not suitable for the film. There might be too much noise on the recording, or the sound that has been recorded might not live up to filmic conventions dictating that some sounds should be exaggerated or modified compared to real-life sound (think, for example, of gunshots and explosions). Also, the film might need sounds for things such as dinosaurs, which do not exist in the real world. Finally, it might be necessary to be able to replace the dialogue (e.g. for films with synchronized dialogue in different languages), and for this purpose, it is more effective or practical to use Foley, which can be recorded and manipulated independently.

This use of Foley and library sounds means that the production method used for sounds in live-action film – at least expensive mainstream film – and animation doesn't necessarily differ significantly, except in relation to films that require extensive use of production sound because of specific genre conventions or budget restrictions, as is the case, for example, with the Dogme 95 films, which do not allow Foley to be used.

Sound effects as mediators of auditory information

In sound studies, the sound of our environment is often referred to as a 'soundscape' that is made up of three different types of sound: 'keynote sounds', 'signal sounds' and 'sound marks' (Schafer 1994 [1977], pp. 9–10). The keynote sound is the 'background sound' and can, for example, consist of waves on the beach, birds singing or traffic noise. It is the sound that you don't consciously pay attention to. The signal sounds, on the other hand, are the sounds you do pay attention to, like a sudden cry of a seagull breaking the relative 'silence' of the waves. The last type of sound is the sound mark, which is a sound that is uniquely tied to a certain place. Church bells will most often be signal sounds, but in cities where the bells play unique melodies, this can be a sound mark.

Sound effects are basically used to create *filmic* soundscapes, using the iconic mode to refer to an extra-filmic reality (as also discussed in the section on radio drama later in this chapter). Soundscapes could be described as the unorganized basic medium that sound effects, a highly organized qualified medium, builds on and imitates. We, therefore, suggest using the terms keynote sound, signal sound and sound mark as one way of classifying and approaching sound effects in film and focusing the analysis on how this filmic soundscape is constructed. The next step is to analyze *what* the individual sounds, in their functions of keynote, signal sound or sound mark, are used to portray about the atmosphere, environment, objects or characters in the scene. We go into more detail next about how these different types of sound add meaning to a film.

The keynote sounds are fundamental for setting a scene in a specific location, while at the same time also contributing to the level of tension in a scene: the sound of an ocean can, for example, tell us that we are dealing with an event that is happening close to the sea, even if the sea is not visible in the shot, at the same time as it creates a peaceful and idyllic atmosphere. A typical use of a keynote sound in film is to use the sound of rain or thunder when lovers in a romantic film are in distress. The sound relies on both the iconic and the symbolic mode for creating meaning – iconic because it resembles sound from our everyday lives, and symbolic because rain and thunder are connected with emotional suffering by convention. An example of this is the scene from the 2005 film *Pride and Prejudice* (2005) when Mr Darcy proposes to Lizzie only to be rejected after a bitter fight. This scene is aptly anticipated by dramatic violins *and* by the sound of thunder. During the two characters' conversation, the music stops to leave room for the dialogue, but the keynote sound of rain and thunder continues and functions to provide a background atmosphere.

Both keynote sounds and signal sounds also provide concrete information about objects and characters in a film. When we listen to sound in our everyday life, we, more or less subconsciously, decode sound to obtain information about the objects and interactions that have created it. Sound is always 'shaped' by the physical properties of its source (Gaver 1993), which makes it possible for us to pick up information about the materiality and placement of a sound source. We use this ability to decode auditory information actively when we knock on a wall to determine its material and thickness before deciding whether to drill into it. Sound thus adds information to the film about the material and spatial qualities of objects and environments, information which is not always provided by the images.

Finally, sound marks will not always be relevant in a film, but you might find examples of films in which a specific sound is associated with a specific place and which thus functions as a symbol of that place.

Even though sound effects are very often exaggerated Foley or library effects, these unrealistic sounds still share characteristics with the sounds they are supposed to be iconic signs of, and if the exaggeration is done in accordance with the specific conventions of a film genre, we tend to accept them as realistic without thinking about it (Langkjær 2010). In this way, sound effects not only gain their meaning through the iconic mode but also through the indexical mode by having a direct relation with the filmed materials (production sound), or simply by having an *imagined* relation to this material (Foley and library effects).

Sound can also be used in an explicitly unrealistic way, however, commonly for comic relief or as a strategy for pointing to the film as a constructed representation. This is a popular strategy in some genres of animation, such as when objects in *Looney Toons* are matched with incoherent sound.

To sum up, one way to approach the analysis of sound effects in film is to ask yourself how the soundscape is composed of keynote sounds, signal sounds and sound marks. What is the function of the keynote sounds? Which signal sounds are designed to stand out, and to what effect? Second, you might ask yourself what the style of the sound effects is. Do they aim to represent or exaggerate what is visually represented or to create an abstract effect, as in

Loony Toons? Other questions to ask are: To what degree do the sound effects represent objects or features, such as thunder, that are not visible in the images? What information about space, place and materiality is provided by the sound How does this auditive information work with the information provided by the images, and how are the sound effects synched with elements in the images? The sound effects might even emphasize something in the images which you otherwise would not have paid attention to. Finally, you could ask to what degree the sound effects are integrated with, or are being substituted for, the use of background music.

This list is not meant to be the ultimate model for analysis, but an inspiration for how to begin to think critically about the function of sound in relation to the other media in film, which we will exemplify briefly next.

Sound and the subjective listening position in **My Neighbor Totoro**

Many of the aspects of sound that we have detailed above can be exemplified with reference to a short clip from the animated feature film *My Neighbor Totoro* (1988). The film is about two girls, Satsuki and Mei, who, afraid and scared while their mum is in hospital, find comfort when they meet a new friend, the fantastical creature Totoro. The scene we wish to discuss occurs about 50 minutes into the film and lasts for a little less than a minute (00:49:42–00:50:32).

Totoro is standing by the bus stop with the two girls; it is raining, and Satsuki has just handed Totoro an umbrella. When Totoro puts the umbrella over his head, he has the experience of hearing rain on an umbrella for the very first time, and this whole scene is a little poetic interlude which shows how different rain can sound depending on the material it interacts with, the listener's position, and the listener's attitude to the rain. In this short clip, there are at least five different sounds of rain: 1) a steady rain sound used as a keynote, characterized as light rain hitting the ground and landing in puddles, 2) the sound of soft splashes of raindrops hitting the head of a frog, 3) the sounds of hard, hollow-sounding drops landing on Totoro's umbrella, 4) the sound of heavy rain hitting the ground far away, and lastly 5) the sound of a cascade of heavy raindrops on the umbrella heard from a short distance away rather than from directly underneath the umbrella.

Although the scene is created by 'cutting' between images of the ground, the umbrella and the frog, raindrops are hard to truly represent only in images. The sound here is (co-)creating our impressions of the size and amounts of raindrops, the placement of the listener in relation to the impact of the raindrops, and what material the ground and objects that the rain is falling on are made of.

Besides giving us all this information about materials and listening position, this scene also shows us something about listening attitude. The first type of rain sound is characterized as a keynote sound, it is continuous without really calling attention to itself, and it keeps playing underneath all the other sounds.

But, as soon as the filmic focus shifts to the different types of raindrops in the next few cuts (the integration and synchronization of sound effects and visual editing is significant here), the sound of raindrops has become the primary focus. The individual drops are signal sounds now that we, along with Totoro, listen to actively. In this way, we are sharing Totoro's auditory attention and wonder concerning the diversity and musical experience hidden in a mundane thing such as falling rain.

Is sound design really a qualified medium?

It should be apparent from the account we have given so far that sound effects are used differently in different genres, and that sound effects are designed both to communicate certain information and to have an aesthetic effect, both of which are subject to conventions. Because sound effects are not just the pure resource of available sound, but are, on the contrary, specifically shaped and moulded to suit specific needs and conventions, we argue that sound effects, or perhaps more accurately *sound design*, is, in fact, a qualified medium with its own creative history.

Foley sounds have existed since the very early sound films, and were used for the first time in the musical *Showboat* (1929) (Theme Ament 2014). As the technology became more advanced, so did sound effects, and Foley and sound editing became a substantial part of film in the late 1960s, and a dedicated Oscar for best sound editing has existed since 1963 (sound editing, here, refers to the selection and placement of sound). From 1930, however, the Academy has been giving out an award for *sound mixing*, that is, for adjusting the volume and other parameters of the sounds on the soundtrack to make it all work together as a whole.

It is clear that sound design, which we use as an overarching term covering the composition of sound effects as it exists in a film (after both editing and mixing), is partly constrained by the technological development but also by the *institutions* that exist around sound design. Besides the Oscars presiding over what a 'good' sound design is in the Hollywood movie, sound design is, and always has been, something that has been taught either through apprenticeship or through specialized programmes at universities or film schools – to which the growing body of specialized literature also speaks. The industry has, furthermore, seen a number of creative individuals who have helped shape the practices and conventions. A few names to highlight here could be Julien Naudin (collaborates with Lars von Trier), Aldo Ciorba (collaborates with Sergio Leone), Ben Burtt (*Wall-E* and most of the *Star Wars* films) and, not least, Walther Murch (*Apocalypse Now*).

The existence of an institutionalized tradition of development as well as role models who serve to regulate sound design to follow communicative and aesthetic conventions means that the requirements of the contextual and the operational qualifying aspects are met – making sound design a qualified medium.

Media combination in radio drama. The integration of sound and music in *The Unforgiven*

We live in a world consisting of narratives of different types: novels, films, films based on novels, TV series based on films, documentary dramas, game plays, etc. Apart from the obvious intermedial aspects of these examples, as media combinations and media transformations, what most of these media products have in common is their dependence on the visual mode in the sensorial modality. One consequence of this presence has led to narrative studies that have largely focused on the 'verbal/textual in combination with visual or audiovisual media', which in turn has created blind spots within the general study of narratology (Mildorf and Kinzel 2016, pp. 1–2). This is the case for radio drama – a sound-based qualified medium. As Hugh Chignell, for instance, asks: how is it possible in a visual culture for 'invisible' drama to exist? (Chignell 2009, p. 26).

The answer might just be that it does exist but that due to its 'invisibility', not enough attention has been paid to it. Radio drama has barely been discussed within intermedial studies until quite recently, and when it has been studied, the view has been that aspects such as the function of sound and music within it are inferior to the narrative structure. In other words, radio drama has been regarded as a literary genre rather than what we are emphasizing that it is here – a sound-based qualified media type (Lutostanski (2016, p. 117), and also see Mader (2007, pp. 179–83)) or a submedium of audio narrative (see Huwiler (2016, p. 99) and Mildorf and Kinzel (2016, pp. 8–9)).

The purpose of this section is thus to 'upgrade' radio drama as a sound-based qualified media type that is equivalent to other narrative media types such as films and TV series by focusing on sound and music but without compromising other key aspects that are typical of narratology, such as narrative events, the relationship between diegesis and non-diegesis, dialogues and monologues, and focalization (Bernaerts 2016, p. 133). This section will discuss a few excerpts from the five-episode crime-fiction radio drama *The Unforgiven* (2018), a so-called prequel to the Emmy Award-winning crime-fiction TV series *Waking the Dead* (2000–11), which investigates cold cases in and around London.[1] A prequel, it should be noted, is, according to the *Oxford English Dictionary*, a 'book, film, etc., narrating events which precede those of an existing work'.[2] This means that the genre (crime fiction) has already been indicated to the listener and that the main characters from the TV series are recognizable within the radio drama. This relation thus frames the listener with a number of given cultural and semiotic codes that are provided beforehand. But what characterizes a radio drama? What are its basic constituent elements?

Radio drama: A hybrid and multimodal narrative art form

Radio drama is a 'hybrid and multimodal form' (Bernaerts 2017, p. 206) in which the story unfolds in time and space through perceived intricate interactions between basic and qualified media such as speech, music, voice, sound and silence. For instance, sound appears in speech in dialogues and monologues as well as in the speech of different types of narrators, not least in the tone of the voice that is central to understanding the characters' different emotional states (Huwiler 2016, p. 103). Dialogue is meant to mean 'talk-in-interaction', just as it is used in everyday life (Mildorf and Thomas 2016, p. 3). The dialogues and sounds thus function to create an effect of realism. Furthermore, on the one hand, sound creates spaces by referring to real-life objects, such as slamming doors or car engines (sound marks). On the other hand, it 'creates spaces of action', such as when an action takes place in a car and that action is marked by the sound of a car engine (soundscape). Sounds may also create 'routes' between different places – here the mixing of sounds and microphone placement function as a framing focalizer for the listener (Lutostanski 2016, pp. 120–1). Sounds also appear in non-diegetic sound effects.

Music functions to underscore specific narrative events, emphasizing emotional states and creating a specific atmosphere, and forms part of the diegetic world. In this sense, radio dramas resemble films. Moreover, words and sounds in combination may create a sense of visual imagery by way of suggestion (Allen 2008, p. 481). Finally, radio drama is also a special type of (technological) mediatized performance, where the actions sometimes take place at the same time as they appear to the listener, either by way of 'showing' or by way of 'telling' what is happening. The way the story is driven, either in the form of dialogues or monologues, thus tells the listener in what mode the narrative events appear. In this sense, radio drama is a typical example of 'liveness' (Huwiler 2016, p. 106).

In the next sections, we highlight four types of functions that sound and music have for the narrative structure in the specific radio drama *The Unforgiven*: 1) sound as a visual marker, 2) words and sound in combination, 3) the use of diegetic and non-diegetic music and 4) verbal descriptions of sound in combination with sound.

Sound as a visual marker

Creating visual imagery by way of words occurs frequently in novels. But how can the same effect be created through sounds? While words are symbolic in character, sounds are most often iconic. As previously mentioned, the function of sound is to create visual imagery through suggestion; this can be done by using original sounds or by mixing sounds and microphone positioning. The issue in these cases is how to become aware of the visual imagery (sound mark), but also what kind of circumstance (soundscape) makes this significant. According to Werner Wolf (2016), the creation of visual imagery by way of words can 'only be perceived in relation to a real or expected presence' (p. 6). In the case of radio drama, there is no visual representation. However, we can explore how auditory basic and qualified media types, sounds, dialogue and music connect to visual imagery. Next we have an excerpt from the title sequence of *The Unforgiven*, which illustrates this. It begins with the listener hearing seagulls in the sky and a police radio in the distance, and then there is a 'speech' by the Head Officer, Det. Supt. Peter Boyd:

> We all know the stats. If a murder doesn't get cracked in the first week, it's probably not going to happen. Unsolved crime. Cold cases. The Met's got more than its share. Which is where we come in.

The absence of visual representation makes the listener particularly aware of the surrounding sound effects. The seagulls and the police radio set the scene in a specific spatial environment and place the listener within a fictional world of crimes: the sounds of the seagulls and the police radio make the listener understand that the story is happening somewhere near water and near a crime scene. The sounds therefore become conventionalized as symbolic signs through their iconic nature, that is, the fact that they represent parts of reality. But they are also examples of indexical signs because of the absence of images – the sounds are pointing to something that is not visually present; that is, we cannot see it with our own eyes. The specific circumstance, the narrative event, makes this significant. This shows at least one difference between words and sounds in terms of the creation of visual imagery: the former do so through symbolic signs and the latter through iconic characters, thereby creating a specific soundscape.

Words and sound in combination and non-diegetic music

The title sequence goes back and forth between two different spatiotemporal settings: between a pub and the crime scene, between dialogues and Boyd's speech. The pub appears as a place for reflection and a 'talk-in-interaction', which is then transformed into the story, where the temporal and spatial distance between the event's actual appearances becomes increasingly present. Musically, the title sequence starts with a single stroke on a cello before we hear a police radio, seagulls and a humming sound. The scene then cuts to the pub, where we hear glasses and voices that are underscored with almost inaudible strings, then 'stitches' back to the first scene, when Boyd is continuing his speech. The speech testifies to a serious crime, which is heard through the tone of his voice. It captures the listener's attention, and the atmosphere is enhanced by dynamically increasing, non-diegetic music.

The story is told through dialogues and monologues from the perspectives of the different characters as if the events had already taken place. This first becomes clear at the pub when Boyd makes a comment in the conversation, saying, 'Hang on, this was my story', then continues when the title sequence has ended; this is marked with a three-note musical motif:

> 15 years before. Day one. Detective Sergeant Peter Boyd's story. February 10th, 1984. My house. My home. Raw winter's day. Sleet dropping out of a snow-filled sky.

So the story begins, and we are displaced in time, to 1984 and to 'a world without DNA, CCTV, mobiles, the internet and databases'.[3] Then there is a call from the commissioner saying that he wants to see Boyd about an old case, about a rapist-killer, a cold case that has now turned into a case of police corruption: Boyd is being accused of framing a killer who is already in prison for raping and killing five girls; the fifth girl's body never was found, but the killer claims he didn't kill her.

As suggested, the story is partly told through monologues. This telling mode often creates a sense of what is happening for the listener, but at a distance. The advantage of this distance is that it can be used to describe the diegetic world in detail, and the showing mode can't always do this. However, sometimes the telling mode merges with sound effects as if the distance to the listener has decreased and the story is happening in the present. An example of this is when Boyd takes the car to the police headquarters to meet the commissioner:

> It was snowing hard. Ice on the road. I enjoyed the risk. I forgot about Jen. My heart raced. There were days despite it all, you're like an athlete on the blocks, the race mentally run. Ahead of the pack coming off the bend, already a winner.

The visual scenery that emerges through the words uttered by Boyd is reinforced by sounds that iconically represent parts of reality. For instance, when Boyd says that it is snowing hard and that his heart raced, we not only hear a car driving off and honking horns, we also hear strong, pulsating music. This creates a spatiotemporal sense – the visual space of snow falling and the time of moving forwards – almost simultaneously. We also hear the sound of an icy wind in the air when he describes how the sky is full of snow. The combination of words and sound frames the whole story's mood here – a cold, barren everyday life. It creates a sense of visual imagery.

Diegetic and non-diegetic music

In episode one, the unit is driving off to an address in London, and this is marked with a comment by one of the unit's members, Spencer, 'OK. Let's go'. It is underscored with a short drumbeat just before we hear a car driving off at high speed. We also hear a voice from either a police radio or the car radio before the music is turned up – it is Maurice Ravel's ballet *Boléro* (1920) with its steady 3/4 rhythm. The other unit members, Grace, Mel and Frankie, are commenting on Spencer's musical choice: 'I didn't know you liked classical music?' 'I don't, it's my fiancée'. Then the music foregrounds as a kind of underscore to this narrative event, blending with sounds representing parts of reality. Since there are no clues through moving images, the microphone placement becomes even more important: it has become a kind of focalizer. In this case, the verbal comments on the music in the car also make the listener understand that the music belongs to the diegetic world. Here, media transformations appear on different levels: partly via basic and qualified media types (sound, words, music), partly via a technical medium of display (car radio). The combination of these media types and the different modalities also creates a sense of spatiotemporality by way of the semiotic modality: the narrative event is moving forward towards the next event.

Verbal description of sound in combination with sound

While the intrigues replace each other with new evidence and new problems, such as a videotape that is delivered showing one of the cold case unit's daughters being abducted. The abducted daughter is holding a newspaper in her hand, and this sends a message to the cold case unit. The information that these (audio)visual media products provide in the diegesis is conveyed primarily by a verbal description of what the characters see on the videotape. As listeners, we don't hear all the diegetic sound elements of the video; instead, they are verbalized through a dialogue, but there are sounds that can be heard. In the following quote, the transcription focuses on the dialogue.

FRANKIE: Kate's [the daughter] video has a background noise, a steady hum.
SPENCE: OK, that's traffic and it has to be moving above 30 miles an hour to create a hum, so we are looking for somewhere near a major road.
MEL: OK, so where the flats run apart there's no big roads.
SPENCE: OK, they have vanished.
FRANKIE: The audio report also picked up an intermittent low-level rumble
SPENCE: Got to be the Tube, surely.
GRACE: Yes, yes.
SPENCE: Where's that on the map?
MEL: OK, I overlay the tube lines. There, Hammersmith and District.
GRACE: And, it doesn't go any near those flats, good.
FRANKIE: There's also a screeching noise near the end of the video.
SPENCE: Let me hear it again.
FRANKIE: And it's a train braking, surely.
GRACE: Does it come to a stop, so held at signal, end of a journey, near a station?
SPENCE: Fast road, near train tracks, over tube, that's this area here.
MEL: Well, the road could be the Westway flyover?
FRANKIE: Yes, that's close enough to the Paddington line. Check the signal points Mel!
MEL: OK, ah, here and here, so, it narrows to round this section here.

When there is a description of the train braking, the listener also hears the sound of something that iconically represents a train braking. What is prominent in this example is that the sounds that the listener hears are followed by verbal descriptions of visual perception: as listeners, we 'see' a train in front of our inner eyes through the combination of words and sounds. But not only that, the verbal descriptions of the sounds also lead the listener to possible places in London – the narrative event is thus an example of how the spatiotemporal modality is made 'visible' to the listener through the semiotic modality. The sounds become narrative agents within the diegetic world.

Although radio drama only consists of sound, the example discussed in this section shows how complex a qualified medium it is and can be. Based on auditory perception in the sensorial modality, the basic media and qualified media types of dialogue, sound effects and music interact in the auditory narrative. Dialogue and sound effects convey visual imagery and mediate between different narratives levels; music is used to create atmosphere. The different ways in which the different media types are combined in radio drama make it a particularly suitable subject to study from intermedial and narratological perspectives.

Songs and singing

Songs are probably the most widespread form of music and definitely one of the most widely consumed art forms. Songs mix words and music and can be mediated in sound or in writing. Singing is the performance of musical sound by the human voice; it is thus an *act* rather than an *artefact*. When analysing a song, we can choose between different medial representations, but the choice has implications for our results. If our analysis is based on a written song, we cannot consider aspects such as tone, timbre, sound effects or visual effects or qualities such as the nasal tone of Rihanna's voice or the guttural tone of Shakira's. If we are making an auditory analysis, we might have trouble hearing the lyrics. As songs are auditory in the sensorial modality, there will be a greater focus on the temporal mode because once we press play, the song starts unfolding in a fixed sequentiality. Even though we can of course rewind, the analysis is being done under wholly different conditions from analysing writing on a piece of paper. In the latter situation, we decide the reading pace and can go back and forth as we please.

The most crucial element of an intermedial analysis of a song is that of interpreting the relationship between the words and the music. Words and music share the same material, sensory and spatiotemporal qualities (see Chapter 4); they only really differ with respect to the semiotic modality in which words tend to make use of the symbolic mode and use the iconic mode less often than music. Some of the most palpably shared features of music and words are rhythm and tonal pitch, which is a good starting point for an intermedial analysis: how do the rhythm and melody of words and music interact? Likewise, the analyst might pursue the question of how music and words, with their different semiotic resources, work together to construe meaning in a song.

The analyst should avoid the common tendency to reduce the meaning of a song to its words. In everyday discourse, the question of what a song is 'about' generally refers to what the lyrics are about. When commenting on the music of a song, we often say that music emphasizes or highlights the text. In the words of musicologist Nicholas Cook (1998), this terminology is dangerous because we thereby 'imply that the music is supplementary to the meaning that is *already* in the words' (p. 54, emphasis in original). An intermedial song analysis needs to steer clear of this trap. One of its most important tasks is to show how the meaning of a song emerges from an *interaction* between words and music and that this interaction is emergent, that is, irreducible to the sum of its parts (Agawu 1992).

Finally, our analytical choices will vary greatly depending on the particular song genre in question. Classical art songs often lend themselves to a visually based analysis because much of their essence or authority as artworks is perceived to reside in their written appearance. Popular song genres such as rock and pop, on the other hand, are much more tied to the medium of the sound recording and thus, in relation to these genres, auditory aspects will often play a larger role in the analysis. These distinctions will be kept in mind in the next sections when we demonstrate how an intermedial analysis of a song might unfold.[4]

Interaction of words and music in a classical art song

German composer Franz Schubert's setting of a German translation by Adam Storck of a Walter Scott poem ('The Lady of the Lake', 1810) known as 'Ave Maria' presents an example of what Cook terms 'conformance' between media; that is, words and music join forces when they are communicating the same message or narrative (Cook 1998, p. 100). Properly titled '*Ellens dritter Gesang*' ('Ellen's Third Song'), this song is part of a song cycle, that is, a musical setting of a number of poems that have been set to music and that tell a consecutive story, a popular format in the nineteenth century (see Mandyczewski 1895, p. 90). If we take a look at the interaction between the words and music in the first stanza of the song, we can see how the melody is constructed to embody the meaning of the words (My own translation of Storck's text comes right below).

> Ave Maria! Jungfrau mild,
> Erhöre einer Jungfrau Flehen,
> Aus diesem Felsen starr und wild
> Soll mein Gebet zu dir hin wehen.
> Wir schlafen sicher bis zum Morgen,
> Ob Menschen noch so grausam sind.
> O Jungfrau, sieh der Jungfrau Sorgen,
> O Mutter, hör ein bittend Kind!
> Ave Maria!
>
> Ave Maria! Maiden mild,
> Listen to a maiden's prayer,
> From these rocks rigid and wild
> My prayer shall to thee blow.
> Safe may we sleep until the morning,

Though people are so cruel
Maiden, hear a maiden's prayer,
Mother, hear a suppliant child!
Ave Maria!

The poem is a prayer that is uttered by Ellen Douglas, 'the Lady of the Lake'. The context is that Ellen and her father have gone to hide in a mountain cave to escape a battle, and she sings this song to urge Mary to help and comfort them. The first line of the stanza containing the anaphoric appeal to the virgin is set to a calm, simple melodic line with straightforward chords. This depicts the confident and hopeful tone of Ellen's prayer. Further, Schubert's composition stretches the words 'Ave Maria' to last more than a whole bar. The two stressed syllables (**A**ve Mar**i**a) are thus significantly prolonged, which makes the listener dwell more on these words than probably would have been the case during a reading of the bare, written poem. The second line, in which Ellen's desperation increases, opens with a gloomy augmented chord that unsettles the hitherto innocuous harmony. The wild and rigid rocks of the third line are portrayed by a tortuously winding melody. In the fourth line, in bar eight, on the word 'blow', (*wehen*), the melody elopes from the words in a long melisma, depicting how Ellen's prayer is blown to the Virgin Mary.

A melisma is a stretching of a single syllable over several musical notes. Whenever a melismatic setting occurs, it has the effect of emancipating music from words in that the melodic movement is conditioned by musical form, not verbal progression. Conversely, syllabic form, in which each syllable corresponds to one musical note, presents a declamatory, verbatim and word-centred compositional style. In this specific case, Schubert lets music escape from the words just at the same time as Ellen's prayer leaves the cave. In the fifth line, Ellen's prayer that they may sleep safely is rendered in a soft, swaying melody that is reminiscent of a lullaby. In the sixth line, the major key shifts to a darker minor one at the same time as Ellen talks about the cruelty of the world. The seventh and eighth lines articulate Ellen's pleading with yearning appoggiaturas (a traditional way of musically expressing longing) on the words 'Sorgen' and 'Mutter'. Finally, the last line brings us back to the comforting state of the opening on the words 'Ave Maria'.

Our analysis demonstrates the close alignment between words and music. At the level of the semiotic modality, Schubert's music provides iconic representations of the narrative that is communicated via symbolic references in words. For instance, the waving melisma, with its rapid tones on the word *wehen* iconically represents a whirling wind. This compositional style, with music iconically miming words, is common in many classical genres, not least in the motets and madrigals of the Renaissance and Baroque styles. In the late Romantic period, we increasingly see examples of music detaching from words and becoming more independent. A poignant example is the last song of Heinrich Heine's and Robert Schumann's *Dichterliebe* (1840), an ironic song of a depraved lover that ends with a musical coda that is in a totally different, mild and optimistic tone from the rest of the song, suggesting a wholly different ending to the story than that of the words.

Another crucial issue in intermedial analyses of songs is discussing positions of enunciation; that is, the question of who is communicating to whom. Pop music scholarship has identified three 'personae' at play in a song (see Frith (1996) and Auslander (2004)); for example, whenever Lady Gaga sings a song, she is simultaneously a real person with a civic name, a culturally and commercially constructed persona who is a star with a stage name, and a character in the narrative of the song. In the case of 'Ave Maria', Ellen is a character in the story of the dramatic poem of which the song is part. She thus stands as the communicator of the uttered words, with the Virgin Mary as the recipient. But the person who wrote the words is obviously in some sense also their utterer – and in this case, we are dealing with a translation, so both the translator (Adam Storck) and the original poet (Walter Scott) must be seen as uttering a message to us in the poem. Then there is the composer – by musically interpreting the words, he is adopting them and making them 'his', so much so that in classical music, we simply refer to 'Schubert's songs'. Finally, there is the performer, who also has some claim to be viewed as the communicator – and in this case we, members of the audience, are the recipients. When a singer sings 'Ave Maria', she is in a sense simultaneously both herself singing to an audience *and* Ellen praying to Mary. In classical music, the same song can be performed by several singers without making one of them 'the original' and the others 'covers', like in popular music. This means that every time a singer sings Schubert's song, she is acquiring it and making its words her own.

Beyoncé's 2008 reworking of 'Ave Maria' retains the 'refrain' and part of the musical accompaniment. This version makes the enunciation structure of the song even more intricate, as Beyoncé's lyrics address both a 'you' and an 'I', but they are very different ones from those in the original poem. In Ellen's prayer to Mary, the personal pronouns are referring to characters in the story (and to the mythical persona of the Virgin Mary); in Beyoncé's version, we can probably accurately speculate that she is addressing a very real person, namely her husband, Jay-Z. The question of who is communicating something to us in a song is complex and involves a vast array of personae.

Contest between sound and sense in a pop song

While 'Ave Maria' is an example of medial conformance between words and music, let's also consider an example of the opposite. The music in a song does not always merely support the message of the lyrics; in some cases, the music and lyrics can seem to contradict each other. Consider these words:

> Oh, we've been together
> But separate is always better when there's feelings involved.
> If what they say is 'nothing is forever',
> Then what makes love the exception?
> So why, oh why are we so in denial
> When we know we are not happy here?

Read as bare text, we are likely to interpret these words as part of a bitter song by someone or about someone who is heartbroken. But when we consider the song as a whole, including its music, the picture changes radically. This song, 'Hey Ya' by the hip-hop group Outkast, has cheerfully upbeat music and is set in a major key. The lead singer, André 3000, sings energetically at a fast tempo and in a bright, slightly nasal tone. The music of the song communicates happy feelings and probably makes listeners want to dance. Music in this instance communicates virtually the opposite of the lyrics, and if we based an analysis on the written words alone, we would come to a conclusion about the meaning of the song that lies far away from the lived experience of listening to it.

Since music and words convey conflicting messages here, we are witnessing what Cook terms a medial 'contest' (Cook 1998, p. 103). In Cook's view, such instances are in fact the most interesting from an intermedial perspective, because the different media involved in the utterance do not just replicate each other but create new meaning through their collision. In the case of 'Hey Ya', we could thus interpret the meaning of the song as emerging from the clash of the melancholy of the lyrics with the optimism of the music: the music provides hope despite the hopelessness of the lyrics. Or perhaps the cheerful music could be heard as an ironic commentary on the disillusioned words. However, we need to consider that the lyrics to pop songs like 'Hey Ya' usually have no independent existence outside the sounding music. The words can thus easily be dominated, outshouted, as it were, by sound. If that is the case, we can say that the material modality exceeds the semiotic in importance. Indeed, it is not even certain that the majority of listeners will actively listen to the lyrics. As such, if there is a contest between the qualified media of music and lyrics here, music is likely to have the upper hand.

Moreover, the lyrics to 'Hey Ya' are full of repetitions. The penultimate line in the above excerpt would be more correctly transcribed as 'So why oh why oh, why oh why oh why oh, are we so in denial [...]?' The repetition of words or phrases leads us to focus on their auditory form rather than on their meaning. The sound of the diphthong 'why oh' only becomes more evocative as it is repeated again and again rhythmically. All the while, the actual question posed here, 'why are we so in denial?', is becoming more and more obscured. Even the subsequent words become sucked into this black hole of non-semantic sound, since 'denial' rhymes with 'why oh'. Rhyme is one of the oldest tricks in the book that can be used to make words more music-like, because rhyming words, like music, exploit the aesthetic quality of sound. Rhyme and repetition are thus devices that draw words towards the medial domain of music. We are used to thinking of the sound of the voice as providing building blocks for uttering meaningful words. But in the case of 'Hey Ya', we encounter the opposite logic: words are employed as sounding building blocks, in line with instrumental sounds and sound effects, and their symbolic meaning subsides.

This effect becomes increasingly pronounced as 'Hey Ya' progresses; towards the end of the song, word repetitions and non-semantic interjections seem to take over, such as when the word 'alright' is almost infinitely repeated or when the phrase 'shake it', syncopated and with great emphasis on the aspirated consonants, becomes a percussive element. It is as though the semantic meaning of the lyrics is gradually dissolving itself as the aesthetic quality of sound takes over. We have a similar effect in other pop songs (Borčak 2017). In Rihanna's 2007 song 'Umbrella', the word 'umbrella' is gradually deconstructed in the course of the refrain, ending in just one repeated syllable that serves only as a means for rhythmically displaying Rihanna's bright, piercing voice: 'umbrella–ella–ella–eh–eh–eh'. These typical traits of pop lyrics are also indicative of the fact that, unlike classical art song lyrics, they are not intended to gain aesthetic attention outside the environment of the sounding music. We could make a full-on literary analysis of Walter Scott's 'Lady of the Lake' because the poem existed prior to being set to song. Although Schubert's music greatly popularized the text and probably saved it from oblivion, the poem has coherent meaning in and of itself. The same cannot be said about pop song lyrics.

Words and music – and beyond

One of the ways in which music creates meaning, apart from including iconic representations of movements or feelings, is by having intertextual references. In Stromae's song 'Carmen' (2015), the lyrics are about how social media are consuming our attention and impounding our social life. Since Stromae sings and raps exclusively in French, it is likely that a large part of his international audience do not understand the meaning of the lyrics, but they get considerable help in this respect from two other involved media: music and video.

The music draws heavily on the famous Habanera aria from Bizet's opera *Carmen* that is sung by the femme fatale Carmen, who leads men astray only to deceive them. The aria titled 'Love is a Rebellious Bird' is about how love cannot be tamed. The intertextual use of the suggestive musical theme is therefore associated with a narrative about seduction and deception; that is, if the listener is well-enough acquainted with a standard Western music repertoire to appreciate this reference.

Both the lyrics and the music in this song thus require specific knowledge (mastery of the French language and/or the Western classical music canon) to be fully understood. Far more palpable and something that has a broader reach is the message communicated visually in the music video, in which a little blue bird, recognizable to most people as the Twitter symbol, becomes increasingly larger as it consumes the social life of the main character until it eats him and others up and then poops them out at the end.

'Carmen' can be considered an example of Cook's third and last type of intermedial interaction: complementation; that is, the different media involved are responsible for different parts of the meaning-making process (Cook 1998, pp. 103). The lyrics warn that social media can be time-consuming. The music adds a dimension that shows that social media are like the rebellious and deceptive bird in Habanera's aria. Lastly, the video visualizes how the negative impact of social media in our life becomes larger and larger the more we engage with them. The importance of the video in this song exemplifies the decisive role that the medium of the music video plays in a great many song genres. The next section will explore the music video in depth.

The intermedial music video

Throughout history there has been a tendency to add something to music, or to perform music in combinations with art, bodies, language and other forms of media. Consequently, when human beings have experienced music of different kinds, there has always been something more than the music to experience. When music is performed, we, the listening and watching audience, see the musicians and their instruments, we might hear other (non-musical) sounds, we see all kinds of visual material, architectural space and we feel the music physically moving through the air and into and onto our bodies, ears, etc. The visual senses, in particular, have been 'the extra' sensorial modality being connected to music as its medial 'package'. This goes for religious as well as non-religious situations, for political, cultural and aesthetic contexts in which music has played an important role through the centuries.

Richard Wagner (1813–83) confirmed his ideas about opera and the *Gesamtkunstwerk* (meaning the 'total work of art'), which should include all art forms and invite the audience to take part in the production of meaning and in the aesthetic experience (Wilson Smith 2007). Later on, different media technologies made it possible to record and store sounds and visual media, and also combine them (sound film appeared as an invention in the late 1920s). Records (and record sleeves), film music, commercials, television and games form the modern mediascape, and today we take it for granted, perhaps more than in relation to anything else in our everyday lives, that we can be connected *online* to all kinds of audiovisual forms of intermedial music.

Thus, the music video has a long tradition and before the music video, there were other ways of combining music and visual media. After the so-called golden age of the music video (during the 1980s and the 1990s), new forms of music video production, new ways of experiencing music videos and new ways of *making use of* music videos have been established in the digital era (see Vernallis (2013) and Korsgaard (2017)). At twenty-first-century big record companies, professional directors and video producers are challenged by amateurs, fans and music lovers (on YouTube, for instance).

What makes the music video a music video is foremost the different combinations of both basic and qualified media involved, but also other qualifying media functions, such as the communication of ideas and values and being primarily a commercial *and* a work of art (at the same time). What is told, and what is sold? These are the questions that we should try to answer when we analyse specific music videos.

In the following section, the central perspectives on the medial and intermedial circumstances that define the music video in terms of audiovisual intermediality are presented so that you can continue your own analyses and explorations in this exciting qualified medium.

The music video must be understood in terms of intermediality. In at least two main ways it can be considered an intermedial kind of communication: 1) it is a (multimedial) combination of different basic media (sound and image), as well as of different qualified media (music and film); 2) it is also a media transformation, being an audiovisual result of the adaptation of a musical composition, in most cases a vocal music composition (Askander 2018, pp. 3–4). Here, the focus will be on the combination aspects.

A music video must include the basic media types of sound and image. It concerns the qualified medium of music being combined with moving images. If those two are not present, then there is no music video to talk about. But words – what about words? Actually, a music video can be produced to fit a non-vocal piece of music. So words are not necessary when defining a music video. But as we know, most of the music videos that have been produced do include words, in the oral performance of the singer in question. Very often, words are also shown on the screen, intra-diegetic words, as well as in the paratexts informing the viewers about the name of the performing artist, the title of the song, the name of the record company, etc. It is worth noting that most music videos that have been broadcasted (on MTV, for instance) do not include information on the director or the scriptwriter.

One of the initial and most crucial questions to raise when studying music videos is what are we looking for? Is it the music video as a whole, and the meaning produced in it? Or is the focus on the comparison between the music video and the corresponding piece of music, which has been released prior to the music video in question?

In this section, we have tried to map out the different kinds of media involved in a music video which enables us to discuss how these media forms work in the modes and modalities of such media. Here, we make use of a very well-known music video: Bob Dylan's *Subterranean Homesick Blues*.

Cards of poetry: Bob Dylan's **Subterranean Homesick Blues**

One of the most famous music videos ever was not even a music video per se from the beginning. Film director D.A. Pennebaker filmed and created *Subterranean Homesick Blues* to be the introductory part of his documentary *Don't Look Back* (*Subterranean Homesick Blues* 1967, one of the first 'rockumentaries' ever). In *Subterranean Homesick Blues*, we see a young Bob Dylan standing in a backstreet, with big paper cards in his hands. Words are written on the cards. When the song starts, Dylan starts throwing these cards to the ground, one by one. The words written on the cards are words from the lyrics of the song. Dylan doesn't mime the singing, and the viewer (and listener) don't see any musicians playing the music that can be heard on the soundtrack. The combination of basic media is here quite obvious: mixed together are written words (on the cards), the sung and orally performed words, the moving images (though they look quite static) and the non-verbal but organized sounds of music (here there is 'only' the music, no other sound effects are used). Dylan is seen standing quite still, and what we primarily see is his small body movements and the cards repeatedly falling to the ground. Everything is shot in one take, adding to the feeling of the static, low-action situation in the clip. The background depicts urban scenery, which goes hand in hand with the rough, noisy rock music in the song. And regarding the words, the lyrics, we initially hear Dylan singing 'Johnny's in the basement, mixing up the medicine/I'm on the pavement, thinking about the government […]'.

It is not just the basic media (words, images, sounds) that are present. The clip can also be understood as a combination of different qualified media: poetry/literature, film and music. In terms of media modalities the Dylan and Pennebaker video discussed here is materialized through the *material* mode of a screen (cinema, TV or computer); that is, a two-dimensional, flat surface, and for the sound, through loudspeakers or earphones. *Sensorially* one can both see and hear the music video as it unfolds. Regarding the *spatiotemporal* dimensions, there are at least three important layers to take into account: the time and space of the watching and listening situation, the time and space of the lyrics' contents, and the time and space represented in the visual material.

What is being depicted visually might extend or narrow down what is going on and what is being represented in words in the lyrics of the song. In the Dylan video, we could say that the lyrics are communicating more time, and more things happening, than is the case in the imagery that we can see. The same goes for space, though the lyrics are also describing a wider perspective than the moving images do here. Finally, the *semiotic* modality should be understood in terms of iconic, indexical and symbolic signs. The moving images, the film clip and the sound recording of real events that actually took place: Dylan did stand in a street while being filmed; he and his musicians did play the instruments we hear. And the video contains symbolic, verbal language, which is written in the field of vision (on the cards, but also in the paratexts, which is the information initially shown in the clip about which artist and which song the clip is about, and so on), and can be heard in the orally performed song lyrics of the soundtrack.

Moving on from these observations on media, modes and modalities, one can interpret this music video in many ways. One of our main suggestions for an interpretation goes as follows. Bob Dylan wants to underline his status of being a poet. He denies the viewer the opportunity to see him (miming) singing and instead emphasizes both the sung and the written words. To that, one can add the fact that the famous American beat poet Allen Ginsberg (1926–1997) can be seen in the background during the whole clip, chatting with a musician in Dylan's band. Ginsberg's presence generates an aura of 'real' poetry because he is an established literary artist who belongs to the production of meaning, from whom Dylan borrows cultural capital.

What can be said about the more or less traditional music video, as we have tried to point out above, will not hold for all music videos in our modern digital mediascape (see Vernallis (2013) and Korsgaard (2017)). Next, we put forward a few modern examples of how music video aesthetics is practised in the twenty-first century. We begin with a digital interactive music video, and then move on to the so-called visual album.

New solutions: the music video in the twenty-first century

In 2010, the American indie rock band Arcade Fire collaborated with Google/Google Earth in the creation of the music video for the band's song 'The Wilderness Downtown' (2010). First, the viewer/listener/user is asked to type the name of the street and town or city where he or she was born. Then the video and the song start. The song is in a low key, with a kind of whispering singing style, and then a young man in a hoodie can be seen in the video, running through the streets of a city. Finally, the man stops and look up, and the viewer of the video sees what the person in the video is now looking at: supposedly, the house where the viewer was born.

This trick is achieved by using Google's project Google Earth and its GPS function; it works by using satellites and its aim is to create a photographic map of the whole world. The trick is also about making the viewer think, 'This video has been made especially for me'. By means of digital technology, the music video becomes personalized, almost intimately connected to the viewer and his or her childhood memories. Through the interactive force of this video, a highly personal experience seems to be made possible At the same time, some viewers may feel that the creators of the video are showing off a little, perhaps to deliberately make many viewers/listeners in the audience ask, 'Wow, how did they do *that*?'

During the 2010s, the concept of 'visual albums' gained more and more attention. Maybe 'visual album' should be replaced by something like 'audiovisual album' or 'intermedial album' to highlight the mix of media involved. Beyoncé (b. 1981) and her fellow directors created *Beyoncé* (2013), and later on *Lemonade* (2016) as visual albums. The first is more like a collection of music videos, without any obvious thematic connections. *Lemonade* is something else. Here we have a fully developed story (even though it is mostly a poetic story) that seamlessly knits together the songs and videos. In between the songs, we hear Beyoncé reciting poetry from poetry books by the Somali-British poet Warsan Shire (b. 1988). These passages are accompanied by visual material showing different settings from both urban everyday life and nature landscapes and sceneries. One could say that *Lemonade* is a collection of music videos, like *Beyoncé*, but here, the videos are not connected to each other in a random way. They are also 'glued' together by the intersections with the recitals of Shire's poetry.

So, *words* are spoken and sung, and visual text can be read in the final credits and in the title signs between the different 'chapters' in the film (like 'Denial', 'Anger', etc.). *Music* is played, and other *sounds* can be heard (both on-location sounds and added sound effects); the moving *images* show the artist performing, old home video clips with Beyoncé's relatives, photos of people and depictions of different surroundings. All these basic and qualified media collaborate in producing meaning in *Lemonade*. Or, rather, they collaborate with the viewer/listener in producing meaning through the material, sensorial, spatiotemporal and semiotic modalities. Several stories and themes can be identified in *Lemonade*: through the lyrics one hears, through the actions and people in and the design of the visual material, and through the music (and other sounds), it becomes clear that this visual album is about race and gender in the history of the US (and maybe globally) but is also about the marriage and relationship of Beyoncé and Jay-Z.

Our suggestion following this investigation is that the best way of approaching music videos by using intermedial theory and concepts is to consider music videos in terms of having the following elements: 1) intermedial combinations of different sorts and 2) media transformations. When analysing music videos, a carefully mapped out description and structuring of qualified media types and modalities is important to understand the many different medial circumstances that are collaborating intermedially. It is just as important to then move on to interpreting and analysing the music videos in question with the aim of gaining an in-depth understanding of how the production of meaning occurs.

Conclusion

To sum up, in this chapter the ambition has been to shed light on intermedial combinations by discussing and analysing different qualified media types, such as comics, sounds in films, radio drama, singing and music videos. These all combine different basic media types but are also set in processes of intermedial transformations, for instance, the adaptation of a graphic novel into a movie, or a TV series that inspires a radio drama. In this chapter, however, we have focused only on the combination functions. In relation to all the combinations of basic media discussed here, we have strived to conduct analyses and to reach for the productions of meaning, which are found in between the media types in question; these productions of meaning collaborate with and/or oppose each other.

In one other aspect, the examples discussed in this chapter also challenge the reader/viewer/listener: one must have different kinds of literacy to really be able to identify certain references and to differentiate structures, forms and content to understand the media product in question. This is a specific challenge for intermediality analysis; if to analyse an intermedial act of communication, must not one, then, have the competence for all the media forms involved? The question is compelling, and should be paid more attention to in upcoming research on intermediality.

Notes

1 In addition to the TV series and the radio drama, the BBC produced a six-part spin-off called *The Body Farm* (2011). These belong to the same storyworld and could thus

be studied with reference to the concept of transmedia storytelling as defined by Henry Jenkins, that is, a representation of 'a process where integral elements of a fiction get dispersed systematically across [different] delivery channels for the purpose of creating a unified and coordinated experience' (Jenkins 2010, p. 944). However, this lies somewhat outside the scope of the present study.
2 'prequel, n'. In *Oxford English Dictionary, OED* Online. December 2020. Oxford University Press. http://www-oed-com.ludwig.lub.lu.se/view/Entry/150546?redirectedFrom=prequel& [Accessed 14 December 2020].
3 Information from the homepage of the BBC 4 radio drama.
4 The analyses in this section in general do not refer to any specific recordings or editions of musical and literary works; rather, they aim at any and all conceivable medial manifestations of a given work, including for example live performances of songs. Therefore, concrete references to works are in general not included.

Further reading: Sound design

Anderson, J.D. and Anderson, B.F. 2005. Part three. Acoustic events. In J.D. Anderson and B.F. Anderson, eds., *Moving image theory: Ecological considerations* (pp. 67–69). Carbondale: Southern Illinois University Press.

Eidsvik, C. 2005. Background tracks in recent cinema. In J.D. Anderson and B.F. Anderson, eds., *Moving image theory: Ecological considerations* (pp. 70–78). Carbondale: Southern Illinois University Press.

Isaza, M. 2009. Ben Burtt special: WALL-E – the definitive interview. *Designing Sound: Art and Technique of Sound Design*. http://designingsound.org/2009/09/ben-burtt-special-wall-e-the-definitive-interview/ [Accessed 1 January 2018].

Kulezic-Wilson, D. 2020. *Sound design is the new score: Theory, aesthetics, and erotics of the integrated soundtrack* (Oxford Music/Media Series). New York: Oxford University Press.

Langkjær, B. 2010. Making fictions sound real: on film sound, perceptual realism and genre. *MedieKultur: Journal of Media and Communication Research*, 26(48), pp. 5–17. doi:10.7146/mediekultur.v26i48.2115

Theme Ament, V. 2014. *The Foley grail: The art of performing sound for film, games, and animation*. Oxford: Taylor & Francis Group.

Thom, R. 2013. Notes on sound design in contemporary animated films. In J. Richardson, C. Gorbman and C. Vernallis, eds., *The Oxford handbook of new audiovisual aesthetics* (pp. 227–232). New York: Oxford University Press.

Whittington, W. 2012. The sonic playpen: Sound design and technology in Pixar's animated shorts. In T. Pinch and K. Bijsterveld, eds., *The Oxford handbook of sound studies* (pp. 367–368). New York: Oxford University Press.

References

Agawu, K. 1992. Theory and practice in the analysis of the nineteenth-century 'Lied'. *Music Analysis*, 11(1), pp. 3–36.

Allen, C. 2008. Radio narrative. In D. Herman, M. Jahn and M.-L. Ryan, eds., *Routledge encyclopedia of narrative theory* (pp. 481–482). London; New York: Routledge.

Askander, M. 2018. Immigration, paper planes, and a ka-ching! Understanding music videos through the concept of iconicity. *M&STE: Elektronisk tidskrift för konferensen Musik & samhälle*, 5(5), pp. 30–40.

Auslander, P. 2004. Performance analysis and popular music: a manifesto. *Contemporary Theatre Review*, 14(1), pp. 1–13.

Bateman, J. 2014. *Text and image: A critical introduction to the visual/verbal divide*. London: Routledge.

Bateman, J.A. and Wildfeuer, J. 2014. A multimodal discourse theory of visual narrative. *Journal of Pragmatics*, 74, pp. 180–208.

Bechdel, A. 2007. *Fun home: A family tragicomic*. Boston; New York: Houghton Mifflin Harcourt.

Bernaerts, L. 2016. Voice and sound in the anti-narrative radio play. In J. Mildorf and T. Kinzel, eds., *Audionarratology: Interfaces of sound and narrative* (pp. 133–148). Berlin; Boston: de Gruyter.

Bernaerts, L. 2017. Dialogue in audiophonic fiction. In J. Mildorf and B. Thomas, eds., *Dialogue across media* (pp. 205–223). Amsterdam, The Netherlands: John Benjamins Publishing.

Borčak, L.W. 2017. The sound of nonsense: on the function of nonsense words in pop songs. *Sound Effects*, 7(1), pp. 28–43. https://www.soundeffects.dk/article/view/97177/145962 [Accessed 16 November 2020].

Chignell, H. 2009. *Key concepts in radio studies*. London: SAGE.

Chute, H. 2008. Comics as literature? Reading graphic narrative. *PLMA*, 123(2), pp. 452–465.

Cohn, N., Paczynski, M., Jackendoff, R., Holcomb, P.J. and Kuperberg, G.R. 2012. (Pea)nuts and bolts of visual narrative: Structure and meaning in sequential image comprehension. *Cognitive Psychology*, 65(1), pp. 1–38.

Cook, N. 1998. *Analysing musical multimedia*. Oxford: Oxford University Press.

Frith, S. 1996. *Performing rites: On the value of popular music*. Oxford: Oxford University Press.

Gaver, W.W. 1993. What in the world do we hear? An ecological approach to auditory event perception. *Ecological Psychology*, 5(1), pp. 1–29.

Grady, C. 2020. 'Space'. *Lunarbaboon*, January 18. http://www.lunarbaboon.com/comics/space-1.html [Accessed 15 December 2020].

Groensteen, T. 2007. *The system of comics*. Jackson: University Press of Mississippi.

Huwiler, E. 2016. A narratology of audio art: Telling stories by sound. In J. Mildorf and T. Kinzel, eds., *Audionarratology: Interfaces of sound and narrative*. Berlin; Boston: de Gruyter. pp. 99–115.

Jenkins, H. 2010. Transmedia storytelling and entertainment: An annotated syllabus. *Continuum*, 24(6), pp. 943–958.

Korsgaard, M.B. 2017. *Music video after MTV: Audiovisual studies, new media, and popular music*. London; New York: Routledge.

Kukkonen, K. 2013a. *Contemporary comics storytelling*. Lincoln: University of Nebraska Press.

Kukkonen, K. 2013b. *Studying comics and graphic novels*. West Sussex: John Wiley & Sons.

Kulezic-Wilson, D. 2020. *Sound design is the new score: Theory, aesthetics, and erotics of the integrated soundtrack* (Oxford Music/Media Series). New York: Oxford University Press.

Langkjær, B. 2010. Making fictions sound real: On film sound, perceptual realism and genre. *MedieKultur: Journal of Media and Communication Research*, 26(48), pp. 5–17.

Lutostanski, B. 2016. A narratology of radio drama: voice, perspective, space. In J. Mildorf and T. Kinzel, eds., *Audionarratology: interfaces of sound and narrative* (pp. 117–132). Berlin; Boston: de Gruyter.

Mader, D. 2007. The descriptive in audio-/radioliterature – a 'blind date'? In W. Wolf and W. Bernhart, eds., *Description in literature and other media* (pp. 179–213). Amsterdam: Rodopi.

Mandyczewski, E., ed. 1895. *Schuberts Werke, Serie XX: Sämtliche einstimmige Lieder und Gesänge*, 8(474), pp. 1823–1827. Leipzig: Breitkopf & Härtel.

Mildorf, J. and Kinzel, T. 2016. Audionarratology: Prolegomena to a research paradigm exploring sound and narrative. In J. Mildorf and T. Kinzel, eds., *Audionarratology: Interfaces of sound and narrative* (pp. 1–26). Berlin; Boston: de Gruyter.

Oxford English Dictionary, OED online. Oxford: Oxford University Press.

Rippl, G. and Etter, L. 2013. Intermediality, transmediality, and graphic narrative. From comic strips to graphic novels. Contributions to the theory and history of graphic narrative. In J. Fotis, M. Martínez and J.P.W. Schmid, eds., *Narratologia. Contributions to narrative theory* 37 (p. 191). Berlin: de Gruyter.

Schafer, R.M. 1994 (1977). *The soundscape: Our sonic environment and the tuning of the world.* Reprint. Rochester, VT: Destiny Books.

Spiegelman, A. 1991. *The complete MAUS.* New York: Pantheon.

Stein, D. 2015. Comics and graphic novels. In G. Rippl, ed., *Handbook of intermediality: Literature–image–sound–music*, vol 1 (pp. 420–438). Berlin: de Gruyter.

Theme Ament, V. 2014. *The Foley grail: The art of performing sound for film, games, and animation.* Oxford: Taylor & Francis Group.

Vernallis, C. 2013. Music video's second aesthetic?. In J. Richardson, C. Gorbman, and C. Vernallis. *The Oxford handbook of new audiovisual aesthetics.* Oxford; New York: Oxford University Press, pp. 437–465.

Wierzbicki, J. 2008. Shrieks, flutters, and vocal curtains: electronic sound/electronic music in Hitchcock's The Birds. *Music and the Moving Image*, 1(2), pp. 10–36.

Wilson Smith, M. 2007. *The total work of art: From Bayreuth to cyberspace.* London; New York: Routledge.

Wolf, W. 2016. How does absence become significant in literature and music? In W. Wolf and W. Bernhard, eds., *Silence and absence in literature and music* (pp. 5–22). Leiden; Boston: Brill/Rodopi.

Radio and TV referenced

The Body Farm. 2011. BBC, BBC 1.
The Unforgiven. 2018. BBC, BBC Radio 4.
Waking the Dead. 2000–11. BBC, BBC 1.

Films referenced

Atonement. 2007. Directed by Joe Wright. UK, France, USA: Universal Pictures, Working Title Films.

Corpse Bride. 2005. Directed by Tim Burton and Mike Johnson. USA, UK: Tim Burton/Laika Entertainment Production.

My Neighbor Totoro. 1988. Directed by Hayao Miyazaki. Japan: Studio Ghibli.

Pride and Prejudice. 2005. Directed by Joe Wright. France, UK, USA: Focus Features, Universal Pictures.

Showboat. 1929. Directed by Harry A. Pollard. USA: Universal Pictures.

The Birds. 1963. Directed by Alfred Hitchcock. USA: Alfred J. Hitchcock Productions.

Music videos referenced

Lemonade. 2016. Beyoncé. Directed by Jonas Åkerlund, Beyoncé, Kalihl Joseph, Melina Matsoukas, Dikayl Rimmasch, Mark Romanek and Todd Tourso. USA: Parkwood Entertainment and Columbia Records

Subterranean Homesick Blues. 1967. Bob Dylan. Directed by Donn Alan Pennebaker. USA: Pennebaker Hegedus Films.

The Wilderness Downtown. 2010. Arcade Fire. Directed by Chris Milk (Created in collaboration with Google).

9 Transmediation

Jørgen Bruhn, Anna Gutowska, Emma Tornborg and Martin Knust

Transmediations are everywhere around us. We meet the same concepts, ideas, narratives and experiences in different kinds of media products every day. TV commercials convey the same advertisement slogans as posters on advertisement billboards. We listen to popular songs on the radio, on Spotify or enjoy artists performing them at live concerts. Whenever a theme, an image or a narrative that is familiar to one media product is mediated again in a different media product we say it is transmediated.

We may not always pay attention to transmediation. When listening to a song being performed live, listening to it on an LP on a record player or listening to it via a compressed MP3 file via a smartphone, the basic media types of organized sound and qualified media types of music remain the same. When a novel is republished as an audiobook, the technical media of display and basic media types (re)construct meaning that was previously mediated by another media type. We might perceive a record, an MP3 file or an audiobook as a remediation, a repeated mediation, of the same media product. However, a change in the technical media of display or basic media type also involves an aspect of change; the change transfers a song or a narrative into a new context and it transforms its experience of the song or the novel. When a novel is adapted into a film, when a poem describes an oil painting, or an opera adapts a drama, all three media aspects change.

This chapter explores transmediation between qualified media types. When we watch a film based on a novel we have read, we recognize the plot that has been transferred into a film. At the same time, something has also changed. The plot finds itself transformed as it has been turned into a film. If we have met the story of a film in the form of a novel before, we start to compare two media products, the one as a source and the other as a target product. The study of transmediation explores the relation between a source media product and a target media product, exploring what is transferred and what is transformed?

In the following cases, we demonstrate how narratives and ideas can only be transferred by being transformed. This is obvious in the familiar case of a novel-to-film adaptation, which is our point of departure. Literature and film are two different qualified media types that use different basic media types: in a novel

DOI: 10.4324/9781003174288-11

the narrative is formed using the basic media type of text displayed on pages or screens. The audiovisual narrative of a film uses moving images and different kinds of sound-based media types displayed on a silver or electronic screen. Printed text is materially static and consists of the predominantly symbolic signs of language, whereas film is kinetic and temporal in the material modality and integrates the symbolic signs of auditive text with the dominantly iconic signs of images. What the novel *describes* with language, the film *depicts* with moving images and shows in dialogue between characters. Also, of course, there are immense differences when it comes to producing and disseminating literature and film. If we look at an adaptation like this, it becomes quite obvious that all adaptations, no matter how faithful they strive to be, involve huge changes. The two media types must by necessity deploy different means to accomplish an equivalent result.

In everyday language, we often speak of transmediations as if they were a transfer of the media product: we discuss how a 'novel is turned into a film'. But strictly speaking, it is not the novel, painting or drama that is transformed. Instead, it is the ideas, narratives and concepts previously communicated in the source media product that are reconstructed in the target media product. And, in the end, although the material source media product remains unchanged, our idea of the source media product is transformed by the transmediation.

The question of transmediation has primarily been explored in the field of adaptation studies. Probably the most well-known examples of transmediation, and definitely the one that has been most thoroughly researched and theorized, are novel-to-screen adaptations (competing with studies of text-to-stage and theatre-to-film adaptations, see Elliott 2020). This field is often simply called adaptation studies, but when we discuss transmediation and adaptation in this chapter we will use it both in the broad sense suggested by Linda Hutcheon (Hutcheon and O'Flynn 2013) followed later by a more intermedial rethinking of the same position by Salmose and Elleström (2020). Hutcheon managed to open the field of adaptation studies to include not only literature and film but also opera, theatre, theme parks and many other qualified media types.

The overarching analytical challenge of adaptation is how to put transfer and transformation in relation to each other. Here, the comparison between source and media product easily leads to some pitfalls. Thomas Leitch has addressed some of these fallacies for the case of novel-to-film adaptation (Leitch 2003); for instance, a one-sided focus on what has changed and media specificity, or applying 'fidelity' towards the source product as a central qualifying criterion when evaluating an adaptation. Instead, Leitch suggests focusing on different kinds of adjustment strategies in literature-to-screen-adaptations (see Box 9.1).

> **Box 9.1 Adjustment strategies**
>
> **Compression**: abridging the plot, for instance, of a novel, so that it fits the format of a 150-page-long screenplay.
> **Expansion**: if a film is based on a short story, then it is the job of the screenwriter to 'bulk up' the plot by adding more material.
> **Correction**: introducing important changes to the source media product, often by changing the ending to fit the social context of the target media product.
> **Updating**: transposing the plot of a classic text into a modern context in a way that demonstrates its contemporary (or universal) relevance.
> **Superimposition**: decisions about what source material to adapt are often made based on reasons other than the literary value of the text. Concerning film, Leitch notes that cinema often 'superimposes' co-authors who are responsible for making the adaptation. Such co-authors are often the stars – actors, writers or directors.
>
> (Leitch 2007, pp. 98–100)

The adjustment strategies can be applied to describe the transformation process of film adaptations but also to other artistic media products. However, if we want to analyse transmediation not only as an adjustment, we have to address how ideas can be transferred by transformation: We then have to investigate the interplay between *medium specificity* and *transmediality* (see Box 1.2).

A first important step when analysing transmediation is to consider the medium specificity of the source media product as well as the target media product in order to understand their medial 'affordances', their medial possibilities and limitations. This first step helps to describe the process of transformation based on the changes of technical media (the basic qualified media types involved). However, if we only consider medium specificity we risk getting stuck stating the obvious, namely that the target media product per definition is different to the source. Therefore, we also have to consider transmedial aspects, including the transfer of ideas, concepts and structural patterns.

Transmedial features can be expressed in several qualified media types. The notion of 'joy' can be expressed with quite different basic media types, with body language, the organized sound of music or the words of a literary text. There are words or phrases that by habit and convention are used to express joy. The image of a laughing person conveys joy. Images of balloons or fireworks are often connected to joyful contexts and conventions. Specific pieces of music are associated with festivity and joy, and certain musical patterns iconically relate to movements we perceive as joyful.

Structures and patterns can be transmedial, too. Narratives can be told in words, conveyed by still or moving images, or the organized sound of music.

Due to the media specificity of written, narrative literature, cinema or graphic novels, the same transmedial narrative of a quest will be told differently in the words of a novel, the moving images and sound of a Hollywood movie or the words and images of a graphic novel.

The analysis of transmediation then addresses how media-specific characteristics are used to convey transmedial ideas or structures. Which concepts and structural patterns of the source media product are easily communicated by the technical media of display and the basic media types of the target media product? Which aspects need to be transformed because of the medium specificity of the target medium?

A model for studying transmediation

To understand such processes, we must recognize the media aspects of each media product and how we interact with them in the four modalities. We will have to discriminate between transmedial and media-specific aspects and between aspects of transmediation and media representation, which will be introduced below. For the study of transmediation we suggest a multistep analysis in order to systematically disentangle and describe important aspects of the transmediation process that takes place between the source and the target media product.

1 The first step is to construct a working hypothesis that *delimits the scope of comparison*. To simply compare source and media target products inevitably ends with the same unsurprising result, namely that the target result differs in many important ways from the source. Therefore, the analysis needs to pursue a specific, well-defined question.
2 The next step consists of a *comparative close reading* of the source and the target media product. The main questions here are what has been omitted from the source media product and what has been added, transformed or developed in the target media product. Differences necessarily include form as well as content.
3 In the third step, the differences and similarities in terms of *transmediality and media specificity* are identified. First, which transmedial traits were transferred? Which aspects do we recognize? Second, which of the changes can be connected with medium-specific affordances of the technical media of display and the basic media types?
4 Fourth, which changes are connected with the *contexts and conventions of the qualified media types*? This depends on the contextual conditions of the different production processes, which can include the producer's intentions and the production circumstances as well as commercial considerations and broader historical, philosophical or aesthetic considerations. This aspect is often overlooked in formally oriented studies: in some cases, to address such questions will of course also require additional methodologies, including knowledge about historical and institutional factors. This level

thus has the possibility to make the analysis more complex but also involves the danger of jumping to conclusions based on limited knowledge. The fourth task, therefore, is to discuss the conditions that may frame the findings of step three.

5   In a fifth and final move, a *new perspective* is employed. Instead of seeing only a transformation of source to target, every new transmediation in another media type affects our understanding of the source media product. This step should open a reflection on which aspects of the originating source may be read in a new way in the light of the target. Do we learn something new about the source?

In the next sections, we modify – or adapt – these five analytical steps to three different media types and three cases, in slightly different ways. We discuss the adaptation of a literary canonical work, Joe Wright's 2005 novel-to-film adaptation of Jane Austen's novel *Pride and Prejudice* (1813) a novel that repeatedly has been adapted into new contexts and audiences. We then explore how poetry expresses the encounter with a piece of visual art, as in the Canadian poet Ann Carson's ekphrastic poem 'Western Motel' (Carson 2001), which describes Edward Hopper's painting of the same name from 1957. Finally, we explore a stage-to-stage adaptation with the example of the German composer Richard Strauss's opera adaptation (1905) of Oscar Wilde's drama *Salomé* (1891). Both drama and opera are performed on stage, but the kind of performance, the use of dialogue and music, and the conventions at play differ widely and inform the adaptation process

Novel-to-film adaptation

Novel-to-film studies were held in low esteem for a long time. It did not belong in the traditional discipline of literary studies but was not considered to be a genuine part of film studies. From its beginnings, film studies strived for the recognition given to the study of established media types like literature. Therefore, film studies investigated and highlighted the medium-specific forms of the still 'new' medium of cinema and was thus less interested in relations of cinema with other media. It was only much later, in the 1990s, that adaptation studies became a broadly recognized academic discipline. At the time of writing, several academic journals specialize in novel-to-film adaptations, and at conferences and on the pages of books, intense discussions take place concerning the history, form and importance of adaptations.

Historically, a classical debate in adaptation studies was about whether adaptations have any aesthetic legitimacy despite their intermedial character: too literary for film enthusiasts and not sufficiently literary for the literati, they questioned the conventional expectations of both qualified media types. Few critics or artists today would doubt that it is possible to produce aesthetically satisfying work that crosses media borders. Therefore, the question of aesthetic purity is partly relegated to the historically dated arguments.

Another recurring question, however, addresses fidelity and refuses to die: the early critics engaged in adaptation studies were already well aware that fidelity was a problematic criterion, simply because any media transformation, by way of its very definition, must infer a change in means and signifying forms (demonstrated in Elliott 2003). Nevertheless, in many popular and journalistic discourses, the demand for fidelity lives on. However, in contemporary parlance, the value-laden notion of 'fidelity' is very often replaced by the more neutral terms 'similarities' and 'differences' when comparisons are made between source and target media products in adaptations or other transmediations. This is not only so in novel-to-film adaptations, but is typical in discussions about all transmediation in the aesthetic realm.

Contemporary adaptation studies proceed on the basis that cinema is inextricably connected not only to literature but also to other arts. In a standard textbook on adaptation studies, the shared history of film and literature is described as stretching all the way back to the very birth of cinema. The first films, produced at the end of the nineteenth century, were heavily influenced by *tableaux vivants*, vaudeville and theatre, and from its inception, cinema illustrated or adapted literary classics. Even today, more than half of Oscar-nominated films are adaptations of previously published literary materials (Albrecht-Crane and Cutchins 2010, p. 10), even though not all adaptations are marketed as such. Other film adaptations explicitly connect to their literary source, as what we here call '*prestige adaptation*': a mainstream film adaptation of a canonical literary work, usually cast with established actors whose status as stars, it is hoped, will mean that the film is successful (see Box 9.2).

Box 9.2 Prestige adaptation

In the context of Anglophone cinema, prestige adaptations encompass adaptations of Shakespeare's plays and canonical English novels (e.g. those of Jane Austen, Charles Dickens, the Brontës) but also classics of genre literature, for example, fantasy (e.g. J.R.R. Tolkien's *The Lord of the Rings*) or crime stories (e.g. Dashiell Hammett's *The Maltese Falcon*). When analysing this type of adaptation, it is important to be familiar with two concepts. Both are different forms of 'corrections' in Leitch's (2007) terms: *gentrification*, which describes the process by which screen adaptations of literary classics are made to fit the confines of contemporary film genres (see Whelehan and Cartmell (2010)) and *heritage film* (a term first coined by Andrew Higson (1993)), which originally denoted films from the 1980s and early 1990s that were set in the nineteenth or twentieth century, mostly adaptations of classics that include meticulously recreated period details and are combined with a nostalgic idealization of the life of the upper classes. Later adaptations of nineteenth- and twentieth-century classics were notably less complacent towards it, and more interested in depicting a realistic picture of the past. These films have been called *post-heritage* films (Monk 1995). The 2005 adaptation of *Pride and Prejudice* can be read within the broader context of post-heritage.

144 *Jørgen Bruhn et al.*

In order to analyse the process of transmediation between novel and film, we will explore a case in which the relation between source and target is apparent: a relatively recent film adaptation of Jane Austen's novel *Pride and Prejudice* (1813). The adaptation, directed by Joe Wright and written by Deborah Moggach, was released in 2005 and is the newest adaptation of *Pride and Prejudice* at the time of writing. It belongs to the category of prestige adaptations by virtue of its sumptuous production values (sets and costumes), as well as due to the star status of the actors involved: Keira Knightley (Lizzie), Matthew McFadyen (Mr. Darcy) and Judi Dench in the supporting role of Lady Catherine. This adaptation of *Pride and Prejudice* also belongs to the category of post-heritage because of its critical attitude to certain elements of the past, such as the inferior status of women in the nineteenth century.

In the subsequent section of the chapter we will analyse the process of transmediation of the source media product (the literary text) to the target media product (the film) in five steps. The analysis will focus on the opening chapter of the novel, and the opening sequence of the film. For the sake of clarity, we decided to study the opening sequence of only one adaptation, without comparing it to other, earlier screen versions, even though such a comparative analysis usually yields interesting results.

At the time of writing, the film is widely accessible via various streaming services. We suggest that before reading on, you read the opening chapter of Austen's novel and watch at least the first five minutes of the film.

The opening of Pride and Prejudice: *From page to screen*

The initial chapter of *Pride and Prejudice* is relatively short. It opens with the celebrated first sentence, 'It is a truth universally acknowledged, that a single man in possession of a good fortune, must be in want of a wife.' This remark turns out to be an observation of the novel's remarkably ironic omniscient narrator who then moves on to relate a rapid-fire conversation between Mrs. and Mr. Bennet, which starts with a piece of local gossip: a large house in the neighbourhood has just been let and the new tenant is a young man. This is tantalizing news to a family which includes five unmarried daughters. In accordance with the inheritance law of the time, upon the death of Mr. Bennet, his property will go to his male next-of-kin, and his widow and children will be left destitute. Finding husbands for the five daughters of the family, who will be able to support them financially after the death of their father, is thus a matter of first importance. The novel's protagonist, Lizzie, is mentioned in the conversation in a way that makes it clear that she is her father's favourite. The dialogue between Mr. and Mrs. Bennet makes the reader privy to their fractious relationship, and this is brought home in the last paragraph, in which the omniscient narrator offers an insight into their personalities:

> Mr. Bennet was so odd a mixture of quick parts, sarcastic humour, reserve, and caprice, that the experience of three-and-twenty years had been

insufficient to make his wife understand his character. *Her* mind was less difficult to develop. She was a woman of mean understanding, little information, and uncertain temper.

(Austen 1991, p. 4)

The narrative structure of the first chapter of the novel displays transmedial characteristics that can easily be transferred to audiovisual cinematic narration, specifically because the presentation of conflict and the characters are based on dialogue. Just like a well-written exposition scene in a film, the opening chapter immediately sets up the story. The very first lines of the novel contain the inciting event (the arrival of a wealthy young man in the neighbourhood), and the dialogue between the Bennets makes it possible for the reader to infer what kind of a world the story is set in. The main characters are a middle-class family living quietly in the country, where the arrival of a new neighbour is exciting news. From the way in which her parents discuss Lizzie, the readers also get a hint of what kind of a girl the protagonist is going to be. From her parents' conversation, we can sense that there is something unusual about Lizzie that sets her apart from her four sisters. All this information is revealed to us in fast-paced dialogue, which gives us insight into the personalities of Mr. and Mrs. Bennet and sets up the dynamic of their relationship, which will later be exploited for comic effect.

Interestingly, even though the first chapter is so effective in capturing the reader's interest and presenting the main premise of the story, no major screen adaptation of the novel has faithfully portrayed this conversation between Mr. and Mrs. Bennet. The opening scenes of all existing film and television adaptations are different, and each finds a way to present the audience with the key piece of information ('Netherfield Park is let at last!'), but the first scene is never just a faithful depiction of the conversation between Mr. and Mrs. Bennet.[1]

The opening of the 2005 film adaptation focuses on the heroine from the very first seconds. The audience enters the world of the film with Lizzie (Keira Knightley) quite literally acting as or guide. The long Steadicam shot, which takes up most of the opening sequence, tracks Lizzie's steps as she comes back from her solitary walk, and we see her family from her perspective. Let us now go through the five-step procedure outlined above to analyse how the opening sequence of the film as a work of adaptation.

1 Delimit the scope of analysis

After reading the first chapter and watching the opening sequence, we decided to focus our analysis on the shift from the omniscient narration in the novel to the 'heroine-centric' storytelling in the screen adaptation. Why does the opening scene of the film shift the focus from the parents' conversation to Lizzie, and how is this shift achieved?

2 Comparative close reading

What information is preserved in the film version? What has been omitted? A marked difference between the novel and the film is that Joe Wright's adaptation opens with Lizzie taking a solitary walk in the countryside. In terms of Leitch's five adjustment strategies, this could be seen as an expansion. For the first two minutes of the film the camera follows Lizzie coming home from her morning walk. As Lizzie approaches her home, the audience gets the first glimpse of the Bennets' residence through her eyes. We see a large, if slightly run-down house, which is messy and full of life. It is only when she passes by the window of her father's study and overhears the famous line 'Netherfield Hall is let at last', after which she and her sisters start eavesdropping on the parents' conversation, which is a compressed version of the dialogue from the novel.

Despite these differences, the opening scenes of the film convey the same crucial information to the audience as the first chapter of the novel: Lizzie's walk towards the house shows her family's social position, she is also introduced as an intelligent young woman with a book in her hand. The dialogue is compressed but also distributed between the parents and the daughters, presenting a close-knit family, discussing exciting news of a new neighbour.

3 Transmediality and medium specificity

Out of all of these pieces of information about the Bennets, only the last one is conveyed in dialogue. The remaining four are presented primarily via moving images. The reasons for the change are rooted in the basic media types of film. The moving images, the dialogue and other auditory media types, *show* in a film what a narrator of a novel can *tell*. The scene described in the novel is completely static, with two characters talking with no background information about the setting. The film privileges movement over description and replaces the scene in the novel with a more dynamic sequence. Put simply, the literary text *describes* with words (using conventional signs), whereas the cinematic images and sounds *show* by way of iconic similarity. What the narrator of a novel tells us, the film will have to show.

In the novel, the dialogue between the Bennets is used to present the conflict and the social context and to introduce the protagonist. In the film, the moving images, dialogue, music, and sound effects communicate information about the family. For example, the view of the house and the characters' costumes allow the audience to gauge their financial status. When Lizzie enters the house, the camera also moves around, emphasizing the bustle of the everyday life of the Bennets. Furthermore, other, auditory media types such as sound design and music add new information. Lizzie's walk is accompanied by music in the style of early nineteenth-century piano music, which builds the atmosphere of the first scene and which even drowns out the sound of Lizzie's sister Mary playing the more old-fashioned harpsichord.

All in all, the visual and auditory media types add up to a rich portrait of Lizzie as the protagonist. In the scenes in which she is shown with her sisters, she is always presented at the centre of the group, which subtly enhances her central role.

4 Qualified media type: Conventions, production and dissemination

The creative decision to open the film with Lizzie walking home also follows the golden rule of screenwriting to open the film by showing the protagonist. Joe Wright's *Pride and Prejudice* is the story of Lizzie, showing her journey as a character, and this journey begins from the first seconds of the film. This means that other elements of the storyworld (e.g. setting, characters) play a supporting role and their most important function is to strengthen and highlight the heroine's journey, which can explain the decision to shift the focus from the conversation between Mr. and Mrs. Bennet to Lizzie's experience of witnessing the conversation.

We can also consider the broader production and reception context for this version of *Pride and Prejudice*. What was the film landscape in the early 2000s? What films were box office hits; what genres were fashionable? In the early 2000s, the British film industry scored two global hits in the romantic comedy genre: *Bridget Jones's Diary* (2001) and *Love Actually* (2003). Their phenomenal success led to a renewed vogue for romantic comedies. In fact, the promotional materials for Joe Wright's *Pride and Prejudice* highlighted the fact that the film was produced by the same studio that was responsible for *Bridget Jones's Diary* and *Love Actually*, and the marketing campaign practically disregarded the fact that the film was set in the nineteenth century, promoting it as 'the ultimate chick flick'.

Additionally *Pride and Prejudice* went into production eight years after the explosion of 'Austenmania', which started in 1995 when several films and television series based on works of Jane Austen became box office hits. Especially the 1995 BBC television series made a great cultural impact and developed a passionate fan following, which was also incidentally referenced in *Bridget Jones's Diary*. The film adaptation of *Pride and Prejudice* in 2005 was thus eagerly anticipated, and instantly began to be compared to the earlier BBC version. The contexts of the romantic comedy boom and Austenmania prove relevant for the analysis of the 2005 *Pride and Prejudice*. In fact, we could argue that the film has a dual identity as both a (post-)heritage adaptation of a canonical novel and a romantic comedy. It is especially tempting to analyse Lizzie, played by Keira Knightley, as a version of a romantic comedy heroine. In the opening sequence of the film, she is singled out thanks to camera movements and framing, suggesting that, in the great tradition of romantic comedy heroines, she is 'not like the other girls'.

5 New perspectives

Every adaptation can potentially influence the interpretation and reception of the source text. After watching an adaptation of a novel, audience members who choose to (re)read the source text will usually imagine the characters and settings as they were presented in the film.

Taking into consideration that step 5 is more suited to analysing complete films than individual scenes, we can still argue that the focus on the heroine in the film's opening scene makes the audience more strongly identify with Lizzie. As the protagonist, she is, literally, presented as the most beautiful and most brilliant of the five sisters. This may change the perception of the character for those people in the audience who will read the novel afterwards.

Ekphrasis, or: What words can make us see

In Ancient Greece and Rome, ekphrasis was a rhetorical term, to mean the art of describing a work of art or other things with *energeia*, with *vividness*. In the twentieth century, the term ekphrasis has begun to specifically denote a verbal description of a work of art (Webb 2009), for example, a literary text, prose or poetry, that in some way represents a painting, a drawing or a photograph, either real or fictitious. One of the most famous examples is Homer's description in the *Iliad* of the making of the shield of Achilles as an outstanding piece of artisanry. Like many other remarkable pieces of art described in literature, the shield is fictive, and Homer vividly describes a piece of work that has never existed, and invites the reader or listener to imagine it (see Heffernan (1993) and Krieger (1992)).

Traditionally, ekphrasis has been seen as a way for verbal texts to compete with and to imitate images – by painting pictures with words – and this might be the reason why writing ekphrastic texts seems to be so alluring to poets and novelists alike. Just as the ekphrasis is a popular trope or genre for writers, it is an attractive subject area of study for literary and intermedial studies, and therefore the concept of ekphrasis is well researched and contested. Many definitions of ekphrasis have been suggested since the study of ekphrasis as a literary phenomenon took off about a century ago, but here we use intermedial scholar Claus Clüver's (1997) definition, which is that ekphrasis is 'the verbal representation of a real or fictitious text composed in a non-verbal sign system' (p. 26). This definition avoids a problem that Lars Elleström (2021, p. 45) has pointed to: a verbal (written) representation is also visual, and a term such as 'visual arts' is thus misleading – even though both images and text are perceived visually in the sensorial modality, they communicate differently in the spatio-temporal and semiotic modality. As Clüver's definition suggests, there are other relations between media that could be and have been defined as ekphrasis, including verbal representations of pieces of instrumental music, film, dance, theatre etc. In this text, however, we focus on the transmediation between a visual, static image and a written text, and for the sake of clarity, a poem is chosen for the analysis.

Ekphrasis is an example of a transmediation between a source media product and a target media product, belonging to different media types that are structured differently on the level of the semiotic modality. A graphic image is constituted by iconic signs, whereas a verbal text is constituted by symbolic signs. In the material and sensorial modality, text and images both appear on surfaces and are perceived visually. However, in most cases the poetic text is structured sequentially (you have to read the words in a certain order for them to make sense), which gives verbal text a fixed sequentiality in the sensorial modality that a static, graphic image lacks. However, both iconic images and words can represent special relations and temporal events in the sensorial modality.

When analysing an ekphrasis there are certain questions that we need to ask. For example, does the ekphrasis describe the image or does it merely refer or allude to it? Does it take the image as a starting point for a narrative or does it linger in the depicted moment? Which aspects of the paintings are verbally represented? Which details are described? Does it describe the media representation – the painting – as a qualified media type or does it focus primarily on transmediating the content? These are all questions that can be asked to gain a deeper understanding of the specific ekphrastic relationship between the source and the target media product. Furthermore, the aim of an ekphrasis is seldom simply to faithfully represent an image – instead, it uses the image to reflect on other issues. What is the role of the image in the poem? How does the description of an image relate to the poem's theme, and the sentiments and the reflections it conveys?

So let's study how the ekphrastic poem 'Western Motel' by Anne Carson (2001) represents and transforms Edward Hopper's painting *Western Motel* (1957). In our analysis, we follow the five analytical steps presented above with some modifications.

1 The scope of analysis

As ekphrastic poems are often comparatively short, we start our analysis with the presentation of the complete target media product.

>Pink bedspreads you say
>are not pleasing to you
>yet you sit very straight
>till the pictures are through.
>Two suitcases watch you like dogs.
>You wear your hair parted
>low on the right.
>Mountains outside
>look like beds without night.
>Two suitcases watch you like dogs.
>Glass is for getaway.
>Hot is out there.
>You seem to know
>the road ends here.
>Two suitcases watch you like dogs.
>
>*Future things then are not yet: and if they be not yet,*
>*they are not. And if they are not,*

150 *Jørgen Bruhn et al.*

they cannot be seen.
Yet foretold they may be
from things present which are already and are seen.
(Augustine, *Confessions* XI)

2 Comparative close reading

What are the similarities and differences between the painting and the poem? The source media product is Hopper's painting depicting a woman sitting on a bed by a large window. The walls, ceiling and floor of the room are green; one can see mountains and a blue sky through the window. In the left-hand bottom corner there are two suitcases, and in the right-hand bottom corner there is an armchair. Calmness dominates the painting: no motion is represented, despite the suitcases and the motel room, which might signal things like 'passing through' or 'travelling'. As for the ekphrasis, Hans Lund (2002) differentiates between two types: the *narrative ekphrasis* and the *ekphrasis of the frozen moment*, and even though it would certainly be possible given the transitory nature of a motel room, Carson's poem does not take the painting as a starting point for a narrative; instead it lingers in the moment, stretching it out over three stanzas separated by one recurring line: 'Two suitcases watch you like dogs'. The repetition in itself underlines the stillness of the painting since it illustrates the lingering and the lack of progression, as the poem concludes: 'the road ends here'. The poem describes some of the objects depicted in the painting: the woman, the bed, the window, the suitcases and the mountains and some of the spatial relations between them (the woman sitting on the bed – even though that is not explicitly stated in the poem, only implied – and the mountains outside, seen from the window). Some details are mentioned: how the woman parts her hair, that the bedspreads are pink and how the mountains look. Overall, the poem is not very descriptive. However, some scholars claim that an ekphrasis does not have to be descriptive as long as it relates to its source media product in a way that it is actualized in the mind of the reader.

3 Transmediality and medium specificity

The most important objects in the painting – the woman, the bed, the suitcases, the window and the mountains – as well as its silent and static atmosphere have been transmediated to the poem. However, due to the specificities of each media type, they are clearly not identical after the transfer: we would never mistake a painting for a poem or vice versa. This has to do with the semiotic sign systems used by each medium: the painting consists of iconic signs and the poem consists of symbolic signs. Therefore, what is depicted in a painting must in an ekphrasis be described by means of words. A motionless and silent atmosphere in a painting can be created by having a balanced composition, geometrical shapes, muted colours, etc. In a poem it must instead be conveyed verbally, for example, by means of short sentences, repetition and a lack of narrative progress.

One way of reading and writing an ekphrasis focuses on how we interact with images, both real and imaginary ones. Some ekphrastic texts are structured so that they imitate how we look at a painting, for example, by means of zooming in and out (see Robillard 2007). In Carson's ekphrasis, two crucial lines are 'yet you sit very straight/till the pictures are through', which refer to the making of the painting: the artist painted the woman sitting on the bed, and she sat still until the painting was finished. These lines function as visual triggers for the reader. They are also intertextually linked to another ekphrastic poem, 'American Gothic' by John Stone (1998), after the painting *American Gothic* by Grant Wood (1930). In Stone's poem, the man and the woman stand patiently while their portrait is being painted, and the man 'asking the artist silently/how much longer'. The ekphrasis thus becomes a representation of the finished painting and of the process of its making, just as in the description of the shield of Achilles.

4 Themes and contexts

When analysing an ekphrastic text it is often fruitful to do a hermeneutic reading and to take relevant contexts into consideration. In this case, 'Western Motel' is one poem in a suite of several ekphrastic poems representing Hopper's paintings, 'HOPPER: *CONFESSIONS*' (Carson 2001). All of the poems are followed by a quote from Augustine's *Confessions*, Book XI, except for the last one ('The Glove of Time by Edward Hopper'), which is not an ekphrasis but a poem that lets Edward Hopper himself reflect on issues such as time, eternity and art. The 11th book in *Confessions* discusses the nature of time: how the present relates to itself, to the past and to the future. By letting a quote from the theologian Augustine (354–430) follow each ekphrastic poem in the suite and by finishing the suite with a poem that explicitly has the word 'time' in the title, Carson points the interpreter in a certain direction: the theme is time, and the nature of time. With that in mind, we might understand the motel room as a waiting room, where the focus is not the 'future things' that Augustine mentions, but the present, which is exactly Augustine's point as well: only the present exists. Paintings and other visual, iconic images are often said to represent just that: a constant now, a moment encapsulated in time. This alleged property of painting has inspired and frustrated poets and thinkers throughout history, and many ekphrastic texts, like this one by Carson, deal with the question of time and timelessness, and, by extension, of life and death.

5 New perspectives

What kind of transformations have taken place in this ekphrasis? Does the ekphrastic poem cast new light on the source media product? The poem performs a transformation from the painting *Western Motel* to a mental image of what it represents. The images the poem conjures up vary depending on whether or not the reader is familiar with the painting. If she is, then the title and description of central aspects of the scene will most likely make her see the painting as a cognitive representation without perception, but not exactly as it is. We tend to forget details, or we transform them in our memories. As the American author Siri Hustvedt (2005) writes: 'Every painting is always two paintings: the one you see and the one you remember' (p. 12). Furthermore, the memories of the actual painting will merge with images conjured up by similes in the poem, for example, 'Two suitcases watch you like dogs' and 'Mountains outside/look like beds without night'. These similes (written comparisons) create a blend where the readers see suitcases and dogs, mountains and beds simultaneously and/or integrated: suitcases that look like dogs and mountains that look like beds.

Thus, much has changed in the process but much is still the same: the stillness emanating from the painting characterizes the poem as well. We still meet a woman in a motel room, her hair parted on the right, sitting on a bed with a pink bedspread. The window shows an outdoor scene that does not really concern her: in the painting she is turned away from the window, and the poem states that '[g]lass is for getaway'. She is not getting anywhere: 'the road ends here'. Is this a reflection on the static nature of painting (as the fictive Hopper says in the last poem of the suite: 'It so happens/paint is motionless')? Or is it an interpretation of this specific painting, or both? Either way, the poem is an interpretation of the painting, and media transformation processes go both ways, as Jørgen Bruhn (2013) points out: the target media product consists of a transformation of the source media product, but the source media product itself becomes transformed by the target media product. After having read Carson's poem, we see Hopper's painting in a new light, as part of the adaptational feedback typical of all media transformations.

Transforming drama to opera

Studies that compare adaptations of literary works in opera have a long tradition that goes back to the nineteenth century. Film and literature studies seem to be rather unaware of this rich body of texts about opera and music theatre that has been written during the past one-and-a-half centuries. The results of studies of, say, adaptations of novels into films overlap in many instances with those of opera adaptation studies. But opera has its genre- and media-specific features as well (addressed, for example, by Stenström (1994)).

Compression and convention: The work of the librettist

As virtually all writers on opera adaptations have pointed out, writing the words for an opera after the model of an existing literary text – which was the work of the librettist – means shortening the original narrative massively, a compression in terms of Leitch's five adjustment strategies. Common compression strategies that librettists pursue are condensing the plot by reducing the action to a handful of crucial scenes, eliminating subplots and minor characters, deleting any retrospective and prospective telling of the story to create a strictly chronological order of events, and sharpening the profiles of characters. These transmedial strategies can also be found in film and dramatic adaptations of novels.

More media-specific is the role of music in the adaptation process. In opera, musical, vaudeville and other forms of music theatre and film, the characters sing, and their songs, the dances and the action are accompanied by instrumental music. Playing music requires time. Instrumental music and singing may sometimes be more in the background – like in melodrama or its modern successor, the spoken dialogue in film that includes background music – or sometimes more in the foreground, like in a virtuoso opera aria. An experienced opera or musical librettist will consider where to put such music highlights when writing the text. Another tradition is that of the choice of the voice range, for instance, tenor parts for the heroes and soprano parts for heroines. When writing a libretto the choice of a certain type of character is implicitly also that of a certain voice range. Conventions also exist about the instruments associated with certain characters. Following or not following these traditions and conventions will give the experienced listener valuable hints about possible interpretations of the opera

Limitations and possibilities of opera

The qualified medium of opera implies certain conventions but also certain limitations of space, time and voice. The natural venue for experiencing an opera is the stage. In a live context, the singers' voices and the orchestra are in precise acoustic balance (see Chapter 14). Composing operas that were not written for live performance, such as the radio operas of the first half of the twentieth century, had to happen within the acoustic limitations that transmitted radio signals offer. This point can be addressed either in step 3 or in step 4 of the adaptation model, depending on whether the media specificity (step 3) or the production conditions (step 4) are in focus.

Opera, perhaps even more than spoken drama, only exists within the very moment of its performance. Its meaning derives from performing and listening to a tone or sound in the very moment of its transitory existence. A composer therefore seldom writes vocal parts that put the success of a performance at risk technically; he or she has to know what can be sung and what cannot. There are limitations of time. An opera should not take longer than a few hours to perform because the voices of the singers as well as the lips of the brass players in the orchestra cannot be overused.

While drama can be performed with very limited resources, such as just one or two actors and a stage, opera involves a large instrumental and sometimes vocal ensemble. This makes opera much more time-consuming and expensive to rehearse and perform. Opera therefore has always required generous sponsorship. These limitations and requirements need to be considered when analysing an opera adaptation. For instance, if a character displays different features in the opera compared to the drama, this may be due to the political view of the sponsors or to the specialization of the singers. Also, a composer may change the profile of a character and add some musical means that change the interpretation of the plot because the music was written in another historical period or for a different audience from the one the drama was aiming at.

Opera adaptation therefore highlights the fact that all adaptation not only relates to a specific source media product but always adapted to a specific target audience and into a new context. The librettist's medial opportunities are musical structures and sounding reality. Opera, for the most part, consists of non-diegetic music (cf. Gorbman 1987 regarding this term), which means music that only exists for the listener and not for the characters on stage. Lines are sung and actions are executed with an orchestral accompaniment. The role of the music can in some instances be compared with that of the narrator in literature because it gives the actions and words a clarity in terms of expression that the spoken word can barely achieve. The action may shift between various emotions within seconds thanks to the instrumental accompaniment or the vocal delivery of a singer. The orchestra may even reveal things that are hidden from the characters on stage, revealing their inner life. The orchestra may look forwards or backwards in the narrative by quoting or anticipating material from other parts of the score, thus creating narratives that run parallel.

The possibilities of using the orchestra's timbre, harmony, rhythm, tempo, volume, instrumentation and so on to create a soundscape with a certain meaning are infinite. Even though the orchestra is usually invisible, it is at the heart of opera, and the tradition of opera music has a successor in mainstream film with its wall-to-wall orchestral soundtracks (cf. Howard Shore's film score for *The Lord of the Rings*). When an opera is an adaptation of a piece of literature, the composer – and thus the music – can be seen as an interpretation of the source text, and the opera may often change the audience's view on this particular piece of literature (cf. step 5 of the proposed analytical model); in some instances, the musical version of the piece may even outshine the literary source, such as Guiseppe Verdi's *La Traviata* (1853) or George Bizet's *Carmen* (1875).

A media-specific possibility that is unique to music drama is the simultaneity of events. Characters can sing different or sometimes completely contrary texts at the same time in the ensembles (duets, trios, quartets, etc.). This would be hard to accept in traditional spoken drama and film. The different texts with their different meanings can be mirrored in the simultaneity of different musical events. European music is essentially polyphonic, which means that different melodies can be sung and played simultaneously, and there is no upper limit for how many acoustic events can occur at the same time. At the turn of the twentieth century, the number of instruments playing together became excessively large, confronting the audience with sometimes dozens of different musical events played and sung at the same time. In short, composing an opera means giving the drama a certain direction, emotional power, clarity in terms of events and hence sometimes a different content. It is an act of interpretation.

> **Box 9.3 From transmediation analysis to opera adaptation**
>
> Each form of transmediation addresses the relation between source and target media product slightly differently. In order to address drama to opera adaptation, you have to consider the following questions that 'adapt' the analytical model to the medium specificity of opera.
>
> - Decide on the scope and form analysis. Do you want to compare the drama text to the musical score and libretto in a more *text-based analysis* compare the drama and the opera as *performed artworks*?
> - Spoken drama and opera share a lot of features. Both present human bodies and their voices to an audience, they are performed on stage and they present a narrative. However, drama and opera integrate the same basic media types and transmedial features in a media-specific way. Especially the way how music contributes to the narrative and its interpretation in opera is a central part of analysing an opera adaptation.
> - In order to grasp how music transmediates the plot, conflict and themes of the drama, you focus on:
>
>   a the main characters: what does their voice range reveal about their gender, age and role in the drama? How do the tempo, range and expression of their vocal delivery differ from each other? Are the characters singing long tones or do they merely speak their parts? Are their psychological profiles similar to or different from those in the source?
>
>   b the orchestra: what 'role' does it have in a certain situation? Does it describe or comment on the action like an external narrator would or does it focalize and tell the story from the perspective of a character? Do you recognize certain melodies that return several times, themes or leitmotifs? Do central themes change shape over time and how? Are there certain solo instruments or instrument groups that are linked to a certain character, situation or action? Where does the composer put climaxes in volume and instrumentation and where does the orchestra remain silent? Does the orchestra follow the movements of the actors' bodies – for instance, like in a cartoon – or does it perhaps tell a story that is different from the one that is visible on stage?

Richard Strauss's (1864–1949) opera *Salome* (1905) is part of a whole chain of transmediations. The story of Salome (who lived during the first century AD) is partly factual and goes back to the New Testament and Flavius Josephus's *De bello judaico*. The legend of Salome's dance in exchange for the head of John the Baptist became part of the medieval literary canon in the early fifth century. What followed was an extraordinary intermedial career of the subject that involves chains of transmediations. Starting in the Renaissance, Salome became popular among painters. At the end of the nineteenth century – parallel with the early women's rights movement, and with symbolism – several painters and writers presented their versions of it. The most infamous one became Oscar Wilde's (1854–1900) eponymous prose drama. Wilde's scandalous play triggered a new era for representing Salome's dance in ballet and opera. Its best-known musical version became Richard Strauss's eponymous opera.

1 Delimit the scope

Richard Strauss's *Salome* belongs to the category of *Literaturoper* (cf. Istel 1914), a musicalization of a drama that leaves the words unchanged. In the opera, the text is a compressed version of Wilde's drama, but there are no major changes in terms of plot. The adaptation of *Salome* can show especially well how music works as a dramatic device; understanding how an opera score is structured also means understanding how a film's soundtrack is structured. The aim of the next sections is to get to grips with the medium of dramatic music – its communicative functions, structures, modes and means of production and reception, and, most importantly, its relation to the action and the story. We delimit our scope of analysis to the question: how does Strauss's music modify the content of Wilde's drama?

Box 9.4 Word and tone in opera

At the beginning of opera history, operas were seen as a form of drama, and hence the writer of the words, the librettist, was regarded as being the author of an opera while the composer was seen as assisting to a greater or lesser extent with the creation of a version that could be performed. The words were the essence; the music was accidental until around 1800. After that, this hierarchy was turned upside down. The music was regarded as essential and the author of the words was only assisting the composer. In contemporary discussions about opera, the fact that it was created in distinct steps by different persons was seen as an aesthetic problem because the quality of libretto and score appeared to be heterogeneous in some instances. Richard Wagner (1813–83) presented a more organic form of music theatre than was produced by following these earlier conventions. He wrote both the libretto and the music himself; vocal lines were to be spoken rather than sung and there were elaborate orchestral parts. This approach was different from the contemporary Italian or French compound form of opera.

2 Comparative close reading

We focus our analysis on the comparison of Wilde's drama text with Strauss's musical score. Strauss drew on Richard Wagner's more organized form of music theatre as a model (see Box 9.4). Strauss took the German translation of Wilde's piece and set it to music without seeking help from a writer (Deppisch 2001, p. 84). If we look at the text, the only change Strauss made was to shorten the text by about half. The action was left intact, with stage directions in their original wording. There are no new scenes and characters added. Strauss's one-act music drama is therefore in many aspects identical to Wilde's one-act play. Its playing time of about one hour and 45 minutes may correspond to that of the spoken drama. Both versions adhere to Greek philosopher Aristoteles' demand for unity of time and space in drama and present their respective version of the events 'in real time'. However, there are more differences than similarities in the distribution of time and the appearance of the work on a detailed level.

3 Transmediality and media specificity

When comparing drama text and opera score, we can notice how Strauss stresses structural patterns that already can be found in the text of Wilde's drama. Salome asks Jochanaan three times to touch one part of his body and he refuses thrice. Herodes asks Salome three times to come close to him and she refuses thrice as well. Salome's wish for a kiss from Jochanaan is repeated ten times ('I will kiss thy mouth, Jochanaan'), and her demand for his head ('Give me the head of Jochanaan') eight times, with the very same words. Symbols, for instance, the half-moon, and identical phrases, recur throughout the work. These repetitive structures in the drama text are enhanced in Strauss's musical setting. Musical structures need repetitions to build relations between the different parts of a piece, on several levels: periods and phrases can be repeated, measures are repeating metric structures, sometimes over a long period of time, and words or lines are repeated in opera arias. In Wagnerian music drama, one important device for creating an instrumental 'subtext' of the drama is the leitmotif, which can comment on a dramatic situation by way of repetition. Strauss presents several leitmotifs and weaves dense thematic structures with them in *Salome*. Some are clearly linked to characters, such as Jochanaan's horn leitmotif (heard for the first time when he enters the stage), and some emphasize some aspects of the characters, such as the rising fourth motif, which is linked to his prophecy (or to that of the Messiah). It is the latter motif that appears at the end of the Dance of the Seven Veils and gives insight into Salome's thoughts while she is dancing.

The choice of voice parts and ranges contributes to the characterization. Salome is a 16-year-old girl, so the lyrical soprano – signifying youth in opera – was a natural choice. The choice of a serious baritone for Jochanaan – the Hebrew name for John – signifies seriousness, masculinity and tranquillity.

Jochanaan has the slowest declamation tempo of all of the characters, which lends serenity to his prophecies. Herodes is a tenor but, as in many other Strauss operas, this tenor part is not heroic. On the contrary, this sick and half-drunk character is presented as weak, unmanly and a coward through his musical declamation. His singing includes squeaking, yelling, barking and shrieking. The young captain of the guards, Narraboth, who is in despair because of his unanswered love for Salome, is also a tenor, but a lyrical one who has to sing expressive melodies rather than declaim and shout like the other tenors in this opera.

The role of the orchestra connects to its four functions in the Wagnerian tradition: 1) the orchestra defines historical time and space acoustically, known as the *couleur locale*; Strauss was proud of being able to compose a humid subtropical night without referring to worn-out formulae in music which were typical of late nineteenth-century exoticism (Deppisch 2001, p. 84). 2) The orchestra gives psychological insights into the inner lives of the characters. While dancing and arousing her stepfather, Salome is thinking about the strange man in the cistern. The orchestra makes her inner thoughts audible. 3) The orchestra comments on what is happening on stage, for instance, through leitmotifs. Feelings and characters can develop over time; the neutral woodwind drill motif, for instance, is linked to the awakening of Salome's curiosity in the first scene that turns into sadism when the head of the dead prophet is shown to her in the last scene. 4) Wagner explained in his programmatic book *Oper und Drama* (1851) that the orchestra in modern music theatre had taken over one important function of the Greek chorus, namely the representation of the audience's emotions (Wagner 1907, pp. 190–1). One theme that is heard for the first time when Salome enters the stage and returns during her dance – a descending line in parallel thirds – may be seen as her personal leitmotif. It appears prominently one last time at the very end of the drama. Here it ends with a shocking bitonal dissonance – two different chords are played loudly and simultaneously, unleashing the entire orchestral force in a brutal way – that reflects the audience's horror at the confrontation with the princess's act of necrophilia when she kisses the dead body and expresses her sexual arousal. This double chord in the orchestra pit has the same hair-raising effect on the audience as the action performed on stage.

Strauss was known for his virtuosity in orchestration and his innovative orchestral effects. They are virtually innumerable in *Salome* and it is often difficult to tell whether the many expressive instrumental effects which resemble sighing, moaning, shrieking, bleating, shrilling, gagging and so on are related to the events on stage, the audience's reactions or perhaps both at the same time.

4 Different performances

Especially the analysis of the role of the orchestra demonstrates how Strauss did not just add music to Wilde's drama but gave it an entirely different shape as a performative artwork, which followed the Wagnerian aesthetic tradition (Knust

2018, p. 43). However, both drama text and opera score are a set of directions fixed in a script but resulting in different kinds of performances. A comparison of a performance of Wilde's drama as it may have looked – and sounded – like in his time and a performance of Strauss's opera could become the point of departure for another kind of adaptation study, which involves the sounds, body movements, stage decorations and lighting and so on with each other as experienced by the audience.

However, one fundamental performative difference that can be addressed based on the score is the disposition of time. Strauss wanted proportions that would give the piece order as a musical principle. This emphasizes his adherence to the forms of instrumental music (Werbeck 1996), which operate using regular proportions of time. He spoke about the 'symphony in the drama' of the *Salome* opera (quoted in Krause 1963, p. 307). Each of the four scenes has double the playing time of the previous one (Schreiber 2000, p. 252) thanks to the elimination of dialogues in the first scenes, the insertion of instrumental interludes and the deceleration of Salome's declamation tempo in her monologue at the end of the drama, which all puts the action in some kind of slow motion.

5 New perspectives

Although the text of the opera remains quite unchanged, the analysis of orchestra and voices has shown how Strauss interpreted the main characters differently from Wilde. The words and the defiant character of Wilde's Jochanaan fit well with those of an Old Testament prophet. In Strauss's opera, some of the musical features make him a little bit like a travesty. Wilde's play leaves it unclear what Salome's motives are for demanding his death. Is she really cruel or just naïve, is she attracted physically or spiritually by the prophet, is her ecstasy at the end just a kind of perversion or is it the symbol of her breaking free from her decadent environment? We don't know for sure in Wilde's drama. In Strauss's interpretation of the biblical legend, Salome ends her life as a pagan ecstatic (pp. 255–6), unaware and even uninterested in the moral values of the new time that is about to dawn. It is the first of his operas with a dominant woman at the centre who leaves no space for a male hero, announcing a new era in the history of the (in)equality of the sexes.

Conclusion

This chapter has discussed the very wide field of media transformations and transmediations, intermedial processes that are everywhere around us in our everyday lives, and which is a crucial aspect of all cultural development. This is not only an important aspect of our high-speed digital age; it is dating back – we must assume – to early human cultures where a story of a successful hunt was transmediated into perhaps a cave painting and possibly later on transformed into parts of a ritual dance performance.

Being less speculative in this chapter, three media transformation types have been described: novel-to-film adaptation, poetry representing aspects of a painting (ekphrasis), and finally operas transforming literary work. The chapter provides models for analysis that diverge slightly, partly depending upon the specific media types involved. What is common to our suggestions for analytical models is the focus on media-specific aspects and how these are being transferred and transformed in the process from a source media product to a target media product. It has been our aim to demonstrate in specific analysis the very abstract idea that all media transformation is an interplay or a negotiation between transmediality and medium specificity.

Notes

1 See Chapter 3, '"First impressions": the screen openings of *Pride and Prejudice*' in Cartmell (2010).
2 For reasons of simplicity, we refer to the characters' names in their German or English original but will only quote their lines according to the English version of Wilde's play, not Lachmann's translation.

References

Albrecht-Crane, C. and Cutchins, D.R. 2010. *Adaptation studies: New approaches*. Madison: Fairleigh Dickinson University Press.
Austen, J. 1991. *Pride and Prejudice*. London: Everyman Classics.
Bruhn, J. 2013. Dialogizing adaptation studies: From one-way transport to a dialogic two-way process. In J. Bruhn, A. Gjelsvik, and E.F. Hanssen, eds., *Adaptation studies: New challenges, new directions* (pp. 69–88). London; New York: Bloomsbury.
Carson, A. 2001. Western motel. In *Men in the off hours*. New York: Vintage Contemporaries.
Cartmell, D. 2010. *Jane Austen's Pride and Prejudice: The relationship between text and film*. London: Methuen Drama.
Clüver, C. 1997. Ekphrasis reconsidered: On verbal representations of non-verbal texts. In U.B. Lagerroth, H. Lund and E. Hedling, eds. *Interart poetics: Essays on the interrelations of the arts and media*. Amsterdam: Rodopi. pp. 19–34.
Deppisch, W. 2001. *Richard Strauss*. Reinbek: Rowohlt.
Elleström, L. (2021). The modalities of media II: An expanded model for understanding intermedial relations. In Lars Elleström, ed., *Beyond media borders. Vol.1. Intermedial relations among multimodal media*. Basingstoke; New York: Palgrave Macmillan, 3–91.
Elliott, K. 2003. *Rethinking the novel/film debate*. Cambridge: Cambridge University Press.
Elliott, K. 2020. *Theorizing adaptation*. Oxford: Oxford University Press.
Gorbman, C. 1987. *Unheard melodies: Narrative film music*. Bloomington: Indiana University Press.
Heffernan, J.A.W. 1993. *Museum of words: The poetics of ekphrasis from Homer to Ashbery*. Chicago; London: University of Chicago Press.
Higson, A.D. 1993. Re-presenting the national past: Nostalgia and pastiche in the heritage film. In L. Friedman, ed., *Fires were started: British cinema and Thatcherism* (pp. 109–129). Minneapolis: University of Minnesota Press.

Hustvedt, S. 2005. *Mysteries of the rectangle: Essays on painting*. New York: Princeton Architectural Press.
Hutcheon, L. and O'Flynn, S. 2013. *A theory of adaptation*. London: Routledge.
Istel, E. 1914. *Das Libretto. Wesen, Aufbau und Wirkung des Opernbuchs nebst einer dramaturgischen Analyse des Librettos von Figaros Hochzeit*. Berlin; Leipzig: Schuster & Loeffler.
Knust, M. 2018. *Sprachvertonung und Gestik in den Werken Richard Wagners – Einflüsse zeitgenössischer Rezitations- und Deklamationspraxis*, PhD thesis (Greifswalder Beiträge zur Musikwissenschaft). Berlin: Frank & Timme.
Krause, E. 1963. *Richard Strauss: Gestalt und Werk*. Leipzig: Breitkopf & Härtel.
Krieger, M. 1992. *Ekphrasis: The illusion of the natural sign*. Baltimore: John Hopkins University Press.
Leitch, T. 2003. Twelve fallacies in contemporary adaptation theory. *Criticism*, 45(2), pp. 149–147. doi:10.1353/crt.2004.0001
Leitch, T. 2007. *Film adaptation and its discontents from Gone with the Wind to The Passion of the Christ*. Baltimore: Johns Hopkins University Press.
Lund, H. 2002. Litterär ekfras. In *Intermedialitet. Ord, bild och ton i samspel*. Lund: Studentlitteratur.
Monk, C. 1995. Sexuality and heritage. *Sight and Sound*, 5(10) (October 1995), pp. 32–34.
Robillard, V. 2007. Still chasing down the greased pig. In J. Arvidson, M. Askander, J. Bruhn and H. Führer, eds., *Changing borders: Contemporary positions in intermediality*. Lund: Intermedia Studies Press.
Salmose, N. and Elleström, L. 2020. *Transmediations: Communication across media borders*. New York: Routledge.
Schreiber, U. 2000. *Opernführer für Fortgeschrittene: Das 20. Jahrhundert I*. Kassel: Bärenreiter.
Stenström, J. 1994. *Aniara: från versepos till opera*. Malmö: Corona.
Stone, J. 1998. *Where the water begins: New poems and prose*. Baton Rouge: Louisiana State University Press.
Wagner, R. 1907. Oper und Drama. In R. Wagner, *Gesammelte Schriften und Dichtungen*. vol. 4. Leipzig: C.F.W. Siegel [K. Linnemann].
Webb, R. 2009. *Ekphrasis, imagination and persuasion in ancient rhetorical theory and practice*. Farnham, Burlington: Ashgate.
Werbeck, W. 1996. *Die Tondichtungen von Richard Strauss*. Tutzing: Hans Schneider.
Whelehan, I. and Cartmell, D. 2010. *Screen adaptation: Impure cinema*. London: Macmillan.

10 Media representation

Film, music and painting in literature

Jørgen Bruhn, Liviu Lutas, Niklas Salmose and Beate Schirrmacher

In Nick Hornby's novel *High Fidelity* (1995), the life of the protagonist Rob revolves around records and popular music. Throughout Virginia Woolf's novel *To the Lighthouse* (1927), the painter Lily Briscoe works on a portrait of her friend Mrs Ramsay. In James Joyce's *Ulysses* (1922), Leopold Bloom's thoughts, memories and associations are informed by newspaper headlines, snatches of songs, advertising slogans and poster headlines as he walks through the streets of Dublin.

These literary examples are signs of a much more general tendency that intermedial studies has a prime interest in: media products represent qualified media types. In media types such as novels, paintings, films, computer games and news articles, we encounter characters, avatars or persons that interact with pictures, musical instruments, photos, computers, record players, newspapers or television sets or go to football games. The choice of media they interact with, just like the way in which they use and think about them, is not only part of a detailed representation of the social world. In *To the Lighthouse*, Lily Briscoe's struggles with material choices and artistic conventions clearly connect to an aesthetic discussion about the representation of reality. In *High Fidelity*, Rob not only sells records but has a specific interest in mixtapes, as cassette tapes allowed listeners to compile their favourite music. Thus, Lily's interest in painting and Rob's interest in music are very significant in the overall interpretation of the novels. Similar to intertextual references, which invite the reader to consider the present text against the background of other texts, these 'intermedial references' (Rajewsky 2002, 2005) invite the reader to consider the narrative in a different medial frame by means of explicit diegetic representation or more implicit structural representation, and often by combining both.

Still, how do we know that the representation of media products or media types *means* something? Or that references to familiar media types have a symbolic value? In this chapter, we will demonstrate how the representation of media can be analysed. We will focus on narrative literature, but the analytical method is applicable to film, computer games, photography and visual art as well.

In the first part of the chapter, we will explore media that are represented inside the diegetic universe. How characters and narrators use and think about media is used to materialize ideas and conflicts, and character development is

DOI: 10.4324/9781003174288-12

often part of a meta-referential discussion about the affordances of literature (Wolf 1999, p. 48–50). In the second part of the chapter, we will turn to novels whose narrative structure and style remind readers of other medial experiences, such as watching a movie, looking at an image or listening to music. The effect of structural media representation is to give the impression that the literary text imitates film, music or images. It changes the experience of reading and draws attention to aspects of literature and language that we usually pay less attention to.

In terms of method, we will draw on previous approaches to diegetic media representation in literature and film (Bruhn 2016) as well as the structural media representation of film (Schwanecke 2015) and music (Schirrmacher 2012) in literature. We propose a three-step model consisting of three basic questions that are designed to trace the significance of media representation in all its variety: what kinds of media are represented? How are they represented? How does the media representation relate to the textual or historical context? The focus of the second two questions can be adapted according to different research focus and interest and we present different approaches of how to interpret and contextualize media representation. In the literary text, the answers to these three questions appear closely interrelated. Still, as always in intermedial analysis, it is helpful to address each aspect in turn to understand how they interact.

We explore diegetic media representation with the help of Jennifer Egan's novel *A Visit from the Goon Squad* (2011), a novel full of technical devices, discussion and reflections about media and reflection about media use. Also, we analyse Jo Nesbø's novel *The Snowman* (2007) as an example of cinematic writing and its close connection to the thriller and horror genre. Günter Grass's novel *The Tin Drum* (1959) is a novel told by a drummer and certain passages are structured by patterns of repetition and contrast, as a representation of musical form. Finally, we provide some examples of how structural principles of painting and photographs can be represented in *Biblique des derniers gestes* (2002) by the Martinican author Patrick Chamoiseau.

Diegetic media representation

In Jennifer Egan's novel *A Visit From the Goon Squad* (2011), fifty years of US history are represented by an intricate web of media in the fictive world (the diegesis) of the novel. Given the fact that music plays a major role in the novel, it has been called a 'music-saturated fiction' (Hertz and Roessner 2014, p. 10) and characterized as a rock novel (Moorey 2014) – these terms are appropriate as general impressions, but less informative about how and why music matters in this novel. By analysing media representation in the novel, we get a better overview of what such broad generic terms mean in a particular case like this novel. Instead of stating that 'music plays a large role in the novel', it is important to ask what kind of music is represented and how it is described and talked about. Moreover, music is not the only medium that is represented.

164　*Jørgen Bruhn et al.*

Once we start to pay attention to media in the diegesis, it is easy to become overwhelmed. Literary texts, almost by default, exhibit quite a messy selection of many instances of media interaction: in novels, characters play music, write emails, watch movies and enter buildings, exactly as most of us do in our real life. If we want to find out what we should qualify as a medium and what each of them might stand for, we have to make them and their role in the plot visible in some way.

We will approach this problem by analysing three consecutive steps: *listing, structuring* and *contextualizing* (first formulated by Bruhn 2016). The analysis registers what kinds of media are represented in the text (step 1, listing). By asking how the represented media are described and how they relate to each other in the plot, we can identify patterns and structures (step 2, structuring); and finally, we ask how we can interpret those patterns in a way that works well with an overall interpretation of aspects of the historical and social context of the novel (step 3, contextualizing). In this third step, contextual knowledge can be brought in: general cultural trends, genre-related questions or knowledge about the author's biography or earlier work.

Listing: What kinds of media are represented?

The first step consists of a broad listing of media products and qualified media types that are represented in the text: what kinds of qualified media are mentioned and what are their basic media types and technical media of display? This is quite a time-consuming exercise even for a short story, and for a novel even more so. Therefore, the first step in this listing process for longer texts should not strive to present an exhaustive list of media representations but should attempt to create an overview of media types that are repeatedly represented.

For Egan's novel, the first step would be to make a long list of the technical media of display that are mentioned (including, for instance, a telefax, computers and guitars). But the novel also revels in making references to artistic qualified media types (antique sculpture, punk rock, modern 'found object art', cinema and photography). Specific media products are mentioned, too, including films and songs that characters discuss, watch or listen to. And different qualified media are referred to in more general terms as forms of communication and expression that differ from and perhaps are compared with other media.

Already in this process of listing, we can find a recurring focus on technical devices and basic and qualified media types of music. Media products such as existing rock songs are mentioned and the songs performed by the fictive rock band are described. Music as a qualified media type is discussed, for example, when a middle-aged character laments the musical tastes of young people. The question of how the basic media type of organized sound communicates is addressed, for example, when a teenager makes a PowerPoint presentation listing 'Great Rock and Roll Pauses' (Egan 2011, Chapter 12).

Structuring: How are media represented?

The second step structures the representation of media. Do we find patterns in the list of technical objects? Do the qualified media types that are mentioned have anything in common? Regarding *A Visit From the Goon Squad*, there are at least two ways in which the listing process may make sense in a way that helps to better understand the novel.

The first way may seem almost too obvious or banal to mention, but it is important. The wide array of different technical devices, which includes anything from letters, via fax and emails, to guitars to computers, mirrors the technical, medial and consequently the cultural changes that have been or will be invented or developed in the US between the late 1970s and the start of the imagined third decade of the twenty-first century. New technical devices from different decades are mentioned, as are qualified media types from the same period, such as 'found art'. Together they draw attention to how communication within society and the organization of society have changed. For example, we write emails instead of letters and a new qualified media type such as 'found art' first challenges and then changes the conventions of visual art in general. Change and development are even more foregrounded in the novel when it points to a possible future by describing how commercial pop music is distributed on mobile phones targeted at babies.

Taken as a whole, the representation of media in the novel depicts a change in media use, which moves from attending analogue punk rock concerts and using tape-recorders and turntables to engaging in distracted communication via mobile phones and emails, and even having absent-minded phone conversations while writing emails. The first step of evaluation that sums up *what kinds* of media are represented is supported by looking at *how* media are described. The different media types are talked about, commented on and described in a way that draws attention to change. Different characters express statements that can be read as epochal characterizations, like 'everybody sounds stoned, because they're emailing people the whole time they're talking to you' (Egan 2011, p. 141). In this general statement about absent-minded emailing, multitasking becomes representative of the interaction with digital media in general.

As the next part of structuring, we ask whether particular media types are explicitly compared with or opposed to each other. Are they integrated into binary oppositions between, for example, the visual and the auditory, or between text or image-based media types? In Egan's novel, we find that the novel represents the historical development from analogue to digital that has taken place, but if we look at how this is described, we can see that analogue and digital media are discussed in terms of being in opposition to each other. If we ask which analogue and which digital media are most frequently mentioned, we find two clusters, concentrated on punk music and punk culture on the one hand and contemporary digital media on the other. Throughout the novel, punk music and digital media appear to be opposed to each other: punk music is described in terms of being 'authentic', whereas digital music is described as soulless, banal, consumer-oriented music. Both punk music and digital media are not only represented, but they are also characterized and even categorized in specific ways. They form a comprehensive dichotomic structure and give sound (so to speak) to a conflict between authenticity and a perceived loss of contact. The fact that the representation of punk music and punk attitudes is closely connected to one of the protagonists (Bernie) and his friends in the past suggests that the text, perhaps a bit uncritically, constructs the notions of authenticity and presence using twentieth-century analogue rock and punk music. The present (or future) situation, on the contrary, is characterized by the fact that medial and technical developments have distanced artists and non-artists from their former values and that an impoverished experience of their art and of life is a result of this.

In the second step of the analysis, we can discern two recurring ideas that structure the list of media types. First, that the representation of media effectively mirrors the development and changes that took place in the US from the late 1970s to some decades beyond that, and even those that will occur in the 2020s (Egan's book was published in 2011). The represented media illustrate a comprehensive history of communication since the 1970s. New technical devices and qualified media types make visible the cultural changes that are connected with them. Yet the representation of media is also connected with a conflict of values that can be seen in the dichotomy between punk, analogue media and authenticity on the one hand, and the depiction of twenty-first-century commercialized, mass-produced mainstream pop, digital media and social media that is connected to inauthenticity, on the other. Thus, media representation in the text connects to a certain amount of nostalgia towards the pre-digital age as a time of non-commercial energy, authenticity and almost naïveté.

Contextualization: How can we make sense of media representation?

In this step, we ask how contextual knowledge can help us better understand the representation of media in the text. How can the novel's historical, social and to some extent biographical contexts help us to understand why the represented media are connected with the ideas we have just analysed? How can we make sense of the analogue–digital dichotomy? Is this a novel that simply wants to demonstrate that music was better in the 1970s? Probably not.

It has been argued that the novel expresses a certain nostalgia. It seems plausible that the experiences and sentiments of a New York City author such as Egan reveal that – like some of the characters in the novel – she may have experienced a multifaceted sense of loss (van de Velde 2014). This loss seems to be related to a post-punk musical scene (with its history of anti-establishment sentiment and political edginess) that turned into infantilized commercial pop music; new digital media entailing new, impoverished communication forms; and the mental and existential post-traumatic stress after the 9/11 terrorist attacks.

However, this argument falls short if we just draw the conclusion that Egan apparently does not appreciate contemporary pop music much. Instead, it is more interesting to spell out that in this novel the sense of loss is connected with how contemporary pop music is described. Presence, contact and some roughness and rawness are equalled with the punk position. This binary opposition between the simplicity and aesthetics of punk rock and digital communication and digital music is then maybe less about the author's personal taste in music. Engaging in this process helps to illustrate what is perceived as lost in the process of digitization and social development. Consequently, the third step may offer at least one possible way of framing and perhaps even explaining (by putting into context) the diegetic representation of media in a novel.

The three steps of listing, structuring and contextualizing provide a systematic way to analyse the diegetic representation of media in narrative literary texts. An intermedial analysis like this may supplement more conventional analytical methods such as searching for symbols and investigating narratological levels or plot structures. The three-step model can be used not only in narrative literature but also in other media types, for instance, cinema (Bruhn and Gjelsvik 2018), or even art exhibitions (Bruhn and Thune 2018). It is, however, possible and even necessary to take the analysis one step further, a step that leads on to the next major part of this chapter.

The structural representation of media

The 13 chapters of *A Visit From the Goon Squad* are quite independent of each other, and some critics even consider the book to be a collection of linked short stories. This particular form of independent yet somewhat linked entities, invites us to see it as analogous to a particular form of organizing and distributing music on the technical device of the gramophone long-playing record, or the LP. The division of the book into two halves, Part A (Chapters 1–6) and part B (Chapters 7–13), mimics the A and B sides of an LP. Thus, the structure of the entire novel, which consists of independent yet thematically interlinked entities, is reminiscent of a pop or rock 'concept album' (see Box 10.1 for more details).

Box 10.1 The LP and the concept album: Technical medium of display and qualified medium

The form and history of the LP (long-playing record) illustrate the close connection between the materiality of technical media of display and qualified media types. Made of vinyl (PVC), the LP allowed for a more lightweight storage and distribution form of recorded music, and soon replaced the earlier shellac discs, which had a 3–5-minute playing time. The LP allowed the storage of up to ten times as much music. From the mid-1960s until the end of the 1980s, the LP was the dominant commercial storage medium for music and was only superseded by, first, the digital CD and later on by digital streaming services such as Spotify.

But in a similar way to how printed books made the qualified medium of novels possible, the LP is closely connected to the development of the qualified media type of a 'concept album', in which the music is not only compiled but is even unified by a theme. *The Beatles* were among the first to not only use the LP to collect a number of random popular individual hit songs (previously issued on single records) but also to design an entire LP as an entity, with either a musical style or a theme, in certain cases even a narrative: that turned the LP into a concept album. The packaging of the LP, the cover and the inner sleeve of the LP, quickly became an integrated part of the design of the entire work and made it possible to include different forms of texts and illustrations.

In many ways, therefore, the album can be seen as an example of the idea of a total work of art where several art forms cooperate to create an augmented aesthetic experience. The implied obligatory switch from side A to side B is not only a material feature of the two-sided record disc but also led to a two-part structure of the album that somehow shifts in character. Thus, the technical medium/the materiality of the storage medium in the form of the LP led to the development of the qualified media type called the album. When the CD took over as the most popular and commercially viable form, the qualified medium of the album migrated to the technical medium of display of the CD.

While the LP is no longer the dominating storage medium, it is still (and increasingly) valued as a strategic aesthetic move in popular music. In digitally produced music, the scratching noise of records has been turned into sounds that are used to express authenticity, for example. The artistic possibilities as well as the 'cultural capital' connected to publishing a well-organized set of songs in a collected form is still a very attractive alternative – sometimes to the degree that album forms spill over into a grand video form, such as Beyoncé's *Lemonade* (2016) (see also Chapter 8).

The LP format needs to be seen in relation to the discussion of music and authenticity in the novel. Does this ordering of the book express a nostalgic longing for the coherence of the thematic concept album in a fragmented time of distress and angst – or is it instead a postmodern device that is meant to relativize the content of the novel and perhaps hint at a distanced narrative voice or a type of agency that is manipulating the protagonists in the novel's diegesis without their knowledge?

There are many examples of novels that structurally remind the reader of the experience of engaging media other than words, text and literature. When reading the novels of the Norwegian crime author Jo Nesbø, for example, we may be reminded of the experience of watching a film. In the novel *Jazz*, by the American writer Toni Morrison (1992), we may perceive a parallel between the novel's structure and the improvisation, expressivity and dialogue between different instrumental voices that are characteristic of jazz.

These structural forms of media representations the semiotician Winfried Nöth would call 'form miming form' (Nöth 2001, p. 18), and they have long been a core interest in intermedial studies. Terms such as cinematic writing, musicalized fiction (Wolf 1999) or pictorialism (Louvel 2011) sum up the impression of reading such texts that are somewhat paradoxical. The texts convey the notion of the presence of a medium that in fact is only referred to. Werner Wolf (1999) describes musicalized fiction 'that points towards a presence of music in the signification of a text which seems to stem from some kind of transformation of music into literature' (p. 51). Or, as Christine Schwanecke (2015) puts it concerning cinematic writing: such writing 'trigger[s] the actualization of the "filmic medium" in a reader's mind while s/he is actually reading and processing nothing but words' (p. 268). We therefore have to deal with the 'illusion' (Schwanecke 2015, p. 268–9), 'imitation' (Wolf 1999, p. 51) and 'simulation' (Rajewsky 2002, pp. 94–103) of the presence of another medium but it is not present in the material and sensorial modality. We still perceive similarities, though, and that is accomplished by way of the literature's own means. We see the words on the page and read them one after the other. But we relate to them differently.

When we analysed the diegetic representation of media, we faced the challenge of how to make sense of the abundance of different media that are always part of the diegesis. When analysing structural representation, the challenge is to pinpoint the specific intermedial quality of the text. Even though the intermedial scholar Irina Rajewsky (2002, pp. 39–40) repeatedly emphasizes the *as-if* quality of structural intermedial references, the focus can easily land on the represented medium that is 'imitated' or 'simulated', which in turn can 'establish the illusion of the filmic medium being (materially) present in the literary text even though it is not' (Schwanecke 2015, p. 268). Illusion catches the reading experience, and imitation and simulation express the relation of how the text is transformed – that it is constructed according to other rules.

Although the texts 'appear to imitate [...] quality or structure' (Wolf 2002, p. 25) of the represented media, their specific intermedial quality cannot be analysed by borrowing the terminology of music or cinema. Thus, although the novel, using titles and metafictional references, suggests a media transformation process, it is not a film made out of words that the viewer experiences. The viewer reads a narrative that draws on the structural principles of film 'with its own means', as Rajewsky (2002, p. 39) stresses. However, if the literary text represents filmic or musical structures 'with its own means', we have to focus on transmedial aspects that the media involved share but that are realized in different media-specific ways. So instead of trying to locate how media-specific cinematic or musical techniques are transmediated into text and to locate literary techniques that would be characteristic of cinematic writing or musicalized fiction only, we have focused on how structural media representation exploits transmedial media characteristics that words, texts and literature always possess but that are more familiar from the represented media.

Cinematic writing: Structural representation of film in literature

Cinematic writing is a literary strategy that has been discussed in literary discourse ever since the advent of modernist experimental writing, and it took a particular turn after Christopher Isherwood (1904–1986) began his 1939 novel *Goodbye to Berlin* as follows: 'I am a camera with its shutter open, quite passive, recording, not thinking. Recording the man shaving at the window opposite and the woman in the kimono washing her hair. Someday, all this will have to be developed, carefully printed, fixed' (Isherwood 1998 [1939], p. 9). Isherwood's narrator suggests a particular literary point of view – that of a distanced, neutral observer who registers what is seen and heard. The comparison with the camera not only announces a specific cinematic way of writing but also reveals the temporal process of writing. Similar to the chemical procedure of analogue film development, it takes time to fix time and space using words on a surface.

The cinematic writing style of Bret Easton Ellis's (1991) postmodern novel *American Psycho* seems to suggest a different parallel with film. It highlights a sense of alienation that is involved in the globalization and commercialization of the modern world, and that goes with modern film production. In the novel, life seems to emulate modern cinematic experiences, similar to the way in which we can describe an experience by saying 'it was just like a film'. Cinematic writing in *American Psycho* thus expresses what Jean Baudrillard (1983, p. 25) has termed hyperreality.

Any analysis of cinematic writing therefore also embraces the experience of literary works from the reader's and reader communities' perspectives. Asking how the strategies of cinematic writing affect and change the experience of reading adds a social component to the usually strictly formal and intrinsic close reading of texts. An intermedial approach offers a more complex and precise understanding of cinematic writing. Apart from exploring how particular cinematic genres connect with the development of certain literary styles, it also seeks to explain why cinematic writing can be partly responsible for contemporary literature's commercial success. This section begins by discussing the more general characteristics of cinematic writing. It presents suitable analytical perspectives that are then applied to a novel that has often been regarded as particularly cinematic: Jo Nesbø's (2010 [2007]) *The Snowman*.

Cinematic writing has usually been discussed from three perspectives: cinematic time and space, shifts in narrative point of view that simulate the view of a camera (as in the quotation from Isherwood above), and the use of montage techniques in literature that are similar to those used in film editing (Cohen 1979, p. 108). So although much attention has been paid to the visual aspects of the film medium, its auditory aspects have been somewhat neglected. Yet film is an audiovisual medium. As the reading of *The Snowman* will show, auditory perception plays an integrated part in contemporary cinematic writing.

The characteristics of cinematic writing are a focus on audiovisual perception, sudden changes in perspective and a narrative point of view that refrains from evaluation and causal connection. None of these techniques are solely or particularly cinematic in themselves. However, if they appear together in a narrative text, they can trigger either involuntary sensations or voluntary cognitive experiences that are similar to those triggered by cinema from narratives that are mediated by moving images and sound and that are connected by the editing montage of individual scenes. In correlation with this chapter's applied method of analysis, we will look into *what kinds* of cinematic references are being represented, *how* these references are being mediated and *where* we find them in the text (we follow the method used by Schwanecke (2015, pp. 274–8)).

What is represented?

The *what* involves which aspects of the qualified medium of film a cinematic reference refers *to*: technical devices of display (cameras, projectors, film screens), basic media types (moving images, verbal language, sound effects, music), structural patterns (like jump cuts, montage, focal lengths, tracking shots) or aspects of qualified media types (specific film titles, film directors, genres). When Isherwood writes 'I am a camera', the text is explicitly referring to a principal technical recording device used in film and mentioned in literary discourse in a way that draws a parallel with narrative point of view and perspective in film. In the novel *Kafka on the Shore*, the Japanese writer Haruki Murakami (2005 [2002]) refers to specific films such as *The 400 Blows* and *Shoot the Pianist* by the French film director François Truffaut (1932–84) in Chapter 34. Regarding the former film, the ending occurs on a French shore and thus engages in the title of the novel and also provides a homage to Truffaut's film. The cinematic references open up a parallel narrative to the novel that is only accessible for those familiar with the film. This is a common way of engaging a particular audience and make them feel that they are smart because they understand the references. Hence, asking *what* is represented also involves drawing conclusions about what aspects of film or which genres are highlighted.

The explicit representation of technical media of display, specific media products and the qualified media type cinema draws attention to the more structural representation that appears to imitate formal elements of film. As an example, the narrator in *Goodbye to Berlin* (Isherwood 1998 [1939]) does not just compare himself with a camera. Throughout the novel, he attempts to use a neutral point of view that focuses on perception and refrains from evaluation or explanation. His extensive use of showing and a lack of telling leads to a point of view that is similar to that used in the audiovisual narration of film. In *The Great Gatsby*, F. Scott Fitzgerald (2003 [1925]) creates a sequence when he introduces the character Tom Buchanan that resembles a filmic tracking shot (moving camera):

> The lawn started at the beach and ran toward the front door for a quarter of a mile, jumping over sun-dials and brick walks and burning gardens – finally when it reached the house drifting up the side in bright vines as though from the momentum of its run. The front was broken by a line of

French windows, glowing now with reflected gold, and wide open to the warm windy afternoon, and Tom Buchanan in riding clothes was standing with his legs apart on the front porch.

(p. 11)

In these two long sentences, the perspective gradually moves from the lawn (that surrounds Tom's house) towards the house until it rests on Tom standing on the porch. In the text, the personification of the lawn, as it starts to move, run, jump and stop, conveys a sense of movement that ends with the reader reaching Tom Buchanan. By using the means of syntactical structures, this passage resembles a film sequence that starts with an establishing shot of Tom's house and ends with a medium shot of Tom himself.

How is it represented?

The *what* of media representation leads us to discuss *how* these references operate. *How* these references are actualized in literature by authors and readers depends on conventions and how they are used in collaboration with the expected response of the reader.

Murakami's references to specific film titles in *Kafka on the Shore* are easily spotted; the next question to ask is what reference to these specific media products contributes to the understanding of the novel. The two films that are referred to can be seen as representative of the French New Wave film genre and auteur cinema, and, as mentioned earlier, the mention of these films opens up parallel narratives to both specific media types and qualified media in a broader sense. The 'tracking shot' in Fitzgerald's novel, however, is a matter of interpretation and analysis. The structural parallel with film becomes visible when we describe the structure of the text. This description provides the parallel with formal characteristics of audiovisual narration in film.

When exploring structural media representation, we can see how simple and more complex forms of media representation interact (Elleström 2014, pp. 28–34). Occasional instances of diegetic media representation, such as the title of a film mentioned in passing and not further discussed, can be considered simple. However, these simple representations, especially if they appear repeatedly or in significant scenes, might signal the more complex representations of structural representation. In fact, as Schwanecke (2015) points out, a certain amount of simple representation is necessary to 'trigger such a "filmic" reception', which includes the 'establishment of iconic analogies between literary structures and filmic conventions, qualities, and structures' (p. 276). The representation of basic media types would mostly involve complex representations. Diegetic media representation that at first glance might look simple can in fact be complex – it depends on the reader's background information. In Malcolm Lowry's (1947) novel *Under the Volcano*, the film with the Spanish title *Las Manos de Orlac* (*The Hands of Orlac*, 1935) is described on film posters and talked about in dialogue, and a screening of it in a cinema is mentioned. We might consider each of these instances to be a simple representation of material aspects of film or media products. However, background knowledge about the film provides the ground for a more complex interpretation. As *Las Manos de Orlac* is a remake of an expressionist silent film from 1924, we can draw a structural parallel between the plot of the film (the growing madness of a former concert pianist who loses his hands in a train accident) and the increasing paranoia of the protagonist of the novel. The reference to expressionist film highlights the importance of subjective perspective in the novel: the focus on visual description combined with the subjective perspective of a stream-of-consciousness style. The diegetic representation of the remake of an expressionist film therefore leads to the unpacking of the subjectivity of Lowry's novel. The fact that *Las Manos de Orlac* is represented with, for example, posters or screenings draws attention to the commercial aspects of cinema (via the advertisement-related aspects of the novel). Thus, diegetic media representation of films in literature can operate on a complex structural level – what Alan Partington (1998) has referred to as the 'snugness effect' – giving the reader the impression that he or she is being invited to share the secrets of the novel, bond with the author and feel smart enough to understand the more complex allusions (p. 140).

Where is it represented?

Finally, there is the issue of *where* in the text the cinematic representations are produced. Schwanecke (2015) argues that they

> can be realized on compositional levels, such as the overall structure, imagery, plot design, or character constellation. References can appear on diegetic levels (within the fictional story), extra-diegetically (elements outside the fictional story, usually a narrator not part of the story world he narrates), and even paratextually (as in titles of plays, poems, novels, or short stories, chapter headings, and tables of contents).
>
> (Schwanecke 2015, p. 278)

Most of these places where references can occur are more convoluted than having a simple reference to a film in the actual literary text (such as mentioning a title of a film) and at times require experience of cinema in order to be analysed. For example, the plot structure of a novel can closely resemble that of a particular film. The description of a particular house can reveal references to either canonical gothic castles from Universal's horror films of the 1930s or the specific house used in Alfred Hitchcock's *Psycho* (1960). A particular character can evoke similarities to Uma Thurman's character in Quentin Tarantino's *Kill Bill: Volume 1* (2003), for example. Again, this illustrates how intermedial theory can unpack a literary text's cinematic qualities that are not perhaps visible at first.

In novels with a structural representation of film, we will find various instances on different levels that interconnect in the way that we described

174 *Jørgen Bruhn et al.*

above. Singular instances of media representation tend to form patterns that deepen understanding of the novel we can get from literary analysis alone. Table 10.1 provides a schematic overview of the different aspects of the representation of cinema in literature.

The *what, how* and *where* variables that are clearly separated in the table for the purposes of analysis are mostly interrelated. When one identifies *what* is being represented, one tends to answer automatically the *how* and *where* questions. It is not always possible to clearly separate the categories in actual analysis, and therefore these variables will be discussed intermittently in the analysis of *The Snowman* (Nesbø 2010 [2007]).

Cinematic representation in Jo Nesbø's **The Snowman**

In the past decade, Norwegian writer Jo Nesbø has achieved huge commercial success with his prolific series about the self-destructive but brilliant Oslo detective Harry Hole. Similar to Stieg Larsson's *Millennium* trilogy, the Harry Hole books display a striking structural representation of the media characteristics of film that might account for at least part of their success. Written from 1997 onwards, the book series caught worldwide attention with the first translation of one of them into English, *The Devil's Star* (2005 [2003]). We will discuss some examples from one of Nesbø's most accomplished and successful novels, *The Snowman*, to illustrate how the novel represents media characteristics

Table 10.1 Different representations of cinema in literature

Representation of cinema	*What*	*How*	*Where*
Technical media of display	Camera 35mm film Film projector Film screens Cinemascope	Simple Complex	Diegetic Extra-diegetic Paratextual
Basic media type	Moving images Sound effects Film music Montage Focal lengths Tracking shots	Simple Complex	Diegetic Extra-diegetic Paratextual
Specific film products	Actors Film titles Directors Film music Composers	Simple Complex	Diegetic Extra-diegetic Paratextual
Social factors and qualifying aspects of contexts and conventions	Film institutions Film reception Film criticism Censorship	Simple Complex	Diegetic Extra-diegetic Paratextual

that are more familiar from film. The novel tells the story of Norway's first serial killer (referred to as the Snowman), who brutally murders women who have had extramarital affairs resulting in children. Oslo detectives Harry Hole and newcomer Katrine Bratt pursue the serial killer in a twisting and suspenseful plot, and Hole becomes personally involved as it turns out that the Snowman is living with his former girlfriend, Rakel, and her son, Oleg.

What? Listing of simple and complex representations

Cinema representation in the novel involves simple diegetic media representation in the form of intertextual references and allusions to cinema, mostly references to conventionally and contextually qualifying aspects and specific film products, such as when Harry Hole and Rakel mention the film titles *The Rules of Attraction* and *Starship Troopers* (Nesbø 2010 [2007], p. 72 and p. 173, respectively), *Mission Impossible* (p. 358) or refer to Wile E. Coyote, one of the two protagonists in the *Coyote and the Roadrunner* series of cartoons (p. 133).

They also discuss Francis Ford Coppola's *The Conversation* (1974), a film that is represented in a more complex form. The film not only inspires the title of Chapter 12, but there are also structural parallels between the film and the aesthetic construction of several of the novel's key scenes. A paratextual media representation is the chronological ordering of chapter titles, from 'Day 1' to 'Day 22', and such chapter titles as '4 November 1992'. They can allude to Stanley Kubrick's use of intertitles in his horror classic *The Shining* (1980) to create temporal intensity and determinism in the narrative. These titles will only be recognized as cinematic references if the reader knows the original film. The paratextual allusion is, however, not the only reference to Kubrick's *The Shining*. It does not seem a coincidence that the initial scene that triggers the serial killer in his childhood is dated to 1980, the year *The Shining* was screened for the first time. Even other aspects of the novel's cinematic style represent plot elements or horror strategies of Kubrick's film.

Even if not all readers spot the intermedial references, the diegetic media representations already clearly frame the crime fiction plot in the context of thriller and horror films. The more complex structural representations, especially of *The Shining*, act as an invitation not only to read *The Snowman* in a cinematic way but to read it in the framing of a horror film, which raises certain expectations. The paratextual framing can therefore draw attention to a narrative style that not only displays characteristics of audiovisual narration in general but also draws on the techniques of suspense used in the horror genre in particular.

How? Representation of editing and montage

The narrative style of the novel displays characteristics that bear a resemblance to cinematic editing and montage. The editing process turns the raw footage into sequences and arranges them into an audiovisual narrative. The editing process is a process of montage as it creates a coherent plot by putting together separate scenes. Montage sequences, a series of short shots that condense space, time and information, intensify this principal characteristic of the audiovisual narration.

Whether or not readers are aware of the cinematic framing of the novel, readers may note or respond to the intensity that structures the plot of *The Snowman*. Nesbø's novel achieves the kind of tempo and suspense often attributed to Stieg Larsson's *The Girl with the Dragon Tattoo* (in Swedish in 2005) (see Bergman 2014, p. 130). When the narrative structure is looked at more closely, the tempo and intensity of the plot appear to be the result of cinematic writing. The tempo and intensity connect to narrative structures that bear a resemblance to editing and montage. Even if the reader does not actively notice the cinematic writing, they are likely to respond to the tempo and suspense it creates, maybe by increasing their own reading tempo.

From the perspective of editing, the narrative structure of *The Snowman* is not chronological. Many literary plots are not chronological but involve flashbacks and flashforwards, but the flashbacks in *The Snowman* display some specific cinematic features. The narrative order of events is arranged around three dominant times, mainly the recollections of the serial killer in 1980, Detective Rafto's search for the killer in 1992, and 2004, when Harry Hole and his colleague Katrine Bratt investigate new disappearances and murders. Within these principal narrative times, there are numerous brief flashbacks: brief, sudden memories of characters or slightly longer returns into past times that resemble shorter, cinematic flashes of past memories and events. At the end of the novel, there is a remarkable recurrence of the first temporal event in the novel, 'Wednesday, 5 November 1980'. The repetition of an event that does not provide new information in literature is unusual, but it is much more common in film, as if it is an aesthetic response to the cinematic production process that often involves several takes of the same scene. The first paragraph of the recap is identical to the opening of the novel, but in the second paragraph, there is a shift in point of view from mother to son. Emotionally, the repeated event's change of perspective satisfies the reader who feels cheated by the lack of explanations in the opening chapter, but the aesthetics of the retake also inhabit a distinctive cinematic character.

The most evident and effective cinematic example of montage in *The Snowman* is the lateral scenes between the investigator Katrine Bratt and the terrorizing publicist Arve Støp while Harry Hole is finding out more about the secret background of Katrine (Nesbø 2010 [2007], pp. 370–91). Here each parallel sequence is separated by a couple of line breaks, not unlike the ellipsis between one frame and another in film (even if these material borders are not visible to the eye while the film is being screened). Even if literary ellipses are common enough, the materiality of the line breaks in this case echoes the materiality of the film frame. Further, these parallel scenes are quite short and similar in length and bear an iconic resemblance to the succession of scenes in a parallel montage in a film.

In this parallel montage, the individual scenes of Bratt's and Hole's storyline are aligned with structural parallels that connect the ending of one scene with the beginning of the next scene. This formal connection of two events that are not temporally aligned is similar to cinematic transitions, also called 'hooks'. The hook should not be confused with the cliffhanger, which is a device commonly used in literature and film to create suspense. Hooks structurally connect two scenes in order to create a seamless and paced temporal movement forward. David Bordwell (2018) explains that hooks are not uncommon in modern popular literature, but they are still mainly connected to the history of cinema. The following example from *The Snowman* illustrates the cinematic technique of the hook. A scene at Rakel's house ends with a question. The following scene at the police headquarters also begins with a question that formally relates to the question that immediately precedes it.

> He tiptoed. 'Can I go now?'
>
> 'Yes, you can go?' (p. 198)

These two questions (although the second question at the same time looks like an answer to the first one) formally connect two unrelated scenes and smooth the transition from one place to the next. This transition forms a coherent structure even if it is a break in time and space. The second transition is also a typical cinematic ellipsis where the same person is present in both scenes but in a different place and time in each.

> 'Get your coat and meet me down in the garage', Harry said. 'We're going for a drive'.
>
> Harry drove along Uranienborgveien [...]. (p. 285)

This kind of ellipsis is not unusual in literature either, but what is particularly cinematic is how the transition between the two scenes is 'smoothed' by the formal parallels that link the two scenes together. The ellipsis is still visible on the page but is noticed less during reading. The use of parallel montage and cinematic transitions leads to an increase in tempo as frequent jumps in place and time are smoothed by structural cohesion. Even in the novel, sudden switches in the middle of events from one scene to the other and formal transitions between two paragraphs have the effect that the reader jumps to the next paragraph. The result of this is that paragraphs lose their usual characteristic of encouraging the reader to pause after reading one paragraph before moving on to the next. Similar to the gaps between singular frames on the filmstrip, the line breaks on the page do not become invisible, but they are ignored. If parallel montage and transitions are used in dramatic and nerve-wracking and thrilling sequences, the effect on the reader could be described as being prolonged and intensified fear regarding what will happen to the protagonists. The aim of eliciting prolonged fear in an audience is a principal characteristic of horror.

The context of horror and crime: Blended qualified media types

What sets *The Snowman* apart from the frequent genre combinations in modern crime fiction is the use of structural patterns that we are familiar with from cinematic genres. In the novel, editing and montage principles are used to achieve a narrative pace and speed similar to a thriller. The novel also draws on horror film aesthetics by using a specific point of view and foregrounds auditory perceptions that are reminiscent of how the camera and sound effects are used in horror films. The focus on graphic violence when describing the murders (Nesbø 2010 [2007], pp. 54, 114–5, 218, 452, 473) is similar to that in splatter film, a subgenre of the horror film genre that puts 'emphasis on displays of gore, extreme violence, and transgressive, opened-up bodies' (Schneider 2004, p. 138). However, the novel's style is more like that used in general representations of the horror film genre than in the splatter film subgenre.

Noël Carroll (1990, pp. 152–5) has defined some key cinematic elements of horror films that will be useful here: unreliable, ambiguous point-of-view shots, visual interferences in the frame, off-screen sound, unassigned camera movement, oscillation between objective and subjective camera shots, and ambiguities concerning natural or supernatural representations. All of these strategies are deliberately used to confuse and unsettle the viewer in different ways. These effects stress the audiovisual perception that we find in the narrative structure of *The Snowman* as well. This sets the novel apart from the more traditional gothic novel and places it more in the realm of filmic horror.

This description is especially relevant to Chapter 8 of the novel, which describes the protracted murder of Sylvia Ottersen. It not only employs the characteristics of cinematic writing in general but also a number of characteristics that fit key elements of horror films: restricted vision, a focus on the auditory perception and frequent switches between the subjective perspective and objective narration. We will have a closer look at how this is done.

Constant switches between subjective and objective positions illustrate especially well how structural representation works with the medium's own means. Including many narrative voices in literary prose changes the focalization (or point of view). Literary prose can confidently communicate the perspective of interiorized experiences and can easily switch between thought and perception. Changes in focalization can be found in many texts. However, the constant switch in *The Snowman* between two different focalizations – Sylvia's inner experience and a narrative voice that only focuses on what can be seen and heard – creates an impression that is similar to a cinematic experience. It results in a similar structural effect to the oscillation between the subjective and the objective camera's points of view that Carroll mentions.

The chapter begins with two short sentences: 'Sylvia ran into the forest. Night was on the way' (Nesbø 2010 [2007], p. 91). These two sentences of identical length that open the chapter create via their brevity two clear and separate images that nevertheless transition into each other like a film cut, from 'forest' (with which we may associate 'dark') to 'Night'. The lack of detail in the two sentences is intriguing and accounts for the immediacy of the vision and tempo that is similar to effects in cinema. Overall, the sentences are shorter in the novel when the pace of the action increases.

Later on, Sylvia stops 'to listen' (p. 91), which launches the excessive use of auditive discourse that is familiar from the sound effects used in horror films. In the darkness of the forest, sound trumps vision in describing the setting and the action. The reference to her motion ('she stopped') underscores the focus on bodies in motion followed by a sudden switch to auditory experience. This is an example of one of the frequent changes of point-of-view narration from (1) an external and less specific perspective to (2) Sylvia's perspective. Her perspective is also focused on through the description of interiorized sounds, such as the description of how her 'heaving, rasping breathlessness rent the tranquillity' (p. 91) or of the sound of her pulse (p. 92). Using interiorized sounds in scenes of great intensity is another popular horror film device, and when it is used in this chapter it contributes to its general focus on auditory perception: Sylvia hears cracking sounds of twigs breaking, and later on, 'quiet footsteps in the snow' (p. 95). There are only a few visual representations, such as '[s]he swept away the branches overhanging the stream, and from the corner of her eye she saw something' (Nesbø 2010 [2007], p. 93). The branches here are both brought into view and obstruct the view at the same time. This echoes one of Carroll's definitions of horror aesthetics, visual interferences in the frame, which operate to confuse and unsettle the viewer (Carroll 1990, pp. 152–3).

The middle section of the chapter is heavy with flashbacks that interrupt the dramatic scene with memories from Sylvia's life, which relate to things like the time she spent at the fitness centre, her first meeting with her husband, and memories involving her children. At the same time, the interrupting memories only increase the sense that her life is in danger, because they may be part of her subjective perspective rather than the narrator providing the reader with flashbacks; if Sylvia is experiencing them, she might be scared that she is about to die. At the same time, the flashbacks disrupt the present action and therefore slow down the inevitable slashing scene. Taken as a whole, the flashbacks create a montage between the present action and the flashbacks. This pattern stresses Sylvia's subjective experience of fear and increases the suspense, since it interrupts the current dramatic scene. The focus on the visual perception and the restriction of the subjective perspective come together when Sylvia sees a fox trap but does not understand its purpose: 'The first thing she had noticed was the strange apparatus, a thin metal loop attached to a handle' (p. 93).

While Sylvia is stuck in the trap (the 'swan neck'), the focus on auditory perception and restricted vision becomes even more prominent. Sylvia hears the killer approaching first before she can see him: 'But in front of her sat a figure; crouched down. It' (p. 96). The focus is on the restricted vision, but at the same time the pronoun is an intertextual reference to Stephen King's novel of the same name and thus directly frames the figure as a menace.

The chapter ends with the serial killer's voice: 'Shall we begin?' (p. 98). The following chapter commences with another rhetorical question, though there is a different mood and setting and the question is asked in Oleg's enthusiastic voice: 'Was that great or what?' (p. 99); Harry and Oleg are in a crowded kebab shop discussing the concert they have just attended. The cinematic transition connects two contrasting scenes with a formal parallelism of the two questions that highlight the contrast between the loneliness and fear of Sylvia and the bustling city centre of Oslo. The use of a cinematic montage here creates the illusion of simultaneity: murder and the everyday at the same time. Robert C. Solomon (2003) states that horror 'is an extremely unpleasant and even traumatizing emotional experience which renders the subject/victim helpless and violates his or her most rudimentary expectations about the world' (p. 253). In the case of Sylvia Ottersen, and how her murder is described through a set of complex media representations of horror films, this is definitely true. Structural representation of cinematic characteristics links the reader effectively to the experience of the victim through the use of frequently changed perspectives and auditory perception and the cinematic handling of space and time, such as the effective use of montage. Taken together, this way of narrating creates a cinematic reading experience. An intermedial analysis of *The Snowman* reveals not only potential explanations of its commercial success, aligning it with the cinematic references of a young generation, but in some ways it also recreates the emotional experiences inherent in the cinematic genres of horror.

Representation of musical structures in literature

In a 1957 poem by Swedish poet Tomas Tranströmer (2011 [1957]), he describes an evening on the seashore, in two stanzas, by day and by night; a bird of prey circles above the shore, and later, the evening star appears to take its place. Both stanzas finish with a nearly identical line about the timeless, rhythmical sound of the breaking of waves. The title of the poem, 'Ostinato', frames the moment of sunset in musical form. An ostinato is a musical motif that is 'stubbornly' (from the Latin *obstinatus*) repeated in the same musical voice. The ostinato forms a repetitive pattern while everything else changes, like the riff in jazz or rock music. In baroque music, this kind of repetitive stagnancy was associated with the timelessness of death and eternity.

In Tranströmer's poem, the title therefore both draws our attention to the stubborn and repetitive sound of the surf and frames the surf as a stable baseline that accompanies the transition from light to darkness. Thus, the title expresses a specific experience of a sunset at the beach and at the same time draws attention to how two things that we perceive as opposites appear interconnected. The constant movement of the surf, the repeated transition from days into nights, and the cyclical patterns of natural time unite continuous change and the notion of timelessness into a kind of contradictory connection. The musical title constructs a succinct and multifaceted metaphor (see also

Prieto (2002) and Englund (2012)). In Tranströmer's poem, the metaphor highlights the acoustic experience of an evening at the shore and uses this experience to make us understand something more about life. However, this understanding can only be reached if the reader is familiar with the conventions of Western classical music.

Tranströmer is not the only author who uses musical titles for literary texts as a kind of intermedial shorthand. In Paul Celan's poem 'The Death Fugue' written after WWII, the voices of victims and perpetrators of the Holocaust repeat and invert each other in motifs in a way that is quite similar to the way in which a musical subject travels through different musical voices of a fugue. In Marguerite Duras' (1958) short novel *Moderato Cantabile*, the repetitive daily routine of a rich woman is disrupted in a series of small (moderate?) steps that slowly builds up into a disruptive scandal. In Toni Morrison's (1992) novel *Jazz*, which is set in Harlem in the 1920s, jazz tunes are heard and played everywhere, yet the plot is not so much about jazz as the title seems to indicate. Instead, the plot circles stubbornly around the violent resolution of a love triangle and revisits it from different perspectives (see also Petermann 2018).

These are just a few examples of literary texts that suggest a structural parallel between the musical patterns referred to in the title and their (narrative) structure. Texts like this can be strikingly repetitive. It might be difficult to identify the development of a conflict in those texts. Instead, the plots of those texts appear to repeat a set or motifs or to move from A to B and then back to A, like a song that returns to a refrain. Different voices in such texts speak about the same subject and repeat it using different variations of it. Certain phrases recur, like the leitmotifs in Richard Wagner's operas.

The titles of works like those just mentioned seem to suggest something like 'read this story just as you would listen to a piece of music', but what exactly does this mean? Reading written words on a page is, in all four modalities, different to the embodied and often very personal experience of listening to music. In this section, we demonstrate how to make sense of plots that are developing a narrative conflict but at the same time are full of repetitive patterns and different conflicting voices. The musical titles or other forms of references to music indicate that something is not only being told but also performed in a specific manner.

Written words and organized sound

Representation of musical structures in literature relies on previous knowledge of conventions and contexts of the music referred to. Spoken words and organized sound are perceived together in sound waves, but written descriptions of organized sounds require previous knowledge. For instance, to the contemporary reader, the numerous quotes of classical and popular songs in James Joyce's *Ulysses* formed a soundscape or soundtrack to the reading experience that a later reading audience may not share.

There are different ways to transmediate the auditory experience of music in literary text. The text can describe the sound of instruments and voices, the causes of sounds, like movements of performers or the reactions of the audience. The text can describe thematical and harmonical structure or music or just refer to the genre. However, describing sound and form of music relies on a reader having previous knowledge of the music described. Thus, interestingly, a description of music sometimes does not focus on the *sound* of the music but rather on the associative imagery it evokes (see Odendahl (2008), pp. 15–17 and Wolf (1999, p. 63)) If Alex in Anthony Burgess's (1962) *A Clockwork Orange* describes a violin solo like 'a bird of like rarest spun heavenmetal' (p. 39), it does not matter that we cannot be familiar with this fictive violin sonata, we provide the suitable auditory imagery, our version of music that is like a bird of heavenmetal.

Different forms of acoustic foregrounding (Wolf 1999, p. 75) can highlight the diegetic soundscape of the plot. The foregrounding of the auditory qualities of words as organized sounds is often referred to as *word music* (see Scher (1968, pp. 3–5) and Wolf (1999, p. 58)). The dada artist Kurt Schwitters's *Sonate in Urlauten* ('Sonata in primordial sounds') from the 1920s would be quite an extreme example, as Schwitter's poem, which via the title already frames itself as a piece of instrumental music, does not consist of conventional words but a series of repeated sequences of sounds, such as 'Fümms bö wö tää zää Uu/ pögiff/kwii Ee'. Sounds that we can only make sense of from how they sound and how they are repeated, varied and contrasted. But even in other texts, the use of onomatopoetic words draws attention to the idea that written words are meant to be sounded, too.

Musical titles: Paratextual representation

When we look at texts that include a structural representation of music, very often the title indicates that we should consider the narrative in the framework of music. In Aldous Huxley's (1928) modernist novel *Point Counter Point*, the title refers to the musical technique of the counterpoint, but the plot does not focus much on music or musicians. The counterpoint is a composition technique that is used to compose the voices to fit the overall harmony primarily but to also be counter voices to each other, as *punctus contra punctum* (Latin for 'note against note'). This suggests that although all of the voices are opposed to each other, at the same time, they can still sound together. The novel presents different narrative strands – including the lives, thoughts, dreams and plans – of a handful of writers, journalists and painters. We read independent storylines that meet and influence each other. At one point, there is a metafictional reference to contrapuntal music, as one of the characters, the writer Philip Quarles, would like to write a novel similar to J.S. Bach's (1685–1750) *The Art of the Fugue*, the baroque composer's last composition that methodically explores all the possibilities of a contrapuntal variation of the same theme.

Reading Huxley's novel gives a similar impression; it is like listening to a piece of music, for example, by Bach: the reader follows the thoughts and associations of different characters, similar to independent, interrupting voices, but they are also structured as a harmonious whole, giving the impression of organized turmoil. In the novel, the different narrative strands unfold independently but are not totally unrelated, similar to polyphonic voices. The different strands repeat and vary similar motives or contrast with each other. They all provide different answers to the same challenge: how to deal with art and life, success and failure and how to cope with life and death.

Modernist writers drew on the patterns of Western art music that were familiar to them as a way of highlighting the sound of language and to structure a hubbub of the conflicting voices of a novel. However, *A Visit From the Goon Squad* demonstrates that even the structure of the concept album of rock and pop music can provide a sense of interconnectedness of the seemingly unrelated. Toni Morrison's *Jazz* (1992) chooses a musical genre that has less rigid rules, which allows for digression and highlights rhythm.

These similarities do not mean that it is possible to analyse the narrative structure by applying the formal rules of music, but a narrative text can be arranged using similar principles to those employed to organized sounds. Instead of trying to analyse a narrative as a fugue or a sonata and trying to find a subject, exposition or modulation in different keys, it is more fruitful to focus on transmedial elements that are fundamental in music and partly in literature. This could be *repetition and contrast, simultaneity of voices*, and events that do not really form causal connections but mirror each other and invert, oppose and vary each other in different ways.

In a novel like Anthony Burgess's (1962) novel *A Clockwork Orange*, we find transmedial characteristics like repetition and multivoicedness. Burgess's novel tells the story of the music-loving hooligan Alex. The short novel includes structures that we recognize from music, such as the repetition and variation of motifs. The novel's three parts mirror the musical ABA pattern. All three parts start with the same phrase: 'What's it going to be then, eh?' The repetition of this opening phrase is like the presentation of a musical theme in instrumental classical music, such as the distinctive and short theme of Beethoven's fifth symphony. Even if we have a similar exact repetition of this phrase in Burgess's novel, it does not make sense to say that this is the theme of the novel. Instead, this exact repetition draws attention to the fact that events, constellations and characters, as the material of narratives, are repeated and varied throughout the three parts.

The plot structure is similar to the sonata form, a tripartite structure of exposition, development and recapitulation that typically structures the first of several movements in instrumental genres of Western art music. In part one, the novel presents Alex as the leader of a violent teenage gang who enjoys music, and violence. The events in part two are contrasted with those in part one: in prison, Alex is subjected to a reconditioning treatment that makes him unable to commit any violent act and falls victim to the violence of others. And at the end of part three, the conditioning is reversed. As Burgess was an art music composer as well as a prolific writer, the structural parallels with the sonata form are quite detailed (Phillips 2010, pp. 88–9). But identifying the sonata structure cannot answer *why* Burgess represents the musical structure in the first place, and trying to work out Alex's hooliganism and its aesthetic framing in art music is puzzling.

A musical structure draws attention to sounds, the repetition of sounds and the simultaneity of different voices. *A Clockwork Orange* uses language in a way that conveys meaning in a more ambiguous and polyphonic way. The novel is written entirely in the fictive teenage slang Nadsat, which is based on Russian. Understanding the novel is therefore based more on repetition, recognition and context and much less on distinct symbolic meaning (which is the conventional signifying structure of language). Even though Alex uses the word 'horrorshow' to mean 'great' in accordance with the meaning of the Russian word 'khorosho', meaning 'good', the English spelling suggests at the same time the very opposite and stresses that to Alex all horror and violence is good. Multiple meanings arise and maybe distract the reader from reacting to what these fascinating words actually describe (assault, violence, rape). Nadsat, like an entertaining melody, can make a reader accept a text that conveys a message they otherwise would object to.

This technique can be compared to that of the Austrian writer Elfriede Jelinek (b. 1946). In her prose, verbal ambiguity instead introduces the structural violence that empty phrases of all kinds are usually supposed to cover. Jelinek's prose is not only filled with different voices, but her ambiguous and associative writing manages to draw the reader's attention to the idea that words that do not have multiple meanings barely exist, and she arranges words in a context that allows for different meanings to be understood simultaneously (see Powell and Bethman (2008) and Schirrmacher (2016)).

When we read *A Clockwork Orange* or Elfriede Jelinek's prose, we focus on the experience of sound, recognize repetitions and contrasts and evaluate how different meanings and associations relate to each other, and writers may draw on this alternative way of storytelling for different reasons. In the case of *A Clockwork Orange*, Burgess's point was not to write a novel that is like a sonata, but to write a novel about the paradox of free will. Contrary to what some critics have argued, the novel does not (and nor does Kubrick's film adaptation) glorify or defend Alex's behaviour. Instead, the musical structure demonstrates the nature of the ethical question: that you cannot have free will without the possibility of making wrong choices. In its repetitive and multivoiced form, the plot performs rather than explains. The plot does not discuss the issues; instead, it shows how categories that one perceives as intrinsically different, such as music and violence, in fact interconnect on a deeper level. Even in this novel, like in the previous examples, the representation of musical structures demonstrates how opposites are interconnected and depend on each other. Consequently, explicit reference to and representation of musical structures are not ends in themselves. The repetition and multivoicedness that we recognize from music can inform our understanding of the narrative, and writers like Huxley and Morrison, Burgess and Jelinek draw on these structures to tell stories about complex and conflicting interrelations.

'An orchestra for ravenous wild men': Representation of musical structures in Günter Grass's The Tin Drum

In the following analysis of a chapter from the German writer Günter Grass's (2004 [1959]) novel *The Tin Drum*, we look closer at how explicit representation of music in a text corresponds with and helps to frame a narrative that is based on structuring principles of music and what these relations bring to our understanding of the literary text.

In Grass's novel, Oskar Matzerath tells the story of his life before, during and after WWII. Oskar stopped growing at the age of 3, and as a child he communicates by beating his tin drum. The title of the novel has already indicated that rhythm is important, and rhythm and repetition become even more prominent in the chapter titled 'Faith, Hope, Love'. This is how the chapter starts:

> There once was a musician. His name was Meyn and he played the trumpet too beautifully for words. He lived on the fifth floor of an apartment house, just under the roof, he kept four cats, one of which was called Bismarck and from morning to night he drank out of a gin bottle. This he did until sobered by disaster.
>
> (Grass 2004 [1959], p. 181)

This chapter tells the story of one of Oskar's neighbours, the musician Meyn, and why he participated in the anti-Semitic pogrom in November 1938, the so-called Night of Broken Glass. But after only two paragraphs, we appear to be back where we started:

> There once was a musician. His name was Meyn and he played the trumpet too beautifully for words […] and from morning to night he drank out of a gin bottle, until late in '36 or early '37 I think, it was, he joined the Mounted SA.
>
> (p. 182)

Nearly the whole of the first paragraph is repeated with a slight variation at the end: the musician has turned into a member of the Nazi organization the SA. In the text that follows, nearly every paragraph goes back to 'There once was a musician' or 'There once was an SA man'. The chapter circles forward in variations like 'There once were four tom cats', cats that Meyn nearly beats to death when he relapses into drinking. 'There once was a neighbour' who reported Meyn's cruelty. 'There once was a musician' expelled from the SA because of his cruelty to animals, and he was not accepted back, although he participated with great fervour in the pogrom. 'There once was a toy merchant', Sigismund Markus, who committed suicide during the pogrom. 'There once was a tin drummer', Oskar, who found his friend dead, and started to tell another fairy tale, a kind of weird foreshadowing of the imminent war based on words he had read on missionary banner: 'Faith, Love Hope'. Yet in the end,

Oskar returns to the initial protagonists, to the toy merchant and the musician, and he sums up as follows:

> There once was a toy merchant, his name was Markus, and he took all the toys in the world away with him out of this world.
> There once was a musician, his name was Meyn, and if he isn't dead he is still alive, once again playing the trumpet too beautifully for words.
>
> (p. 190)

What kind of music is represented?

The chapter tells the story of an alcoholic trumpeter, but it also deals with his violence against animals and fellow humans. It is told by a drummer, but apart from that, the performance or sound of music is not explicitly mentioned. At the end of the previous chapter, however, Oskar mentions that people have complained about his endless drumming, which helps him to remember what he wants to write, and he promises to 'try to dictate a quieter chapter to his drum even though the subject [...] calls for an orchestra of ravenous wild men' (p. 181). The chapter is therefore framed as a piece of music to be played loudly and disturbingly. More specifically, the German original talks of a 'roaring and ravenous orchestra' ('*brüllende[s], ausgehungerte[s] Orchester*'). The 'roaring' orchestra is associated with the sound of jazz from the roaring 1920s, or the jazz age, and in fact Oskar becomes a jazz percussionist after the war. Jazz music thus provides a first possible frame: a lively musical style with characteristic syncopated rhythms, involving improvisation and cyclical formal structures. Two typical jazz instruments, the trumpet and the drum, feature in the plot. Grass was a percussionist in a jazz band during the 1950s, so was familiar with jazz. But he also compared the structure of the chapter to a rondo, a genre of instrumental classical music. The structure of a rondo is similar to that of a song; it has different stanzas, but the first and main section, A, always returns, like a refrain. Thus, it is possible to frame the chapter in two kinds of very different musical traditions. Finally, the 'ravenous' or 'famished' orchestra, in the context of anti-Semitic persecution in Nazi Germany, already leads the thoughts to the prisoner orchestras in Nazi concentration camps, where music was played to stop the screams from the gas chambers from being heard. The 'famished orchestra' description indicates that the Holocaust forms an undertone for the whole chapter.

How is music represented? Which transmedial characteristics are used?

The repetitive structure is obvious. The initial phrase 'There once was ...' returns like a refrain throughout the chapter. Even the way in which the chapter always falls back on the initial paragraph, like a chorus, is reminiscent of the cyclical structure of both certain jazz styles and rondo, where the initial section will always return after variations or digressions, specifically in traditional jazz styles, such as New Orleans and Dixieland jazz, which had a revival in post-war Europe in the 1950s. Both the parallel to New Orleans jazz and the classical rondo of classical music fit the refrain-like repetition of not only a phrase but a whole paragraph. The rondo stresses the turning in circles. Jazz provides an understanding of the improvisational character of the final section. When Oskar discovers his dead friend the toy merchant, the rhythm of repetition changes and Oskar digresses into a new and eerie fairy tale that is still based on some snatches from what has been told until then but creates a fairy tale about the arrival not of Santa Claus but the gasman, who hands out nuts and almonds. Faith, love and hope are degraded into empty phrases, interjections, and constantly interrupt a narrative thread that becomes increasingly difficult to entangle and increases in tempo as the phrases become shorter and shorter. This processual exploration of motifs that Oskar performs as narrator is similar to improvisations in music. These structures of repetition variation and contrast, as well as multivoicedness and circularity are transmedial characteristics; they are, however, more familiar to us from the structuring of organized sound in music.

Why is music represented?

What do the structural patterns we recognize from music do to our understanding of the story? They make the structure much stronger than the linear tale of Meyn's misfortunes, a muddle of coincidences that happened to end up in Meyn's participation in the pogrom. The repetitive pattern always falls back to the beginning, so each event that is presented as a variation of the initial situation undermines the linear storytelling. The storyline appears to make excuses about why one of the neighbours participates in the riots and destruction that led to Markus's death. Meyn only joined the Nazi SA to get sober. He only killed his cats because he happened to drink again. He only beat fellow citizens during the pogrom because he hoped he would be forgiven for having beaten his cats. In fact, the reasons why Meyn took part in the pogrom are presented in a structure that invalidates them. These misfortunes of Meyn mirror the excuses and explanations that were given by ordinary Germans after the war to try to explain their part in Nazism. The repetitive structure stresses that regardless of the reasons provided by these citizens, they were still part of the crimes that were committed. The causal connections are superseded, and we perceive the structural parallelism: one man is dead and the other is living 'happily ever after'. One man is a murderer and the other was murdered.

A similar point is made when we look closer at Oskar's interruptive improvisation. The talk of gas and the smell of almonds leads the thoughts to the almond-like smell of cyanide used in the gas chambers. While on the surface the passage is talking about dreary everyday life in wartime, the verbal ambiguity forms an uncanny echo of constant and ongoing death in the concentration camps. The verbal ambiguity points out that some people were living an ordinary life while millions were sent to the gas chambers. The representation of musical structure enables a kind of narration that circles

188 *Jørgen Bruhn et al.*

around the German responsibility for the Holocaust but does not accept any explanations, reasons or excuses. Personal motifs or knowledge are not valid.

Thus, the chapter uses repetitive structures that are more common in music. They undermine the inherent causality of narration, because usually each time we tell a story, we explain it. We provide reasons for a sequence of connected events. Narratives are a way of understanding the world; the order of events provides an explanation of why we ended up where we are. Representation of musical structures invites the reader to perceive similarities between causally unrelated events and to perceive contrasts as interconnected. By means of verbal ambiguity and semantic multivoicedness, different perspectives are present simultaneously.

In all the examples discussed above, the representation of musical structures is used to tell stories differently and to present complex and contradictory connections to the reader. In modernist novels, they represent the experience of modern life as fragmented – constructed of incoherent but at the same time interconnected events that take place at the same time or in the same place. In *A Clockwork Orange*, musical structure is used to demonstrate that what we perceive as oppositions, such as violence and music, and order and domination, are in fact two sides of the same coin seen from two different perspectives. Musical structures lend themselves to expressing that which resists narrative explanations. Not only in Grass's fiction but in that of other authors, they tend to appear in the context of war, violence and trauma. The musical structures are not used to make suffering beautiful. Instead, they are used because the repetitive pattern expresses something about the experience of trauma. Reasons and explanations *why* cannot express the overwhelming experience and pain of the fact that it *did* happen.

Pictorial narration

To demonstrate the variety of structural representation that is used, we conclude with an example of what could be called pictorial narration. It is one of the possible cases of so-called interpictoriality, which means that pictorial images are represented in literature 'as an explicit quotation, a form of plagiarism, an allusion or even in its iconic form' (Louvel 2011, p. 56). Pictorial narration corresponds to the last of these cases, that is, when pictorial images not only describe or refer to visual representations but when the text itself starts to display iconic similarities with the qualified media type of painting. Even here, structural forms of representation are framed with more explicit forms of media representation, more simple but explicit references or implicit allusions to paintings or photographs that, once again, provide a frame for the more complex structural representations. As in our previous examples, the representation of media in the plot combined with structural parallels interact and support each other.

The following example illustrates this. It is an extract from the novel *Biblique des derniers gestes* by the Martinican author Patrick Chamoiseau (2002). The novel *Texaco* (1992) established Chamoiseau's reputation as a defender of postcolonial ideas. In his novels, Chamoiseau criticizes more or less openly the dissolution of the authentic Martinican identity into a continental French identity. The main character of *Biblique des derniers gestes*, Balthazar Bodule-Jules, is one of the last champions of the authentic Martinican culture and a representant of the island's traumatic history, as was the traditional Martinican bard Solibo in the earlier novel *Solibo Magnifique* (1988). But Balthazar Bodule-Jules is not only a bard; he has also taken part in a number of wars against colonization. The ways in which he talks about these episodes, and the ways in which the narrator, a certain Petit Cham who interviews him, puts them in print, raise suspicions about their truthfulness. Media representation, and more specifically representation of images, is one of the devices used in the narration of these episodes.

In one of the interviews given to the narrator, Balthazar Bodule-Jules pretends to have seen the dead body of the revolutionary leader Che Guevara (1928–1967) (Chamoiseau 2002, p. 681). However, his description of what he claims to have seen with his own eyes resembles the famous photograph taken by Freddy Alborta and published in newspapers around the world on 10 October 1967 (see Figure 10.1). The way in which the narrator relates what the character has said thus gives the reader the impression that the character has not really seen the

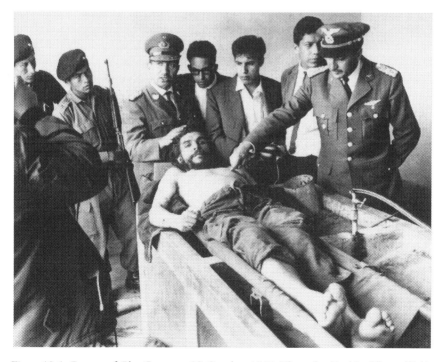

Figure 10.1 Corpse of Che Guevara, 10 October 1967 (Photo by Freddy Alborta/Bride Lane Library/Popperfoto via Getty Images/Getty Images).

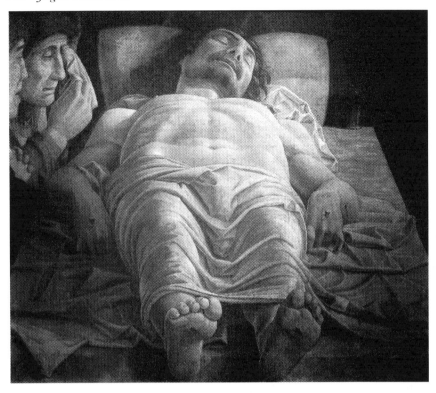

Figure 10.2 Lamentation of Christ by Andrea Mantegna (1430–1506) (Photo by Jean Louis Mazieres. CC BY-NC-SA 2.0).

body but is describing it with reference to Alborta's photograph. Indeed, the details of the description correspond exactly to the details shown in the photograph: the body is tied to the stretcher, the eyes seem open and the face seems to smile. This conclusion is also supported by the fact that the narrator makes an explicit reference to Andrea Mantegna's Renaissance painting *Lamentation of Christ* (see Figure 10.2) when describing Che's body, a reference that has been made by many commentators when analysing Alborta's photograph. The explicit reference to the painting establishes the association with Christ and thus highlights Che Guevara's martyrial and mythical status. Thus, it is not only the physical appearance that is transmediated, but also what Che Guevara stands for. The explicit reference to the *Lamentation of Christ* also signals that the narrator's description is a transmediation of the photograph it has been compared with and that Bodule-Jules probably used the same photograph when talking about this episode, which would mean that he does not draw on the memory as an eye-witness. If he cannot describe more than we can already see from the photograph, how do we know if he is indeed an authentic eye-witness? The reference to the painting and the structural representation of the photograph is therefore a way of suggesting the character's unreliability.

While we have seen earlier how Ellis's *American Psycho* frames the experience of life in film, this passage from *Biblique des derniers gestes* frames memory in visual representation – in painting and photography. Thus, the structural representation of Alberta's photograph not only suggests the unreliability of the protagonist. More generally, it draws attention to how photographs tend to support (and maybe even replace?) memories. Memories are in fact supported and influenced, perhaps even shaped, by photographs, since they not only document the past but replace it in our minds, as Linda Henkel (2014) showed in a recent study.

Conclusion

The structural representations of film, music and images that we have discussed here not only draw attention to the characteristic affordances of other media. These texts draw our attention to the abilities of literary language. This kind of writing exploits traits that language, text and literature already share with the media referred to, but these are traits that we do not usually pay much attention to. These similarities link back in one way or another to the general intermedial idea behind this book: that all media are mixed media. The fact that all media are interrelated and by their very definition share characteristics found in the four modalities is the reason why texts can convey similar experiences to watching films, listening to music or looking at pictures.

References

Baudrillard, J. 1983. *Simulations*. Paul Foss *et al.* (Trans.). Los Angeles: Semiotext(e).
Bergman, K. 2014. *Swedish crime fiction: The making of Nordic noir*. Barnsley: Mimesis International.
Bordwell, D. 2018. The hook: Scene transitions in classical cinema. http://www.davidbordwell.net/essays/hook.php [Accessed 25 January 2018].
Bruhn, J. 2016. *The intermediality of narrative literature: Medialities matter*. London: Palgrave Macmillan.
Bruhn, J. and Gjelsvik, A. 2018. *Cinema between media: An intermediality approach*. Edinburgh: Edinburgh University Press.
Bruhn, J. and Thune, H. 2018. 2014. In S. Petersson, C. Johansson, M. Holdar and S. Callahan, eds., *The power of the in-between: Intermediality as a tool for aesthetic analysis and critical reflection* (pp. 25–48). Stockholm: Stockholm University Press.
Burgess, A. 1962. *A clockwork orange*. London: Heinemann.
Carroll, N. 1990. *The philosophy of horror, or, paradoxes of the heart*. London: Routledge.
Chamoiseau, P. 2002. *Biblique des derniers gestes*. Paris: Gallimard.
Cohen, K. 1979. *Film and fiction: The dynamics of exchange*. Yale: Yale University Press.
Egan, J. 2011. *A visit from the goon squad*. New York: Anchor Books.
Elleström, L. 2014. *Media transformation: The transfer of media characteristics among media*. London: Palgrave Macmillan.

Englund, A. 2012. *Still songs: Music in and around the poetry of Paul Celan*. Farnham: Ashgate.
Fitzgerald, F.S. 2003(1925). *The great Gatsby*. Matthew J. Bruccoli, ed. New York: Scribners.
Grass, G. 2004 [1959]. *The tin drum* [*Die Blechtrommel*]. 3rd ed. R. Manheim (Trans.). London: Vintage.
Henkel, L. 2014. Point-and-shoot memories: the influence of taking photos on memory for a museum tour. *Psychological Science*, 25(2), pp. 396–402.
Hertz, E. and Roessner, J. 2014. Introduction. In E. Hertz and J. Roessner, eds., *Write in tune: Contemporary music in fiction* (pp. 1–16). London: Bloomsbury.
Isherwood, C. 1998 [1939]. *Goodbye to Berlin*. London: Vintage Classics.
Louvel, L. 2011. *Poetics of the iconotext*. L. Petit (Trans.). Farnham: Ashgate.
Moorey, G. 2014. Aging, death, and revival: Representations of the music industry in two contemporary novels. *Popular Music and Society*, 37, pp. 65–84.
Nesbø, J. 2010 [2007]. *The snowman* [*Snømannen*]. D. Bartlett (Trans.). London: Vintage.
Nöth, W. 2001. Semiotic foundations of iconicity in language and literature. In O. Fischer and M. Nänny, eds., *The motivated sign: Iconicity in language and literature* 2 (pp. 17–28). Amsterdam: John Benjamins.
Odendahl, J. 2008. *Literarisches Musizieren: Wege des Transfers von Musik in die Literatur bei Thomas Mann*. Bielefeld: Aisthesis.
Partington, A. 1998. *Patterns and meanings: Using corpora for English language research and teaching*. Amsterdam: John Benjamins.
Petermann, E. 2018. *The musical novel. Imitation of musical structure, performance and reception in contemporary fiction*. New York: Camden House.
Phillips, P. 2010. *A clockwork counterpoint: The music and literature of Anthony Burgess*. Manchester: Manchester University Press.
Powell, L. and Bethman, B. 2008. 'One must have tradition in oneself, to hate it properly': Elfriede Jelinek's musicality. *Journal of Modern Literature*, 32, pp. 163–183.
Prieto, E. 2002. *Listening in: Music, mind, and the modernist narrative*. Lincoln: University of Nebraska Press.
Rajewsky, I.O. 2002. *Intermedialität*. Tübingen: Francke.
Rajewsky, I.O. 2005. Intermediality, intertextuality, and remediation: a literary perspective on intermediality. *Intermédialités / Intermediality*, 6, pp. 43–64.
Scher, S.P. 1968. *Verbal music in German literature*. New Haven: Yale University Press.
Schirrmacher, B. 2012. *Musik in der Prosa von Günter Grass. Intermediale Bezüge – Transmediale Perspektiven*. Stockholm: Acta Universitatis Stockholmiensis.
Schirrmacher, B. 2016. Musical performance and textual performativity in Elfriede Jelinek's *The piano teacher*: *Word and music studies – New paths, new methods*. *Danish Musicology Online*. Special edition, pp. 93–108. https://www.researchgate.net/publication/313172304_Musical_Performance_and_Textual_Performativity_in_Elfriede_Jelinek's_The_Piano_Teacher
Schneider, S.J. 2004. Towards an aesthetics of cinematic horror. In Stephen Prince, ed., *The horror film* (pp. 131–149). New Brunswick: Rutgers University Press.
Schwanecke, C. 2015. Filmic modes in literature. In G. Rippl, ed., *Handbook of intermediality: Literature – image – sound – music* (pp. 268–286). Berlin: de Gruyter.
Solomon, R.C. 2003. Real horror. In Steven Jay Schneider and Daniel Shaw, eds., *Dark thoughts: Philosophical reflections on cinematic horror* (pp. 227–259). Lanham: Scarecrow Press.
Tranströmer, T. 2011. *Samlade dikter: 1954–1996*. Stockholm: Bonniers.

van de Velde, D. 2014. Every song ends: Musical pauses, gendered nostalgia, and loss in Jennifer Egan's *A visit from the goon squad*. In E. Hertz and J. Roessner, eds., *Write in tune: Contemporary music in fiction* (pp. 122–135). London: Bloomsbury.

Wolf, W. 1999. *The musicalization of fiction: A study in the theory and history of intermediality*. Amsterdam: Rodopi.

Wolf, W. 2002. Intermediality revisited: Reflections on word and music relations in the context of a general typology of intermediality. In S.M. Lodato, S. Aspden and W. Bernhart, eds, *Word and music studies: Essays in honor of Steven Paul Scher and on cultural identity and the musical stage* (pp. 13–34). Amsterdam: Rodopi.

Films referenced

Kill Bill: Volume 1. 2003. Directed by Quentin Tarantino. USA: Miramax Films.
Mission Impossible. 1996. Directed by Brian De Palma. USA: Paramount Pictures.
Psycho. 1960. Directed by Alfred Hitchcock. USA: Universal Studios.
Shoot the Piano Player [*Tirez sur le pianist*]. 1960. Directed by François Truffaut. France: Les Films du Carrosse.
Starship Troopers. 1997. Directed by Paul Verhoeven. USA: Touchstone Pictures.
The 400 Blows [*Les Quatre Cents Coups*]. 1959. Directed by François Truffaut. France: Les Films du Carrosse.
The Conversation. 1974. Directed by Francis Ford Coppola. USA: Paramount Pictures.
The Hands of Orlac. 1935. Directed by Karl Freund. USA: Metro-Goldwyn-Mayer.
The Rules of Attraction. 2002. Directed by Roger Avatar. USA: Lions Gate Films.
The Shining. 1980. Directed by Stanley Kubrick. USA: Warner Bros.

Part III
Applying intermedial perspectives

11 Introduction to Part III

Jørgen Bruhn and Beate Schirrmacher

What is now known as intermedial studies developed from interart studies, which explored the relation between literature, art, music and film. Due to this historical development, intermedial research has been mostly interested in analysing artistic media products, and the analytical methods that we presented in Part II were primarily exploring artistic communication. This third part intends to widen the scope of intermedial studies in several ways. First, we want to stress how intermedial theory, although developed in the context of artistic communication, is not restricted to analysing works of art. Instead, we demonstrate in different ways how intermedial analysis can be used to understand the combinations and transformations of all kinds of media types. In different ways, this third part means to highlight the importance of interaction across theoretical fields, across media borders and in the digital sphere in particular. We therefore take a closer intermedial look at the workings of social media and of computer games. We also present an intermedial approach to performance that can combine the focus on the body from performance studies with an intermedial analysis of media types. We use the spatiotemporal modality as a lens to describe the interaction of different kinds of spaces and bodies in theatre and performance. Furthermore, we focus on transmedial phenomena that are not restricted to only one qualified media type but which cross conventional media borders and may need new productive methods to analyse the way communication is transformed in these processes. Therefore, we explore several transmedial storyworlds in popular culture. We also claim that understanding the social challenges of communication needs an intermedial approach and a transmedial perspective. This is the reason why we explore how intermedial analysis contributes to understanding societal challenges, here exemplified by the communication of climate change, on the one hand, and the destructive spreading of disinformation, on the other.

DOI: 10.4324/9781003174288-14

12 The intermediality of performance

Per Bäckström, Heidrun Führer and Beate Schirrmacher

In the street, you see a person standing on a box, motionless like a statue. When someone throws a coin into a hat on the pavement in front of her, she starts to move. The same evening at a bar, a young man gets onto a makeshift stage, grabs the microphone and starts to talk. After only a few moments, the audience responds by laughing. In the city's theatre, the whole audience listens silently to how Hamlet, Prince of Denmark, struggles with the question 'to be or not to be'. Meanwhile, in the concert arena, a pop artist sings his or her latest songs in a show that includes lights, different costumes, dance and video in front of thousands of cheering fans.

Pantomime, stand-up comedy, drama and pop music concerts are different experiences and follow different conventions, but they are all artistic performances that take place in a marked, specific performative space: a stage, a theatre or an arena. Even in everyday life, people perform to reinforce and communicate identity in front of an audience. The so-called performative turn in social sciences and the humanities discovered the role of performance in all kinds of human interactions. In a way, performance is everywhere and '[a]ll the world's a stage', as Shakespeare wrote in his play *As you like it* (written ca. 1600). Performance studies explores all kinds of events, from theatre performances and artistic activities outside institutional framing to sporting contests, ceremonies, informal gatherings, everyday rituals and daily interaction. This performative aspect of everything we do and say has become even more prominent in social media interaction today (see Chapter 16).

In this chapter, however, we will focus on performance as an aesthetic or communicative event that unfolds at a specific time and in a specific space and where at least one person performs a series of movements that we perceive as meaningful in front of an audience. In traditional theatre, the audience is accustomed to sitting and watching passively and silently. However, when we look at the audience of a pantomime acted out in the street, a stand-up comedy act, a festival or a football match, we understand how the audience takes an active part in the construction of a performance. The co-presence of performer and audience creates a performative space that is set apart from the social world. Performance scholar Jill Dolan highlights the utopian potential of live performance as 'a place for people to come together, embodied and

DOI: 10.4324/9781003174288-15

passionate, to share experiences of meaning-making and imagination that can describe or capture fleeting intimations of a better world' (Dolan 2005, p. 2).

However, it is not only people who come together in a performance, but also many different kinds of materialities and media. In the unique moment of performance that unfolds in time and space, the performer interacts with an audience but also with other objects: props such as the famous skull that Hamlet holds in his hand or technical devices such as the microphone in a stand-up act. In this chapter, we will look closely at how different kinds of bodies and objects interact in a performance and at how the presence and emergence of an event interact with mediation and transmediation. Pantomimes, stand-up comedy acts, drama and music concerts can be understood as different qualified media types that take place in the context of different architectural framings that already in themselves indicate which conventions are at play, what kind of performance the audience should expect and what kind of response is expected from the audience (see also Chapter 14).

We explore the interaction between performers and technical devices and other basic and qualified media by analysing different kinds of performances of lyrical poetry and their media transformation to YouTube videos and discuss different levels of entanglements by looking at the performance of a football game.

By doing so we want to go beyond Philip Auslander's concept of mediatized performance (Auslander 2008 [1999]). Instead of differentiating between a performance and its mediatization, we explore how mediation and, in many instances, media transformation are part of the performance itself. From an intermedial perspective, mediation and transmediation does not first take place when electronic media of amplification and reproduction come into play. Instead, these aspects already are part of the qualified media type performance. By exploring performance as a qualified medium, we also highlight the importance of performative key concepts such as presence, process and entanglement in all kinds of intermedial relations. This opens up the possibility of considering the performative aspects of other media products as well.

Performance, mediation and performativity

If we define performance primarily as unfolding in the present moment, and understand media products primarily as tangible material objects, then the performative event and media products appear much more opposed to each other than they actually are. The seemingly clear distinction between presence and representation stems from the ideological need to demonstrate the importance of presence. Performance studies focuses more on the processes that develop a 'transformative power' (Fischer-Lichte 2008) rather than on specific repeatable content that performances communicate as well.

From an intermedial perspective, however, performance can be described as a media product in the form of an event, characterized by its specific spatio-temporality that involves affecting bodies in the sensorial modality. Seen from this perspective, performance and mediation seem no longer opposed to each other. Instead, they appear as different aspects of the complexity of communicative situations. Performance can then be described as a qualified media type that combines or integrates many technical devices and basic and qualified media types: bodies interact with, for example, props, screens, speech, text, images, costumes, colours, video and music. In fact, the multimodality of a performance has the potential not only to integrate with but also to transform any other media type, which has provoked the idea that theatre should be understood as a 'hypermedium' (Chapple and Kattenbelt 2006).

In the communicative event of a performance, binary distinctions, such as doing and meaning, presentation and representation, are undermined. Bodies and objects on stage communicate not only by representing things and pretending to carry out acts, but they also communicate by being present and carrying out acts. If we approach performance with binary distinctions, they start to 'oscillate' or 'fold into each other'. This oscillation between concepts that we perceive as being opposed to each other is called performativity and is one of the main characteristics of every act of performance.

Box 12.1 Performativity

The term performativity originates from linguistics. In the 1950s, the linguist J. L. Austin drew attention to the fact that verbal language is not only about representation of meaning. In his book *How to Do Things with Words*, Austin (1962) describes how certain words (such as 'to baptize' or 'to marry') not only represent certain acts are also part of the social actions they describe. This performative aspect of language is not only restricted to the relatively small group of performative verbs that Austin draws attention to but is also an aspect of all language use. When we use words, we want to cause (re)actions. A person can say, 'It's cold in here' with the aim of making someone else shut the window. These kinds of speech acts are studied within linguistic pragmatics. The performative aspects of verbal language have been explored further by post-structuralist philosopher Jacques Derrida, who points out how every word we choose carries out a performative act that repeats conventions but also has the potential to change them (Derrida 1988 [1977]). Derrida's philosophical approach to language made it possible for Judith Butler to explore further how we perform gender (and social identity in general) by means of repetition and change (Butler 1990). Performativity has become what Mieke Bal calls a travelling concept (Bal 2002) that changes the perspective from representation of conventional meaning to social acts that are being carried out. Binaries like meaning and doing, representation and presentation, repetition and change are enmeshed and cannot be told apart from each other to the extent that it is neither possible nor productive to clearly separate them (for an overview, see, for example, Bal (2002) or Velten (2016)).

The concept of performativity highlights how acts of representation are able to change the world around us and made it possible for performance and theatre studies to highlight the performer's presence and his or her acts as an intrinsic part of the performance. Our intermedial approach allows us to explore more in detail the entanglement of presence and representation, of performance and media products, of performativity and intermediality. After all, both performance studies and media studies are interested in the role of material presence in communication, be it the presence of bodies and their interaction or the material presence of objects that we interact with.

Even the concept of a performance as a 'live' event depends on the existence of media products that represent and transmediate performances. Still, there is a difference between a live performance and its representation in other media. However, from an intermedial perspective we see that it is not enough to dismiss the media representation of a performance as just a 'reproduction' or as 'unreal'. Instead, we can explore it as an instance of transmediation. The film clip that you recorded at a concert transmediates basic media types of the performance, but it cannot really transmediate the co-presence of affective bodies, the experience of being there.

In many kinds of performances, different technical media and qualified media types are a deeply integrated part of the live experience. The audience of a rock concert or of a football game are both attending a live event but at the same time gather a lot of their impressions from video screens on or around the stage or pitch. In the light of this, how can we tell where the live performance ends and the media representation begins? And is there a producer of any live performance in the digital age, especially in the social media age, that is not aware that it has the potential to be extended and reproduced beyond the here and now – that it can be filmed and shared instantly?

The performer's body as a medium

In the study of the intermedial aspects of performance, the live body and its interaction with other technical devices and qualified media types stand in focus. The poet William Butler Yeats (1865–1939) famously asked: 'How can we know the dancer from the dance?' (Yeats 1996). His question illustrates that it is hard to distinguish between the performer's body and what we call in this book the qualified medium of dance. Nor is it easy to understand how the performer's body can *act like* a medium, which cannot be separated from the presence of a human being per se.[1] At the same time, we realize that the situation is rather complex, since at least one other medium is involved: the body is not usually moving of its own accord but is seen moving in relation to music of some sort – be it tapping a rhythm with a hand or foot, humming, a musical instrument or an entire orchestra.

Hence, the material human body is the main medium we must focus on when we are analysing a performance. But the body also interacts with technical devices like microphones and other basic media types like sounds and organized sound, as well as media products of other qualified media types like music, or film. Because of this, the analysis becomes more and more complex, and in the end, we have to acknowledge that an increasing number of media constitutes a particular performance.

It is clearly not easy to come to terms with the idea of the body being a medium in a performance. To put it simply, the perspective of performance studies on the body corresponds to what we call in this book a technical medium of display; in contrast, intermedial studies observes the body in all its intermedial aspects and relations, but at the same time, the presence of the body tends to be neglected. At first sight, these look like two mutually exclusive fields of research, but on a closer look, mediation is not necessarily opposed to presence, because the main medium in a performance is the body, and the body is directly connected to questions about presence and authenticity. Amalgamating these two analytical fields is therefore a good idea, because it could introduce a richer analysis focusing on the body, other media *and* presence. The body is not only a technical medium of display in a performance, but also much more. For example, the body displays the semiotic modality such as the embodied or body-related codes that are needed to experience presence; these codes imply the sensorial modalities of seeing and hearing, for instance, the wearing of long black leather coats and growling respectively in black metal. According to Lars Ellestrom (2021), the body can be seen as a basic medium in a performance, since we perceive the bodily movements of a performer in a spatiotemporal performative space as meaningful – as a performance by a moving body, which, in this special case, is a qualified medium. When the specific purpose of a performance is to express an aesthetic utterance or a communicative act with the body, the body becomes a technical medium of display. We can communicate multimodally by using the body through clothing, facial expressions, body posture and movements, gestures, our voice, verbal text, etc. The body has a variety of uses, and while those that are driven by nature and instinct have a biological function that is common to all fauna, it also has uses that are more developed in human beings that we will focus on next: orality and gestures (see Box 12.2).

Box 12.2 Bodily performance: Orality and gestures

Orality refers to both verbal expressions (the actual words) and extra-verbal expressions, such as the pronunciation of these words (intonation, pitch, etc.) and non-verbal sounds, such as guttural expression, expressions of astonishment, hesitation or thoughtfulness ('er ...') and emotions, emotional expression, etc. Verbal language is a complex area of research, but to gain an understanding of the orality of a performance, only a fairly simple question about its function needs to be considered: which words do the performer(s) actually articulate? Extra-verbal expressions and non-verbal sounds have mostly been neglected until recently, both by linguists and performance studies scholars, despite the fact that these expressions add value to a performance. In music studies (Barthes (1981) and Frith (2002 [1996])), this phenomenon is receiving increasing attention, which should be self-evident after decades of pop music that includes nonsensical sounds, such as Little Richard's 'A-wop-bop-a-loo-bop-a-wop-bam-boom!' in the song 'Tutti Frutti' (1955).[2] For an intermedial and performance studies analysis of a performance, it is therefore important to pay more attention to both non-phonetic ('sniffs, lip-smacks, grunts, moans, sighs, whistles, and clicks') and nonsensical expressions (Keevallik and Ogden 2020, p. 1).

By gestures, we mean the non-verbal modes of embodied communication. It is easy to disregard gestures in performance studies, or even to take an approach that views gestures as subordinated to orality, as in traditional linguistics, but such a way of thinking neglects the decisive importance of non-verbal expressions in our communication. The *Oxford Latin Dictionary* describes gestures as something in-between: 'Neither *praxis* nor *poiēsis*, Gerere – from which "gesture" is derived – means "to bear", "to carry", but also, "to show", "to reveal", "to perform the function", "to administer an office"' (Glare 1982, p. 762). The philosopher Giorgio Agamben (2018) also sees 'gesture' as the middle way, in between 'to do' (*facere*) and 'to act' (*agere*). He explains this by pointing to the importance of gestures in a performance, where they have parity with verbal language: '*Gesture* is the name of this intersection between life and art, act and power, general and particular, text and execution' (Agamben 2000 [1996], p. 79). Gestures that have often been regarded as subordinated to speech and of no significance are in fact constitutive of a performance. And gestures not only work with, against or separately from verbal language but also take part in the production of language before it turns into verbal expressions (Goldin-Meadow and Alibali Wagner 2013). It is therefore of the utmost importance for an intermedial and/or performance studies analysis of a performance to observe the gestures and posture of the performer(s) (see also Kendon (2004) and Michel Guérin (2011 [1995])).

A bodily performance of any kind is mostly constituted by two main basic media types, orality (verbal and extra-verbal expression) and gestures (non-verbal expression), where gestures can work in tandem with extra-verbal expressions. In a multimodal analysis, these two basic media types could be divided into an even more fine-grained analysis of modes, such as intonation and pitch, hand gestures and body posture, etc. However, even if we sum up these various modes of the basic media types of gesture and orality, we use gesture(s) in this chapter in a broader sense to include movement and posture, because it is practically impossible to distinguish between different parts of non-verbal communication.

What complicates things when we think about the body as a medium, however, is the fact that we also perceive all kinds of mediated communication through our own bodies And, to complicate things even more, two kinds of bodies are always present at a performance: the body of the performer and the bodies of the audience (see Chapter 14, Box 14.2). This double function is very important, but it also constitutes a challenge when we consider intermedial aspects of a performance, because we have to consider which aspects of the bodily interaction with other media we should focus on – the body as the performing instance or the body as the recipient of sensorial data? Here we will focus on the first aspect, because the second aspect is hard to analyse when the material is a film clip. Rather than postulating that the body is a medium, it's more important to understand how the body can function and be used as a medium, especially if we want to understand how embodied performance presents and interacts and connects with other forms of mediated communication.

Poetry performances

In this section, we analyse the intermedial interaction between the body and different media in three different poetry performances. In our step-by-step analysis, we explore the following aspects:

1   The presence of the body.
2   The qualifying aspects of the performance.
3   The interaction with other media types and the expansion of the performative space with the use of technical devices and different media.

The first step explores how bodily presence, that is, how the orality and gestures of the performer, contributes to our understanding of the words performed, and here we focus on the body as a basic medium. The second step discusses the qualifying aspects of a performance, that is, aspects that contribute to our initial understanding that what we see and hear is a performance in the first place. The final step includes the interaction with other media types, both those that are 1) part of the performance and thereafter those that are 2) not part of the actual performance, but the technical devices that make it possible for us to observe the performance. While two of the performance analyses focus on the performer, the third analysis looks at the interaction between the performer's body and the audience's bodies. The result of these analyses is the recognition that a performance that at first sight seems fairly uncomplicated almost always involves a more complex intermedial situation.

Different kinds of poetry performance

We use the term 'poetry performance' in this chapter to serve as an umbrella concept for every performance of a poem (without music), which can be divided into subgenres such as poetry-reading, lyrical performance and spoken-word/poetry slams. A 'lyrical performance' is a performance in which the poet does not read the poems from a written text but performs them after having memorized them (Bäckström 2003). Lyrical performance and spoken word are overlapping concepts, but they describe two different strategies that can be illustrated by Lydia Lunch's more inspirational act versus Henry Rollins' memorized performance. The three examples of subgenres noted earlier belong to two different kinds of aesthetic performances. A poetry-reading is a performance that stems from a literary media product. In performance art, however, the media product is a performance that has an aesthetic intention *in itself*, which makes it an artwork in its own right. A seemingly spontaneous street performance fits this description, and this type of performance art first came into prominence in the 1960s. Lyrical performance and even more so spoken word, which is based on improvisation, are also kinds of performance art.

In poetry performances, in general, there are at least three different ways in which orality and gestures can relate to each other: 1) orality overshadows the gestures, as in many poetry-readings, 2) orality and gestures have equal status, as in lyrical performance and spoken word, and 3) orality is subordinated to the gestures, such as when rock singers growl in death metal and black metal. We will look into these three aspects and their different demands in the context of an intermedial analysis of three poetry performances by the American poets Lydia Lunch, Henry Rollins and Allen Ginsberg, respectively (see Box 12.3). All of the performances have been recorded and published on YouTube.

Box 12.3 Poets

Allen Ginsberg (1926–97) was one of the main Beat poets who revolutionized the American poetry tradition when they introduced poetry-readings and performances and suggested that they were as important or even more important than the printed poems. Ginsberg is most famous for *Howl and Other Poems* (1956), but equally important is the title poem in *Kaddish and Other Poems* (1961).

Lydia Lunch (b. 1959) is an American rock singer (Teenage Jesus and the Jerks, 8-Eyed Spy, the Contortions, solo), actress, poet, spoken-word artist, etc. She has published several books, including *Paradoxia* (1997) – a kind of autobiography – but her main act is spoken word, regarding which she has released more than 15 recordings.

Henry Rollins (b. 1961) is an American rock singer (Black Flag, Rollins Band), actor, author, poet, spoken-word artist, etc. He has published several books, a selection from them is published in *The Portable Henry Rollins* (1997), but like Lunch, he prefers spoken word to rock music and has released more than 15 spoken-word records.

Performance – The body

In her spoken-word performance of the poem 'Fuck',[3] Lydia Lunch describes the 'meat market' that she welcomes the audience to. The market metaphorically signifies men's obsession with sex, a theme she scorns the audience for, teasing the men in explicit language until one of her last statements: 'you can't afford it, and I'm not selling it'. How do orality and gestures in her performance contribute to our understanding of the poem? Lunch clearly performs her poem, and her enactment seems to rely on improvisation. She is wearing a glittering black dress and bright red lipstick and has dyed bright red hair; that is, she is dressed for this performance in a way that fits with the female gender role she will criticize an instant later. She raises herself with the microphone in her hand and a neutral but nevertheless friendly expression on her face and smiles sweetly towards the audience – or maybe someone among them; the smile, again according to a stereotyped female behaviour, quickly turns audacious and forbearing at the same time. In a few seconds, she has established the necessary presence and contact with the audience, because she has looked and even stared directly at them, and then she starts to recite the poem with an offensive expression on her face.[4] Here orality and gestures are clearly emphatic, and her obligatory but sarcastic 'Welcome, Ladies and Gentlemen' reveals a wish to shock. She begins as if she wants to introduce somebody else, but instead she presents a powerful self to the audience, a self that does not comply with the expectation that she will display compulsory female behaviour. Instead, she is a strong woman with sexual desires, complaining about men. Her articulation is exaggerated, with excessive lip movements that make her speech both ardent and provocative. Her arm movements are vigorous and she takes up space; that is, she behaves in a way that a woman is not traditionally supposed to behave. Her left arm is either drawn against her chest in a gesture of anger and vitality or is pointing out towards the audience as if she is indicating someone in the audience, challenging the man she has selected. The audience is in shadow; it is only possible to see a line of dark heads in the front row and to hear the audience cheering or mocking her. Her sometimes vulgar expressions and gestures, combined with her explicit poetry, show the audience, and the viewers of the video, a powerful woman. Lunch's performance is deliberately disturbing, as she establishes a stereotyped female gender role only to undermine it profoundly with her orality and gestures.

When Henry Rollins performs his poem 'Family Man',[5] he stands in front of a screen showing slides and confronts the audience with a fierce monologue scorning gender roles. Rollins rages against the family man, who is an incarnation of suburban family life. Rollins' face is seen in a close-up, and at the very start he has his face turned sideways and his eyes closed. The performance is clearly staged, beginning in darkness and ending in light. When the first slide is projected, accompanied by the sound of the projector, he abruptly 'wakes' up, opens his eyes to stare at the audience and then slowly turns his head towards us. A fiery presence is immediately established, even though there might be no other audience than the people watching the clip. He starts to recite his poem 'Family Man' and then – probably involuntarily – he blinks for the only time in the whole sequence. The expression 'family man' has a neutral connotation when Rollins uses it, even though it is usually loaded with the positive connotations of a trustworthy husband and father. When Rollins pronounces these two words, his expression, especially the grimace he makes with his mouth and the minimal movement of his eyebrows, changes them from forming a neutral description into an expression of hatred and utter contempt. At the end of the performance, the last slide is projected and then the blank screen takes over, although this is not completely synced with his last words. Rollins' face is then lit up as if by the projector, but the glitch in the syncing reveals that it is probably a second light source. There are not many gestures except his lips pronouncing the words in a sinister and threatening way while he stares at the camera without a single blink (after the first and only one), which means that he is staging himself as a very threatening figure. Rollins has memorized the poem,[6] and from the very start we focus on his face. In many ways this is a minimal performance; there is not an abundance of movements or other distractions (if we concentrate on his body, although we can only see his face), and in this sense it is a perfect example of a lyrical performance. In fact, he only performs using his face, with orality and a minimum of facial gestures. Even though there is not much movement except for his lips, there are facial expressions that we can interpret as gestures that both change and specify the meaning of the verbal statements. Therefore, the main gesticulation in this performance takes place in Rollins' face, where his mouth and eyebrows are in motion. This makes his facial gestures even more threatening, because they exaggerate the sinister mood of the performance. This is an exemplary illustration of the power of gestures and intonation, because Rollins' gestures change a phrase that can have either neutral or positive connotations into an expression of utter contempt.

Contrary to Lunch and Rollins, Allen Ginsberg *read* his poems at the Royal Albert Hall in 1965.[7] But even in this performance of the literary media product of a written text, Allen Ginsberg's orality and gestures have an impact on our understanding of the poetic situation. His reading starts after a prelude, but his performance is already qualified because he is one of a group of poets reading their poems. Ginsberg reads his poems with emphasis. To show that he is a Poet, he reads from sheets of paper he is holding in his right hand, and after a while he picks up a book and reads from that instead.[8] His face is animated, and he underlines the words of the poem with facial expressions and grimaces and by using his left hand to mark the rhythm and underscore important words. Here the body clearly guarantees the presence and authenticity of the performance, since Ginsberg's orality and gestures establish a lively and engaging performance, and, more importantly, so do his actions of looking directly at the audience before he starts reading and very soon after that looking up and smiling again. Most of the time his face is bent down towards the book, though, and he looks up at the audience only occasionally, which makes his facial gestures less visible for both the audience and the viewer of the film. But Ginsberg demonstrates the combined value of the voice and arm and hand gestures and how they can animate a performance. His hand gestures are, accordingly, the most flamboyant part of his performance; they mark the rhythm, flapping like a bird, and his index finger reprimands the audience and he points at one of the other Beat poets on the stage. He gets more and more agitated and heated, and then he abruptly stops his reading to calmly ask 'Andrei' if he would like to read.

Performance as a qualified medium – Institutional framing

In these three examples, we can see how the body language of the performers contributes to and enhances our understanding of the spoken word and also guarantees the necessary authenticity and presence of each performance. One important question remains, though: why do we interpret these activities as performances at all? And how do we know that we have to expect that poetry will be performed? We are not only watching performers speaking and using their bodies; we are also seeing a *body acting out 'something' in the spatiotemporality of a performative space in front of an audience.*

Lydia Lunch performs in front of an audience, which makes it possible for us to rapidly determine the situation as a performance of some sort, even if we are not part of the co-present audience but are only watching the YouTube clip. There appears to be no proper stage, but rather a performative space around her, a clear division between the performer and the audience, which situates Lunch as a body in a certain space at a specific time. We must add here that the microphone, besides being a technical device (which will be discussed next), also enlarges the performative space, simply because it ensures that Lunch will be audible from further away. Despite this, we still have to decide if she is performing at this moment as a rock artist or as an author, and because there are no instruments on the stage, the conclusion must be that she is very probably performing as an author. This is immediately confirmed when she starts to speak, because first of all she does not sing, and second she addresses the audience as 'ladies and gentlemen' at the beginning of her performance. The rest of the stage lies in darkness, and we can only distinguish something that seems to be a table and that eventually turns out to be a Xerox machine, with crumpled sheets of paper on it. This implies that the only valid criteria for this being performance is the situation itself: we can see an individual in front of other individuals, speaking words that by convention usually introduce performances of other sorts (vaudeville, circus, etc.). There is of course something else that causes us to make this decision, which is drawing on the contextual qualifying aspects of Lydia Lunch being known as an actress, poet and rock artist. She is also a spoken-word artist and very likely it is poetry we will hear, and consequently she is the main attraction and not just the person announcing the show.[9]

Henry Rollins doesn't perform his poem on a stage, or in front of a co-present audience, but it is clear to anyone who watches the film that it is still a performance, because the staging, with its carefully fashioned soundscape, makes it an ephemeral presentation that occurs at a specific time and in a specific space. Having prior knowledge of Rollins is of course of great importance, but even someone who does not know that he is a rock singer and author would still recognize the situation as a performance. Why is that? Well, we see Rollins *as if* he was on stage, addressing an audience, so the situation is fairly similar to that of Lunch's performance even though we do not know whether there is an audience in front of Rollins or not. We sense a performative time more than a performative space, because Rollins begins with his eyes closed and then suddenly opens them. So even in this case, the framing of the performance makes us decide that this is the qualified medium of performance, and after hearing Rollins speaking, we also deduce more or less instantly that it is a lyrical performance, that is, he is not singing or performing drama. In Rollins' case, the fact that we cannot see the microphone, a technical device, in the film, makes the performance more direct, which reduces the performative space and makes it even more claustrophobic because the head of the performer is so close to the audience.

Allen Ginsberg climbs onto a traditional stage when it is his turn to read. The stage is not just any stage, but one of the main performance stages and perhaps the most famous in the UK, the Royal Albert Hall, where artists have performed for about 150 years. It is *the* exemplary institutional frame, not least because most members of the audience sit in the stalls and balconies, like the audience should in a theatre. Unlike Lunch and Rollins, Ginsberg reads from a manuscript and then from a book, devices that work as genre markers, making us qualify the media type faster. At the same time, they are intermedial references that are included in this qualified medium, and as technical media of display they become part of the performance. Before Ginsberg starts reading, he turns over the sheets of paper, decides which poem to read and slams the remaining papers down on the music stand; he hesitates slightly until the audience stops booing the poet who has just finished performing, and then he starts to read forcefully from the book. It seems as if several cuts may have been made in the film, because in one frame Ginsberg is sitting down throwing pieces of paper at the partner of the poet who has just performed, Ernst Jandl,[10] and in the next he suddenly stands up in front of the microphone. We interpret this lacuna as editorial, because the booing seems to be superimposed on the later frame of Ginsberg, so in reality there must have been a short pause before he entered the stage. The same happens with the sheets of paper he seems to start reading from, because when he actually reads, it is from the book and *not* from the sheets that we have seen first, which means that there must have been an editorial cut here as well. It is interesting to reflect on the interaction between the audience and the poet, because Ginsberg so clearly reacts to the audience and stages himself as a serious poet. He hesitates while they are in an uproar booing, and he starts reading when he gets a signal that the audience has started to calm down, which forces all of the audience members to do so and then even more gradually to become quiet and start to listen.

The performer's intermedial relation with other media

All of the performers we have discussed interact with different kinds of media and devices. Some of these technical devices or physical media, such as Lunch's microphone or Ginsberg's book, are also qualifying aspects of the lyrical performance or poetry-reading. The choice of device in itself indicates whether we can expect a lyrical performance or a performance of poetry, but other media are also involved in these performances.

The main technical media in the case of Lydia Lunch are fairly simple to identify: first of all, she holds a microphone in her right hand through which she addresses the audience, so this medium is necessary for the performance itself. The microphone in Lunch's hand is therefore a qualifying aspect of this kind of modern performance. There is one more technical medium in all three examples, however, which we do not usually reflect on, because this medium is more or less 'transparent': light. All three shows are illuminated to various degrees, which can be most clearly distinguished in the case of Lunch, because she definitely has a spotlight focused on her – highlighting her and putting the audience in shadow.[11] And in the case of this film-recorded performance, the video is a transmediation of Lydia Lunch's performance. Video technology changes the modalities of the performance significantly; most notably, those viewing the video clip are not attending a unique event with 'free' spatiality but have access to a media product that displays a performance, but that in itself is sequential and repeatable and the visual and auditory experience is decided by the position of the camera (and the recording microphone).

When it comes to Henry Rollins, we can't see devices such as microphones, cameras and so on, and his performance is staged in a closed room. It seems as if there is no co-present audience in the room; instead, the film extends the performative space to include us as part of multiple video audiences. Even if there are no spotlights visible, light contributes to the performance. Rollins is filmed in front of a projector screen (another technical medium of display), on which an old-fashioned slide projector displays amateur slides (according to the sound, which is clearly audible and part of the performative space). These images are obviously chosen to contrast with Rollins' reading of 'Family Man', and therefore they add a communicative level to the embodied message, since they show scenes that could be found in any conventional family photo album (the qualified medium of family slides). These photos work in contrast to Rollins' aggressive and threatening performance, which sets the scene in two ways: first of all, they display an atmosphere of naïveté and harmony that is *uncanny* (in the same way as in David Lynch's movie *Blue Velvet*, released in 1986); second, they give depth to Rollins' anger, because he so obviously attacks what they depict. There is one more medium in his performance, a circular sound whose source is hard to determine, but it is similar to the sound of a metronome or a clock with its rhythmical markings. The sound is more industrial and therefore more aggressive, though, so it is probably being produced by something other than a metronome or clock; in any case, the circularity and simplicity suggest repetitiveness, boredom and menace (the sound is louder before and after the performance, which shows that the sound has been edited to create a particular effect). It is hard to decide what qualified media type the basic media type of organized sound belongs to in this case, but the function may be one of two kinds: maybe Rollins wanted a rhythm to read to because he is a musician, but it is more likely that it was chosen to intensify the atmosphere, which is both threatening and tedious at the same time.

Allen Ginsberg is filmed from a distance as a full figure, a half figure and as a close-up on stage; there is a microphone standing in front of him and he also has, like the other poets who perform before him, a microphone hanging on his chest, both of which probably amplify the sound and are recording the poet. The fixed microphone augments the performative space and reduces the poet to an appendage to it, since he so clearly directs himself to it from a slightly bent-over position.

The media transformation of the live performance

When we analyse live performances, we are utterly dependent on the recorded sounds and images, because most people cannot attend a particular performance that is only going to take place once. And even if technical media had been used for these recordings, we would still have been at risk of not being able to access them so easily if the internet had not been developed, and with it social media such as YouTube. The media products discussed here thus involve several levels of transmediation and media representation. All three examples of live performances are analysed by way of film clips uploaded on YouTube. The kind of media we discuss next as augmenting and documenting media are by no means last in a hierarchical order, but rather the opposite, as they are the level of mediation that we are usually most aware of and that are discussed in terms of mediatization (Auslander 2008 [1999]).

However, seen from an intermedial perspective, live performance is already a media product; it uses the body as a basic medium and a technical medium of display that expresses the performance in movements and in spoken language together with extra-verbal oral utterances and gestures. The stage and the audience as qualified media indicators are the levels of mediation that make us decide what genre we are looking at and/or listening to, and this media product is then transmediated into a recorded performance, permitting us to analyse the live performance. Both film and sound, recorded by the camera and/or the microphone, have the properties of extending or augmenting the performative space and time. When we study live performance, we interact with a media product of film while focusing on the media product that is transmediated. This is a bit like reading a translation of a novel that we cannot read in the original. Thus, we have to consider how the transmediation affects our experience of the performance, which of course makes it important for our decision about which kind of qualified medium we are watching. However, because they do this to a minor extent in relation to the stage/audience divide, we do not explore in the next sections the YouTube clips in relation to the social media context, but instead focus on the transmediation of the performance.

Filming introduces a question about immediacy, which is the kind of media interaction that does not pay attention to the presence of the medium but only interacts with what we perceive as 'content'. Lunch is filmed head-on and the shots are edited to include her as a full figure, a half figure and a close-up. This style is used throughout the entire performance, and the only cuts involve shifting between two different cameras. When we watch the performance on a screen as an edited film, we are attending a different kind of performance from the one we would be attending if we were part of the co-present audience. The media representation of a live performance, however, transmediates many of the basic media types of performance, such as orality, gestures and the speech of bodies that are also moving, and hence we are able to decide which kind of performance we want to watch. Though the experience of the performance changes, the film makes it possible for us to watch Lunch's performance after the real-time performance has ended. We do not know if the microphone generates the sound for the film, or whether the camera does, which seems more likely, or both, but this had no real consequences for our previous analysis as we focused on analysing the speech and orality of the live performances and not their transmediation by means of sound recording (and sound editing).

Rollins is filmed head-on and in close-up. There are no cuts between different camera perspectives, and in this static perspective we can perceive the changing slides in the background. It seems as if the camera provides the sound as well because we can't see any handheld or pinned microphone, but sound has been recorded (and edited) in a way that makes it possible to discern the interaction between Rollin's speech, the sound of the slide projector and the rhythmical sound effect. Without the filming, though, it would not be possible for anyone to analyse his performance, since it seems to have been staged for the camera only.

In the case of Ginsberg, the recording film cameras and microphones are not visible, but the film has been heavily edited and cut before being put together again as a whole. According to a comment on YouTube, the film was cut considerably to form the circa 25-minute long clip we can watch now, because the readings went on for hours. This seems to be correct, because Ginsberg's reading is far too short if we consider his status as one of the main Beat poets at the time, and we have already mentioned the visible cuts in the reading. What is striking, as we have disclosed earlier, is that although the film makes it possible for us to experience parts of the reading, at the same time we are more exposed to someone else's editing of the same event. What we see is not documentation straight off, but a narrative that has been planned and realized for a film audience by an anonymous film editor.[12] Thus, although the film recordings at first glance seem to be transparent, we can see when we look more closely how the media characteristics of film inevitably transform the media product of a live performance.

Poetry performances: Concluding words

As we have seen, the body is not the only medium in a performance, but it reacts to and interacts with other media, some of which are constitutive of our decision concerning which qualified medium or which genre we are watching. Other media are not part of the performance but make it possible for us to see it – they augment the performative space, but they also transform and transmediate it. Through a combination of the perspectives of performance studies and intermedial studies, we have achieved a richer analysis, which focuses on the performer's body as a medium and the presence it establishes. At the same time, the body is discussed in its multimodal complexity and in terms of its intermedial relations. Whereas performance studies are inclined to disregard various media because they are seen as being hindrances to the necessary presence that a performance must establish, according to intermedial studies, we can now see that mediation and mediatization are necessary means to establish the very same presence. At the same time, it is not enough to focus on the different media involved in a performance, because one then tends to miss the presence of the performer and sometimes even the message. It is therefore clear that intermedial studies can offer a very useful toolbox when it comes to different kinds of analyses, and especially so when it comes to analyses of live arts.

Football as an intermedial performance

A ball being playfully kicked by a few players towards a goal seems enough for us to recognize a football game even when it is played informally in a backyard or a street. But the institutionalized, professional game follows a set of specific rules. Twenty-two players who form two teams compete in a stadium for the highest score by trying to get the specifically designed ball into the opponent's goal. Each move is carefully observed and analysed by the referees, an audience and multiple technologically extended eyes and ears. Despite all of the rules and control, a lot of training and well-planned strategies, a football game is an exciting performance without being too predictable. A large audience is therefore emotionally engaged, cheering in a stadium, in pubs, in city squares or at home. Football is transformed into various qualified media products such as video games (*FIFA 15*), books, films and music videos about football, or football songs in different languages.

In this part of the chapter, we examine the criss-crossing multimodality of an international football match as a *mediatized* public performance and as qualified media products. The social and political qualities of football cultivate specific social identities that are inseparable from neoliberal consumer culture. By reading this section, you will gain a more differentiated perspective on how cultural artefacts in our (post)modern culture are enfolded in complex mediatizing processes.

Football: A game, a form of play or a performance?

What do we gain when considering football as a performance and not only as a game or a form of play? How does an intermedial approach differ from the statement 'That's football: sometimes the better team wins' (attributed to the German professional player Lukas Podolski, quoted in Werron 2015, p. 24)?

When played informally, the game can be performed at any time, by any number and any kind of player; bins can be either used to mark goalposts or instead of a ball. This type of competitive leisure activity may be studied in terms of traditional play theory, as done by the Dutch historian Johan H. Huizinga in his seminal book *Homo Ludens: A Study of the Play Element in Culture* (Huizinga 1949). He regarded the human species as players, *homo ludens*, and culture as a purposeless and self-referential play. Football favours the educational ideals of fair play and sociability while presuming that football involves the truthful play of free people making free choices. However, it is doubtful if modern elite football equals this idealist view. Elite football is not only a game; it is also a competitive performance following inherent structures of power and commerce.

Football has been criticized not only for being a mass media event but also for its sociopolitical, military and ideological issues concerning national identity (Law 2014, p. 30). International football games are unmistakeably similar in some ways to military battles: players have to strictly obey the rules of the game. A game is often mentally dominated by aggression and violence. Moreover, it is embedded in national rituals such as the waving of national flags or the singing of anthems or national football songs. International football games are both multimodal performances and qualified media products. They affect the audiences and they (re)produce, at the same time, particular antagonistic sociopolitical tensions between competing and cooperating groups and norms. Football games and political power struggles cannot be disconnected. No wonder that football is a common metaphor for war. It is not only applied to the Gulf War in 1991 but also to other ideological and cultural battles foregrounding antagonistic arguments.

A football performance as a qualified multimodal medium

Let us start by focusing on the complexity of a football game when it is performed in the material and the spatiotemporal modality of a stadium. When attending such a performance, we interact with (1) the materiality of the stadium, (2) the materiality of moving bodies and (3) the materiality of multiple integrated technical media of display. The latter dissolves the opposition between football as a live performance and as a media product.

The sociopolitical impact of the stadium

The stadium is not a container in which a football game, as an aesthetic media product, is materialized. Rather, as a technical medium of display, the stadium institutionalizes football by giving it an economic value and by conditioning the social gathering for the identity formation of football fans.

In general, the stadium creates a material borderline between the inside and the outside, between the football performance that promises a unified entity and the everyday reality outside. Similar to a theatre, the stadium seems to offer a self-referential performance, controlled by its own rules enclosed by the architectural frame. It invites the audience to immerse itself in the enchanting and meaningful acts of a symbolic world. This perspective allows us to analyse football with the Greek concept of *catharsis*. Traditionally, it promises a releasing and cleansing of the spectators' emotions or violent affects. However, this idealistic concept presumes a clear separation between the safe, ordered and meaningful play-world inside and the contradictory 'real life' outside.

Meanwhile, a modern stadium, such as the German football team Bayern München's Allianz Arena, is more than an architectural frame. The aesthetically designed roof over the stands offers not only a material shelter. Rather, it integrates many technical devices, such as the lighting, microphones and cameras; most of them invisibly for the spectators. This functional equipment strengthens the visual and acoustic details of the events for the spectators. However, it also gives an advantage to those who observe and control the movements on the stands, the pitch and the surroundings of the stadium. Moreover, the installed microphones foreground the typical soundscape of football, the cheering and whistling noises. This technically enhanced sound intensifies the fans' emotional involvement and guarantees the authenticity of the live game. However, the characteristic soundscape of fans is also added as an isolated component to so-called ghost games to improve those media representations of football games that are not played for real spectators. Technological devices can be used to manipulate or simulate the interactivity of the game.

Not only the soundscape but also the inner and outer safety fences strengthen a clear border between the closed world of a football game and the otherness of an open and unstable 'reality'. This antagonistic thinking between the inside play-world and the otherness of the life-world outside affirms the process of othering, that is, the difference between 'us' vs. 'them'. However, having in mind that all people experience the game and the world differently, it seems better to assume a 'pluralization of life-worlds' both inside and outside the stadium (Bausinger 2000, p. 56). Some act as fans, supporting one team or the other, and some are critical observers of both teams or just contemplate the aesthetics of the play.

The sociopolitical impact of the material and spatial organization of the stadium shapes the live experience of a football match. For instance, the stands at the goal ends, commonly called the Kop, are the cheapest places to watch a match because of their limited view. They are also the ones with the closest connection to the favoured team and their other fans. Thus, these seats support the feeling of identity with one group in competition with the fans of the other team. Already the term Kop introduces another popular war metaphor into the world of football (Odell 2019). It derives from the similarity between these fans and the soldiers that had lined up in front of the steep hill of Spion Kop in the Second Boer War (1899–1902) (Pakenham 1979).

The distinctive material and spatial organization of the spectators in the stadium produces social differences as the more distanced and seated stands are also more expensive. The sociopolitical aspect becomes even more recognizable when regarding the shifting organization of the stands in the historical context.

In 1989, a game in the overcrowded Hillsborough stadium became a total disaster,[13] in particular, due to the poorly organized policing. However, thereafter, all UK stadiums were reshaped into modern all-seater stadiums. This reduced the intensity attributed to the Kop but diversified also a former mostly male working class audience. It opens the stadium not only for women and children but gave also higher-ranking groups separated and comfortable seats of the VIP areas in the 'sky boxes' to see from above without being seen. On the other hand, the material–technological organization of space through barriers and fences now delimits the visitors' coordinated tactile movements (such as swaying and surging down the slope). The safety equipment of the stadium domesticates and disciplines human behaviour. and visitors can be tracked and observed. Seen from the view of the technological safety system, all visitors are considered to be 'rioters' (King 1998, p. 161).

The materiality of the body

During a football performance, bodies interact with other bodies in a spatio-temporal and sensorial experience and a constant meaning-making process. The body, as a basic medium, becomes a mode of production and is seen as an 'object' that transforms a place into a stage by acting and interacting with other bodies (see Chapter 7). Even a football performance constructs such a dynamic interplay between the bodies performing as subjects and objects both on the pitch and on the stands. Even for the intensive but limited time of the performance, football has some qualities of the theatre.

During a performance in a stadium or a theatre, bodies represent different roles. On the pitch, the players and the referee are actors who are performing their roles according to their specific function and spatial position on the pitch. They are 'goalkeepers', 'defenders', 'midfielders', attacking 'forwards', or 'strikers'. The fixed number of the dramatic actors matches that of the players. They are identified by their football kit, which is comparable to the ancient masks that used to be seen on the stage. The identity of the football club is symbolized by the emblem and colours on the kit, while the numbers are indexical signs pointing roughly to the player's position on the pitch.

The 'agon' of a competitive performance

When we compare a football performance with a theatrical performance further, we also immediately see differences, such as the relevance given to the basic medium of words. Traditionally, verbal signs are prioritized when qualifying cultural media products and meaning. However, the intermedial performance discourse foregrounds the multimodal potentiality of creating meaning. Therefore, it also explores the non-verbal staging of football and its agonistic or competitive structure (*agon* is a Greek term for struggle) as an aesthetic event. The analogy between football and theatre is based on this 'powerful communicative poetics' (Pyta 2015, p. 262), also known as *agon* aesthetic (Borge 2015).

In this case, the focus is on the structural similarities between the theatre with its staged aesthetic interaction (called *praxis*) and the football play as staged aesthetic performance on the pitch (called *agon praxis*). In theatre, the prot*ago*nist and the opponent, the ant*agon*ist, interact and push words and arguments in competitive dia*logo*ues back and forth (*logos* means both the word and the aesthetic of order). In football, the staged *agon praxis* intertwines the aesthetically interacting and competing bodies kicking and passing the ball into the opponent's goal. Thus, while the basic medium of the body organizes an *agon* performance, the beauty of composing an order (*logos*) that guarantees the aesthetic of the game is not restricted to words. Instead, the *order* of a performance is constituted by the presence of bodily actions following the invisible rules of the game during the performance of embodied meaning-making.

For instance, the football prot*agon*ist Zidane, representing masculinity, power, and tactical knowledge, can figure as a tragic hero when competing with his ant*agon*ist Materazzi.[14] Although Zidane intended his famous headbutt in 2006 as a punishment for Materazzi's verbal insult, this action was against the football rules. Zidane's tragic leaving of the pitch exemplifies the tragic *agon* aesthetic. Moreover, it implies also a competition between different rules and ethical codes of different time-spaces and cultural groups.

However, professional players, such as Zlatan, Beckham or Mbappé, can be regarded either as actors, heroes, protagonists or commodities. In any case, they are never private individuals. Rather, they always play at the front of the stage and brand themselves like movie stars and cultural icons. Football players are not any longer bound to a club by loyalty, but by money. Sold and purchased by different clubs, a football player is, like his kit, both a media platform for advertising and a commodity. Players increase their so-called transfer value not only through their success on the pitch but also through networking and mediatized discourses of sports journalism. Moreover, countless interviews on social media or TV, advertisements or fan discourses create dramatic narratives and myths. This discourse also intensifies the sociopolitical value attributed to specific players and football performances in capitalism.

The body of the '12th man': The audience

Despite the before-mentioned ghost-games, the atmosphere of a live football performance depends on the co-present audience. It participates as the so-called 12th man and creates the specific atmospheric tension between order and disorder in a stadium. As soon as you enter a stadium, you participate in the dynamic structure of a mutual and performative self-constitution: you choose a role such as critical observer, connoisseur, supporter, fan or ultra, and you participate as one of the multiple voices of an interactive communication. Some fans on the stands use their moving bodies as a basic medium to instigate group-based emotions. This affective communality often stipulates a rivalry and dissensus between different groups battling for the 'best' choreography. The multimodal fan performances consist of ritualized movements, such as cheering, handclapping, of instrumental and vocal sounds as well as of well-organized responding football chants. Thus, the noisy fan groups compete with the visual body performances of the players on the pitch. The specific atmosphere of a live performance affects the communication between the players and the spectators of which some groups so actively participate in the performance. This interplay creates the pluralization of life-worlds by shaping multiple sensual (rather than rational) meanings and emotions. In the social-relational situation in and outside the stadium, the performing players and the performing spectators elicit different forms of a mutually 'transformative aesthetic' (Fischer-Lichte 2008, p. 38), ending in an 'emotional repertoire' of social bonding and identity formation.

Football – Live performance and media product

All technical media devices and media of display change the social experience of the space where football is experienced. The impact of diverse media technologies, used by the organizers to broadcast the play and by the fans to communicate, subdues an important traditional opposition: that between the idealized *live* performance of football in a stadium as an *immediate* and ephemeral experience of presence on the one hand and the qualified media product on the other. Usually, the media product is linked with the idea that the football game is merely a representation of a game and produced by the recording and disseminating media technologies. Even outside the stadium, at home in front of the TV or at the pub, the viewer can still experience the stadium's noisy atmosphere, either alone or with their friends.

However, this view needs to be reconsidered. The transmitting media technology constitutes an important part of the live experience in a stadium. To emulate the mediated TV show, the stadium improves the affective sensation of football also by incorporating and combining modern technical media: mobile video walls shall overcome the visual limits of a fixed, distanced pitch in the stadium. They provide the spectators with close-ups of the players, with the shifting visual frames of the cameras, and repetitions of scores and fouls. While the fans and the players are co-present in the stadium, the fans in the stands also watch the players on screens in the etymological sense of television (*tele* meaning far and *visio* meaning sight). Thus, the mediating sight percieved via the eyeball is mixed with the mediated sight that is framed through technical media. Thus, the stadium's technological elements do not only enhance the immersive effect of an autonomous football world. Rather, the only partly visible technological devices can also control the performance and change its 'natural' sensual perception. The microphones in the roof, for instance, stipulate the sound of the fans and the ball to intensify the immersive effect but repress other phenomena that disturb the order and unity of the play-world. Important are the cameras and the video assistant referee (VAR) that distribute information merely to selected groups rather than to all visitors and thus illustrate the agency and social power of technical media in its encounter with humans. The collected data of the VAR – interpreted by experts in a command centre, an elevated separate zone of power in the stadium, and transferred to the referee's headset during the game – exclude not only the spectators from the information for his decision making. More important is the fact that measurable technological data collected from an 'objective' position in the sky is given priority over the human decision making in a game, performed by humans according to ethical rules.

In these moments, technological media transform the human subjects controlling the technical media and the human subjects performing both on the pitch and on the stands into hybrid subjects/objects. The technical data collection becomes agency and a resource of social power that affects the players, the coaches and the audience. Technological data that cannot be seen with the naked eyes now shape how humans shall experience and evaluate the live performance of the game in front of them. Using the sociopolitical modality, we can interrogate the social power given to the technological media infrastructure, deciding what counts as 'neutral' or 'objective' information. This materiality of knowing can be used either in opposition to or in accordance with a mutual dependence on humans' rights and their ethical values.

The commercialization of football

'Modern football is highly commodified – something to be bought and sold to consumers' (Bale 1998). The physical space of the modern stadium transformed the ideal 'flow of the game' into a 'flow of money'. Due also to the increased costs for advanced technological devices, broadcast rights were sold to public or private channels. As fans constantly practise a highly valued loyalty to their local club and its stadium, they are the ideal consumers or *fansumers* that produce reliable data for the advertisements visible on high-tech LED screens alongside the pitch. In the all-embracing experience economy of popular culture, this commercializing practice creates a synergetic relationship between football, leisure and consumerism. Rather than being merely a game, football is intersected with the sociopolitical rules of the neoliberal and globalized consumer culture. Thus, it has also an ideal symbolic surplus value as a commodity.

The embodied experience of a football performance is always bound to a place, a time and diverse technical media. However, also public places other than the stadium can become attractive spatiotemporal and material frames for football. Lately, public viewing events are popular public spaces where huge mobile video screens provide an open-air football experience for a community of enthusiastic spectators. They provide the feeling of presence and of *being there*, similar to an experience in a stadium, and dissolve the opposition between a performance and a media product. However, these events never deliver neutral audiovisual footage. Any broadcasting of a live football performance reconstructs, frames, enhances and comments on the game and the affective atmosphere of the stadium.

To conclude, the experience of immediacy and presence draws the feeling of authenticity from the collective experience of co-performing spectators rather than from the spatial and temporal closeness to the performing players.

Spatiotemporal modality: Perception of time frames and the space of the turf

We usually think that a game of football lasts for 90 minutes. However, if we look more closely, a football performance is staged in a relative rather than a fixed time frame. This time frame is set by the *Laws of the Game* (LOTG) and established by the referee. The referee directs the play with simple tools and symbolic signs of power. His or her body gestures and the sound of the whistle are audiovisual signs announcing the beginning and end of the playtime. The referee not only keeps the time but can add time for any unpredictable stoppage and two extra time slots of 15 minutes if a match has no winner at full time. Thus, the referee's position represents tension against the quantitatively measurable clock time, which is visually displayed in running numbers on digital screens. A football performance also makes us aware of the quality of time as an emotional resource; in particular, the last few minutes of the game or the extra time are periods of excitement. In an unexciting game, the quality of time is also negatively felt and made audible by the fans' sonic practice.

The space on the turf is outlined with several white lines, partly defining the surface of the playing field and dividing it into different zones. While these lines seem to limit the pitch to a two-dimensional surface field, the players' performances explore it as a three-dimensional stage: the players jump to attempt headers, for example. A particular use by Zlatan Ibrahimović of the third dimension of the pitch and the aerodynamics of a ball can be appreciated for its elegance and aesthetic: against all probability, he scored with his famous overhead kick, called a 'bicycle kick', in 2012.[15] The quality of time and space (*kairos*) and the player's body skills came together in a way that could not have been anticipated. In football, space is also closely linked to the time that players are in possession of the always-moving ball. The dribbling of the ball along the touchline of the pitch visualizes the different qualities of the space, as only the player, not the ball, is allowed to move outside the pitch, in between the pitch and the spectators. The value of this movement lies in the emotional closeness to the co-present audience, reinforcing their desire to 'play football together'.

So, multiple lines transform the pitch not only into a measurable space, distinct from the spectators, but also into different qualitative zones of intensity, such as the spaces close to the goal or the penalty area. Also, different tactical principles of creating and occupying space attribute special values to these zones. Often, the attacking team will spread out over the field to find an empty space in which to get a shot, while the defending team will strive to compress the space around the ball. Bayern München's player Thomas Müller is celebrated as the 'interpreter of space' because he can anticipate a qualitative time-space, *kairos*, fitting for a shot, and the right partner running into the right zone. Space, time, bodies and the ball create here a dynamic performative agency.

The large stadiums and the attention paid to international football also attract political protest performances that make the inherent social rules and the *Laws of the Game* visible by disturbing them. Such an unexpected performance was organized by the Russian group Pussy Riot, as three of their members invaded the pitch in the second half of the 2018 FIFA World Cup Final match between France and Croatia. Dressed up as police and thus representing legal authority, they demonstrated the rules and structure of power that only become visible when they are disturbed. In this sense, the antagonistic game inside the space equals the game and the invisible power rules outside the stadium, in particular, in the Russian authoritarian regime where the official Russian media channels neither showed nor commented on this interference. Instead, the Russian internet forums rapidly created supporter groups to disseminate the political message of this otherwise suppressed invasion. This resistant performance of Pussy Riot exemplifies the potentiality of the dissemination of diverse technical media. Moreover, it illuminates the invisible policing structure of international football and the potentiality of the antagonistic rhetoric of 'we' and 'them' inherent in the competitive football performance. These aspects can be explored when analysing the space, time, materiality and technology of football performances in the modern stadium by applying the sociopolitical modality.

Football as an intermedial performance: Concluding words

This chapter explored international football as a multimodal performance played in various contested (time) spaces. While football enfolds the traditional concepts of an antagonistic game into the broader intermedial concept of a qualified media product, the power structures, inherent in the material–technological modality of the stadium, modify the encounter of the football fans with the performing bodies of the players during the limited but dynamic time-space of a football game. Rather than regarding the stadium as a neutral container for the *live* performance, the material and technological aspects of the stadium actively organize the spaces along with the invisible but important *sociopolitical* power structures.

Notes

1. When we refer to the body in this chapter, we are referring to the performer's body but choose to use only the word 'body' to avoid making the text repetitive.
2. See the BBC website for a list of ten great songs that got away with nonsense: https://www.bbc.co.uk/music/articles/2d67dd79-7603-46ef-ba55-b46cd2884f8b (accessed 1 October 2021).
3. See Lydia Lunch's performance at: https://www.youtube.com/watch?v=gDvWrp xpJ8U (accessed 1 October 2021). We use the conventions of spoken word and call the performed text a poem.
4. How the performance is filmed makes it nearly impossible to observe the reactions of the audience. We therefore exclude audience reaction from the analysis, which will focus on Lydia Lunch as a performing body.

5 See Henry Rollins: https://www.youtube.com/watch?v=r3S-IuxseAI (accessed 1 October 2021).
6 There is a slight chance that Rollins reads the poem from a written version of it placed somewhere in front of him, but he had performed the poem frequently with his rock group Black Flag, so it is more likely that he knew it by heart.
7 Allen Ginsberg reads at the Royal Albert Hall in 1965 (the original clip withdrawn, this one shows the reading also, though): https://www.youtube.com/watch?v=JiQQ0DljjJ4 (accessed 1 October 2021)
8 It is hard to decide, but it seems as if the poets are reading from a protruding stage, because Ginsberg turns his face in different directions and gestures energetically in the same directions.
9 Her very modern reading has – paradoxically – ancient roots in the 'bard battles' of, for instance, the Celtic or Scandinavian traditions, where one kind of battle involved competing to see who could insult the other party the most harshly.
10 His partners were also poets. The mockery of concrete poetry was probably experienced as a threat to the dead serious Beat poets, who, even though they sometimes jest, clearly want to give the impression of being Poets.
11 When it comes to Rollins, it is hard to discern whether the light is natural or comes from another source, and Ginsberg stands on a stage that has ordinary stage lighting.
12 According to one comment, Peter Whitehead filmed the poetry-readings, but there are no indications about who edited the film, even though it was probably done by Whitehead too.
13 You can find a short introduction to the disaster in the short video titled *What happened at Hillsborough?* by BBC News. Available at https://www.youtube.com/watch?v=MNS26Oj9B4o (Accessed 1 October 2021). For more critical background information, see Pyta (2015).
14 You can see Zidane's headbutt, an aggressive reaction caused by Materazzi's offensive words about Zidane's mother or sister, here: https://www.youtube.com/watch?v=zAjWi663kXc (Accessed 1 October 2021).
15 You can see this famous bicycle kick here: *Zlatan Ibrahimovic's Famous 30-yard Bicycle Kick vs England*: https://www.youtube.com/watch?v=RM_5tJncHww (Accessed 1 October 2021). For more details about the performance of this skilled kick, see O'Brien (2005, p. 69).

Further reading

Agamben, Giorgio. 2018. *Karman: A brief treatise on action, guilt, and gesture*. Meridian, crossing aesthetics. Stanford: Stanford University Press.
Auslander, Philip. 2008 [1999]. *Liveness: Performance in a mediatized culture*. London/New York: Routledge.
Bal, Mieke. 2002. *Travelling concepts in the humanities: A rough guide*. Toronto: University of Toronto.
Barthes, Roland. 1981. *Le Grain de la voix: Entretiens (1962–1980)*. Paris: Gallimard.
Chapple, Freda and Kattenbelt, Chiel, eds. 2006. *Intermediality in theatre and performance*. Amsterdam: Rodopi.
Fischer-Lichte, Erika. 2008. *The transformative power of performance: A new aesthetics*. London: Routledge.
Frith, Simon. 2002 [1996]. *Performing rites: Evaluating popular music*. New York; Oxford: Oxford University Press.

Goldin-Meadow, Susan and Wagner Alibali, Martha. 2013. Gesture's role in speaking, learning, and creating language. *Annu. Rev. Psychol.*, 64, pp. 257–283. doi:10.1146/annurev-psych-113011–143802

Guérin, Michel. 2011 [1995]. *Philosophie du geste*. Arles: Actes sud.

Keevallik, Leelo and Richard Ogden. 2020. Sounds on the margins of language at the heart of interaction. *Research on Language and Social Interaction*, 53(1), pp. 1–18. doi:10.1080/08351813.2020.1712961

Kendon, Adam. 2004. *Gesture: Visible action as utterance*. Cambridge: Cambridge University Press.

Krämer, Sybille. 2014. Connecting performance and performativity. Does it work? In Laura Cull and Alica Lagaay, eds., *Encounters in performance philosophy*. Basingstoke: Palgrave Macmillan.

Velten, Hans Rudolf. 2016. Performativity and performance. In Birgit Neumann and Ansgar Nünning, eds., *Travelling concepts for the study of culture* (pp. 249–266). Berlin; Boston: de Gruyter.

References

Agamben, Giorgio. 2000 [1996]. *Means without end: Notes on politics*. Minneapolis: University of Minnesota Press.

Agamben, Giorgio. 2018. *Karman: A brief treatise on action, guilt, and gesture*. Meridian, crossing aesthetics. Stanford, California: Stanford University Press.

Auslander, Philip. 2008 [1999]. *Liveness: Performance in a mediatized culture*. London; New York: Routledge.

Austin, John Langshaw. 1962. *How to Do Things with Words*. Oxford: Clarendon.

Bäckström, Per. 2003. *Aska, Tomhet & Eld. Outsiderproblematiken hos Bruno K. Öijer*. Lund: Ellerström (diss.).

Bal, Mieke. 2002. *Travelling concepts in the humanities: A rough guide*. Toronto: Univiversity of Toronto.

Bale, John. 1998. Virtual fandoms: Futurescapes of football. In Adam Brown, ed., *Fanatics power, identity and fandom in football* (pp. 265–278). London: Routledge,.

Barthes, Roland. 1981. *Le Grain de la voix: Entretiens (1962–1980)*, Paris: Gallimard.

Bausinger, Hermann. 2000. Kleine Feste im Alltag: Zur Bedeutung des Fußballs. In Wolfgang Schlicht and Werner Lang, eds., *Über Fußball: Ein Lesebuch zur wichtigsten Nebensache der Welt*. Münster: Hofmann, pp. 42–58.

Borge, Steffen. 2015. An agon aesthetics of football. *Sport, Ethics and Philosophy*, 9(2), pp. 97–123.

Butler, Judith. 1990. *Gender trouble: Feminism and the subversion of identity*. New York: Routledge.

Chapple, Freda and Kattenbelt, Chiel, eds. 2006. *Intermediality in theatre and performance*. Amsterdam: Rodopi.

Derrida, Jacques. 1988 [1977]. Signature event context. In *Limited Inc* (pp. 1–24). Evanston: Northwestern University Press.

Dolan, Jill. 2005. *Utopia in performance: Finding hope at the theater*. Ann Arbor: University of Michigan Press.

Elleström, Lars. 2021. The modalities of media: A model for understanding intermedial relations. In Lars Elleström, ed., *Media borders*. Houndmills; New York: Palgrave Macmillan.

Fischer-Lichte, Erika. 2008. *The transformative power of performance: A new aesthetics*. London: Routledge.

Frith, Simon. 2002 [1996]. *Performing rites: Evaluating popular music*. New York; Oxford: Oxford University Press.

Glare, P.G.W. (red.) 1968. *Oxford Latin dictionary*. Oxford: Clarendon Press.

Goldin-Meadow, Susan and Wagner Alibali, Martha. 2013. Gesture's role in speaking, learning, and creating language. *Annu. Rev. Psychol.*, 64, pp. 257–283. doi:10.1146/annurev-psych-113011-143802

Guérin, Michel. 2011 [1995]. *Philosophie du geste*. Arles: Actes sud.

Huizinga, Johan H. 1949. *Homo ludens: A study of the play element in culture*. London, Boston and Henley: Routledge & Kegan Paul.

Kendon, Adam. 2004. *Gesture: Visible action as utterance*. Cambridge: Cambridge University Press.

Keevallik, Leelo and Ogden, Richard. 2020. Sounds on the margins of language at the heart of interaction. *Research on Language and Social Interaction*, 53(1), pp. 1–18, doi:10.1080/08351813.2020.1712961

King, Anthony. 1998. *The end of the terraces: The transformation of English football in the 1990s*, London: Leicester University Press.

Law, Alex. 2014. Playing with tension: National charisma and disgrace at Euro 2012. *Soccer & Society*, 15(2), pp. 203–221.

O'Brien, Richard. 2005. *The ultimate sports handbook*. Philadelphia: Quirk Books.

Odell, Joseph. 2019. The legend of 'Spion Kop'. *Tales of two halves*. https://taleoftwohalves.uk/featured/legend-spion-kop (Accessed 15 August 2020).

Pakenham, Thomas. 1979. *The Boer war*. New York: Random House.

Pyta, Wolfram. 2015. Football memory in a European perspective: The missing link in the European integration process. *Historical Social Research/Historische Sozialforschung*, 40(4), pp. 255–269.

Velten, Hans Rudolf. 2016. Performativity and performance. In Birgit Neumann and Ansgar Nünning, eds., *Travelling concepts for the study of culture* (pp. 249–266). Berlin; Boston: de Gruyter.

Werron, Tobias. 2015. How are football games remembered? Idioms of memory in modern football. In Wolfram Pyta and N. Havemann, eds., *European football and collective memory* (pp. 18–39). Basingstoke: Palgrave.

Yeats, William Butler. 1996. *The collected poems of William Butler Yeats*. Richard J. Finneran, ed. New York: Scribner.

13 Truthfulness and truth claims as transmedial phenomena

Jørgen Bruhn, Niklas Salmose, Beate Schirrmacher and Emma Tornborg

Emmanuel Levinas (1906–1995), a French philosopher, argued that the human face has a direct connection to the ethical dignity of individuals, thus theorizing a widespread idea. Face recognition is already evident in newborn infants; we learn, very early, to 'trust' a face. Face perception not only relates us to and communicates with friends, families and foes but plays an extraordinary role in our interpretation of our social role. Cultural practices may change how we perceive faces, which has been conspicuous in recent debates about the wearing of niqabs to the requirement to wear a face mask in certain situations. The important bond between individual assurance and face recognition can be temporarily disturbed, as evidenced by the widespread use of masks and the unsettling, distorted faces often seen in horror films.

Nevertheless, until recently, faces have been fairly stable and convincing entities in a rapidly changing and fragmented world. Human faces – which we are used to rely upon and to trust – suddenly seem to be malleable, changeable. AI and advanced image-processing techniques have radically changed this. We can no longer trust a face. Faces are altered in films: dead actors are seen acting in blockbusters, old actors become young (as in Martin Scorsese's *The Irishman*) and AI-driven face apps redesign our faces. A machine operated by artificial intelligence can create faces that we do not recognize as fake. So-called deep fakes not only create fake news but fake events, fictional events that never took place. The digital face determinedly questions what is real – what is truthful.

By way of the terminology suggested in this chapter, we advocate that these changes to a human face are so utterly disturbing because in our everyday life we perceive the human face to have very strong *truth claims*: based on earlier experiences and cultural contexts, we connect a face to a person and to their identity and intentions. If we sense that there is a risk that the nature of a human face is fake, this puts at risk the perceived *truthfulness* of several central psychosocial aspects of everyday life. The fact that we recognize people, that we trust what these particular people say, that we interpret their feelings and attitudes through facial expressions and that we can rely upon their identity, creates strong bonds that are violated through their loss of truthfulness. We realize with sudden despair the potential risk of a lacuna being created between what is being said and who, or even *what*, is stating it.

DOI: 10.4324/9781003174288-16

This question of when and how we can trust a face is part of a larger problem. A general agreement on how and under which circumstances we can trust a face, a news article, a photograph, a film appears to have gone missing. Information society appears to have turned into a disinformation society, which actualizes the question of when, how and why we know that mediated information is true? This chapter addresses this sense of loss of reliability by exploring the concepts of truth claims and truthfulness across media.

We understand *truthfulness*, in the most general sense, as a reliable representation of the world around us: the social world as well as the physical world. The concept of *truth claims* refers to the reasons why we should trust a media product.

Together, these concepts enable us to describe how we perceive a particular media product to be truthful and what kind of knowledge of the world we derive from it. News or novels, poetry or scientific articles can be truthful to different aspects of the world around us and we derive different forms of knowledge from each media type. Truthfulness is a transmedial notion and when we speak of truth in different contexts, we refer to different kinds of knowledge.

Therefore, instead of speaking of 'post-truth' and 'alternative facts', and of telling facts from fiction, we use the concepts of truth claims and truthfulness to be more specific about our expectations of truth in different contexts. In the digital age, where different forms of information, narratives and ideas more easily than ever spread between different media types, we can map how different particular media products contribute to our knowledge of the world.

We begin this chapter by exploring different relations of truthfulness and discuss the truth claims of the different qualified media types. Discussing the truthfulness of fiction, we illustrate how the concept helps to get beyond troubled binaries like fact and fiction. We demonstrate how different qualified media types of popular science communication (Rachel Carson's *Silent Spring*), ecopoetry (in particular Swedish poet Jonas Gren), mainstream Hollywood film (*The Day After Tomorrow*) construct different truthful relations to scientific knowledge. Finally, we discuss how different forms of disinformation draw on the truth claims of news media and construct a perception of truthfulness that is based more on internal coherence than on events that actually have taken place.

Truth, facts, authenticity, fiction and truthfulness

In a way, truthfulness has been a perennial question throughout the history of media, whether in the form of a general media distrust (just think about Plato's discussions about whether writing could be trusted as compared to face-to-face speech), or a critical media stance that points out how media construct what they communicate. Questions of truthful media transformation have been discussed, for instance, within a discourse of authenticity (Enli 2015). Particular truth claims have been discussed in relation to specific qualified media types, like truth claims of photography (Gunning 2004), or the construction of journalistic authority (Carlson 2017). From an intermedial perspective, however, we want to pursue truth claims and truthfulness as exemplified in a variety of media types.

Describing, analysing and comparing truthfulness as a transmedial phenomenon both broadens the field of research and at the same time makes it more specific, so let us briefly point out how a transmedial approach to truthfulness in media can be used to clarify our understanding of related concepts like truth, facts, authenticity and fiction. Truth, facts and authenticity are often used in everyday discourse as part of apparently clear-cut binaries like truth–lie, authentic–fake, fact–fiction. However, in different contexts, these concepts are used differently according to different truth claims and refer to truthful relations to different aspects of the world, to experience, to events, to emotions, or to coherence between events. With the transmedial concepts of truth claims and truthfulness we can better describe and compare which elements in a media product respond to the truth claims of a particular media type.

The concept of truth, for instance, is not only relevant in philosophy, as the inherent logical truth of a specific philosophical proposition. When we speak of truth in religious, literary, scientific, legal and news media contexts the concept is based on different aspects of truthfulness. Another term relevant in this context, objectivity, connects to the production of 'facts', of something that has an actual existence. Objectivity as a working method is often connected to the analytical methods of the natural sciences. Objectivity in that context means that similar experiments that are repeated at different times and in different spaces would produce identical, and thus 'objective', data or results. In other disciplines and professions, different working methods are used for the same aim, to gain objective results. In addition, not everything that someone speaks of as 'a fact' does have actual existence and instead is merely *presented* as having an objective reality.

Questions of truthfulness have been discussed in tandem with the concept of authenticity. However, depending on whether we speak of a historical object, a piece of art, a person, or a commodity, authenticity refers to different relations (see Box 16.3), for instance, as a truthful representation of an original, as a truthful representation of inner feelings, or the promise of the natural in a customized product. Authenticity always constructs an experience of immediacy that is constructed in communication and it often implicates an interaction between different truthful relations that need to be differentiated. Finally, truthfulness and truth claims help to describe the difference between fictive and factual narratives. Instead of trying to differentiate between the concepts of fiction and non-fiction, we can differentiate how a news article is expected to relate truthfully to an actual event, and the fictive events of a fantasy novel can be a truthful representation of causes and effects we recognize from our actual world: that might actually be one of the reasons the reason why we read fiction!

The truth claims of media

Media products give us access to what we do not know from our own direct experience. In order to gain knowledge from media products, we have to trust the sources. When we read books, journals or newspapers, watch television news or google a question, we trust the testimony of the experience of others. According to media philosopher John Durham Peters, media is 'a means by which experience is supplied to others who lack the original' (Peters 2001, p. 709). When we elicit knowledge from media products, we trust the people involved in its production. Every qualified medium is framed by a set of gatekeeping acts through which a media product gains credibility. A printed novel in a bookshop confirms that the author, the editors at the publishing house and the owners of the bookshop all consider the story in the novel relevant and important enough to be published and sold. Every professional film affirms the collective belief in the project, ranging from that of the film directors, cinematographers, editors and producers to its distributors. A scientific article confirms the relevant evaluation and critique of the findings of the study produced by the authors, peer-reviewers and editors. Implicitly, each and every media product contains a warranty, or a guarantee that specific acts have been carried out. When we respond to the truth claims of a media product, we rely on knowledge about the qualifying aspects of context and convention, and we try to confirm what kinds of acts are involved in creating this particular media product.

This means that the truth claims of media relate to our knowledge about the production process. All media convey truth claims based on their materiality (Gunning 2004). These truth claims are seldom made explicit. Implicitly they provide the reasons for what kind of truthfulness the audience can expect. For example, generally we say that a photo is an indexical sign or even proof that somebody was actually at the place where the photo was taken. This is based on the materiality of photography: by 'taking a picture' at a certain place and time, a person has opened a camera's lens and thus let light in and, if it is an analogue camera, made an imprint on camera film that can later on be developed and turned into a photo. The truth claim of photography, therefore, is that 'someone was there' and was able to see and capture something in front of the camera. The problem is that a fake media product, a photoshopped image or a deep-fake, makes this claim too. A fake photograph is produced with the aim to convince the audience of the actual existence of something or somebody at a particular time and place. The history of photography, from its beginning as analogue technology to the present digital age, has therefore constantly been haunted by the risk that its truthfulness can be undermined. Hence, one of the first lessons to learn is that the general truth claims of a qualified media type are not a guarantee that each media product is truthful.

Truth claims are not only based on the production processes but also on the material qualities of the basic media types. For instance, Tom Gunning stresses how the detailed iconicity of photographic images makes it look so similar to what is represented, that the level of detail provides a truth claim in itself

(Gunning 2004, p. 45). Similarly, the characteristic layout of text and image of newspapers provides a truth claim because we normally associate newspapers with reliable information (Carlson 2017, pp. 50–93). Fakes draw on the material characteristics of basic media types without being grounded in the actual production process.

Truth claims and qualified media types

Different media types are associated with different kinds of truth claims depending on their qualified properties, which is the historical, operational, aesthetical aspects of the medium (Elleström 2021). We ascribe greater credibility to a scientific article than to a poem when it comes to factual, scientific matters, just as we would rather trust a televised news programme than an avant-garde theatre performance to get an accurate weather report. On the other hand, we do not expect any deeper revelations about the human condition in the daily weather forecast, but that is often what we look for in avant-garde art. We do this because it is the contract we have with these types of media and their qualifying aspects. However, we constantly renegotiate our relationship with media. For example, not everything that looks like news is credible, and the privileged authority that news media has to tell truthful stories about actual events is no longer uncontested (Carlson 2017). This has caused disturbances within news communities on a global scale, and the mistrust and lack of agreement about what can be a credible source of information cause conflicts between groups as well as between individuals. For instance, during the COVID-19 pandemic, the practice of academic peer-reviewing has been at the forefront of news when discussing the eligibility of scientific publications on the virus. Some of these reports have been rejected since they have not had time to undergo the important scientific scrutiny of an academic peer-review process. Hence, the discussion of the most recent scientific publications on the virus acquainted even the non-academic public with peer-reviewing as a qualifying aspect of a scientific report that contributes to the truth claims of scientific communication.

Perception of truthfulness

Specific media characteristics convey certain truth claims that contribute to how and when we perceive communication to be truthful. The truth claims of media can be employed in communication to produce a *perception of truthfulness*. Our perception of truthfulness is the subjective evaluation of the truth claims and it can be manipulated.

This evaluation can connect to different aspects of a media product. A media product can be experienced as truthful in relation to the social and physical world. It can also be evaluated as truthful in the way it represents inner experiences, or complex connections. When we say something is 'true', this is in fact a short cut for saying, 'I perceive this as being a truthful representation of something' and thereby accepting the truth claims conveyed by the media product. When we accept a media product as 'true', we perceive it as truthful in relation to either external perception or inner experience.

Objective and subjective truth claims

As media products can be truthful both in relation to external perception or inner experience, another way to look at truth claims is to divide them into objective and subjective truth claims. Objective truth claims relate to existing objects and events, whereas subjective truth claims are related to cognitive and affective states. And these two kinds of truth claims are not only opposed to but also dependent on each other.

Georgia Christinidis (2013) argues that subjective truth claims concern subjective responses to an exterior world. She states that 'the choice to sincerely represent one's subjective reaction to outside events can be termed "authentic"' and uses authenticity 'to designate the fictional representation of subjective responses to external events' (p. 35).

Emma Tornborg divides objective truth claims into two categories: those *in* a media product and those *with* a media product. A truth claim made *in* a media product is manifested in the specific media characteristics in the modalities of a particular media type. A truth claim made *with* a media type, as Tornborg (2019) argues, is a 'result of a negotiation between audience and media form: certain types of media have a high number of objective truth claims because we historically associate them with a high degree of factuality [...] This association is based on earlier experiences of that media type' (p. 241). A manipulated photograph or a deep-fake video rhetorically makes a truth claim with a media type to convince its audience of the existence of events that never took place.

This suggests that there are two different aspects to take into consideration when analysing truth claims from an intermedial perspective: specific media characteristics of the media product and qualifying aspects of media. Based on both media characteristics and conventions, certain kinds of media products have traditionally been believed to be more apt to communicate objective truth claims, such as a photographic image, a recorded voice or a scientific figure.

By describing the interaction between truth claims and truthfulness, we can start to understand better the clash of different and conflicting 'truths' in contemporary public (and private) debates. In the following, we map different possibilities to establish truthful relations to different aspects of communication. We discuss how truth claims connect to the conventions of qualifying media types, truth claims that relate to external perception and subjective experience, and how truth claims connect to different acts of indexical relations. What happens to truth claims in transmedial communication?

Truthfulness as a transmedial phenomenon

Media scholar Gunn Enli (2015) has stressed that the question of reliable communication must be seen as part of the 'communicative relation between producers and audiences' (p. 1), and she argues that we must see authenticity and truthfulness as 'a social construction' which 'traffics in representations of reality' (p. 1).[1] Truthfulness, then, is part of the communicative context of senders and receivers; it relates to evaluations in its relation to reality – and it is mediated. Truthfulness can be understood as a contract between sender and receiver. When discussing truthfulness in mediation, we have to consider the specific truth claims that are in play and that are conditioned by the production process and media characteristics of each specific media type. But how are aspects of truthfulness transmediated between different qualified media where different truth claims are at work?

To transfer the objective results of a scientific journal article from the media type of a scientific journal article to a climate-fiction novel is in several ways comparable to how aspects of a Jane Austen novel are transmediated into a film. In the studies of film adaptation, the concept of 'fidelity' (as discussed in Chapter 9) is often a rather conservative and not very productive demand. In film adaptation, part of the pleasure 'comes simply from repetition with variation, from the comfort of ritual combined with the piquancy of surprise' (Hutcheon 2006, p. 4). This is different regarding media transformations where truthfulness to external perception is central: we don't want the news journalist reporting from a war zone or witnesses giving evidence in court to be too 'creative' or subjective; we are expecting them to relate what happened rather than to tell a good and creative story.

If we want to explore transmedial aspects of truthfulness, we have to keep in mind that we establish different forms of truthfulness in different media contexts. If we want to explore, for instance, how the plot of a climate-fiction (cli-fi) novel is truthful to the results of a scientific report this will be different to the way a news report is truthful to actual recent events: this is because different forms of (objective and subjective) truth claims are made in literature and news media

Truthfulness and indexicality

For a methodological investigation of how truthfulness is actually established *by* communication, Ellestrӧm (2018) discusses how what we call objective and subjective truth claims create different forms of indexical relations. The indexical sign points beyond itself, to the actual existence of something or someone, and like the footprint marks that somebody has been present. Elements in communication can point towards the existence of external objects but also to the inner experience, emotions, or beliefs and thus affirm the relevance of world views.

But indexical signs can also point towards the existence of other signs and provide coherence. As a heuristic short cut, confirmation bias makes us believe that something is true because it aligns with what we already know, or what usually tends to be true. In languages, indices like pronouns point towards names and nouns and thus provide coherence in an utterance. When we perceive something as 'true', it is not only about facts, evidence and the perception of the world. In order to accept something as true it has to make sense to us as well, to be presented in a way to provide understanding and coherence. Relations of truthfulness in communication, cannot sufficiently be explored by trying to determine whether it is fact or fiction, authentic or fake, truth or lie. Instead, Elleström suggests, we have to describe different relations between external truthfulness and internal coherence.

The grounding of communication in the experience of the world, and the creation of understanding by coherence thus interact both when we read a cli-fi novel or a fantasy novel, a news article, a poem or a scientific report, but in different ways.

The truthfulness of fiction

The concepts we have described more generally above also help to describe the truthfulness of fiction in a more nuanced way.

The debate of the truth of fiction is a perennial question. Plato (428–348 BCE) suggests that poets cannot be truthful, since they are merely imitating or making copies of the real True ideas, which places them far from the truth of the ideal forms. Even though we do not believe in the ideal forms, the very term 'fiction', from Latin *fingere*, 'to form', refers to something that is 'put together' (*ficta est*). Fiction is constructed and thus appears opposed to objects of the social world that exist. Hence, the suspicion that poetry or fiction are not truthful remains. As philosopher Emar Maier points out:

> [T]he idea that both lying and fiction are just assertions of known falsehoods can be traced back to eminent philosophers such as Plato, who wanted to ban poets from his ideal society, David Hume who called them 'liars by profession', and Albert Camus who wrote that 'fiction is the lie through which we tell the truth'. It is apparent today in the common usage of fiction-related phrases such as 'story', 'pretend' and 'made up' to characterise lying.
>
> (Maier 2020, n.p.)

Traces of this line of thought, that fiction is not 'really true', are especially visible at the time of writing, when 'based on a true story' is a successful marketing phrase and a reason why this particular story matters and autobiographies by celebrities or people who have experienced unusual things are extremely popular. Research has shown that many high school students prefer this mix between fact and fiction – 'faction' – to regular fiction, because they do not see the point of reading about events that did not happen in real life.

Still, fiction time and again appears as a role model for real events. As already Aristotle (384–22 BCE), a pupil of Plato, pointed out in his *Poetics*, fiction should tell stories of what may happen and what is possible; we could say that fiction should relate truthfully to the law of probability or necessity. However, the boundary between real events and fiction seems to have become blurrier than ever in the late twentieth and early twenty-first centuries. People, for example, compared the 9/11 bombings in Manhattan 2001 with images from the film *Independence Day* from 1996. New technologies in photo and video imaging and processing have undermined the conventional notion that *the camera never lies*. This is not a totally new phenomenon, of course; the infamous 1917 series of five photos of 'fairies' called the *Cottingley Fairies*, assumed to have been taken by two young cousins in England, fooled a whole generation, including the author of *Sherlock Holmes*, Conan Doyle. The fraud was finally uncovered in the 1980s when reports noted that the fairies were identical to similar creatures in *Princess Mary's Gift Book* from 1914. The reason this hoax was so convincing was because it was a truth claim made with a media type – the analogue photograph – which was considered the most trustworthy media type at the time because of its supposedly steadfast indexicality, that is, analogue photos' 'real connection' to reality.

Fiction and science

While fiction lands in between what is 'true' and 'made up', another tricky question is to position fiction in relation to science. How can one compare a novel and a scientific article? The novel tells a made-up story and a scientific article tells facts, or so it seems. Yet, both a novelist and a scientist connect events and construct a narrative. The difference is that the truth claims of a novel do not entail that the events have taken place. The truth claims of a scientific article are based on observations of real events. Nevertheless, we can productively approach the differences between fictive discourse and discourse representing scientific facts. Philosopher Paul Ricœur (1985), claims that scientific and poetic speech are different solutions to the same problem, the ambiguity of language:

> At one extremity of the possible range of solutions, we have scientific language, which can be defined as a strategy of discourse that seeks systematically to eliminate ambiguity. At the other extremity lies poetic language, which proceeds from the inverse choice, namely to preserve ambiguity in order to have it express rare, new, unique […] experiences.
>
> (p. 63)

Although Ricœur is referring to poetic speech, a similar parallel can be drawn to formal and representational elements of fiction in all media. While scientific discourse focuses on a truthful representation of events that can be confirmed in external perception, poetic and aesthetic discourse involves truthful representations of inner experience, a truthful response to the world and its many ambiguities. Truthful representations of the ambiguity of the world, are not only restricted to poetic language in fiction, but can be found in many qualified media types, via music in film or material in sculpture. The issue of ambiguity is thus central to Ricœur's work, as he claims that 'scientific statements have an empirically verifiable meaning. Poetry, however, is not verifiable' (p. 68). Hence, scientific truth claims, according to Ricœur are preferably connected to media types that use representations that are provable, or at least give the impression that they are provable. Scientific truth claims tend to be objective, while aesthetic truth claims often operate in both objective and subjective domains. Where science attempts to bring order in a complex world, the poetic truth of aesthetic communication in itself captures the complexities of an ambiguous reality.

Objective truth claims and internal coherence

Fact and fiction have mostly been discussed from the viewpoint of truthfulness through questions like *Is this work of art convincing?* Truthfulness then relates to the degree that plot, setting and characterization feel authentic – what we called 'internal coherence' earlier, in Aristotle's terms, the events appear probable and necessary. This kind of truthfulness in relation to coherence and probability has therefore been given precedence over facts and documentary accuracy. Some fictional aspects can be considered important for fiction's truth claims. So-called metaleptic elements, such as a pronounced awareness of the fiction's own form and fictional constructions, signal a critical and ironic approach to fiction which in turn simulates objectivity and grants fiction a sense of sincerity and critical openness. This is evident in much postmodern fiction, in film and literature alike, where the very construction of fiction is stressed for the benefit of a 'suspension of disbelief' (the poet Samuel Coleridge's definition of fictive imaging, from the early nineteenth century). In the opening sequence of Jean-Luc Godard's 1963 film *Le Mépris* (1963), we experience a long take with a movie camera on tracks coming towards us and following Brigitte Bardot, the female lead in the film. The sequence is accompanied by a voice informing us about the credits of the film, and the take ends with the camera turning towards the audience. This opening sequence clearly defines fiction as something constructed and made up, not a depiction of reality, which opens up a critical analysis of what film and fiction are. This is a critical perspective that is, paradoxically, similar to a scientific investigation.

Different genres, or qualified submedia, function as taxonomies of truth claims. Horror films, for example, are generally considered less truthful regarding the external reality than realist fiction. Unfortunately, such divisions are rather superficial, since science fiction films and horror films of the 1950s – to take two of many possible examples – were closer to scientific discourse and concerns than traditional Hollywood cinema at the time. In the end, truthfulness is all about gaining the audience's trust in terms of the audience being able to believe that the film is true; this creates a contract between producer and consumer that assures authenticity and truthfulness even if this turns out to be a highly subjective truth claim. And in the terminology of this chapter, it is about producing a number of truth claims in each media product that add up to a conviction that there is (more or less) truthfulness in relation to certain specific questions.

The different focuses on the perception of objective or subjective truth claims are perhaps the most essential differences between a scientific and a fictive discourse. While a media product communicating the results of natural science, or historic research, predominantly strives to convince the audience of its objective, quantifiable truth, a work of fiction is about immersion and subjective affective experience. Consider, for instance, the difference between reading the entry on WWI in the *Encyclopaedia Britannica* and reading *All Quiet on the Western Front*, published in 1929, by Erich Maria Remarque. The former deals in facts, whereas the latter is all about being submerged into the interiority of events and experiences from the WWI trenches. Facts are void of experience, but experience is anchored in facts that can be perceived by many. This is one of the major appeals of fiction.

Perhaps a better approach to understanding the truthfulness of fictive narratives is how objective truth claims of actual events and internal coherence blend into either mixed media products or mixed qualified media types. Literary auto-fiction is becoming increasingly popular, since the autobiography denotes truthfulness both to an external reality and to the inner psychological life of the writer. Or, to put it another way, the connection between the author and the content is understood as direct and explicit: it feels 'honest'.

We find a comparable but not identical constellation of fiction and truthfulness in cinema. The documentary film, for instance, has long held a status as truthful and authentic, beginning with Robert Flaherty's *Nanook of the North* (1922). The cinematic truth claims consist in the apparent objectivity and in the depiction of close-up experiences of the life of Inuit people; these aspects convinced the audiences that this is a truthful account of Nanook and his family in the Canadian Arctic, almost as if they were not aware that there was a camera filming at all. However, it later became known that this film was highly staged and almost directed, not unlike a traditional drama film. So although truth claims are made in *Nanook*, the film is not based on but is emptied of real indexical relations. In fact, it is what we would call a docudrama today. Nevertheless, the aesthetics of *Nanook* – fake or not – were successful and separated it from more traditional fiction films, so it became a standard for a 'realistic' filmmaking tradition that could be seen in Italian neorealism and the French New Wave in the 1940s to the 1960s. Later on, these modernist genres in their turn inspired a tradition of documentary and fiction films that operated with truth claims that aimed at producing a truthful impression: long takes, avoidance of spectacular camera angles, framings and perspectives, diegetic sound only, use of amateurs (in fiction films), and so on. The Danish Dogma manifesto from 1995 resembles these cinematic truth claims.

Truth claims of media, truthful representation in media products and understanding the way different media products convey knowledge, are not only of theoretical interest. Urgent societal challenges like the climate crisis and the spreading of disinformation put questions of truthful communication at centre stage. In the following, we demonstrate how intermedial analysis provides the tools to approach the complex communication crisis of the twenty-first century.

Truth claims in climate fiction

The climate crisis is the most critical encounter that humans have ever faced, and hence communication between science and global populations (including politicians) is of the utmost importance. But the overwhelming and in fact quite unusual consensus among the scientific community that the climate crisis is a fact and that it is caused by human action does not have a sufficiently wide reach. In polarized public debates, climate change is still not accepted as a fact but is contested. It is clouded by and questioned by discourses of fake news, accused of being left-wing alarmist propaganda and, perhaps most importantly, stalled by the very medial qualities of scientific documentation and reporting. The words of scientist Gus Speth (2014) went viral when he claimed:

> I used to think that top environmental problems were biodiversity loss, ecosystem collapse and climate change. I thought that thirty years of good science could address these problems. I was wrong. The top environmental problems are selfishness, greed and apathy, and to deal with these we need a cultural and spiritual transformation. And we scientists don't know how to do that.

Speth's wording echoes the analysis of environmental problems and representations that fall under the broad category of ecocriticism. Greg Garrard (2012) defines ecocriticism as 'the study of the relationship between the human and the non-human, throughout human history and entailing critical analysis of the term "human" itself' (p. 5). While originally ecocriticism focused on literary representations (Clark 2015), today it includes analyses of other aesthetic practices and media types. This 'cultural and spiritual' transformation is closely connected to concepts of agency. Ecofeminist Val Plumwood (2002) has addressed the acute situation of humanity and the need to renegotiate the traditional narratives of the Western world. This need for redemption is often referred to as 'the crisis of humanity'. 'If our species does not survive the ecological crisis', writes Plumwood, in an attempt to encourage environmental activism,

> it will probably be due to our failure to imagine and work out new ways to live with the earth, to rework ourselves and our high energy, high consumption, and hyperinstrumental societies adaptively [...] We will go onwards in a different mode of humanity or not at all.
>
> (p. 1)

Plumwood, thus, identifies the crucial importance of agency in ecological discourse, and the concept of agency becomes essential when discussing the Anthropocene through media. Scientific discourse includes high-level truth claims by way of its claim that it is based on objective perceptions, but it scores low for representations of how individual human agency may act upon the threats. Scientific truths about our climate therefore need to be transformed into a media type with better prospects when it comes to agency: literary and cinematic fiction are exactly such media types.

The usual definition of climate fiction, often called cli-fi, is fiction that represents the consequences of man-made climate change and global warming (for a broad overview, see Goodbody and Johns-Putra 2019). This definition can be seen as too limited, since there are climate phenomena that are not only man-made conditions but caused by volcanic eruptions, plate tectonics and solar radiation. We can now encounter the climate crisis in a variety of media: films, documentaries, news reports, activist happenings or protests, novels, poems, art exhibitions, games and popular science, some of which would fall into the cli-fi category. Thus, the climate crisis is a transmedial phenomenon; it is not restricted to the media of natural sciences but is transformed from the media of traditional science into many other media types. It is, however, as Tornborg (2019) writes, 'not a case of a transmediation from one specific source to one specific target. Instead, it is factual media concerning anthropogenic issues in general that constitute the source' (p. 235).

If the goal of transmediations of climate change is to keep these new forms close to a certain scientific truth, a media type conventionally connected to solid claims of truth communication should be the most suitable format: examples of this could be different genres of film and literature such as docufiction, docudrama, pure documentary or realist fiction. This idea would, however, be strongly rejected by critics such as Amitav Ghosh. Ghosh (2016) offers a harsh criticism of bourgeois literature in *The Great Derangement: Climate Change and the Unthinkable*, in which he reads the literary tradition of 'realism' as intertwined with the concept of probability and thus not a suitable candidate for representing or mediating anything out of the ordinary, such as extraterrestrials, unknown monsters or extraordinary aspects of humanity, which would destabilize relations between humans and nature. Weird climate phenomena caused by climate change would in our current historical situation, ironically, be part of such 'weird' content (pp. 16–17). 'Here, then', writes Ghosh, 'is the irony of the "realist" novel: the very gestures with which it conjured up reality are actually a concealment of the real' (p. 23). Instead, Ghosh is in favour of a literature that captures the uncanny, such as the strangeness of the familiarity of rain with a dash of toxic waste, since the images of climate change are 'too powerful, too grotesque, too dangerous, and too accusatory to be written about in a lyrical, or elegiac, or romantic vein' (pp. 32–3) – and even the conventional 'realist' model would not, Ghosh argues, be able to capture the experience of the weirdness of the environmentally deranged and changed planet. It took a partly scientific, partly literary text to be able to deal with the weird new nature: *Silent Spring* by Rachel Carson (2002).

Silent Spring: *Popularizing science by way of narrative*

The publication of *Silent Spring* in September 1962 sparked a national debate in the US on the use of chemical pesticides. When the author and marine biologist Rachel Carson died 18 months later in the spring of 1964, she had set in motion a course of events that would result in a ban of the domestic production of DDT and the creation of a grassroots movement demanding protection of the environment through state and federal regulation. The success of *Silent Spring* was due to its careful balance in communicating scientific facts in a hitherto popular way, stimulating human agency around environmental issues among the public as well as the US authorities.

Silent Spring is a work of popular science narrative, and as such a work of blended genres and a mixture of truth claims based on scientific observations from the institution of the natural sciences: these produce a specific truthfulness that is characteristic of this media type of popular science. Carson borrowed formal and generic ideas from science fiction and fairy tales and incorporated them into her book, merging discourses of science and popular communication. The term *popular science* does not suggest a particular technical or basic medium; popular science can be communicated by a textbook, a podcast, a film or, less often, a dance. The qualified aspects cannot be specified very precisely either: popular scientific narratives can be presented through fiction film, documentary, experimental film, and so on. In other words, popular science narratives constitute a rather broad genre, squashed in between journalism and literature and characterized by a certain medial homelessness. Genre definitions seem to unfold within the qualified aspects of media without being media-specific, since popular science has a well-defined aesthetic history and formal structure.

The *popular* in popular science narratives suggests a departure from the customary scientific practices and conventional claims, meaning that every scientist tends to operate on their own without necessarily needing a proper understanding of, or desire to comprehend, how their findings are situated in a larger framework. Carson, writing in the early 1960s, criticizes what she understood to be increasing compartmentalization and states that '[t]his is an era of specialists, each of whom sees his own problem and is unaware of or intolerant of the larger frame into which it fits' (p. 13). And, according to Linda Lear in her introduction to the new edition of *Silent Spring*, in Carson's view 'the postwar culture of science that arrogantly claimed domination over nature was the philosophical root of the problem. Human beings, she insisted, were not in control of nature but simply one of its parts' (p. xviii). This statement foregrounds the most essential issue in recent ecocriticism, namely human interaction with nature, and is further echoed in Carson's belief in the ecology of the human body, which was a major departure at the time in the thinking about the relationship between humans and the natural environment. Popular, diverse media such as book reviews, speeches and TV 'allowed journalists to cover the pesticide debate not as a complex scientific *issue* but as a series of *events*' (Parks 2017, p. 1218), and this pays tribute to the intermedial aspect of *Silent Spring*'s aftermath, which created a clear boundary with monomedial scientific discourse.

The popularization of the originally scientific knowledge about DDT, the first modern, mass-produced synthetic insecticide, is evident in the formal aspects of the essays collected in *Silent Spring*. First, the chapters are structured according to a dramaturgy defined in the theory of drama; we can identify the inciting incident, 'Elixirs of Death', the rising action, 'Rivers of Death', the climax, 'Nature Fights Back', and the denouement, 'The Other Road'.

Second, most of these titles imply the literary submedium rather than the scientific one; 'The Other Road', for example, alludes to the famous poem 'The Road Not Taken' (1915) by American poet Robert Frost, which discusses the choices we have as human beings. The transmediation of a literary style in a scientific work grants it something that science denounces: the improbable, the unknown and the mysterious that are involved in human interaction with scientific facts. This intertext of Frost's poem, common knowledge at least for citizens of the US at the time, opens up conceivable solutions to the threat the book discusses. Hence, it situates the book in a historical and cultural context, as well as a literary one, that goes beyond science into the very deepest emotional and individual concerns of humans. *Silent Spring* thus mixes at least three different qualified media types (scientific writing, popular fiction and science fiction) and blends them into the media type of popular science writing.

Third, *Silent Spring* is also an intermedial product in which several illustrations play an essential part in conveying the message of the book. The nature of these illustrations bolsters the blending of the genre even further, since they are not the typical illustrations we expect from a work of science, which would be diagrams, statistics, tables or detailed representations of flora and fauna. Rather, they are artistic, visionary sketches in black and white.

We certainly notice a set of different intermedial and transmedial aspects in *Silent Spring*: an illustrated book, popular science, the use of science fictive narrative and formal attributes of science fiction (such as the big-bug films of the 1950s), and elements of fairy tales. It is not far-fetched to claim that the impact and success of *Silent Spring* are owed to its intermedial and transmedial features. *Silent Spring* reveals itself to be a transitionary work between the science fiction of the atomic age and the dawn of the environmental movement in the age of countercultures. This is science fiction aesthetics in the name of scientific communication.

The very success of *Silent Spring* (it resulted in the banning of certain pesticides, the emerging environmental movement and a public awareness of toxicity) can thus be traced back to the very medial form of the book. The qualified aspect of scientific truth (Carson's scientific background, the scientific reports and references) is present in specific truth claims concerning scientific facts and a scientific discourse, comingled successfully with medial aspects with a stronger appeal to individual and collective human agency (illustrations, literary narrative strategies, allusions to fairy tales). What was lost because of a lack of conventional scientific truthfulness was gained in the insistence on human agency.

Poetic truthfulness in ecopoetry

Poetry as a literary genre, as compared with the broad field of narrative literature, occupies a unique place in the discussion of truthfulness in literature. As previously discussed, thinkers and writers have engaged with the issue of the truth of literary fiction for a really long time, so how can we approach the specific question of truthfulness in poetry from an intermedial point of view in a fruitful way?

For the most part, even if poetry does refer to verifiable facts about objects or events, poetry even more than fiction conveys a strong subjective truth claim: a 'deeper', more subjective, perhaps intuitively grasped insight about love, God or the human condition. It is perceived truthfulness of another sort. This is probably the most common understanding of the relation between truthfulness and poetry, and it is a position that in modern thinking relates to, for instance, many modernist ideas about poetry's privileged access to the meaning of existence. For the German philosopher Martin Heidegger, for example, it is even the case that an exclusive selection of poets offer privileged access to the philosophical truth about the world. Facts, not to mention hard science, seldom enter this discussion. However, there is a reason not to exclude facts from the discussion of truth or truthfulness in poetry, not least since there is a growing body of poetry, often motivated with ecological concerns, that incorporates scientific sources, references and quotes.

What poetry reveals to a reader, or what she or he regards as authentic or sincere, is – more or less – subjective experiences, or in Christinidis's (2013) words: 'the fictional representation of subjective responses to external events' (p. 35). These complex issues that concern poetry and truth claims will be addressed further in the next section, which is about ecopoetry.

Poetry can go against conventions and expectations and renegotiate the relationship between subjective and objective truth claims; it can pave the way for the development of different media types and genres. Take, for example, ecopoetry, which is often written out of a desire to affect the reader in a specific way – to make the reader understand the severity of the ecological crisis. The poet is often well informed about the subject and this knowledge is conveyed in different ways, often by means of scientific facts, either in the poems or as footnotes. Anglophone examples of this type of poetry have been written by Ted Hughes, Gary Snyder and, more recently, Adam Dickinson: some examples of Swedish poets who write in this genre are Jonas Gren, Åsa Maria Kraft and Agnes Gerner. Terry Gifford (2011) discusses ecopoetry's relationship with scientific facts: 'I have a feeling that we need to adjust our aesthetics for our times and that our criteria for the evaluation of ecopoetry does need refining' (p. 11); he continues: 'Don't we now need to know the data in our poetry? Don't we need to adjust our aesthetic to allow for the poetics to be informed' (p. 12).

The issue boils down to two questions: how do we as readers regard poetry that includes scientifically produced facts (not just facts such as water boils at

100 degrees Celsius or that a dog has four legs, but facts that belong to a more specialized scientific discourse, 'gained from scientific, academic inquiry' (Haiden 2018, 10)) – is it still aesthetically appealing? And how do we regard the scientific facts referred to in ecopoetry – are they still credible? Regarding the first question, Yvonne Reddick (2015) notes:

> The question of whether or not scientific data should be included in ecopoetry remains problematic. In the opinion of the present critic, if scientific data can be deployed in a way that adds to the aesthetic value of the poem without sounding propagandist, it can enhance the quality of the writing in a startling and unsettling way.
>
> (p. 265)

In other words, if poets use scientific facts in an overly didactic or propagandistic manner, it will affect the quality of the poem negatively. Since at least the Romantic era, a good poem is supposed to be multivalent, ambivalent and open for individual interpretation. A poem with a distinct cause that exists outside the text and the poetic context has often been regarded as less interesting from an aesthetical point of view. This does not mean that a poem cannot have a message or a cause, even a political one, but it should not be the poem's only raison d'être and must be conveyed so that it is open to many different interpretations. This, in turn, has to do with Cleanth Brooks's (1947) notion of 'the heresy of paraphrase': if we could capture the essence of a poem by paraphrasing it, it would not be a good poem. The subject matter of a poem is intimately intertwined with the poetic language, the rhythm and the imagery.

However, even if a poem incorporates scientific facts, it does not necessarily mean that the whole poem is riddled with them – they might be present in just one or two verses. Besides, regardless of how many facts a poem includes, what matters is their role in the poem. Do they emphasize the poem's theme, enhance its sensations and atmosphere and contribute to making it original and new? In that case, it is an aesthetical win.

The second question has to do with the facts and the credibility that we ascribe to them. As discussed earlier, we are accustomed to believing what we read in a scientific journal (or even if we never read such journals, we imagine them to be truthful), but we are not used to regarding poetry as a medium for conveying facts. When we come across a scientific fact, or a scientific discourse, in poetry, we might tend to look at it as something else, as Jerome J. McGann (2002) puts it: 'In poetry facts are taken to be multivalent [...] They are open to many readings and meanings, and any effort to explicate them by a historical method, it is believed, threatens to trivialize the poetic event into a unitary condition' (p. 223). The scientific fact that is transmediated from a factual source media product transforms into something else, a symbol, when it is mediated by the target media product, the poem. How can poetry overcome this situation? One way of doing so is to employ the same method as the source medium: referencing. By referencing, the poem can 'prove' its own credibility, its own truthfulness, despite what media and genre conventions lead us to believe. The transmediation of a factual discourse combined with a reference to the source media product is the only way that poetry can be truthful in a positivistic meaning of the word and thus make objective truth claims, as well as subjective ones. If this method is successful, the objective truth claims strengthen the subjective truth claims and vice versa.

Let's look at a poem by Swedish ecopoet Jonas Gren and see how it treats facts, truth claims and truthfulness:

> Behold the human
> Hide Hollows Guts
> *Enterococcus faecalis*
> *Helicobacter pylori*
> Ninety percent of
> the cells in a human
> belong to microbes
> I'm
> in a minority
> within myself
> (Gren 2016, p. 14)[2]

This very short poem concerns the abundance of microorganisms in the body. In 'The Anthropocene Within', Johan Höglund (in press) describes the human body as an ecosystem of its own:

> What new microbiological research argues is that the human cannot be imagined as this bounded biological and psychological entity. The human body, this research argues, is an assemblage of thousands of species the members of which outnumber the cells of the human body. According to the most recent estimates, the human body is made up of roughly 3–3.7 trillion human cells, but it is also inhabited by 3–4 trillion bacterial cells belonging to 500–1000 different species.
>
> (Höglund, in press, p. 3)

In Gren's poem, these data are transmediated into poetic reflections: 'I'm/in a minority/within myself'. The poem has a lyrical tone and the data and scientific names do not change that but instead add to the overall poetic atmosphere. The binomial names *Enterococcus faecalis* and *Helicobacter pylori* are correct, and furthermore they are explained in the anthology's glossary. The fact that there is a glossary points to the scientific and factual intent of the collection. For example, the main title of the collection is *Anthropocene*, and the term Anthropocene is lengthily explained in the glossary, with references to scholars in the field.

The scientific terms and data emphasize the poem's post-humanist motif of the dissolved self (who am I if my cells belong to someone else?), which in turn makes us reconsider the invocation to 'behold the human' (*ecce homo*), which has a long Christian tradition, originally ascribed to Pontius Pilate when he presented Jesus to the crowd. *Ecce homo* suggests that the human being is a solid unit, separated from other beings and superior to them. In Gren's poem, we are invited to see the human as an ecosystem of microbes in which the human body forms the habitat for trillions of life forms. The human body becomes a feeding ground, landscape and nature: there is a transformation from culture to nature, that is, from foreground to background.

The glossary, which provides adequate references to and explanations of scientific terms and concepts, gives the poetry collection credibility; the collection makes objective truth claims and, furthermore, proves itself objectively truthful through the glossary. Because of the new context, the reader is not solely focused on the factual content of the transmediated phenomena but on their aesthetic function as well: how they sound, their placement on the page and how they connect structurally and thematically with the rest of the verses. They have transformed into poetic units and have been placed in a poem and in a poetry collection that truthfully conveys topical scientific information without ever losing their multivalency and lyricism.

Hollywood Environmentalism in *The Day After Tomorrow*

If poetry operates on a smaller, more intimate scale, Hollywood blockbusters bang out their messages with a hammer. In the past few decades, several Hollywood ecological disaster blockbuster films have addressed the issue of the climate crisis (see *Waterworld* (1995), *The Day After Tomorrow* (2004), *Geostorm* (2017), *Interstellar* (2014), *Mad Max: Fury Road* (2015)). The modern adventure blockbuster, with its all-inclusive potential, huge budgets and advanced technology, should, it seems, be suited to communicating the need for an altered direction for humanity. As Ailise Bulfin (2017) observes,

> given that a significant number of people derive a good deal of their information on and understanding of the threat of climate change [...] from popular culture works such as catastrophe films, it is important that an investigation into the nature of these popular representations is embedded in the attempt to address the issue of climate change.
>
> (p. 140)

One of the aesthetic challenges a subject matter of climate change poses, is the difficulty of representing and transmediating a scientific phenomenon of such gloomy magnitude (end of the world) and infinite temporality (deep geological time as opposed to the short time frames of human time) in art and popular cultures. Images of melting icebergs and starving polar bears infiltrate popular media since these are intelligible illustrations of the climate damage that can be comprehended in human time. The format of the blockbuster cli-fi film rearranges the sense of deep time very conveniently, a fact that has drawn a lot of criticism from scientific communities.

One of the early, trendsetting cli-fi blockbusters was Roland Emmerich's *The Day After Tomorrow* (2004).[3] The film depicts the disappearance of the Gulf stream and the following collapse of the polar icecaps, which rapidly initiates a new ice age. This resonated with a debate in the news in 2004 on human-induced short-term variation in ocean circulation and its effect on the climate. Most palaeoclimatologists (they study past climates) were highly sceptical of the melting polar icecaps theory, but many of them probably immensely enjoyed seeing a palaeoclimatologist in one of the main roles of the film. Daniel P. Schrag, a palaeoclimatologist and professor of earth and planetary science at Harvard University, said,

> On the one hand, I'm glad that there's a big-budget movie about something as critical as climate change. On the other, I'm concerned that people will see these over-the-top effects and think the whole thing is a joke [...] We are indeed experimenting with the Earth in a way that hasn't been done for millions of years. But you're not going to see another ice age – at least not like that.
>
> (cited in Bowles 2004)

Likewise, the film was scientifically scrutinized by ClimateSight.org (ClimateSight 2012). Nevertheless, using scientists as characters in these films is common enough in feature films, be they cli-fi films or not: it is an economic way to grant these films a notion of truthfulness. Having scientists as film characters facilitates the presentations of the truth claims related to scientific facts presented at conferences, in political venues and within scientific communities themselves.

Even if these films incorporate media types usually associated with the scientific community as a means of framing the climate crisis in a believable scientific context, the realism of these films is more due to the suspension of disbelief mentioned earlier. However, in terms of truthfulness, these films aim less for scientific rigour and more for affective immersion. Scientific discourse can tell us how things are, but fictional discourse can make us *feel* these figures, schemes and calculations. In these films, the action sequences, as well as more contemplative and prophetic images of destruction, successfully create a physical and phenomenological experience for the viewers through the cinematic embodiment of the severe threats of climate change. Through images of the end of the world, these catastrophe films initiate a particular emotional reaction, which Salmose (2018) has termed the 'apocalyptic sublime', as a way of representing the effects of climate change (pp. 1418–24). Sublime here refers to the definition of sublime as a combination of awe and horror, or 'delightful horror'. An apocalyptic sublime, then, is a sublimity that is invested in the sense of the apocalypse of the world.

There are primarily two variants of the apocalyptic sublime in the blockbuster cli-fi as a media type. The first, and most frequent, variant is related to traditional action sequences: they are narrative and protagonist driven and work inclusively through embodiment, for example, the body's reactions to aesthetic experiences. This is the 'action apocalyptic sublime' (pp. 1419–22). The second variant is more existential and affective (in the sense of poetic, affective qualities), and emphasizes the more universal dimensions of catastrophe. This is what Salmose (2018) calls the 'poetic apocalyptic sublime' (pp. 1422–4).

The action apocalyptic sublime is immersive, sensorial and embodied: it makes people feel and experience the climate catastrophe in an entirely different way to watching a starving polar bear. In the action apocalyptic sublime, the camera is rarely still; impatiently, it tracks the horrible experience of our heroes through a crumbling civilization. The use of advanced CGI 'places' viewers in the filmic diegetic universe very effectively. Watching films in cinemas or home cinemas especially exaggerates the bodily experience of the action. The apocalypse of the world is haunting and cool and is supported by a pompous musical score. There is a sense of awe when popular icons and emblems are part of the cinematic catastrophe; items symbolizing the coherence of the world which we take for granted are suddenly lost. In *The Day After Tomorrow*, this is evident when both the Statue of Liberty and the Hollywood Sign are demolished. The destruction of the latter by numerous tornadoes is part of the initiation of the catastrophe, and the gravity of the event is underscored by the Fox News reporter from a chopper: 'Liissaa, ah, are you getting this on camera? […] It erased the Hollywood Sign […] the Hollywood Sign is gone!' Although such an attempt at apocalyptic sublime might initiate a sense of comedy that could distance the viewers from the catastrophe rather than embody them, the result is still quite overwhelming. The truth claims here are not so theoretical or abstract; instead, the film produces a physical experience that concerns the truthfulness of the situation.

Perhaps more effectual in terms of agency is the 'poetic apocalyptic sublime'. This would include visions of rising water and magnificent waves that are the after-effects of the geological disasters these narratives represent, such as the melting of the polar ice caps due to climate change in *The Day After Tomorrow*. The use of flooding images makes the slow violence of climate change visible and felt, even if these changes occur in a less dramatic fashion in reality than in the movies. These representations reproduce a universal mythical narrative of the revenging or wrathful flood that occurs in many religions and mythologies, such as in Plato's allegorical depiction of Atlantis. Therefore, the poetic apocalyptic sublime carries a stronger intertextual and symbolic vitality than the cataclysmic images of inland earthquakes.

Scenes that can be described as the poetic apocalyptic sublime are also constructed in a very different style from the action-driven variants. Alexa Weik von Mossner (2017) describes the opening sequence showing Antarctica in *The Day After Tomorrow* in a similar fashion but without using the term sublime: 'we feel the emotional impact of both the beauty of nature […] and its destruction' (pp. 154–5). In this way, the scene targets the very sublime interplay between awe and horror. Mossner goes on to say that '[t]he evocation of a spectacularly beautiful but suddenly also threatened environment cues awe for the sheer beauty of the images and sadness in relation to a vulnerable ecological space at risk' (p. 155). This latter reading, which parallels the experience of that scene, suggests exactly the kind of introspection and reflection that differentiates the poetic apocalyptic sublime from the action apocalyptic sublime. The affective result is perhaps even more convincing in the magnificent scene in *The Day After Tomorrow* when the camera, in one long, breathtaking shot, circles around the deluged Statue of Liberty (which has also been struck by lightning) in the underwater New York City to the sounds of lightning, water and sudden frantic, orchestral bursts. It opens up an opportunity for feeling the true angst of the destruction. The poetic sublime is less violently physical and more affective and reflexive; the truth claims deal more with feelings of despair and nostalgia than with violent upheavals.

Hollywood cli-fi films promulgate a sense of hyperreality. Through a superbly technically constructed point-of-view experience, these films maximize, even override, conventional truthfulness. The creation of a total subjective experience is made possible because of the truth claims of its own cinematic method. Although Hollywood cli-fi films have the potential to create a temporary emotional shock regarding ecological disaster, these affective affirmations are contradicted by the sentiment 'do not worry, everything will be as it has always been', which is an inherent part of the adventure narrative genre, wherein quest, conflict, heroism and resolution contradict the sensual impact of the apocalyptic sublime and diminish any kind of agency to change human behaviour. Consequently, and typical of many mainstream representations of future climate disasters, *The Day After Tomorrow* ends in smiling reunions, a newly constructed heterosexual couple and a strangely intact Manhattan skyline in bright sunlight in front of a blue sky. The film suggests both a longing for past times and a strong desire to preserve what is imagined to be the essence of the Western world. The genre, thus, disregards a necessary shift of focus to the negative aspects of the Anthropocene condition, and the potentially sensational warning effects of these spectacles are short-lived.[4]

In the end, the qualifying media aspects of Hollywood commercial cinema, and its narrative structures, appear to severely reduce the hard facts of climate science even if the inclusion of scientific characters and qualified media types attempts to bridge this gap. The truth claims related to the presence of the scientists and, in particular, to their discourses and multimedia presentations that are part of the film are downplayed in the more comprehensive (and economically dominant) Hollywood plot. What we can acknowledge here is the transition from scientific objective truth claims to Hollywoodesque subjective truth claims. Nevertheless, the medial possibilities inherent in Hollywood cinema (embodiment, immersion, affect) manage to create an experience that concerns the effects of climate change that scientific discourse cannot.

How do we know it's true? Fake(d) news and the truth claims of news media

In 2014, a story about a schoolgirl spread across Swedish social media. The article that was shared told how a 9-year-old girl was kept in after school because it was held that the Swedish flag on her mobile phone case could be offensive to migrants. And although the story was soon debunked as satire, one user angrily retorted in a commentary field discussion: 'I don't care if it's a fake, it's still a f**ing scandal' (Werner 2018, p. 27). This comment is symptomatic of how objective and subjective truth claims collide, and bears similarities to the debate about the climate in the 2010s. It is an example of how the hierarchy between subjective and objective truth claims, between a truth claim involving a 'personal, local approach to truth' and emotional, personal experience and truth claim involving objective knowledge 'gained from scientific, academic inquiry' (Haiden 2018, p. 10) has become unstable. If a story feels right, why bother about whether it actually did take place?

This comment is also symptomatic of how digital communication and digital social interaction have complicated the practices of evaluating truth claims. We often ground our evaluation of truthfulness in our knowledge of and our trust in the source. We also evaluate the truthfulness of media products according to the conventions of qualified media types. But in front of the computer and on the internet, we access and easily switch between different kinds of qualified media types. News, science, satire, gossip, fiction and education are often only separated by a mouse click or two. When read in its original context, the 'news' on a website called *The Stork* (which offers 'Real news and gossip') about punishing a schoolgirl because of the colours on her mobile phone case is easily recognized as news satire. Once the article is shared on social media, it might be mistaken as news.

In the following, we explore conflicting truth claims in the current infosphere by analysing how we ground our evaluation of truthfulness in different interacting indexical relationships between external indexical relations and internal coherence. After this analysis, instead of just being baffled by the fact that some people accept as true what to others is clearly fake news, we will be better able to describe how fabricated news stories are manipulated.

Different kinds of qualified media convey different forms of truth claims. Thus, we evaluate narratives differently depending on whether we read a novel or the news. A news article tells the story of a particular event that has taken place. In the news, the cohesion of narrative patterns is used to put this particular event into context (Carlson 2017, p. 54). However, the difference between fictive and factual narratives does not help when it is uncertain which truth claims apply and which are made up.

True stories: The truth claims of news media

What are the truth claims of news media? Matt Carlson (2017) conceives journalistic authority as being established and confirmed with every single piece of news that conveys what we call truth claims here. There is the truth claim of professionalism – news stories are true stories because they are based on research, on interviews with sources and a journalist's own observations. The truth claims of news media are also to a large extent based on and performed by the visual and narrative forms and conventions employed. Last but not least, the news article is the result of an editorial evaluations process: the event is selected and evaluated as relevant news. The position of news within the structure of the TV news or the newspaper already signals an evaluation of its importance and context.

These truth claims of news media are challenged in digital media. A printed news story and its position in a printed newspaper claims relevance and the public's attention. In digital media, news stories that are shared become isolated and interchangeable texts. Actors other than journalists draw on the visual and narrative truth claims of news media for other reasons than simply informing readers or viewers about recent events.

In the current infosphere, trust in journalistic professionalism or heuristic short cuts cannot be applied. We cannot easily differentiate between true and false, or that facts are replaced by fiction. We cannot understand different forms of disinformation by simply pointing out that they ignore facts. Nor does it help to label media products that manipulated the truth claims of news media as fake news. 'Fake news' is a rhetorical term often used to attack opponents and always the problems of others (Tandoc 2019). To make things even more difficult, this kind of pseudo-journalistic disinformation is not totally fabricated. Instead, actual events and facts are connected in a way that conveys a distorted impression that is not truthful. Truth claims are made, but they are made on false grounds.

In the following, we explore the manipulation of truth claims of news media by describing how disinformation manipulates the relation between different indexical relations, between external experience, the narrative and the confirmation of world knowledge. We analyse two different cases of disinformation. These stories draw on the truth claims of news media but do not comply with all of them. We explore the possibilities that are offered to ground the article in experience, previous knowledge and coherence. Which facts and actual events are mentioned? Which structural patterns of cohesion are created? How does the event relate to previous knowledge and belief? Through this we may begin to understand how we end up in conflict about whether a piece of information is a true story or fake news.

Alternative truths and narratives

In October 2016, news media in Sweden reported that the Swedish Transport Administration would no longer allow Christmas decorations to be fastened to the lamp-posts owned by the administration in minor localities for safety reasons and due to organizational and legal changes. When Swedish Television covered the story on a regional news site on 23 October, the web article included the uncomprehending reactions of local politicians (Renulf 2016). On 24 October, the alt-right news site *Fria Tider* (*Free Times*) published an article that integrated the event into a strategic narrative, and provided an alternative explanation and context for the reported event, already presented in the subheading 'War on Christmas' (Fria 2016). Journalist Paul Rapacioli has traced how the actual event in the context of alt-right media was reported on as a symptom of Sweden's problems after the so-called refugee crisis in 2015 (Rapacioli 2018, pp. 15–27). *Fria Tider* thus anchored the event into the same anti-Muslim and anti-migration narrative that the article from *The Stork* about the banned mobile case satirized. The *Fria Tider* article presents the ban on fastening Christmas decorations to the administration's lamp-posts as an indexical sign of an ongoing fight against Christian traditions. This is not only indicated in the subheading but explicitly repeated in the article. 'The change is a victory for those who want to tone down the remainder of the country's Christian traditions' (Rapacioli 2018, p. 17). These lines are added to an otherwise quite faithful account of the report on Swedish television.

This anchoring in the audience's worldview is supported by different forms of structural coherence. For instance, the article reduces the complexity of the matter by creating the structural parallel that the ban on Christmas decorations equals a ban on Christmas traditions. The phrase 'War on Christmas' echoes those of existing campaigns such as the 'war on terror' and the 'war on drugs', which conveys a certain authority to the phrase. However, the claim that there is an ongoing campaign against Christian traditions is not grounded in the specific quote of a source that could confirm the claim put forth. Still, the text is grounded in something that is presented as factual external evidence, as it points out that there had been no reports yet of lamp-posts collapsing because of the weight of Christmas decorations. This external fact, which points towards an event that has not taken place, can in turn be read as indexical evidence that the official reasons cannot be valid.

Thus, the article is not merely anchored in a strategic narrative that confirms the previous convictions of the intended audience. The article aligns all three forms of indexicality. The article anchors the claim of a War on Christmas in other observable facts, connects a fictive event to existing events by parallelism and increases all forms of coherence to reduce complexity and create an impression that it all fits together.

Recognition effects

Different indexical relations also cover up for each other in the manipulated feature stories of the former German star reporter Claas Relotius. In 2018, Relotius had to admit that he had manipulated many of his prize-winning reportages that had mainly been published in the highly respected German news magazine *Der Spiegel* (Fichtner 2018). In the wake of the scandal, many wondered why nobody had noticed earlier that Relotius's stories were, in fact, a bit 'too good to be true'?

In Relotius's feature stories, we can see how different indexical relationships are grounded in each other. 'The Story of Ahmed and Alin: Syrian Orphans Trapped in Turkey' (Relotius 2016) is mostly made up of fictive events. It tells the story of two Syrian siblings who had fled from Aleppo to Turkey aged 10 and 11, were separated and now worked as child labourers. *Der Spiegel*'s internal fact-check revealed that Relotius and his photographer had met a boy named Ahmed, but he was not orphaned, did not have a sister and did not collect scrap but worked in a relative's car repair shop.

Narratologist Samuli Björninen (2019) has analysed in detail the literary narrative strategies of this article. The story is told mainly from the point of view of the alleged sister Alin, that is, from a fictive point of view. It is told by an omniscient narrator who not only observes people but focalizes from their point of view and prefers to mediate their words in his own words in free, indirect discourse. As he quotes the children only in short phrases, the narrator feels obliged to ensure that 'they tell their stories vividly and honestly – in the way only children can' (Relotius 2016, p. 128); this is a quite remarkable self-referential statement ensuring the (falsely claimed) authenticity by simply stating their authenticity. Still, these literary narrative techniques might be consistent with the style of New Journalism that advocates literary and subjective storytelling in journalism, and they are a hallmark of the magazine *Der Spiegel*.

Thus, a reportage can comply with the truth claim of journalism that it is telling a story based on research, on interviews with sources and on a journalist's own observations despite the fact that it draws on literary techniques. However, in the case of Relotius's texts, the increased coherence between fictive events that are constructed to fit, covers up the absence of facts that could be checked. The details that appear to be external facts are minor details, such as the 15 steps to a cellar or the number of children working at a sweatshop. The text is vague on exact dates that could be checked, such as when it is claimed that war arrived in the children's life 'a summer's day, two years ago' (Relotius 2016, p. 128). If the text referred to the 'summer of 2014' instead, the inconsistency would be more obvious, as the siege of Aleppo had already started in 2012. The patterns of cyclical time, such as day and night, increase coherence, because Alin is said to sew by day and Ahmed to collect scrap metal by night.

Instead of being grounded in facts that can be observed and checked by others, the reportage is anchored in the general knowledge and experience of the German audience. In a surprisingly inconsistent way, the text mentions small details for the German audience to recognize. On second glance, these details are obviously wrong for a Middle Eastern context, such as when Alin, who is a Muslim, is said to fold her hands in bed for her night-time prayers (which is a Western Christian tradition). When the children are said to escape from Aleppo in the boot of a car, this description creates a recognition effect in relation to stories of escape from the GDR. The siblings keep in contact via smartphones, although at least Ahmed is said to live in a makeshift shed in the forest without electricity, and Alin is said to be hungry but must have spent money on mobile data. It takes time to notice these inconsistencies because smartphones even provide opportunities to highlight other forms of allegedly factual evidence, such as films and images. The phones provide internal narrative coherence as well, as they connect the Syrian past with the present and the two siblings' narrative strands via text messages. All these appeals to the audience's world knowledge about what *usually tends to be true in a German context* do not add up to an appeal to confirmation bias but create more of a vague recognition effect. In marketing strategies, the recognition effect will nudge customers in a shop to choose the brand they recognize. In this text, the fragments of inconsistent familiarity appear to nudge the reader into acceptance of the story.

The article does not confirm any strategic macro-narrative. Instead, it is anchored in literary intertextuality. Alin is said to sing a Syrian folk song about children who lost everything but end up as King and Queen of Syria. The song thus connects both to the sibling's alleged situation and to the title of a German folk song, *Es waren zwei Königskinder* (There once were two Royal Children). The folk song creates coherence as it works as a *mise en abyme* for the entire reportage. The German title *Königskinder* in turn also evokes the above mentioned well-known traditional folk ballad about 'two Royal Children' that 'held each other dear' but 'they could not come together' because 'the water was far too deep' (Nagel 2018). Even in this article, the structural parallel with existing phenomena, here an existing folksong, anchors the made-up story. In the German ballad, the prince tries to cross the water and drowns in the attempt. The intertextual reference does not create an exact parallel but connects the invented fate of the Syrian siblings with the actual stories of refugees drowning in their attempt to reach Europe. The structural parallel in the intertextual reference grounds, via a kind of family likeness, the invented events in actual reported events. Therefore, a made-up feature story is indexically grounded in literary intertextual references. Once again, different external and internal indexical relations appear to refer to each other and thus cover up the fact that they are all made up.

In both of these cases, the line between fiction and fact is not easy to draw. Both cases present a story that is more based on the world knowledge or world view of the audience than on the factual experience of the reported event. However, facts are not merely replaced by an invented story that confirms the opinion of the audience. There is no radical shift from truth to lie. Instead, both texts reveal an alignment in the different forms of indexical relations that provide coherence. Instead of pointing to actual events, they connect to each other and provide coherence. Thus, a closer look at indexical relations can describe the mechanisms that explain in more detail how news stories are manipulated.

Conclusion

Questions of truth, authenticity and objectivity have long been discussed in media-specific contexts. In this chapter, we touched upon some of those questions, like the truth of fiction, the indexicality of photography, the objectivity of the camera. With the concepts of truth claims and truthfulness in different media types, however, we presented in this chapter a transmedial approach. Truthfulness and truth claims allow us to connect different but related discourses on truth, authenticity, objectivity and to explore more specifically the implicit appeals made in different media products concerning why, how and when we should trust them.

Throughout this chapter, we explored different forms of truthful representations in poetry, popular science narratives, literature, mainstream cinema and the news media. We highlighted the interaction and interrelation of truth claims and truthfulness. The truth claims of qualified media types influence what kind of truthful relation we expect and respond to. In specific media products we perceive interaction of objective and subjective truth claims, of truthful representations of external perception and inner experience.

The truth claims may vouch for different kinds of truthful representations in different media types, but they are always framed by production and reception contexts, and based on constellations of basic media types and technical media of display (as is all communication by way of qualified media).

Exploring truth claims and truthfulness across media are thus useful tools to address the societal challenges of the current communication crisis. In this chapter, we explored the communication of climate change and the spreading of disinformation. But questions of scientific truth production and truthful communication grew more and more prominent during the time of writing, due to the COVID-19 pandemic. And generally, as we can combine different media types and transfer information between different media types more easily than in the digital age, we need to better understand the transmedial dimensions of truthfulness. Identifying truthfulness, therefore, is definitely an issue that demands a high degree of intermedial literacy to avoid getting lost in the labyrinth of truths, fake news and half-lies.

Notes

1 Enli discusses the question of 'mediated authenticity', but we gently transplant her arguments into the very similar (but not identical) questions of truth claims and truthfulness.
2 Se människan/Huden Hålorna Tarmarna/*Enterococcus faecalis*/*Helicobacter pylori*/Nittio procent av/cellerna i människan/tillhör mikrober/Jag/är i minoritet/i mig själv (p. 14). Translated by Jonas Gren and Dougald Hine. The translation has not been published at the time of writing.
3 For an extensive analysis of the differences between scientific media and cinematic media, and the transmediation from the scientific article 'The "Anthropocene"', published by Paul J. Crutzen and Eugene F. Stoermer in 2010, to *The Day After Tomorrow*, see Lars Elleström's 'Representing the Anthropocene: Transmediation of narratives and truthfulness from science to feature film' (2020).
4 In the case of *The Day After Tomorrow*, this is also supported by Mike Hulme's analysis of five different reception studies of the film. Hulme (2009) explains that the film 'cannot be said to have induced the sea-change in public attitudes or behaviour that some advocates had been hoping for' (p. 214).

References

Björninen, S. 2019. The rhetoric of factuality in narrative: Appeals to authority in Claas Relotius's feature journalism. *Narrative Inquiry*, 29(2), pp. 352–370.
Bowles, S. 2004. 'The day after tomorrow' heats up a political debate: Storm of opinion rains down on merits of disaster movie. *USA Today*, 26 May.
Brooks, C. 1947. *The well wrought urn: Studies in the structure of poetry*. New York: Harcourt, Brace & World.
Bulfin, A. 2017. Popular culture and the 'new human condition': Catastrophe narratives and climate change. *Global and Planetary Change*, 156, pp. 140–146.
Carlson, M. 2017. *Journalistic authority: Legitimating news in the digital era*. New York: Columbia University Press.
Carson, R. 2002. *Silent spring*. 40th anniversary ed. Boston: Houghton Mifflin.
Christinidis, G. 2013. Truth claims in the contemporary novel: The authenticity effect, allegory, and totality. In D. Birke and S. Butter, eds., *Realisms in contemporary culture: Theories, politics, and medial configurations* (pp. 33–48). Berlin: de Gruyter.
Clark, T. 2015. *Ecocriticism on the edge: The Anthropocene as a threshold concept*. London: Bloomsbury.
ClimateSight. 2012. The day after tomorrow: A scientific critique. *Climatesight.org*, 26 April. https://climatesight.org/2012/04/26/the-day-after-tomorrow-a-scientific-critique/ [Accessed 4 December 2020].
Elleström, L. 2018. Coherence and truthfulness in communication: Intracommunicational and extracommunicational indexicality. *Semiotica*, 225, pp. 423–446.
Elleström, L. 2021. The modalities of media II: An expanded model for understanding intermedial relations. In L. Elleström, ed., *Beyond media borders, volume 1: Intermedial relations among multimodal media* (pp. 3–91). London: Palgrave.
Enli, G. 2015. *Mediated authenticity: How the media constructs reality*. New York: Peter Lang.
Fichtner, U. 2018. Der Spiegel reveals internal fraud. *Spiegel.de*, 20 December. https://www.spiegel.de/international/zeitgeist/claas-relotius-reporter-forgery-scandal-a-1244755.html [Accessed 8 December 2020].
Fria Tider 2016. Trafikverket förbjuder julpynt. *Fria Tider*, 24 October. https://www.friatider.se/trafikverket-f-rbjuder-julpynt [Accessed 13 November 2020].
Garrard, G. 2012. *Ecocriticism*. 2nd ed. London: Routledge.
Ghosh, A. 2016. *The great derangement: Climate change and the unthinkable (The Randy L. and Melvin R. Berlin family lectures)*. Chicago: University of Chicago Press.
Gifford, T. 2011. *Green voices: Understanding contemporary nature poetry*. Manchester; New York: Manchester University Press.
Goodbody, A. and Johns-Putra, A. 2019. *Cli-fi: A companion*. Oxford: Peter Lang.
Gren, J. 2016. *Antropocen. Dikt för en ny epok*. Stockholm: 10TAL.
Gunning, T. 2004. What's the point of an index? Or, faking photographs. *Nordicom Review*, 25(1–2), pp. 39–49.
Haiden, L. 2018. Tell me lies, tell me sweet little lies. In J. Althuis, L. Haiden and A. Reynolds, eds., *Fake news: A roadmap* (pp. 7–14). Riga: NATO Strategic Communications Centre of Excellence.
Höglund, J. in press. The Anthropocene within: Love and extinction in M.R. Carey's The girl with all the gifts and the boy on the bridge. In J.D. Edwards, R. Graulund and J. Höglund, eds., *Gothic in the Anthropocene: Dark scenes from damaged earth*. Minneapolis: University of Minnesota Press.

Hulme, M. 2009. *Why we disagree about climate change: Understanding controversy, inaction and opportunity*. Cambridge: Cambridge University Press.
Hutcheon, L. 2006. *A theory of adaptation*. London: Routledge.
Le Mépris. 1963. Directed by Jean-Luc Godard. France: Rome Paris Films et al.
Maier, Emar. 2020. Making up stuff. *AEON*, 13 January. https://aeon.co/essays/how-to-tell-fact-from-fiction-in-fiction-and-other-forms-of-lies [Accessed 18 August 2021].
McGann, J.J. 2002. *Byron and Romanticism*. New York: Cambridge University Press.
Nagel, G. 2018. Es waren zwei Königskinder. *lieder-archiv.de*, 12 August. https://www.lieder-archiv.de/es_waren_zwei_koenigskinder-notenblatt_300454.html [Accessed 4 December 2020].
Nanook of the North. 1922. Directed by Robert Flaherty. USA: Robert Flaherty.
Parks, P. 2017. Silent spring, loud legacy: how elite media helped establish an environmentalist icon. *Journalism & Mass Communication Quarterly*, 94(4), pp. 1215–1238.
Peters, J.D. 2001. Witnessing. *Media, Culture & Society*, 23(6), pp. 707–723. doi:10.1177/016344301023006002
Plumwood, V. 2002. *Environmental culture: The ecological crisis of reason*. London: Routledge.
Rapacioli, P. 2018. *Good Sweden, bad Sweden: The use and abuse of Swedish values in a post-truth world*. Stockholm: Volante.
Reddick, Y. 2015. 'Icthyologue': Freshwater biology in the poetry of Ted Hughes. *Interdisciplinary Studies in Literature and Environment*, 22(2), pp. 264–283.
Relotius, C. 2016. Königskinder. *Der Spiegel*, 28, 7 July. https://www.spiegel.de/media/a3a46a28-7ac2-480e-b3a8-97366f1f4c1e/CR-Dokumentation.pdf.
Renulf, K. 2016. Ingen julbelysning i småorter till advent. *svt.se*, 24 October. https://www.svt.se/nyheter/lokalt/jonkoping/ingen-julbelysning-i-smaorter-till-advent [Accessed 13 November 2020].
Ricœur, P. 1985. The power of speech: Science and poetry. Robert F. Scuka (Trans.). *Philosophy Today*, 29, pp. 59–70.
Salmose, N. 2018. The apocalyptic sublime: Anthropocene representation and environmental agency in Hollywood action-adventure cli-fi films. *Journal of Popular Culture*, 51, pp. 1415–1433.
Speth, G. 2014. Connection will be the next big human trend: Interview with Daniel Crockett *Huffington Post*, 22 August.
Tandoc, E.C. 2019. The facts of fake news: A research review. *Sociology Compass*, 13(9), pp. 1–9. doi:10.1111/soc4.12724
The Day After Tomorrow. 2004. Directed by Roland Emmerich. USA: 20th Century Fox.
Tornborg, E. 2019. Transmediations of the Anthropocene: From factual media to poetry. In N. Salmose and L. Elleström, eds., *Transmediations: Communication across media borders* (pp. 235–253). New York: Routledge.
Weik von Mossner, A. 2017. *Affective ecologies: Empathy, emotion, and environmental narrative*. Columbus: Ohio State University Press.
Werner, J. 2018. *Ja skiter i att det är fejk det är förjävligt ändå: Om myter på nätet, fejkade berättelser och vikten av källkritik*. Stockholm: Bonnier.

14 Media modalities of theatrical space

Heidrun Führer and Janneke Schoene

When 'theatre' is mentioned, very different experiences can come to mind: one might recall seeing a specific play at a particular theatre, for example, attending a performance of Richard Wagner's opera *The Flying Dutchmam* (1843) at Malmö Opera in 2019 or watching the musical *Beauty and the Beast* in Disneyland's Royal Theatre (repeatedly staged there). One might consider theatre to be an embedded environmental situation: the architecture of the building in which the performance took place or a long evening with friends when one watched a staged performance. One might even think of theatre being public performances in galleries or happenings in the street, where one can suddenly encounter any kind of performance such as a flash mob or pantomime. This chapter focuses on 'theatre' in its plural forms and its intermedial modalities. It aims to link concepts stemming from ancient philosophy and post-dramatic theatre with modern intermedial theory.

What is theatre? Intertwining buildings and events

As just indicated, the notion of theatre might refer to the theatre or to a specific theatre play, such as Wagner's *The Flying Dutchman* or Shakespeare's comedy *A Midsummer Night's Dream* (1595/96). Both of these plays were written to be performed in specific theatre buildings – Wagner's in the Bayreuth Festival Theatre, built in 1876, and Shakespeare's in the Globe Theatre, probably constructed in 1599. Often, though, theatre plays are not considered to be bound to a specific materiality, technical medium or a specific building. Rather, theatrical performances are known to travel from place to place and from group to group throughout time. They are always transformed to fit specific historical situations, languages and audiences of a particular place and in a particular context. Still, these theatrical performances gain their identity also via their architectural information. Theatre is more than a cultural 'text' that can be identified by the authors' names, the title and the story. Even when theatre is classified according to the intermedial basic media of word, image, or music, often, no further attention is paid to the surrounding material and additional technical conditions that stipulate the 'atmospheric' condition of theatre as a form of human communication. In this chapter, we explore the

DOI: 10.4324/9781003174288-17

media and modalities of theatre with a special focus on the material space and the technical medium of display.

Traditionally, theatre is divided into multiple literary submedia such as comedy, tragedy, image theatre, opera, musicals, etc. These genres distinguish different types of drama with respect to the dominating basic medium solution of the dramatic conflicts. However, when considering the material and technical conditions or modalities of theatre more in detail, some problematic oppositions become visible: that between live events, mediated in the presence of the theatrical stage, and a disseminated media product, displayed on TV or another technical medium occurs for example. The concept of theatre comprises multiple media products that can be considered both as 'live' and as reproducible media products.

Since the material and technical conditions of theatre continually change with the times, these variable conditions influence the semiotic modality of theatre as a technical medium of display. A famous Beatles performance from 1964 can exemplify this complex intertwinement. The performance was recorded as a live event for a TV show in a setting that imitated the Globe Theatre, a historical building that underlines the symbolism which can be attributed to the technical medium of display. In the case of the Beatles performance, the theatre supported not only the remediation of a famous scene from *A Midsummer Night's Dream* but also the parody of established theatre conventions by the Beatles. Thus, apart from the pre-written literary texts representing a fictitious storyworld, also the building sets the spatiotemporal, material and semiotic frame that includes the symbolism of this theatre building. An intermedial consideration of the performing stage also considers how a specific architectural space as the technical medium of display affects the interaction of performing bodies on stage, and how the performers and the auditorium create both shared and divergent time-spaces. Thus, in our intermedial perspective, theatre is a multimodal media type of multiple qualified media products and performative cultural events which are not only shaped by the basic and technical media but are also transformed by time, space, architectural conditions and the specific sociohistorical context.

To explore theatre as a multimodal transformative process of *becoming*, we need to give up such conventions as studying merely the content of written language as a cultural text on its own, separated from the specific material and spatiotemporal conditions of the actualized performance on stage. Instead of marginalizing these phenomena as surrounding 'context' or 'form', we emphasize the suffusion of the abstracted categories of 'text' and 'context', of 'form' and 'content' within any discourse. In other words, we integrate the space (form) of the architectural building and the actual event as material and spatiotemporal modalities of theatre instead of regarding them merely as 'institutional and technical submedia' (Wolff 2011, p. 2). This can be done by focusing on the complex intertwinement of the technical and basic media aspects with particular sociohistorical discourses and the non-linguistic performative space of a theatrical atmosphere.

We can, for example, consider how the architectural material as a technical medium of display interplays with Disney's and Wagner's musical dramas and intensifies the communicative and affective impact on the audience. The spatial arrangement of the Royal Theatre in Disneyland harks back to an entertaining medieval theatre on the street or in a tent, where people and actors more informally meet and communicate, while Richard Wagner's theatre in Bayreuth is modelled after the idealized form of Ancient Greek theatre. How can the role of the theatre building be described in intermedial terms? Indeed, Wagner consciously changed some spatial arrangements to intensify the emotional impact on the audience. For instance, in his architectural arrangement of a proscenium theatre, the audience is separated from a single stage, as he transformed the ancient 'orchestra' into a purely instrumental performance place that disappears from the direct view of the spectators into a darkened space lower than the illuminated stage. This spatial organization enhances not only the sound and atmosphere of Wagner's music drama, but it also makes the single performance centre stage and helps the spectators to immerse in the theatrical event. However, when post-dramatic theatre gives up the unifying spatiotemporal arrangement of the proscenium theatre (see below), it explores the medial character of the body and the performative agency of the material and spatiotemporal modalitiy of the performance differently.

The space and technology of Ancient Greek theatre

It is always instructive to see how our modern understanding of theatre is related to specific cultural and historical discourses. Greek theatre has existed since at least the sixth century BC. The very term theatre highlights the importance of space and place for theatre to take place: the Greek 'theatron' means 'a place of seeing' or 'viewing place'. When sitting in a semi-circle-like architectural space in a concave shell-shaped area, the spectators could both see and hear the public performance of how human bodies presented spoken or sung dialogues and how they performed on two interrelated stages, the main stage for the actors and a second stage for the ancient chorus. On the second stage, called 'orchestra', which means the 'dancing space', the chorus had an intermediary function commenting for the watching audience on the performers' words and action on the first stage. The intermediary function of a chorus in a Greek drama is easier to grasp if a contemporary reader not only considers the dialogue and action of a contemporary play but also the complex spatial modalities of the theatre, that is the spatial arrangement and the material modality of the second stage. This creates the presence of three different spatiotemporal 'worlds': that of the spectators, that of the singing and dancing chorus, and that of the actors and the spatial design conveys their relation towards each other.

These material and spatiotemporal aspects also influence how the actors and the spectators perform and interact with each other. Additionally, the tradition of performing religious and ritualized processions complicates the spatiotemporal modality even further. When performing both inside and outside the theatre, the moving bodies alter the imaginative, affective, sonic and social qualities of the space and produce a complex semiotic modality of theatre. Accordingly, the material building is not to be understood as a housing with a fixed borderline opposing the real world (outside) and the fictive world (inside). Rather, it creates a dynamic line that produces different qualities and intensities of whatever is seen, heard and experienced as different modes of performance. In this regard, theatre is a heterogenous 'lived space', splittable into zones of different intensities. Similarly, also modern theatre architecture explores the design and experience of space broadly. The interaction of space with the material and the technological modalities also makes surprising sound effects possible (see post-dramatic theatre below).

In case you have the opportunity to visit an Ancient Greek open-air theatre and you try to speak from such a scene, you will be surprised how far you can hear the sound travelling up even to the highest places. The ancient masks decorating the actors' faces supported the transmission of soundwaves over spatial distances, whereas the basic features of standardized character types and repeated staged patterns helped the audience to recognize the acting both in the sensorial modality and understand their significance in semiotic modality.

The effect of theatrical events on the spatiotemporal co-present ancient spectators has often been technologically intensified. For instance, the stage(s) were modified to change the symbolic effects of the scenery to represent not one but multiple virtual time-spaces. This was and is done by applying more and more advanced visible or invisible stage technology. It influences the logic of the performed action as much as the theatrical codes and conventions stipulate the process of semiosis of the spectators. The best-known example of how ancient mechanical technology could influence the action on stage was for centuries a hand-powered flying system called '*deus ex machina*'. It displayed and materialized the immaterial 'divine' power by staging unexpected appearances of 'a god coming from the machinery', as the Latin implies. As this technological stage device was most often used in comedies to bring the staged confusion to a neat end, there are doubts about how seriously the audience took the transcendent power that mystically intervened to solve the problems of the human beings.

Box 14.1 Ancient Greek theory of theatre

The understanding of Ancient Greek theatre, and theatre in general, has been much informed by the first theoretical treatise describing and analysing the praxis of different ancient performances, namely the *Poetics* by Aristotle (384–322 BCE). According to him, a dramatic, an epic and a lyrical mode can be distinguished. All three modes belong to the larger concept 'mimesis' ('to make and to bring something into being' and 'to imitate'), often merely called 'representation'. These different types of representation are recognized by their consistent and closed form and their well-structured matter or 'content'. While the lyrical and the epic form of enactment operate both with a narrative voice, the dramatic mode seems 'to bring something into being' by doing, by staging events, and by characters that directly communicate with

> their voices in a way that creates a plot or a story. This plot is also called 'diegesis'. On these grounds, comedy and tragedy are distinguished concerning the types of dramatic characters, the structural elements, such as their tragic or happy ending, as well as the rhetorical style of the language used. As these categories became normative genre distinctions, the theatre was reduced to a self-contained, intentional and meaningful media product. Thereby, the interactive performances of embodied humans in a specific spatiotemporal environment, the shifting media technology, and the spatial and social conditions of the theatre were disregarded. However, these elements influence actively the immaterial atmospheric elements of theatre and the experience of a performance.

The qualifying modalities of a proscenium theatre

In an intermedial perspective on theatre and performance, the influence of the material, sensorial and spatiotemporal qualities of theatre are considered. It analyses not only the written text but also the performative space, the stage technology and the architectural condition of theatre. All these conditions affect the potential interaction of actors and audiences and their sense of identity and community as an ephemeral event, unique in time and space. Thus, the question is not only whether the audience is absent or co-present, but also how the architectural conditions allow the spectators to interact other than mentally. More than being merely a material shelter, a theatre building becomes an influential technical medium of display. As such, it organizes multi-layered social and virtual time-spaces.

In general, the material modality and the architectural design of a theatre form the expectations and experience of the visitors and shape multiple layers of the (time-)spaces, sensorial and semiotic experiences. For example, one's first impression of the Malmö Opera, which was built during the first half of the twentieth century, might be that it is an innovative, modern theatre. Still, like a proscenium theatre, the architectural construction directs the audience into the heart of the building, namely the auditorium that faces the theatre stage. Nevertheless, the huge foyer provides more than a transitory space. It also has a representational function and provides communicative possibilities – before, in-between and after the performance. This material and spatiotemproal potentiality is very much part of a theatre experience. For some visitors, the mingle in this social space might add another meaning to the play performed on stage.

The material design of the proscenium theatre appeared in the Western middle-class culture of the eighteenth century and transformed the ancient theatre into what is called the representational theatre. This understanding restricted theatre and performance to a (mostly verbal) representation or a text that was played in front of an undifferentiated and disembodied audience. Moreover, this material and spatial arrangement also separates the stage from the auditorium, where the bodies of the spectators disappear in the darkened space. Without moving they can merely gaze towards the central and illuminated stage where the storyworld unfolds, consisting of the bodies of the speaking or singing actors.

The proscenium theatre provides two physically separated spaces, the stage, and the auditorium, and arranges an invisible, so-called fourth wall that is symbolically marked by the curtains and the stage lighting. This spatial design favours the understanding of performance as 'mimesis', representation, or as a 'cultural text'. As this text is played in a metaphorical time-space on stage, it is regarded as 'fiction' according to the convention of the so-called 'suspension of disbelief'. This contract invites the disembodied audience to immerse in the staged make-believe world with a coherent event construction and significant speeches (see Box 14.2.).

This intermedial concern of the material, spatiotemporal and semiotic aspects of theatre and the represented storyworld also reveals the specific historical conventions of the eighteenth century. At this time, the audience was taught to contemplate the aesthetic artwork by following specific social codes of behaviour in theatre. These codes differ not only from codes associated with other buildings and places that are not housing art, such as churches, marketplaces, shopping centres or football stadiums, but also from other forms of theatre, such as the Royal Theatre in Disneyland. Its tent-like structure and spatial arrangement hark back to a more informal medieval theatre tradition when all kinds of people gathered in the street or in a tent to be entertained by different kinds of spectacles for a while. This architectural material and spatial modality of the Royal Theatre can be unfolded in its semiotic modality: a tent implies not the same restricting social codes as a pompous theatre building grounded in ancient rituals and culture. One can understand that a Disney performance is made 'for all people' rather than for an elite gathered to see a serious opera in a proscenium theatre. As the spectators of a Disney theatre expect to be entertained rather than morally educated, they also interact both with the actors and the other spectators differnetly. They are not expected to contemplate and immerse in a distinct or fixed unity of performance.

In general, theatre grants or attributes agency to both humans and non-human things taking place in between the architectural construction, the stage technology, the staged performance and the interaction with the audience. The material arrangements do not only influence how the audience behaves and positions itself in space but also how the audience members experience and interact with the performance they are attending. Post-dramatic theatre breaks with these conventions in different ways.

Box 14.2 The body as subject and object

The spatiotemporal modality of architecture establishes many conventional expectations about what theatre means. Some of these conventions concern the role that human bodies play in theatre involving both performers and audience. The human body is a main and complex medium (see Chapter 12), and theatre performances often explore the tension between bodies felt as subjects and bodies experienced as objects.

When you consider yourself as a *subject*, you assume that you have a body of your own and that you can sense and experience the space, the atmosphere and the emotional energy of your surroundings. Feeling embodied like this means that your body seems to disappear in its task of coordinating the complex process of mediation (sensual and bodily perception, memory and imagination). However, when you consider your body as an object, you draw attention to its own materiality, its form and practice. As soon as you watch your body in the mirror, it becomes a sign and an object for you as for other spectators.

Traditionally, the bodies of the human actors are regarded as *objects* staging an autonomous fictitious world and the spectators as disembodied *subjects* who are silently immersed in the spatially and materially framed storyworld. However, no audience is a coherent mass of bodies outside history and social change. We know, for instance, that spectators of the ancient theatre talked, ate and continually came and went in search of even better entertainment, and that the visitors of Shakespeare's Globe Theatre were rowdy crowds and behaved according to sociohistorical codes so different from today.

The modern silent audience that obediently follows an accepted established theatre etiquette is a result of the material design of the proscenium theatre and an unspoken 'theatre contract' from the nineteenth century that defines a binary relation between two spatiotemporal worlds, that of the actors on stage, performing from the script, and that of the spectators, who learned to quietly contemplate the make-believe world of a 'representational' theatre. The post-dramatic theatre challenged in particular the idealized concept of the disembodied spectator.

Post-dramatic theatre

During the twentieth century, so-called post-dramatic theatre broke with multiple conventional practices, including the primacy of the dramatic text, the fourth wall, the 'suspension of disbelief', and the Aristotelian definitions of dramatic forms and norms. Post-dramatic theatre foregrounds the 'material situation of the performance on stage' (Lehmann 2006). It eventually even leaves the conventional architectural space and the figurative space of a theatrical stage to explore how people perform in their everyday physical and social spaces in real time. When city centres, public spaces, shopping malls, etc. are used as stages (e.g. by flash mobs), the distinction between performance art and the performance of everyday life is blurred. In this, post-dramatic theatre is in many regards linked to the development of performance art and the avant-garde practices of the Futurists and Dadaists.

A key aspect of post-dramatic theatre is to stress the ambivalence of the human body being both subject and object (see Box 14.2). It often incorporates not only the audience as co-subjects but also a metacommunicative reversal of roles in the plays. This shall be exemplified with some works of Christoph Schlingensief (1960–2010), German director and artist, who emphasized, among other things, the agency of material objects and spaces that have an impact on human bodies. Many of his plays and installations make those spaces interact that are traditionally kept apart. His constantly growing and changing installation *Animatograph*, for example, was a performative installation that travelled to different places. First shown in 2005 on the occasion of an art festival in Reykjavík, it was also set up in traditional theatre contexts such as the Burgtheater in Vienna and the Volksbühne in Berlin as well as in public places, such as a woodland in Germany or a small township nearby Lüderitz in Namibia.

The title of this installation refers to early types of animatographs or rather theatrographs from the nineteenth century. Back then, different images like photographs or paintings were projected both on actors on the stage but also on the audience. As a result, not only the staged play but also the audience became the object of the gaze and an integrated part of the 'real' play (Berka 2010). Thus, the installation consists of *and* generates different wooden segments and spaces with screens and projectors, each being used as a potential projection surface itself. When installed somewhere, overlapping images as well as sounds were constantly projected on and woven into the installation that came across as a living organism that includes bodies as basic media and potential technical media, again breaking conventional theatre structures. The audience could enter the maze-like and slowly moving 'stage' that became then an intermedial web of images, visual impressions, references and connotations. The use of modern technologies, parallel screenings and projections, and even revolving stages in Schlingensief's work, are neither bound to functionality nor the perfect illusion of a fictive make-believe world. Rather, they emphasize the mediality of the theatre performances. However, as theatre performances are often connected to fictionality, at least to some degree, the post-dramatic tendencies of Schlingensief's theatre foreground the sociopolitical functions of performances rather than frames of illusion. In this regard, it rejects traditional differentiation between subject and object (see Box 14.2). In emphasizing the material and spatiotemporal modality, his theatre concept breaks down the fourth wall. Besides, by interconnecting all present bodies (both acting and non-acting) the complex process of mediation and the mediatization of self-referentiality becomes present.

As mentioned earlier, post-dramatic theatre particularly questions the conventional entanglement between bodily performances and theatre buildings, implying a distinction between reality and fiction. How this convention is disturbed, shall be exemplified with another work by Schlingensief. During his project *Passion Impossible – 7 Day Emergency Call for Germany*, Schlingensief left the classical theatre building of the Schauspielhaus Hamburg in 1997 and, dressed up as a police officer, interacted with other characters, the audience and people in the centre of the city. While Schlingensief's 'staging of the city' strived to emphasize the mediality of reality as a practice of representation itself, this appearance and acting was not clearly framed as art/theatre/performance. Therefore, also 'other' police officers did not stay in the conventionally passive role of spectators, but became active: they investigated Schlingensief's status as a police officer and thus explored the distinction between reality and play/illusion that is normally fundamental for separating qualified media products from the everyday life.

In short, any space can potentially become a stage. Thus, both material and non-material phenomena can create a multi-layered symbolic situation that can oscillate between the physical space and the fictional place. Even the performing bodies of actors and spectators oscillate between different roles: between being present in the 'here and now' and referring to an immaterial narrative of another 'reality' at the same time. Later, so-called flash mobs take up these post-dramatic tendencies although these ephemeral pop-up performances outside of the institutionalized, architectural spaces of theatres are less theoretically grounded in theatre studies. They also demonstrate that subjects can suddenly be turned into objects and the other way around. By drawing attention to themselves as unexpected interventions in public spaces (see Box 14.1), they, ideally, create 'zones' of a certain spatiotemporal intensity to supersede other institutionalized or even economic structures of partly organized, partly randomly co-present human bodies in public.

This development complicates the theoretical analysis drawing on fixed and generalized categories. A dynamic intermedial understanding of theatre emphasizes that performers and spectators 'act' together in performative spaces and times (Bowler 2015). In the words of theatre historian David Wiles, performative events should not be analysed separately from where they take place: 'the play-as-text can be performed *in* a space, but the play-as-event belongs to the space, and makes the space perform as much as it makes the actors perform' (Wiles 2003, p. 1). In addition, performances in and outside institutionalized theatrical buildings are shared perceptual and imaginative efforts of spatiotemporal and semiotic modalities that become entangled in the spectators' process of semiosis.

In summary, this chapter explored the shifting concept of theatre and theatrical performances from an intermedial perspective by foregrounding how the material and spatiotemporal modality becomes performative value. Theatre transforms the body into a technical medium of display. At the same time, the body is also a basic medium that oscillates between actor and spectator, active and passive, subject and object, fictitious and real. In particular, post-dramatic theatre draws from this tension. Therefore, theatre can be considered a collaborative media product whose dynamic borders challenge any fixed conceptualization.

References

Berka, R. 2010. Schlingensief's animatograph: Time here becomes space. In T. Forrest and A.T. Scheer, eds., *Art without borders* (pp. 169–186). Bristol: Intellect.

Bowler, L.M. 2015. *Theatre architecture as embodied space: A phenomenology of theatre buildings in performance*, PhD thesis. München: Ludwig-Maximilians-University München. https://edoc.ub.uni-muenchen.de/20310/7/Bowler_Lisa_Marie.pdf [Accessed 1 February 2021].

Lehmann, H.T. 2006. *Postdramatic theatre*. New York: Routledge.

Wiles, D. 2003. *Short history of Western performance space*. New York: Cambridge University Press.

Wolf, Werner. 2011. (Inter)mediality and the study of literature. *CLCWeb: Comparative Literature and Culture*, 13(3).

15 Transmedial storyworlds

Mikael Askander, Anna Gutowska and Péter Kristóf Makai

When the writers of the television series *Game of Thrones* asked George R.R. Martin (b. 1948), the author of the *A Song of Ice and Fire* series of novels, about some of the changes he made, Martin shot back with a question of his own: 'How many children did Scarlett have?' This retort is meant to remind audiences that there is a discrepancy between the book and film version of the American classic *Gone With the Wind*. Famously, Scarlett O'Hara has three children in Margaret Mitchell's novel, but only one in its film adaptation.

Martin's remark brings us into the territory of *transmedial storyworlds* and *transfictions*. Throughout history, many influential cultural texts gave rise to series of adaptations, appropriations and references across a range of different media. Popular stories get endlessly adapted, appropriated and reinterpreted across a range of media, from literary works to paintings, sculpture, music, film and television, thus creating vast, interconnected universes of stories. We could also call such texts *palimpsests*. The Greek term *palimpsestos* originally referred to a piece of parchment from which the old text has been scraped off and the parchment reused for a new text. Since parchment was made from treated animal skin, the old text could not be erased perfectly, so traces of the old letters were still visible under the new layer of text.

In the 1980s, the influential French literary critic Gérard Genette gave new meaning to this term in literary criticism. In his book *Palimpsests: Literature of the Second Degree* (Genette 1997), he used it to describe a process wherein writers refer back to earlier texts and 'overwrite' or 'rewrite' them. Genette coined the term 'hypotext' to refer to the source text and 'hypertext' to refer to the later text that is inspired by the original (1997, p. 5). For example, Charlotte Brontë's novel *Jane Eyre* (1847) would be a hypotext, and Jean Rhys's novel *Wide Sargasso Sea* (1966), which is a prequel to/retelling of *Jane Eyre* from the perspective of Mr Rochester's estranged wife Bertha, would be a hypertext. More loosely, *Jane Eyre, Wide Sargasso Sea* and other ancillary texts inspired by Brontë's novel as well as its many stage and screen adaptations could also be analysed as an example of a transmedial storyworld.

The terms transmedia (or transmedial) storyworld and transfiction are sometimes used interchangeably, even though their focus is slightly different. A transmedia storyworld emphasizes the shared elements of a universe that exists across a range of different media (for example, the *Star Wars* franchise includes feature films, live-

DOI: 10.4324/9781003174288-18

action and animated television series, comic books, novels, video games and theme park attractions). The term *transmedia*, made famous by Henry Jenkins in *Convergence Culture* (2006), literally means 'across media', and thus – as specified by Jan-Noël Thon's overview of the relevant literature (Thon 2015) – it describes phenomena that are not media-specific, but which exist across a range of different media types.

In contrast, *transfiction* is narrower in scope: it is a term used to describe a situation in which 'two (or more) texts share elements such as [...] characters, imaginary locations, or fictional worlds' (Saint-Gelais quoted in Ryan 2012, p. 612). The term emphasizes the fictional nature of the migrating entities, whereas *transmedial storyworld* can also apply to non-fictitious phenomena. Thus, we can talk about the huge *Star Wars* transmedial storyworld in general or the Han Solo transfiction specifically; the latter is a part of the whole universe and encompasses the nine feature films and the character's origin story (the film *Solo: A Star Wars Story* (2018), as well as novels, graphic novels and video games featuring the character.

Transmedia storytelling is another related term that has been pioneered by the influential cultural studies scholar Henry Jenkins. It is strongly connected to the term transmedial storyworld, but, unlike the latter, it emphasizes the process of storyworld creation rather than the product. Jenkins defines transmedia storytelling as 'a process where integral elements of a fiction get dispersed systematically across multiple delivery channels for the purpose of creating a unified and coordinated entertainment experience' (Jenkins 2006, p. 17). While Jenkins researches contemporary popular culture and uses *Star Wars, Harry Potter* or *The Matrix* as his case studies, the narrative model he describes can also be used to describe transmedial storyworlds throughout history.

Another pioneer of transmedial narratology, Marie-Laure Ryan, develops Jenkins' theory and suggests that in fact transmedia storytelling constitutes a special case of transfictionality, one where the migration of fictional entities operates across many different media. According to Ryan, *transmedial storytelling* can encompass three possible relationships between the text and the storyworld: (1) one text/one storyworld; (2) one text/many storyworlds; (3) many texts/one storyworld (Ryan 2012, p. 365). Ryan also distinguishes between 'top-down' and 'bottom-up' transmedial storytelling (Ryan 2015, p. 5). In the former case, the transmedial universe and the ways in which it is going to be revealed across different media are planned in advance, and in the latter, it starts in an unpremeditated way, motivated by the creators' desire to exploit the success of a narrative originally conceived as autonomous (Ryan 2015, p. 6). The *Matrix* franchise, which was envisaged as a transmedia universe from the start, would be an example of the top-down approach, and the *Star Wars* franchise, which followed organically from the success of the first three films, would be an example of the bottom-up approach. Following Ryan's analysis of transmedia, Jan-Noël Thon also notes that transmedial storyworlds can be varying mixtures of canonical media products (that have either a single author, or many authors) and fan-produced material (Thon 2015, p. 45).

The transmedial universes that rule today's popular culture, such as the Wizarding World (the Harry Potter Universe) or the Marvel Cinematic

Universe, all belong to the many texts/one storyworld type. They are commercial media franchises, constructed by the producers to whom the intellectual property belongs, in order to maximize audience engagement. Its main strategy is to split an overarching grand narrative into smaller storylines, each of which contributes a piece of the larger puzzle. They coordinate the evolution of the storyworld across media to reach audiences with different demographic characteristics and also to expand the range of associated material products (toys, collectibles, clothing, etc.) that are available for purchase.

Although transmediality, understood as migration of information across different media, has been an important feature of cultural production in many eras and societies, it is worth noting that in the last few decades much of contemporary entertainment media almost exclusively relies on adaptations or transmedial storyworlds. Virtually all the franchises that dominate the global box office, like the Wizarding World, the Marvel Cinematic Universe, the DC Comics universe, the Game of Thrones or The Lord of the Rings franchises, exist across a range of media.

These cultural giants can be studied from a range of critical perspectives that focuses on the question of authorship and authorial control and considers the relationship between the official canon and the fan communities, fan fiction and fan art, emphasizes media affordances (which stories work best in which medium and why) and studies the industry-relations (focusing on production aspects, financial aspects and creating brand loyalty by adding new media to a transmedial franchise).

In the rest of the chapter, we will use intermedial theory to elucidate the creation of the following transmedial storyworlds that were made from the late nineteenth century to the twenty-first century:

- *Sherlock Holmes* – a transfiction that started in the late nineteenth century with Arthur Conan Doyle's detective stories. It features new additions, including multiple reinventions, reimaginings and the reappropriations of the main character (e.g. in the TV series *Sherlock* (2010–17) and *Elementary* (2012–19), or the movie franchise starring Robert Downey Jr. as Holmes). Our case study discusses how Sherlock Holmes becomes transmedially recognizable as a character through the standardization of his attributes and his attitudes towards sleuthing and technology across the centuries (for transmedia characters and Holmes, see Thon 2019).
- *Penny Dreadful* (2014–16) – a transmedial franchise (incorporating a television series and several graphic novels) that also has its roots in the nineteenth century. However, in contrast to the *Sherlock Holmes* transfiction, *Penny Dreadful* is a mash-up that draws its inspiration from a range of nineteenth-century 'monster narratives'. In our case study, we analyse how sources in the public domain were used by the showrunners to create a coherent storyworld through the palimpsestic reappropriation and re-righting of the originals.
- *Welcome to Night Vale* (2012–) – an intellectual property that began its life as a series of podcasts about the fictional American town of Night Vale, where

every conspiracy theory is true; Night Vale was later portrayed in several novels and staged as a live tour. Our case study investigates how the sensory unimodality of the audio drama format left much open to the audiences' imagination, which the producers capitalized on when they added to the Night Vale storyworld in subsequent live performances and novels.

All three cases discussed in this chapter include fairly recent additions to their transmedial worlds. While the *Sherlock Holmes* transfiction is over 100 years old, it is still very vibrant and has recently been rejuvenated with new media products which attained international popularity (this is especially true of the BBC television series *Sherlock*, starring Benedict Cumberbatch, which became a global cultural phenomenon). The three cases were chosen to shed light on a variety of strategies used in a transmedial expansion of their storyworlds.

The transmedial Sherlock Holmes

Since Sherlock Holmes first appeared in Arthur Conan Doyle's novel *A Study in Scarlet* (1887), the world-famous detective has been omnipresent in culture and public discourse all around the globe. Although there are several key attributes that make Holmes immediately recognizable to modern audiences, such as the meerschaum pipe, the deerstalker hat and the phrase 'Elementary, my dear Watson!', they do not appear in the original stories of Conan Doyle, but were later additions to the character. To understand Holmes, you have to consider the original stories as part of a much larger web of cultural texts. Just a few years after Doyle's first Holmes story, the detective had already moved on from the page to the stage, to the radio play, to the cinema screen, to the TV series, and later on to the gaming industry (see Boström 2017). An interesting example of his presence in the gaming industry is found in *Sherlocked* (2015–), an escape room in the city of Malmö, Sweden. You can visit this room with your friends or colleagues and form a group that will be locked in the room for an hour. You will be dressed up in period clothing to properly fit into Sherlock Holmes' era, and during that hour, you will be asked to find clues, solve a riddle, etc. to escape from the room.

Through the decades, Sherlock Holmes appeared in many different forms of storytelling and media constellations, so we can analyse the character in terms of transmediality. He is a predecessor to transmedial franchise models of the twentieth and twenty-first century such as Disney, Star Wars and the Wizarding World. In the 2010s, this becomes obvious through a variety of productions that were more or less obvious rewritings of Doyle's canonical Sherlock Holmes universe. Many of them seem to strive to both connect to the 'real' Sherlock Holmes and develop new angles on the beloved character. In the TV series *Elementary* (2012–), Holmes and Watson solve crimes in New York, and the Watson character is not a John but a female doctor named Joan. A less obvious example is *House M.D.* (2004–12), a TV series in which the names of the protagonists are changed to House and Wilson. They do not fight crime but diagnose medical conditions and work in a hospital, facing mysterious illnesses to be identified and understood. The hospital context is fitting: Doyle himself was a doctor, and in his creation of Sherlock Holmes, he is said to have been inspired by one of his teachers.

Steven Moffat and Mark Gatiss's TV series *Sherlock* (BBC 2010–17) is another success story: it has run for four seasons since it started in 2010. Here, Sherlock Holmes (Benedict Cumberbatch) and his sidekick Dr John Watson (Martin Freeman) are placed in contemporary London to solve crimes. Much of the plot is based on Doyle's stories, but parts of the story have been rearranged and modernized. An example of this is the first episode, 'A Study in Pink'. The title has been changed from Doyle's 'scarlet' to 'pink' (which is the favourite colour of the murdered woman in the story). In Gatiss's vision, the detective is also a genius when it comes to the use of different digital devices, such as mobile phones, computers and satellite navigation systems.

Holmes' intermedialities

Plenty of intermedial dimensions can be identified within the storyworld of Sherlock Holmes: in the written and published books we find combinations of words and images (illustrations), and we also find references within the stories themselves to other art forms and media, such as music, for example when Holmes and Watson go to a concert or when Holmes plays the violin, etc. Doyle's original stories are therefore already intermedial because they are combinations of words and images. Sidney Paget's illustrations influenced which actors were chosen to play Holmes in film and TV versions. Of course, *Sherlock Holmes* is also intermedial in the sense that it has generated many adaptations, rewritings and transmedial processes.

So let's focus on the BBC's *Sherlock* for a while. In this series, the viewers meet Holmes and Watson as they are living in the digital mediascape of the twenty-first century. In Doyle's stories, Watson is the narrator. He writes up his experiences of solving cases with Holmes with a pen and paper in books and a traditional diary. In *Sherlock*, Watson writes a blog. Holmes publishes his reflections on different scientific discoveries on his homepage, 'The Art of Deduction', while in Doyle's stories he submits scientific articles to different journals. The blog and the homepage are part of *Sherlock*, the diegetic world of Holmes and Watson. When the series aired, however, these sites went up on the internet. On these pages, Watson and Holmes communicated with their followers as if they were living in our world. This was not a unique occasion; the same kind of transmedia storytelling was put to great use in the Lionsgate Television series *Mad Men* (2007–15), when characters from the story tweeted on Twitter about their fictional lives.

Sherlock Holmes has travelled across media borders extensively: from technical to technical medium, from basic to basic medium, and from qualified to qualified medium. Some examples could be identified like this:

- from technical to technical medium: from paper and ink (book) to screens;

- from basic to basic medium: from the printed words of the novels to the orally performed words on film and TV;
- from qualified to qualified medium: from crime fiction novel to theatre play and to film.

So, we have this detective, Sherlock Holmes, who is depicted in different media types, and consequently the modalities of the media in question also differ.

A good way of discussing the transmedial Sherlock Holmes is by way of the concept of cultural icons (see Lund (2012) and Brooker (2001)). A cultural icon may appear in several media. It does not have to be a single story, character or real person, but can also come in the shape of a poetic expression, a piece of music, a building (like the Eiffel Tower) or something else (e.g. images of the double helix). Famous cultural icons are found in every qualified media type, from Frankenstein's monster to Marilyn Monroe, Hamlet with Yorick's skull, or the intro to a very famous rock song such as Deep Purple's 'Smoke on the Water'.

In *Sherlock*, there are plenty of references to the fan cultures of Sherlock Holmes as they have appeared throughout the decades. Lyndsay Faye explains this phenomenon by pointing at the 'opacity' of Sherlock Holmes: he becomes a riddle, a gap for everyone to fill in, reflect upon and dream about. That, according to Faye, is part of the mystery of the transmedial power of Sherlock Holmes:

> Sherlock Holmes as a popular heroic figure displays a remarkable level of tantalizing opacity [...] Therein lies the magic, I would posit, both for fans and for Sherlockians, at least for those inclined to create their own transformative works.
>
> (Faye 2012, s. 5–6)

If this is true, this opacity will probably continue to be at work for a long time to come and Sherlock Holmes will continue to be a cultural icon and an intermedial and transmedial construction in many different media.

Appropriating the nineteenth-century icons: The storyworld of *Penny Dreadful*

In our discussion of the Sherlock Holmes transfiction we touched on the notion of character recognizability. How many features (and which features?) of Conan Doyle's character do we need to decide that a given fictional character is recognizable as a version of Sherlock Holmes? Is Doctor Gregory House, the protagonist of *House, M.D.*, recognizable as a reinvention of the iconic character, even though he is a medical doctor and not a detective? And is *Elementary*'s Joan Watson, an American Chinese woman living in modern-day New York, still a version of Dr John Watson?

The question of character recognizability becomes even more interesting in the case of mash-ups, which are storyworlds that take their inspiration from various earlier texts and thus simultaneously contribute to multiple transfictions. In this section we discuss one such example: *Penny Dreadful*, which originated in 2014 as a television series created by the acclaimed Hollywood screenwriter John Logan. The series ran on Showtime for three seasons (2014–16), garnering a string of accolades, including BAFTA awards and Emmy nominations. When it was cancelled, the creators decided to continue expanding the storyworld with graphic novels, and they have also produced a spin-off television series called *Penny Dreadful: City of Angels* (2020), which is thematically connected to the original series but set in a completely new setting with a new cast of characters.

The creation of the spin-off means that technically *Penny Dreadful* should be considered an 'anthology series', meaning a type of television, film or radio series which presents a new set of characters and a new story in every episode or season that are unrelated to the previous ones. It should be noted that *Penny Dreadful* is not a typical anthology series, because its first three seasons constituted one coherent story, but the existence of the spin-off seems to move the series in that direction. However, in this section we are only going to discuss the original television series (seasons 1–3, released between 2014 and 2016).

What is interesting about *Penny Dreadful* from an intermedial and transmedial perspective is that the series is not a straightforward case of the adaptation of one nineteenth-century text, and it does not add to just one existing transfiction (as is the case with *Sherlock*). *Penny Dreadful* is a *mash-up* in which characters from various out-of-copyright novels coexist in a shared storyworld. These characters are the protagonists and villains of iconic nineteenth-century 'monster narratives': *Frankenstein* by Mary Shelley (1818), *The Strange Case of Dr Jekyll and Mr Hyde* by R.L. Stevenson (1886), *The Picture of Dorian Gray* by Oscar Wilde (1890) and *Dracula* by Bram Stoker (1897).

The scope of *Penny Dreadful*'s world-building ambition is perhaps not on the same scale as that of the creators of *Star Wars* or *Harry Potter*'s fictional universes, but what is notable about this television series is how it uses the different 'building blocks' from iconic nineteenth-century novels. As a consequence, the series can be said to add new material simultaneously to as many as four separate transfictions related to the four novels that it appropriates.

Penny Dreadful's production history is a little bit unusual in contemporary television practice, in that it just had one writer, who was also one of the producers and thus had an unusual amount of creative control. For a high-end television series, typically there is a lead writer or a showrunner working with a team of other writers. But in the case of *Penny Dreadful*, John Logan wrote all 27 episodes. He already had a distinguished career as a screenwriter, having written scripts for a number of Hollywood blockbusters and two James Bond films.

When Logan talks about the genesis of *Penny Dreadful*, he often repeats that what started him off was a very simple realization – that three of the most iconic nineteenth-century novels 'about monsters' – *Dracula*, *Dr Jekyll and Mr Hyde* and *Dorian Gray* – were published within a few years of each other. To this list he adds another, much earlier but probably still more influential nineteenth-century 'monster narrative': *Frankenstein* (1818). Once he decided on the material to be appropriated, he started to envisage a universe where the characters from all these novels could coexist and interact. He pitched the idea to Sam Mendes, with whom he had collaborated on the James Bond film *Skyfall*, and they managed to find a television studio interested in the project. A decisive factor was the phenomenal success of the first seasons of *Game of Thrones* (2011–18), which opened the door for other expensive fantasy projects because they had demonstrated that there could be a global mainstream audience for such projects.

But what is fascinating about *Penny Dreadful* from a transmedial perspective is not only that it appropriates characters and storylines from multiple novels but also that it includes references to their culturally significant adaptations. It can thus be said to appropriate the source texts as well as their subsequent adaptations. In fact, analysing the inspirations for *Penny Dreadful* can be compared to an archaeological excavation: it is all about unearthing subsequent layers of appropriation. The very bottom layer is constituted by the out-of-copyright nineteenth-century novels. The expiration of copyright often means that there is an opportunity to greatly expand a now cheaply accessible storyworld, as we have also seen with H.P. Lovecraft's (1890–1937) universe of weird stories recently.

As we said before, Dracula, Dr Frankenstein and his creature, Dr Jekyll and Dorian Gray coexist in *Penny Dreadful's* storyworld. They are accompanied by a range of lesser-known characters from the original novels, especially from Bram Stoker's *Dracula*: Dr Seward (here turned into a female 'alienist'), Renfield (Dracula's hapless first victim in Stoker's novel), Mina Murray and Dr Van Helsing all appear in *Penny Dreadful* in minor, though crucial, roles.

The next layer of the palimpsest that is *Penny Dreadful* are the canonical Hollywood adaptations of *Dracula* and *Frankenstein*: the Universal Monsters franchise (1920s–40s). A clear proof that Logan wanted to reference the Universal movies as inspiration is the character of Ethan Chandler, played by Josh Hartnett. In a plot twist towards the end of season one, the character is revealed to be a werewolf, and his real name turns out to be Ethan Talbot – 'Talbot' being the real name of The Wolfman in the Universal Monsters universe.

The third layer of inspiration is Francis Ford Coppola's adaptation of *Dracula* (1992), visible in the TV series' portrayal of Dracula in season three and in some more subtle references in costume and stage design.

The fourth major layer of inspiration is steampunk, notably *The League of Extraordinary Gentlemen* comic book series created by Alan Moore (1999). The similarities between *Penny Dreadful* and this graphic novel and its rather disappointing screen adaptation are so pronounced that *Penny Dreadful* was actually accused of plagiarism by some reviewers. And given the fact that *The League* itself is also an appropriation of late-Victorian material (the inspirations for its characters include Dracula, Dr Jekyll and Mr Hyde, Jules Verne's Captain Nemo and Henry Rider Haggard's Allan Quatermain), we are dealing with an interesting question: if an appropriation appropriates an earlier appropriation of a source text which is now out of copyright, can we still talk about plagiarism?

Finally, there is one additional source of inspiration: the literary genre of the penny dreadful itself. In the mid-nineteenth century, the 'penny dreadful' was a derogatory term for long-running, serialized novels that often featured supernatural elements. One of the most famous penny dreadfuls, *Varney the Vampire* (1845–7) is explicitly referenced in the series as a part of its storyworld.

The existence of these manifold layers of inspiration also means that *Penny Dreadful* can rightfully be called a palimpsestic appropriation. The term 'palimpsest' highlights a text's references to earlier texts (possibly in an oblique or allusive way), and appropriation is described by Julie Sanders (2006) in her *Adaptation and Appropriation* as a practice requiring 'a more decisive journey away from the informing source into a wholly new cultural product of domain' (p. 26). According to these definitions, then, the difference between adaptation and appropriation is one of degree: bolder and freer adaptations would be called appropriations.

There is also another technical term that describes John Logan's strategy even more precisely, especially when it comes to his approach to *Frankenstein*. 'Re-righting' is a term that was coined by the French adaptation scholar Chantal Zabus (2001) and that denotes a kind of rewriting or adaptation 'that aims at redressing certain wrongs and restoring an apocryphal script that has been suppressed due to ideological pressures present at the time of writing the original text' (Zabus 2001, p. 195). Re-righting becomes a political and ideological practice: it sets right the perceived wrongs in the original text and rescues characters and storylines that were treated 'unfairly' by the original writers. Zabus' theory is deeply rooted in postmodern discourse, especially in Gérard Genette's narratology and his notion of the palimpsest. Zabus' re-righting seems imminently applicable to many recent adaptations/rewritings that clearly have a political agenda, for example, the ITV television series *The Frankenstein Chronicles* (2015–) and *The Great* (2020), a quasi-biographical television series about the Russian ruler Catherine the Great, which plays fast and loose with historical facts.

In very general terms, the three seasons of *Penny Dreadful* can be seen as an attempt to re-right the plots of its two main inspirations, *Dracula* and *Frankenstein*. With regard to *Dracula*, the series achieves this by giving the protagonist Vanessa Ives (who is a stand-in for Bram Stoker's female protagonist, Mina Murray) more agency, and with regard to *Frankenstein*, by asking the audience to sympathize or even identify with the creature. The series' sympathetic treatment of Frankenstein's creature, who here initially uses the name of Caliban and then adopts the name of a historical figure, a minor Romantic poet called John Clare, bears a strong resemblance to many iconic twentieth-century rewritings of canonical texts whose mission is to 'rescue' the Other in the story. They include Michel Tournier's novel *Friday, or, The Other Island* (a 1967 rewriting of *Robinson Crusoe* from the perspective of Friday) and Jean Rhys's *Wide Sargasso Sea* (1966), which rewrites *Jane Eyre* from the perspective of Rochester's estranged wife, 'the madwoman in the attic' of Brontë's original novel. A more recent example is *Indigo* by Marina Warner (1992), which rewrites Shakespeare's *The Tempest* to restore dignity to the play's purported villains, Caliban and his mother, Sycorax.

Why do creators of modern cultural texts so often resort to palimpsestic appropriation? Why do so many contemporary novels, graphic novels, films and television series adapt and build on earlier works? There are many factors that make such a practice attractive from the creators' point of view. Appropriating a successful and influential cultural text means that there will be at least some 'in-built' audience for the new media product, which will consist of fans of the original, which the new project's marketing campaign can capitalize on. This goes a long way to explaining the proliferation of remakes, sequels, prequels and spin-offs at the box office. A new version of *Dracula*, *Sherlock Holmes*, *Pride and Prejudice* or *Robin Hood* will be easier to finance and promote than a completely original idea and will be guaranteed to have a captive audience.

Additionally, in the case of texts that exist in the public domain, using them for inspiration is cost-free, and therefore even more tempting. While the legal situation may vary in different countries, the general rule of thumb is that if more than seventy years have elapsed since the death of the original author, all their works enter the public domain and can thus be freely adapted and appropriated. Naturally, today that 'out-of-copyright' category includes almost all texts written in the nineteenth century and before. All Greek myths, medieval romances and Shakespeare's plays are now in the public domain and constitute a shared cultural heritage of all humanity, which anybody can appropriate in any way they like. The proliferation of these adaptations creates the rich, interwoven tapestry of today's culture that forms a kind of master-palimpsest.

The spirit of community radio: The case of *Welcome to Night Vale*

When judged against the worldwide success of the universes of *Star Wars*, *Star Trek* or Marvel, most other transmedia storyworlds pale in comparison. However, these less obvious examples of transmedial worlds are still worth considering, because their niche appeal and less commercial approach to building a storyworld offer more room for formal experimentation and original content. One such example is the transmedial world built by the hit podcast *Welcome to Night Vale*. In this section we discuss the Night Vale universe and how the modalities of the qualified medium of the audio drama podcast allowed for world-building opportunities and the engagement of the audience with the storyworld as these opportunities were expanded.

The brainchild of Jeffrey Cranor and Joseph Fink, *Welcome to Night Vale* (2015, WTNV) is a twice-monthly podcast that details the disturbingly weird life of a mysterious, fictional desert town in the Southwestern United States, Night Vale. It is a place 'where all conspiracy theories are true, where the mundane is extraordinary and the extraordinary is mundane' (Kelso 2018). Delivered in the style of a typical US community radio broadcast, *Welcome to Night Vale* is hosted by Cecil Gershwin Palmer (via the sonorous voice of Cecil Baldwin), and is released in 25–30-minute segments on the 1st and 15th of every month. The show has been downloaded more than 220 million times

(Heathman 2019) and has a cult following which helped propel the podcast to international fame. Often compared with the likes of TV series *Twin Peaks* (1990–1) by way of *A Prairie Home Companion* (1974–2016), it is a narrative universe where the core of the world-building is fleshed out in the 150-odd episodes of the podcast, with additional stand-alone stories featuring the main characters in the two published *Night Vale* novels and the yearly, self-contained live shows, performed in Europe and North America.

As an audio drama podcast, *Welcome to Night Vale* exists primarily as a digital audio recording, accessible on the internet via computers, smartphones and related devices (technical media of display). An audio drama can vary in format and length as well as in its formal properties, from a single narrating voice to a cast of characters. It is recorded by other devices, such as microphones and audio mixers (Heater 2019) that leave particular traces of their recording unless edited out. In the diegetic world, Cecil is in the recording studio of the Night Vale Community Radio building, which is equipped with 'a recording booth, a production booth, a bloodstone circle, a broadcasting tower [...] a break room where dead interns are buried [and] the office of Station Management, which seems to be larger on the inside than its external dimensions should allow' (Night Vale Community Radio 2020), among other eldritch features. Podcasts differ from traditional radio dramas in that they are broadcast instead of narrowcast, and although original releases are scheduled, earlier episodes can be accessed on-demand, whereas traditional radio shows are broadcast only once, perhaps with a few reruns.

The audio-only format means that WTNV conveys the entirety of civil life in Night Vale via the use of sound. This leaves a lot of room for the imagination, and listeners readily immerse themselves in the fictional world of the show, since they are addressed as citizens of the town. The power of the radio format lies in the medium's capacity to 'bring life to imaginative landscapes that have been rendered impossible to stage by the realist tradition' (Hill 1996, p. 112). And there is no shortage of impossibly imaginative landscapes and situations: sometimes a large pyramid suddenly appears in the middle of town (episode 9, 'Pyramid'), and there is a cat, Khoshekh, floating exactly 4 feet above the ground in the station's bathroom (episode 2, 'Glow Cloud'). The medium's lack of visual information also allows the audience to use their imaginations to fill in notable visual and spatial blanks (e.g. 'What does Cecil look like?', 'How is the town laid out?'), which results in a surge of creative interpretations of what is audio canon, ranging from consensus fan art (so-called fanon) that depicts what Cecil might look like to detailed maps of the town (Davis 2013) featuring the iconic locales mentioned in the broadcast (see Hancock (2018) and McCumber (2018)).

In terms of media modalities, a contemporary audio drama that mimics a community radio broadcast uses a single sensory modality: all information reaches the listeners through the ear. Thus, WTNV has a limited toolkit for the representation of space, because the medium 'does not possess the essential concreteness of the theatre space' (Hill 1996, p. 116). For example, world-building is restricted to verbal descriptions and utterances about spatial features and physical circumstances. However, due to the sprawling nature of the podcast (which has released over 170 episodes at the time of writing, close to the end of 2020), there is ample room to develop the storyworld into a living, breathing town. In a talk given at Google's headquarters, leading man Cecil Baldwin stated:

> [W]hat's interesting about doing a show that is ongoing and episodic and epic is that you always have the chance to change things [and] worldbuild […] to go off on tangents and explore little cul-de-sacs, and then maybe go back to the main plot.
>
> (Baldwin 2017, 22:52)

Nonetheless, the audio format allows the producers to give voice to the townsfolk, with trained voice actors lending personality to recurring characters. Besides the DJ, we also hear the voice of the citizens in interviews and on-the-spot reports, including the voices of Dylan Marron as Cecil's husband, Mara Wilson as the Faceless Old Woman who secretly lives in your home, Symphony Sanders as 16-year-old militia leader Tamika Flynn, and Wil Wheaton as chef Earl Harlan. Their stories unfold and intermingle with the larger life of the community, and the podcast format, as Joseph Fink states, allows a more experimental style of writing:

> With podcasting, you can do all sorts of things you can't do on radio. We've done things like release two different episodes which tell the story from two different points of view. We've released an episode that has three different endings depending on how you download it.
>
> (Brennan 2019)

With regard to time and temporality, the show is uploaded at the beginning and the 15th of every month, but within the fictional universe, Cecil gives the audience hints that he is on air more often, even if real-world listeners are not privy to those broadcasts. In the podcast, time follows the progression of the primary world, like a Christmas edition around our Christmas time (episode 120, 'All Smiles' Eve'), or a Thanksgiving edition in the lead-up to real-life Thanksgiving (episode 78, 'Cooking Stuff'). In every show's storyline, complications within the show build up in the first 12–15 minutes, followed by a non-narrative portion, the weather report, which exclusively features music. During the weather segment, narrative time passes (sometimes five minutes, sometimes five weeks), just enough for the plot to resolve itself in the remaining 7–10 minutes. Unlike with traditional broadcasts, such as the community radio format WTNV is patterned after, the streaming audience can skip and rewind parts of the recording to gloss over particular segments (i.e. advertisements) or to listen again more intently to bits and pieces they might have missed.

Materially speaking, WTNV's stories are mediated via sound waves that are digitally recorded by microphones. Raw recordings are stored on computers during the editing phase, when audio software is used to edit and polish the recordings to make them suitable for broadcasting. They are then uploaded onto the internet, from where they are available on platforms such as Podbean, Podbay, Spotify or YouTube. Here, users can stream or download episodes to listen to them on their own devices.

Finally, the words and sound effects that make up the show convey cognitive import through semiotic means. As noted media scholar Mary Hill observes, 'being an aural medium, [radio] grants extra signifying power to words, silences, and rhythms' (Hill 1996, p. 112). This is exploited in the podcast to the full extent. The show naturally makes use of all three main categories of semiotic relationships. Hill reminds us that '[r]adio signifiers [...] do not replace that [which is absent] with a thing and thereby produce an illusion of presence. The radio sign works indexically – causally, or as an indication – rather than iconically' (p. 114). When listeners hear the shock or excitement in the voice of Cecil Baldwin as he plays the character Cecil Palmer, they hear a real person's voice, and it is indicative of play-acted shock or excitement. Similarly, sounds of ruffling paper, closing doors and other trivial sound effects are recorded with actual paper and doors and so on.

Other sounds effects are iconic: in episode 47, 'Company Picnic', announcers from Night Vale's rival town, Desert Bluffs, take over Cecil's place at the microphone, and at one point during the broadcast announce that a corporate-mandated, 15-second sound clip is to be played, described as 'a deep rumbling sound, like a giant dragging its prone, misshapen body across baked, waterless earth' (14:00–14:15). Due to the unfortunate lack of recordable giants in our world, the sound clip only mimics the sound of the fictional event. In some cases, voice modulation is used to provide an additional layer of meaning. In episode 42, 'Numbers', we hear the announcer of a numbers station calling out numbers with added static to simulate the low sound quality of spy broadcasts – it's *as if* the voice was coming from an actual station. Lo-fi sound quality is also used to suggest that something has been recorded on another medium, such as old tape, as in episode 33, 'Cassette', in which Cecil finds his childhood tape recordings.

On some occasions, however, voice modulation is used to signal that a shift or transformation has taken place in the diegetic world. One conspicuous example is episode 61, 'BRINY DEPTHS', in which Cecil is asked to utter the eponymous phrase. The words 'BRINY DEPTHS' are spoken in a clear, unmodulated voice at first, and then, as the broadcast progresses, it becomes more distorted and is sometimes accompanied by a piece of instrumental string music, suggesting that someone might be using it for an occult reason. The same episode is notable for other sound effects that fulfil symbolic purposes. A letter is sent to Cecil, but the address to which it is sent is not written in the standard postal format. Instead, it is represented by an audio recording, described by fan transcript site Cecil Speaks – Night Vale Transcripts (2015) as '[Perhaps the sound of ocean waves and birds played at 8kbps, followed by what sounds to me like three blows on a party horn, then a few moments of ambient crowd noise]', which might imply the presence of an alien intelligence which does not communicate using human words.

After the surprise success of the podcast, the cast has gone on to perform *Welcome to Night Vale* live as well. Initially, performances featured live readings of earlier scripts, and on the first anniversary of the show, a special episode was made (episode 25, 'One Year Later'). These performances have been noted to bridge the medial gap between the radio and the theatre: 'Despite it being a live reading of the podcast, the vibrance of the voice actors made it seem more like a stage production. Baldwin's stage presence was captivating. He encouraged dialogue and audience participation throughout numerous parts of the show' (Shin 2018). Since then, live shows and world tours are regularly produced with original scripts that allow for Rocky Horror Show-style audience participation.

Since there are no video recordings of such live performances, because the showrunners forbid them in an effort to preserve the intimacy and exclusivity of the live shows, we can only speculate how the cast and the audience interact with each other. In interviews, Cranor has intimated that 'sometimes we have call-and-response, or somebody from the audience who has to be addressed in some way' (Oyeniyi 2017, n.p.). Nonetheless, it stands to reason that *Night Vale* performances on stage break medial barriers and use the physical bodies of the audience members to incorporate them into the world of the live show. In a report about the 2018 touring live show 'A Spy in the Desert' in Tennessee, journalist Ainsley Kelso (2018) noted that 'one fan was brought up onto the stage to perform with the cast', and the writers of the live performance asserted that 'we are obviously thinking about what the audience is seeing. What the audience is feeling. How we can use the benefit of being in a room together. We have the option to use physical comedy' (n.p.).

In a stage performance, audience members can see and touch cast members, which might engage people more at the cost of having their mental images of the fictional characters shattered. Cecil Baldwin has stated that the script of the performance 'acknowledges that everyone is in the same room [...], if you are live on stage, you can't deny that', and the use of stand-alone scripts 'allows people who are not super-fans of the podcast to walk in and get what's going on' (Baldwin 2017, 43:14). These concessions are worth taking into consideration when analysing *Welcome to Night Vale* as an intermedial phenomenon. There is also a financial incentive, according to Joseph Fink: 'a podcast is free so in order to make money from it, you have to figure something else out [for the live shows]', hence the exclusivity and the audience participation (Brennan 2019, n.p.).

Similar growing pains hallmarked the creation of the first novel, simply titled *Welcome to Night Vale* (Fink and Cranor 2015). Most of the difficulties with the writing process were caused by the fact that Cranor and Fink were tackling a new medium. Describing their dilemmas candidly, they admitted:

> You can't write a novel the same way you write something people listen to. We thought a lot about visual rhythm, you know, sentence length,

paragraph length and how that is related to how people read it in a way we don't have to when we write for audio. The biggest thing we really had to think through was how to end it, because the way a continuing podcast works, it's kind of a juggling act. You are constantly landing stories, but at the same time, you are constantly throwing stories in the air, because otherwise you don't have anywhere to go. You always need to have something in the air. But with a book, everything needs to land at the end. You can't leave a bunch of stuff hanging in [the air].

('Welcome to Night Vale' Goes from Podcast to Page, 2015, n.p.)

The most obvious consequence of the medial change is that the novel brings the familiar setting alive on the page without Cecil Baldwin's vocal performance. Nonetheless, interspersed in the narrative, we find segments titled 'The Voice of Night Vale', which are put into the mouth of Cecil but lack the surefooted delivery associated with Baldwin. A more traditional narrator takes over Cecil's role as the main mediator of events, flitting from character to character to tell the story of the novel. The narrator often knows more than the character it follows, providing direct insight into the thoughts of the characters. When one of the protagonists, Diane, talks to the angels (who are all named Erica, as established by the podcast), we are given a look into the Ericas' minds: 'This was not why they were sad. Their sadness was unrelated to the conversation. It was not unrelated to the dirt-covered bundle on the kitchen counter' (Fink and Cranor 2015, p. 61). In line with the unsettling, mind-bending atmosphere of the podcast, sometimes the narrator involves the reader more directly than we would expect, based on our familiarity with classic, third-person, past-tense narration:

> Imagine a fifteen-year-old girl of mixed-race parents. That's pretty good. That's very close, she might say to anyone who described what she looked like. Diane didn't know what she looked like. She never cared to know. Many people would tell her anyway.
>
> (Fink and Cranor 2015, p. 71)

The lack of a clear, unambiguous external description owes something to the original broadcast format that treasures the listener's imaginative gap-filling, as does the direct, imperative address of the audience.

In summary, *Welcome to Night Vale* is a media franchise that has been transmediated from the airwaves to the page and stage. In the process, characters and locations which audiences have originally heard about and imagined in their own heads successfully grew more fleshed out. Fan communities have attempted to create a shared set of images and facts that anchor the disembodied voices in a pseudo-physical environment. As the original performers went on tour, they used their physical presence to complement their vocal performances and brought their audience materially into the world of Night Vale. Subsequent novelizations have attempted to bring the intimacy of the original vocal performances onto the page using the toolkit that novel writers have had for centuries to give a glimpse into the inner lives of the characters through the use of narration. The three different approaches show that different media are capable of realizing different material, sensorial, spatiotemporal and semiotic configurations to provide their audiences with a shared sense of fictional reality.

Conclusion

The very same processes of worldmaking that have made *Welcome to Night Vale* successful have enabled the creation of the transmedial worlds of the Sherlock Holmes universe and the transfiction *Penny Dreadful*. The reason why transmedial worlds have proven so popular is undoubtedly due to the alliance of the human imagination and the profit motive. Audiences who like stories set in a particular fictional universe will crave more of the same, by extending the stories of characters and places previously known, or by exploring the gaps of earlier cultural texts, or by reinventing their old premises for new sensibilities and audiences. Whatever the impulse behind the expansion, revision or reiteration of storyworlds, new media products garner attention and circulate in communities so that old intellectual properties may be judged anew.

References

Baldwin, C. 2017. Welcome to Night Vale. *Talks at Google* [video online]. https://www.youtube.com/watch?v=wdkwpZOyNEw [Accessed 27 April 2021].

Boström, M. 2017. *The life and death of Sherlock Holmes*. London: Head of Zeus.

Brennan, M. 2019. How 'Welcome to Night Vale' creators turned a podcast into a live event. *Irish Examiner*, 29 January. https://www.irishexaminer.com/breakingnews/lifestyle/culture/how-welcome-to-night-vale-creators-turned-a-podcast-into-a-live-event-900682.html [Accessed 27 April 2021].

Brooker, W. 2001. *Batman unmasked: Analyzing a cultural icon*. London: Continuum.

Cecil speaks – Night vale transcripts. 2015. Episode 61 – BRINY DEPTHS. https://cecilspeaks.tumblr.com/post/109756725541/episode-61-briny-depths [Accessed 27 April 2021].

Davis, L. 2013. A series of maps of the freaky city of Night Vale. *Gizmodo*, 9 August. https://io9.gizmodo.com/everyone-keep-looking-at-this-and-then-grabbing-their-e-1272878630.

Elementary (CBS, 2012–). TV series.

Faye, L. 2012. Prologue: Why Sherlock? Narrator investment in the BBC series. In L.E. Stein and K. Busse, eds., *Sherlock and transmedia fandom: Essays on the BBC series*. Jefferson: McFarland.

Fink, J. and Cranor, J. 2015. *Welcome to Night Vale: A novel*. New York: Harper.

Genette, G. 1997. *Palimpsests: Literature of the second degree*. Lincoln: University of Nebraska Press.

Hancock, D. 2018. Our friendly desert town: Alternative podcast culture in Welcome to Night Vale. In J.A. Weinstock, ed., *Critical approaches to Welcome to Night Vale: Podcasting between weather and the void* (pp. 35–50). Basingstoke: Palgrave Macmillan.

Heater, B. 2019. How I podcast: Start with this/Welcome to Night Vale's Jeffrey Cranor. *TechCrunch*. https://techcrunch.com/2019/05/08/how-i-podcast-start-with-this-welcome-to-night-vales-jeffrey-cranor/ [Accessed 27 April 2021].

Heathman, A. 2019. Welcome to Night Vale's creator on how to make a successful podcast. *London Evening Standard*, 25 January. https://www.standard.co.uk/tech/welcome-to-night-vale-jeffrey-cranor-interview-live-london-shows-a4047571.html [Accessed 27 April 2021].

Hill, M. 1996. Developing a blind understanding: A feminist revision of radio semiotics. *TDR*, 40(3), pp. 112–120.

House (FOX, 2004–2012). TV series.

Jenkins, H. 2006. *Convergence culture: Where old and new media collide*. New York: New York University Press.

Kelso, A. 2018. Podcast live show brings conspiracy theories to Bijou Theater. *Tennessee Journalist*, 5 October. https://tnjn.com/2018/10/05/podcast-live-show-brings-conspiracy-theories-to-the-bijou-theater/ [Accessed 27 April 2021].

Lund, H. 2012. *Kulturella ikoner*. Stockholm: Carlssons.

McCumber, A. 2018. 'It would make more sense for it to be there than not': Constructing Night Vale as a 'place'. In J.A. Weinstock, ed., *Critical approaches to Welcome to Night Vale: Podcasting between weather and the void* (pp. 69–82). Basingstoke: Palgrave Macmillan.

Moore, A. 1999. *The league of extraordinary gentlemen*. New York: DC Comics.

Night Vale Community Radio. 2020. Welcome to Night Vale wiki. https://nightvale.fandom.com/wiki/Night_Vale_Community_Radio [Accessed 27 April 2021].

Oyeniyi, D. 2017. Jeffrey Cranor welcomes you to Night Vale. *Texas Monthly*, December. https://www.texasmonthly.com/the-culture/jeffrey-cranor-welcome-night-vale/ [Accessed 27 April 2021].

Penny Dreadful. 2014–16. TV series created by John Logan. USA: Showtime.

Ryan, M-L. 2012. Transmedial storytelling and transfictionality. *Poetics Today*, 34(3), pp. 361–388.

Ryan, M-L. 2015. Transmedia storytelling: Industry buzzword or new narrative experience? *Storyworlds: A Journal of Narrative Studies*, 7(2), pp. 1–19.

Sanders, J. 2006. *Adaptation and appropriation*. London: Routledge.

Sherlock (BBC, 2010–) TV series.

Shin, P. 2018. Review: A vibrant presentation of Welcome to Night Vale Live at Athenaeum Theatre. *Third Coast Review*, 12 October. https://thirdcoastreview.com/2018/10/12/review-a-vibrant-presentation-of-welcome-to-night-vale-live-at-athenaeum-theatre/ [Accessed 27 April 2021].

Thon J.-N. 2015. Converging worlds: From transmedial storyworlds to transmedial universes. *Storyworlds: A Journal of Narrative Studies*, 7(2), pp. 21–53.

Thon J.-N. 2019. Transmedia characters: Theory and practice. *Frontiers of Narrative Studies*, 5(2), pp. 176–199.

'Welcome To Night Vale' Goes from Podcast To Page. 2015. *WBUR*. https://www.wbur.org/hereandnow/2015/11/24/welcome-to-night-vale [Accessed 27 April 2021].

Zabus, C. 2001. Subversive scribes: rewriting in the twentieth century. *Anglistica*, 5(1), pp. 191–207.

16 Intermediality and social media

Signe Kjær Jensen, Nafiseh Mousavi and Emma Tornborg

It is probably just a matter of the blink of an eye for you to capture an Insta-worthy image or video of an enjoyable moment, combine it with a suitable caption and post it on Instagram, punctuating the caption with hashtags that connect your post to a pool of other images and notes, or to sign into a location to connect to a physical spot outside your phone. No wonder your friends use emojis to react to your post the moment it is aired: heart-eyed, laughing little creatures that speak words. And a year later, when you are reminded by the app about your long-gone memory-image, how about turning it into a short-lived story, maybe flavouring it with another layer of words, emojis or GIFs, and posting it at the top of the interface for 24 hours of glimpses and reactions?

This is such an easy, almost automatic task to do and yet – now that you are well acquainted with the intermedial toolbox – you understand the level of intermedial literacy and intermedial skills that go into it! Several basic media and semiotic modes are combined and integrated: still or moving images, voice, sound, written words, hashtags, emojis and frames; and one media product is transmediated into another with different temporal and semiotic arrangements. This is only one of the many different intermedial navigations that we engage with in our everyday life across social media, be it Facebook, Instagram, YouTube, Twitter or numerous other platforms.

It wouldn't be an exaggeration to say that a considerable part of e-literacy, the knowledge and skills used to navigate the internet, is indeed intermedial literacy. But intermediality is not just latent knowledge you happen to have without knowing what forms your e-navigations. A systematized knowledge of intermedial and multimodal relations becomes especially important when social media become the subject of analysis and research. In addition to being studied in media and communication studies, social media have been a hot topic and a popular field of observation in disciplines as diverse as public relations, ethnography, psychology, digital humanities, and many more. The ability to grasp and analyse complex intermedial relations would be a prerequisite to understanding processes of meaning-making across social media as communication is increasingly hybridized and diversified for users of these platforms.

DOI: 10.4324/9781003174288-19

In this chapter we will provide you with examples of basic analyses of macro and micro levels of intermediality in social media: YouTube entertainment, an example of a multi-layered social media practice, and GIFs, which derive from other media and migrate across different platforms on the internet. Before delving into these cases, let's begin by taking a general look at social media through an intermedial lens.

We all have an idea of what the term 'social media' is referring to. It probably ignites in our minds an image of the navy-blue Facebook logo or the lighter blue of Twitter's or some other iconic, globally used social network: Tumblr, WeChat, Instagram, Weibo, TikTok, you name it! But how can we actually define social media? What is it that is *social* about it and differentiates it from other media? How can we describe social media from an intermedial point of view?

Carr and Hayes, two communication and social media scholars, offer the following quite comprehensive and interesting explication of social media:

> Social media are *Internet-based* channels that allow users to opportunistically interact and selectively self-present, *either in real-time or asynchronously*, with both *broad and narrow audiences* who derive value from *user-generated content* and the *perception of interaction* with others.
>
> (Carr and Hayes 2015, p. 50; our emphasis)

With this definition, they distinguish social media from both traditional media – which is not interactive or internet-based – and other new media, such as email and messaging apps that are not sufficiently *social*. Indeed, what is social about social media is the 'multi-directionality of communication flow' or a phenomenon formulated as 'masspersonal communication' by O'Sullivan and Carr in another article (O'Sullivan and Carr 2018, p. 1161). The notion of masspersonal communication refers to the way in which communication is in a one-to-one, one-to-many, many-to-many and many-to-one form on social media. The idea behind this concept is that we should dismiss the dichotomy between mass communication as a one-to-many communication performed by mass media as opposed to interpersonal communication defined as a two-way, one-to-one form of communication. Instead, we should understand communication in social media as consisting of people simultaneously engaging in mass and interpersonal communication. Rather than being either interpersonal or mass communication, masspersonal communication differentiates across a scale and is determined by its level of 'accessibility' and 'personalization': a public post on Facebook with no specified audience is more accessible and impersonalized, while a personal tweet in a private Twitter account which directly addresses the account-holders' followers is less accessible and more personalized; however, neither of the two can be categorized as solely mass or solely interpersonal communication.

This also links to the importance of (a perception of) interaction on social media. Our interactions on social media are shaped and determined by algorithms. These interactions can happen in real time (live-streaming on Facebook, Instagram or YouTube and receiving live comments and reactions) or asynchronously (commenting on a friend's post from yesterday). Moreover, we do not only interact with other people but also increasingly with various types of bots, in such a way that it is not always easy to distinguish between human and nonhuman interaction on social media.

Using social media is closely tied to the developments of mobile communication. As Rasmus Helles (2013) argues, 'the central affordance of mobile phones is not the mobility of the device per se, but rather the fact that the user becomes a mobile terminus for mediated communicative interaction across the various contexts of daily life' (p. 14). Social media are accessed through a varied set of electronic technical media of display like laptops, smartphones, tablets, smartwatches, etc. These devices are generally portable and have made media use less location-bound than ever.

Accordingly, the material dimension of social media can be formulated as an integration between physicality (of the devices) and digitality (of software, apps, etc.). Although there is a common tendency to talk about the virtual versus the real world when we are discussing social media, or the web in general, it is becoming almost impossible to detach online life from offline life. Scholars such as Nathan Jurgenson believe that although the two spheres are distinct, we should avoid 'digital dualism' or the virtual vs real dichotomy. Instead, he suggests considering social media and social media practice as 'implosion[s] of atoms and bits':

> The physicality of atoms, the structures of the social world and offline identities 'interpenetrate' the online. Simultaneously, the properties of the digital also implode into the offline, be it through the ubiquity of web-connected electronic gadgets in our world and on our bodies or through the way digitality interpenetrates the way we understand and make meaning of the world around us.
>
> (Jurgenson 2012, p. 86)

In this way, social media follow us via our mobile devices and frequently pop up in our everyday practices in a shifting and fluid spatiotemporal frame. They engage our touch, hearing and sight and make all categories of semiotic relations work: the iconic value of photos and emojis, the symbolic value of words, signs and hashtags, and the indexical value of location markers, to name a few basic ones among many. The high level of hybridity and mixedness in social media is an outcome of the constant mixing, coexistence and integration of various basic media texts, moving and still images, sound-specific and more social-media, elements such as hashtags and locations, on various platforms:

> the way we present ourselves to our online audiences is no longer only by textual and visual cues such as status messages, photos, or videos but also through geocoded digital traces, geographical data visualizations, and maps of individual patterns of mobility.
>
> (Schwartz and Halegoua 2015, p. 1644)

Apart from media combination and integration, even the two aspects of media transformation, transmediation and representation, are also persistent intermedial processes in social media practice as content creation. As you will see in the case studies, other media are engaged with in the form of quotations, framings, recycling, etc. in the everyday social media practices of entertainment, education and self-representation. Online fan culture has provided opportunities for people to transform their favourite films, novels and comics and put their own trace on them. Even more traditional ways of media consumption such as reading a book or watching a film have been reframed on platforms like Letterboxd and Goodreads, where the practice of watching or reading obtains another interactive layer for users, who are able to respond to the media products in a way that has been further legitimized and made even more systematic.

Social media provide an exciting scene where we can put our intermedial toolbox to use. They are not only a new type of media but offer a new understanding of mediation in which life and media are intertwined more than ever. This new notion and experience are best explained by what Kember and Zylinska (2012) suggest is 'the vitality' or 'lifeness' of media, 'that is, the possibility of the emergence of forms always new, or its potentiality to generate unprecedented connections and unexpected events' (p. xvii). Following this brief glimpse at social media and its intermedial dimension, we will now take a look at our two cases of applying the intermedial perspective of analysis to YouTube entertainment and GIFs.

Media transformation on YouTube: Social media entertainment as an intermedial practice

YouTube might best be described as a 'platform'.[1] It is a website that enables 'professional' as well as 'amateur' media producers, and all those in between, a *space* in which to share and distribute video material in a variety of different forms and genres. This platform allows for both relatively 'traditional' video content, but also new types of media, which build on pre-existing material and media genres, for example, 'honest trailers', 'react videos' and 'Let's Play videos'. YouTube thus enables, and perhaps even encourages, the distribution of a range of different practices of combining and transforming material, that is, the distribution of different intermedial practices. Because the videos themselves share the same basic media modes as traditional film (cf. Chapter 2), many consider the innovative aspects of the platform to be the inherent possibilities for 'amateurs' to upload and distribute their own productions within a social community, creating an open and *social* practice that is in opposition to the closed processes of the traditional media of broadcasting companies and film studios. In this respect, YouTube has also often been hailed for its democratic potential, a potential which, however, exists in tension with YouTube's still more commercial profiling (see Box 16.1).

It can be hard to draw a distinct line between 'professionals' and 'amateurs' in the context of social media. On the one hand, there is no doubt that a TV channel, such as NBC, uploading content is professional and that a teenager uploading videos from his or her bedroom is an amateur, but what about Casey Neistat, who, besides being a vlogger, is also a professional film-maker? And what about Felix Kjellberg (b. 1989), aka, PewDiePie? PewDiePie has no official degree in media production, but he still decided to pursue a YouTube career as an alternative to going to university and making a foundation for a more 'traditional' career. At the time of writing this chapter, towards the end of 2020, PewDiePie is one of the most famous YouTubers, and he makes millions of dollars each year from his YouTube videos, in which he plays video games or talks about internet memes. PewDiePie is a professional in one sense of the term because he makes YouTube videos for a living, but at the same time, he has not been professionally trained as a media producer (although he is undoubtedly highly skilled in digital editing techniques and employs people to help with media production) and he produces a type of content that many people would still associate with 'amateur' content. In this chapter, we focus solely on the type of content that is created by individuals or groups located outside the traditional media companies. We discuss how to understand this social practice of content production within an intermedial framework, and lastly, we provide a brief analysis of how PewDiePie engages with his content and viewers in his Let's Play Minecraft videos.

Box 16.1 YouTube and the tension between democratization and commercialization

In contrast with traditional media such as film and television, having a platform for media-sharing and consumption implies an ideology of equal access and opportunity for everybody, and YouTube has often been thought of as a democratization of media distribution and as a hub where individuals can express and share their opinions within a larger community. The democratizing and equalizing potential of YouTube, and other platforms, has also been critiqued and problematized in recent years (see, for example, Allmer (2015), Burgess and Green (2009), Graham and Dutton (2019), Snickars and Vonderau (2009) and van Dijck (2013)) not least because of its increasing commercialization and professionalization. YouTube's guidelines and selective algorithms, which ultimately exercise control over what kinds of videos are being uploaded and which videos are shown to users, also problematize this democratic ideology. As a consequence, YouTube still allows everyone with access to a computer and an internet connection to upload content, but it does not allow everyone's content to be distributed to the wider population. This both entails that not everyone has equal access to be 'heard', but it also causes problems with 'filter bubbles' and 'fake news'. YouTube and other social media platforms are also being increasingly problematized in news media and popular culture, for example, in *The New York Times* podcast series 'Rabbit Hole' (Roose 2020).

Characteristics and conventions of 'social media entertainment': The qualifying aspects

We will use the term 'social media entertainment', as suggested by Craig and Cunningham (2019, p. 4–5), to refer to a range of potentially profitable but non-traditional media content on YouTube. According to Cunningham and Craig's definition, social media entertainment is characterized by conventions of a high level of audience interaction, a sense of authenticity regarding the content creator, an appeal to community-building and, lastly, by being distributed in a 'commercializing space' (Craig and Cunningham 2019, p. 149), by which the authors mean the whole culture of commercialization and professionalization around this content. As we take an intermedial approach in this book, we wish to add one dimension to this characterization, namely the notion that social media entertainment is very often characterized by an extreme level of transmediation of pre-existing media content together with the representation of 'old' media types and genres in a new context. This type of transmediation might metaphorically be described as a recycling of content and genres to create something which is new and unique to social media entertainment.

YouTube as a hub for an interactive, social community

What formally differentiates YouTube videos from other types of film is the potential for interaction and communication between different parties: 1) between the producer and the audiences, 2) between different producers, and 3) between individual audiences of the videos. All of this interaction is afforded through the platform, and despite the very small number of people actively engaged on YouTube through uploading or commenting compared with the number of users on the site (cf. Snickars and Vonderau 2009, p. 12), this interactive feature has been part of shaping the content on YouTube, most notably, perhaps, through vlogs. This has created an affordance for content creators to explicitly address and encourage interactivity and community-building and has also created a higher demand for 'authentic' and visible creators.

When entering into any kind of medial analysis of YouTube content, it thus becomes relevant to ask whether it is the video itself that is the real content or whether the video has to be analyzed in the context of the larger framework of sharing, commenting and responding on the YouTube platform. When viewers comment on a video, they can be seen to *transform* the video into something new, making it a topic in a discussion forum rather than 'just' a video, as they evaluate and potentially negotiate and co-create meaning around what they have just seen. Sometimes, the content creator will even participate in these discussions or respond to comments in a follow-up video, further strengthening the sense of *interactivity, community* and *co-creation*. These interactions are all part of a chain that can be considered in the light of an intermedial transformation, as the meaning around the video develops through new comments and (video) reactions. In our case study of PewDiePie later in this chapter, we concentrate on PewDiePie's ways of encouraging these interactions, as we focus on 'textual' strategies in the videos themselves, and we therefore only refer sparingly to his followers. This is an analytic choice on our part, and other choices regarding the balance between the inputs by the content creator and his or her audiences can be a legitimate strategy, depending on your research interest and theoretical framework. For an example of a study with a more socially oriented focus that concentrates on what happens in the chain of comments and reactions, see Ruth Page's (2018) *Narratives Online*.

Media transformation on YouTube

One of the most popular video types on YouTube is the vlog, but within the form of the 'vlog', many different formats are possible, and 'vlog' can be hard to define clearly, as we discuss in Box 16.2. Taking a glance at a list of 12 recommended vlogs in an online article by social media manager Rob Nightingale (2017) reveals YouTube videos that are based on a range of antecedents. Most obvious is perhaps the older brother, the blog, which has its roots in written diaries and oral confessions, but antecedents in the form of qualified media such as video games, films and home videos are also evident. It is, moreover, interesting to note the number of qualified media types and genres which are being transmediated through vlogs. That is, genres that were initially mediated through writing technologies and later by video are now being taken up by internet platforms, and both basic and qualified media types from before the invention of the internet are being represented through social media entertainment. These genres are travel logs, educational content and news coverage, and it is evident from the list of vlogs recommended in the article by Nightingale (2017) that they cover everything from personal stories to climate-aware travel and videos aimed at informing viewers about psychic illness or politics. Consequently, what characterizes these particular YouTube videos, and what seems to be a general tendency for a lot of social media entertainment, is that they *transform* of 'old' media content, types or genres into social media, taking on the qualifying aspects of social media entertainment in addition to the pre-existent characteristics. In a way, what social media entertainment does, is to creatively recycle pre-existing media content, types and genres in a new context.

This is very explicit when pre-existing material is used to make a new product, which we see with 'honest trailers', and sometimes the practice of recycling is more implicit in the form of media representations of older types of media, such as the blog. Thus, the transformation happening on YouTube, and similar platforms, means that 'old' qualified media types are now being mediated by social platforms, which encourages a sense of interactivity and community, as discussed above, but also of authenticity (which we will turn to next), which did not exist in the original form of the 'recycled' material.

When we use the metaphor of 'recycling' to describe these transformation processes involving both transmediation and media representations (see Chapters 9 and 10), it is to highlight that social media entertainment often has a much more extensive and explicit reuse of media content and/or qualified media characteristics than what we usually see in 'traditional' fields such as literature and film. Let's Play videos are, for example, much more than 'just' an adaptation or representation of a gameplay, as entire sections of gameplay are 'quoted' at length in Let's Play videos and become the topic of the videos. Likewise, the 'travel vlog' is not just *representing* travel logs and blogs but fully appropriating these genres in a social media entertainment format.

These kinds of creative uses and recombinations of existing content, which we see in social media entertainment, are also studied in the growing discipline of 'remix studies', taking their name from the popular musical practice. As remix studies constitute a distinct, albeit related, discipline to intermediality studies, we will not discuss this concept further here, but the interested reader is encouraged to consult Navas, Gallagher and Burrough (2014, 2021).

Box 16.2 What is a vlog?

The word vlog is a contraction of the words video and blog. The concept thus names an intermedial *combination* of the qualified medium of blog with the *basic* medium of video (we refer to video as a basic medium here because it is not the qualified dimensions of *film* that are relevant but the pure resource of video recording). Another way to look at this is to see the vlog as a *transformation* of the blog into an audiovisual form – a transformation that adds the affordance of emphasizing the content creator's face and voice, adding to the authenticity dimension, which is so characteristic of social media entertainment.

With regard to both form and content, the term vlog has been used ambiguously and can refer to the style of the earliest videos uploaded to YouTube, to videos on social media which more generally showcase personal content, or to any video which is produced by individuals or groups located outside the traditional media. Most often, however, vlog refers to a video in which a content creator speaks directly to the camera, making a *seemingly* personal, sincere, authentic and direct address to the followers of a channel. The camera tends to be used as a 'window' through which the content creator can speak to the audience, rather than making the audience feel like an 'observer', as in traditional media content.

Authenticity and bodily presence in opposition to traditional media

One of the primary ways in which these videos succeed in terms of their social transformation, and authenticity, is by being produced by *seemingly* 'ordinary' people located outside the traditional media industries: content creators who use themselves, their own bodies, voices, lives, and interests to communicate in a space where 'talking back' is allowed (see also Craig and Cunningham 2019, p. 148–83). Even though the most popular YouTubers are indeed 'professionals' who make a living from their social media content and who hire trained personnel to assist with editing, marketing, legal concerns, etc., they still put themselves in front of the camera and speak to their audiences as if they were friends. As such, a specific type of authenticity, which is created through a perceived distance to traditional media and through an acknowledgement of and direct address to an audience, as well as through the bodily presence of the main content creator(s), seems to be a convention of social media entertainment.

The concept of authenticity always has to do with the implied representation of what is not present or cannot be seen. This is, e.g., also the case when a media product conveys an authentic representation of the 'real' world (i.e., the non-mediated world) and when personal communication involves authentic outward expressions of invisible inner feelings. When new media appear, the relation between what can be constructed by mediated authenticity and what are signs of personal authenticity has to be renegotiated and can easily be mixed up (Enli 2015). The short history of YouTube has revealed instances where YouTubers have gained large followings from uploading seemingly personal stories, which have later been accused of being scripted. The most extreme case of this sort was probably when the famous YouTuber LonelyGirl15 was discovered to be an actor in 2006 (see Burgess and Green 2009 for a discussion of this 'fake' vlogger). Even when the stories are not scripted, however, a YouTuber *always* chooses what we see and what we don't see and what types of glimpses we get into their personal lives. Therefore, the people we see on YouTube can be considered to be constructed media *personas*, i.e. what we see is a specific version of a person and not the whole truth. That is why we prefer to talk about authenticity with regard to social media *personas* rather than with regard to 'real' people. Ultimately, we can only analyze and discuss a YouTuber based on what they have made publicly available (the persona) and not who they are outside social media.

Box 16.3 Authenticity

When we speak of authenticity, this concept always involves both the notion of immediacy and construction/staging. Authenticity refers to a kind of representation that is constructed, staged or enacted in a way so that it conveys an experience of immediacy and presence – a kind of 'natural enactment' (van Alphen, Bal and Smith 2009) – a representation that is truthful in respect to different phenomena in different contexts (see Chapter 13).

In the case of historical and artistic objects, authenticity is perceived as a property of the material and stands for the object's '*originality*', or unbroken connection with something that is perceived as original. In interpersonal communication, a *personal* authenticity, in the sense of *sincerity*, refers to outward expressions that are consistent with inner feelings, convictions and involves the assurance that the speaker stays true to oneself.

> In media contexts, authenticity involves a focus upon how the experience of immediacy is constructed by media. The accusation of inauthenticity is a common feature of media criticism and derives from the fact that many media products are fundamentally *materially* inauthentic in relation to what they mediate. Still, a theatre play, a film, a novel, a vlog can be perceived as a truthful representation of real-life experience. Gunn Enli (2015) lists a number of strategies such as spontaneity, immediacy, the use of confessions, ordinariness, ambivalence and imperfection that all function as authenticity markers and help to construct mediated authenticity.
>
> In the authenticity discourse of social media entertainment, YouTubers pose themselves as an alternative to traditional media. Traditional media are perceived as driven by commercial interests, presenting fictional experiences and as not being open to audience involvement. In contrast, the norm for creators of social media entertainment involves showing a genuine, personal interest in their own content and community, as well as using *real* feelings and experiences as background for their videos. However, when a certain type of personal behaviour becomes necessary to gain success, then this behaviour can be *staged* to gain popularity.
>
> In Craig and Cunningham's review of authenticity as a concept in cultural studies, there is an emphasis on the problematic relation between authenticity and commercial interests, also explored in business studies (Gilmore and Pine 2007), which is relevant when approaching authenticity in social media entertainment. There arises a tension between the promise of an authentic personal behaviour on the one hand and authenticity as a commercial selling point on the other (for a broader discussion of authenticity on social media generally and in relation to PewDiePie, see Craig and Cunningham 2019, Chapter 4).

Summing up social media entertainment

Based on the previous discussion, one could argue that social media entertainment is a specific type of qualified medium, characterized by the conventions of (1) extreme levels of transmediation (extreme compared to 'traditional' media) in the form of a recycling of content, genres and media types, (2) interactivity, (3) community, (4) authenticity and (5) by being distributed on a social media platform. It is a qualified medium that is stratified into several genres or submedia, however, such as Let's Play videos and DIY tutorials.

Social media entertainment even has a unique history of developing these conventions through its short history. Although social media entertainment does not belong exclusively to YouTube, it is interesting that these conventions can all be traced back to the very first YouTube video, 'Me at the Zoo', which was uploaded by one of YouTube's founders, Jawed Karim, in 2005 (Jawed 2005). The video is only 18 seconds long and shows Karim at the zoo in front of some elephants (see the still in Figure 16.1). Karim is mostly speaking directly to the camera, saying (this and all following transcriptions of speech in videos have been made by the chapter authors):

Figure 16.1 Screenshot of the first YouTube video, 'Me at the Zoo', posted by YouTube co-founder, Jawed Karim, in 2005.

> Alright, so here we are [looks left] in front of the [gazes into the camera again] ah ... elephants. [looks over his shoulder to the elephants and back to the camera]. Mhmm the cool [emphasizes with a hand gesture] thing about these guys is that, is that [sic] they have really, really, really [emphasizes with rhythmic movements of hand on each 'really'] long, uhm, trunks [illustrates with hand gesture]. And that's cool [looks over his left shoulder to the elephants again and back]. And that's pretty much all there is to say.

The quotation from the video shown in Figure 16.1 is an example of a simple *multimodal* transcription that transcribes the words verbatim along with simple gaze and hand gesture notations. Our multimodal transcription helps to make it clearer how Karim relates to the camera and how he uses his body when he is conveying his personal experience of being at the zoo. His language and body are directed at the audience behind the camera, except for a few glances he makes towards the elephants (perhaps showing that he is a bit shy in front of the camera), and his language and body are, unlike an actor in a film, unpolished and natural; there are spontaneous pauses and gestures. This unpolished address to the audience creates a sense of authenticity, unscripted personal expression and invites community-building and interaction. The video represents structures familiar from the blog format and perhaps also news reporting because of how Karim is placed in relation to the elephants and the camera, as if he is 'reporting' on the elephants at the zoo, a media practice associated with authenticity and trustworthiness in relation to a journalist. These patterns that refer to conventions of blogging and news reporting thus help create an impression of personal authenticity.

To sum up, social media entertainment can be described as a qualified medium that transforms previously existing media types and genres, mainly diaries, blogs and home videos, into audiovisual content on a social platform. Furthermore, social media entertainment stages the body, voice and personality, or persona, of a content creator outside the traditional media and acknowledges, or even addresses, the social community directly. One approach to the intermedial analysis of YouTube videos would therefore be to look for ways in which a video establishes these dimensions of transmediation, authenticity, interactivity and community. Questions to ask yourself are: which media types or pre-existing content, e.g. narratives, images or structural patterns, are being transmediated and represented? What kind of meaning potential is being transferred along with the recycled material, media type or genre? Are practices from different 'old' media types combined (e.g. if Karim had inserted animation or music into his report on the elephants)? How are the content creator's body language and voice quality used and combined with the images? How is the video being interpreted and negotiated in the comments, and does the content creator react to comments, thereby allowing the followers to influence the content? We explore these questions in a brief example analysis by taking a closer look at the Let's Play genre and how the YouTuber PewDiePie engages with the social media entertainment dimensions and with his audiences.

PewDiePie plays Minecraft, and 37,000,000 watch

PewDiePie is a Swedish gamer and YouTuber whose real name is Felix Kjellberg. He started his career in 2010, and in 2019 he hit 100 million subscribers. PewDiePie's channel was for several years the largest channel on YouTube (from late 2013 to early 2019 – briefly surpassed by *YouTube Spotlight* in 2013), and as such, he has been widely influential. He is also one of the most controversial personas on YouTube, however, with several scandals in his wake, making people either love him or hate him (see, for example, BBC Newsbeat 2019). The main content of PewDiePie's channel (PewDiePie n.d.) is Let's Play videos, but he has also done a substantial amount of other types of social media entertainment, such as react videos, rants about current trends and updates on his personal life. In this section, we briefly discuss PewDiePie's recent Let's Play Minecraft series (uploaded 21 June 2019–28 April 2020) (PewDiePie 2019g) consisting of 45 publicly available videos, which we will refer to as 'episodes' in the following analysis because PewDiePie himself refers to the individual videos as episodes in a series.

'Let's Play' refers to a social media entertainment genre in which a gamer plays video games while talking to his audiences and commenting on the game, and the gamer's face and upper body are often visible in the video along with the gameplay. Through the gamer's comments, Let's Play contains an address to the audiences and showcases the personality (or persona) of a gamer; there is also a focus on the gamer's face, which is filmed up close – all typical tools of social media entertainment. Let's Play is thus also an obvious case of media transformation, where a video game is transferred into a new context and thus transformed into social media entertainment, and it can be considered both a transformation of the videogame and also a combination of video games with the basic medium of video and the qualified conventions of social media entertainment (see also Chapters 5 and 17).

Let's Play is one of the most popular video types on YouTube, but platforms dedicated to live-streaming, particularly of gameplay, also exist, e.g. Twitch, on which PewDiePie also has an account. The difference being that Twitch is used for live-streaming sessions, and YouTube, at the time of writing, mainly for pre-recorded material, which, unlike the live streams, might be substantially edited, as we will see with the analysis of PewDiePie's Minecraft videos.

One of the absolute strengths of PewDiePie's videos is his very strong invitation to interact and build communities. Not only does he speak directly to his followers as if they were friends (referring to them as 'bitches', 'gamers', 'bros' or '9-year olds'), but he also named his Minecraft world 'Broland' in reference to his followers, allows them to have a direct influence on the gameplay and responds to their comments. In the opening of 'Im actually having… FUN? In MINECRAFT (hacked) – Part 2', for example, PewDiePie addresses comments which his followers posted for the first video in the Minecraft series:

> Broland continues. You guys have been making fun of me in the comments, don't think I don't read those [waving a pointed finger at the camera], saying I don't know how to play a game, I don't know how to make Minecraft. Me, I'm a veteran okay? I was born to play Minecraft. I've played Minecraft before you [points at the camera] were born. Okay?
> (PewDiePie 2019d [00:00:07])

Here we can see that the audience is clearly being addressed by PewDiePie, who is speaking into and gesturing towards the camera. These words also speak to how he creates authenticity by 'staging' a particular persona. The lines here contain a classic, self-ironic joke about PewDiePie being a veteran and basically a master of Minecraft, and the lines are said in a light-hearted way in PewDiePie's characteristic, exaggerated, Swedish accent. Even though he is Swedish, the exaggerated accent is something that he adds on and off for comic effect, and it is part of his unique YouTube persona to play on this Swedishness. This is perhaps most obvious when PewDiePie decorates his buildings in Minecraft with the Swedish flag, when he refers to blue birds as 'Ikea birds', and when he decides to build a huge 'Ikea tower' and a giant meatball.

Even more important to this persona is when he talks openly about himself as a private person. On these occasions, the comedic act is dropped, and PewDiePie normally uses a more calm and sincere tone of voice. He does this several times during the series, not least at the beginning of episode 29 (PewDiePie 2019e), when he shares some of his actual wedding photos. He also talks to his audiences about the very recent wedding and his feelings about it later in the episode, letting his followers get a glimpse into his personal life. This build-up of a credible and likeable YouTube persona is an important strategy for creating authenticity and encouraging community, as it invites the audiences to come a little closer, not just to PewDiePie but to the person behind PewDiePie, Felix Kjellberg. It is important to remember, however, that we can't tell how well this self-ironic Swedish PewDiePie corresponds to the 'real' Felix Kjellberg – to the way he would speak and act in private. But by sharing private thoughts and emotions and by showing seemingly spontaneous thought processes and reactions while playing, PewDiePie's persona comes to *seem* real, as if he is a close friend of his audiences and is on equal terms with them.

Coming back to the interactivity and community-building, PewDiePie also responds to advice and suggestions from his followers, sometimes with more success than others. An example of his followers managing to 'troll' PewDiePie is when it was suggested that he should sleep in Nether (a hellish subworld of Minecraft), which he attempts to do in episode 5 'I slept in the Nether in Minecraft':

> Okay Jörgen [PewDiePie's first Minecraft horse] wish me good luck, we're going to the Nether. 'Cause everyone said there is a secret achievement [zoom in and enlargement of PewDiePie's face] if you sleep in the Nether [cuts back to small visual of PewDiePie in the corner of the screen]. Why would anyone do that? Oh God this place is SO creepy dude. Why on earth would I sleep here? This is awful. Alright fine, we'll make a little Nether realm house. How about that? It's gonna be so cute. Oh my God I am scared [laughing]. Alright good night gamer – AAHHHHH [PewDiePie screams as his character dies, and the screen shows 'sub2pewdiepie12 was killed by (Intentional Game Design)'].
>
> (PewDiePie 2019c [00:04:43])

PewDiePie was thus tricked into killing himself in the game. After this happens, PewDiePie goes silent for a few seconds, sighs, and then a black and white, highly transparent recording of his face is superimposed on the screen, taking up almost half of the space. The brightness of the colours of the gameplay is turned down, and melancholic, simple piano music is played in the background. PewDiePie continues: 'My own audience, my own supporters. Can you believe this?' (PewDiePie 2019c [00:05:19]).

Here, PewDiePie again addresses his audience directly, and he also takes the chance to use visual and auditive editing techniques familiar from film and TV to create a somewhat ironic, emotional and comic effect. PewDiePie's voice, face and overall reactions become part of a joke but also give the impression that we are seeing PewDiePie's genuine emotional responses. This is just one example of PewDiePie's heavy use of editing techniques in his videos, which points to a tension between the seemingly 'authentic' gameplay and the 'finished' YouTube video. When this tension still works in the context of PewDiePie's authenticity, it is because the edited media product emphasizes PewDiePie's emotional reactions, self-irony and humour.

These editing techniques and references to film and TV are not only added as an authorial comment on the gameplay or as response to seemingly bad advice from PewDiePie's followers (which is allowed through the social interaction) but also to create a narrative coherence across the episodes. Towards the end of the series, in the final moments of 'Married in Minecraft Epicly – Part 29' (PewDiePie 2019e), one of PewDiePie's pets, a pig called Peepeepoopoo, nudges him into a portal, behind which the dreaded Ender Dragon is waiting (the final boss and biggest enemy in Minecraft). The episode ends abruptly on this 'cliff-hanger'. This ending is replayed at the start of episode 30, 'I challenge the Ender Dragon in Minecraft (Ending)' (PewDiePie 2019a), representing structural patterns familiar from TV series to create drama, coherence and audience engagement across episodes. As the replay ends and the 'real' episode begins, PewDiePie delivers a dramatic monologue, backed up by solemn music and sound editing, which adds a little bit of reverb to selected sentences of his speech:

> My own ... friend, my best friend in the whole world. Peepeepoopoo. Peepeepoopoo. He betrayed me! Oh my God. Peepeepoopoo! I'll get you for this! I'll get you for this one day [PewDiePie rubs his eyes, as if in distress]. He pushed me in. Surely it must have been a mistake? There's no way Peepeepoopoo would deliberately betray me? Oh God.
> (PewDiePie 2019a [00:00:31])

Here, the difference between 'PewDiePie as authentic Felix Kjellberg' and 'PewDiePie as a persona' becomes particularly blurred, as PewDiePie is 'acting' as his Minecraft character but in a way that is coherent with his YouTube persona, and he seems to express genuine feelings of betrayal and hurt.

Peepeepoopoo is quickly forgiven, though, and when he dies later in the same episode, we get to see an edited montage sequence, showing the best moments with Peepeepoopoo along with melancholic piano music (PewDiePie 2019a [00:12.48]) (a stable technique that PewDiePie uses every time a Minecraft pet dies). Towards the end of this montage, the music changes into a more active and dark sound, reminiscent of action films when a hero is getting ready for battle. This music plays while we see an edited gameplay of PewDiePie getting ready to fight the Ender Dragon (PewDiePie 2019a [00:14:18]). Thus, the editing and choice of music here create a clear parallel between PewDiePie's Minecraft character and the trope of action heroes from film and TV.

It is clear that PewDiePie's different combinations of the gameplay with film and TV conventions have several effects: they create narrative coherence across episodes, they 'import' meaning potential through associations with emotionally charged editing techniques, conventions and character tropes, and they provide a base on which PewDiePie can showcase his self-ironic persona in an authentic manner.

Regarding PewDiePie's tendency to 'narrativize' his Minecraft series, he explicitly comments on this 'strategy' in episode 31, referring to the defeat of the Ender Dragon as the 'end' of the *series* but not the end of the gameplay videos:

> So technically, for me the series is over. It ended on episode 30 [a small image of the YouTube title of the episode moves across the screen from the bottom up and back down]. I want to keep it intact that way you know, in terms of 'storytelling' [makes quotation marks with his hands] […] The thing is, there's a lot of stuff in the game I can do […] So basically, to explain it, the series is over, but the series continues [emphasizes and illustrates by moving his hands to opposite sites on 'basically', 'the series is over' and 'continues'].
>
> (PewDiePie 2019b [00:02.43])

Here, PewDiePie shows a self-awareness of the story-like qualities of the previous episodes, and just the fact that PewDiePie refers to the individual Minecraft videos as 'episodes' within a series adds to this sense of narrative coherence and once again builds on a reference to the medium of TV series.

Several of PewDiePie's followers also comment on this narrativizing and 'TV-dramatic' strategy. For instance, a commentator appreciates '**story driven episodes, drenched with character and emotion**' (emphasis original), while other followers perceive 'a soap opera' or a 'drama horror show' (PewDiePie 2019h, comments online).

Many more of the comments on PewDiePie's videos, however, focus on highlighting particularly funny comments PewDiePie has made, perhaps showing that the main attraction for them is PewDiePie's unique persona and sense of humour. The gameplay thus functions to provide a topic for PewDiePie to work from, but the real enjoyment for audiences of PewDiePie's Let's Play Minecraft comes from him visually reacting and verbally narrativizing his 'journey' through the game. The combination of the gameplay, references to film and TV *and* the unique format of social media entertainment video provides a space for PewDiePie to stage himself with acts that express his self-irony and his emotions and humour, in turn creating authenticity, interaction and community by doing so.

Social media entertainment on YouTube and intermedial literacy: Concluding remarks

As we noted in the introduction to this section, users of social media rely on an intermedial literacy in their everyday interactions with the different platforms. In this chapter, we have argued that social media entertainment on YouTube is a particular qualified medium that often takes this intermedial literacy to an extreme level, showcasing a high level of transmediation, or recycling, of previously existing content, media types and structural patterns familiar from other media types. Furthermore, what characterizes social media entertainment on YouTube is how the multimodal affordances of the video medium and the dialogic affordances of the social platform are used to create authenticity (particularly through the distance that exists between social media entertainment and the traditional media and by emphasizing the content creator's face and voice), interactivity (through an address and response to the audiences) and community. As such, the intermedial combination of the basic medium of video with the qualified medium of social media entertainment and different media representations becomes productive because it allows the dual focus on the content creator's bodily presence and the meaning content associated with the referenced media.

PewDiePie is an example of a YouTuber who employs a range of different tools in the way he utilizes conventions used in film music, visual editing, narrativity, discourses of authenticity, community-building and gaming. He nurtures a specific 'authentic' YouTube persona by being present in body and voice, speaking openly about his life and being self-ironic about being a Swede. He also encourages interaction by speaking directly to his audiences, making 'brofists' with the camera, referring to his followers as a community (e.g. as an army of 9-year-olds), and reacting to their responses. Finally, he transmediates gameplay as well as conventions from film and TV to create engaging, coherent and humoristic content.

The intermediality of GIFs – How to express yourself with another face

Most people are probably familiar with GIFs at this point. Born in 1987, and therefore four years older than the internet itself, the GIF initially functioned as a space-saving format that could be used to send colour images digitally via companies such as CompuServe (Boissoneault 2017, n.p.). In 2012, Katherine Brown argued that the GIF is 'an outdated, retro, online bitmap image format that was prevalent in the early popularization of the internet as a kitschy animation often representing flames or glitter for an email signature, the background of a website, or as an icon' (p. 6). However, in recent years, the GIF's popularity has increased enormously, and technical media such as smartphones and social media platforms such as Facebook and Twitter have facilitated the use of GIFs in text messaging, chats, posts and comment sections. The GIF is a qualified medium that is mainly used as a communicative tool in everyday digital communication. The most common type of GIF is the reaction GIF. From an intermedial perspective, there are many aspects of the GIF that can be studied: for instance, the transmediation of images but also of emotions, representation of qualified media types like film, temporal aspects of a loop, the tension between movement and stillness, the performativity of posting a GIF. In this section, we are going to discuss some of them.

Intermedial performativity

Chiel Kattenbelt (2010) asserts that 'intermediality is very much about the staging (in the sense of conscious self-presentation to another) of media' (p. 29). This is what the GIF does. It represents – points to – its source media product, most frequently a short scene of a film, and it stages it by repeating a certain moment in an infinite loop. Hampus Hagman (2012) claims that the GIF liberates the pure movement that is inherent in film and suppressed by narrative cinema. Thus, according to Hagman, the GIF performs through one of the essential properties of its source medium film, the moving gesture: 'Posted online, another viewer recognizes the strange and altered form a (possibly) familiar moment from a film has taken, and hence becomes aware of movement as pure potential. Quite literally, it gestures to him or her' (Hagman 2012, n.p.). This is a fruitful way of regarding the performative potential of the GIF: as an estrangement that emphasizes the media characteristics of the source medium but by doing so transforms it and provides it with new properties and new meaning.

The representative aspect of the GIF is emphasized by Tolins and Samermit (2016), who investigate GIFs in text messaging. They see the reaction GIF as a kind of substitute for the sender's own gestures or expressions. When posters use a GIF to perform a reaction, they are 'borrowing' someone else's expressions and gestures and making them their own. The substituting role of reaction GIFs is essential. If online communication does not include the use of camera or microphone, we do not see the face or hear the voice of the person we are communicating with. This can easily cause misunderstandings, since body language and tone of voice are important tools that we use to get our message through. Rhetorical devices such as irony can be especially difficult to convey in writing, which everyone who has ever looked through a heated commentary section knows. To facilitate communication, different strategies have been employed over time. Twenty years ago, posters often described their reactions verbally, like this: *smiles*. Another method, still in use, is to use manual emojis, such as :-), when letters and punctuation form ideograms of a smiling, laughing or sad face. GIFs use iconic signs but are often combined with symbolic signs when captioned. The basic media type of moving images is used to visually represent the poster's sensations or reactions, enhancing the message and clarifying the poster's position in the communication. Tolins and Samermit (2016) argue that 'GIFs can be analysed as a novel form of embodied re-enactment or demonstration [...] These GIF demonstrations are meant to be taken as the contributor's own actions' (p. 76).

However, the GIF is not a medium that only represents pre-existing content or ideas. According to Miltner and Highfield (2017), '[m]ore than just representing affect, GIFs have the capacity to augment and shape our affective performances', because 'selecting and using the GIF format is a performance in and of itself' (p. 4). This relates to Brown's (2012) study of how GIFs are used to construct sexual, political and ethnic identity in online communities such as Tumblr. For example, within fandom communities, fans can create and share

GIFs that suggest that characters that are straight according to the official description are in fact having relationships with each other that might be described as LGBTQ+. This is how fan fiction works, but using such GIFs is also a way for a poster to position themselves within a community – to construct and perform an identity, which is not necessarily identical to their IRL identity.

Hence, the GIF can be understood and studied as a performative medium because of how it turns, for example, gestures or facial expressions that are performing an emotion in one context to performing it in a completely different context. A GIF represents the poster's reaction in an exaggerated manner, since it isolates what G.E. Lessing in his essay 'Laocoon' (1766) describes as 'the pregnant moment' (or at least one of them) from the scene it derives from in the source media product (for example, short excerpts from TV series, interviews, films and home videos): facial expressions, gestures and movements that indicate strong emotions such as surprise, anger, joy, embarrassment, love, excitement, etc. The repetitive nature of the GIF underlines the sentiment it embodies. Another common feature is the zooming-in element: the GIF often only shows a section of the camera frame in the film, zooming in on the face of a person pulling a face. This zooming in is constantly repeated, which adds to the sense of exaggeration.

The GIF is meant to provoke a reaction in the responders or amuse them, and most of the time, there is no doubt what reaction the poster wants to convey, even in cases where the responders are not familiar with the source of the GIF. However, the essence of the GIF is that it transmediates another media product and knowledge about that product is important: for the poster to display cultural knowledge and cultural affinity, and for the responders to understand the full meaning of the reaction. Miltner and Highfield (2017) call the demonstration of cultural knowledge one of 'two core aspects of digital communication' (p. 3), the other being the performance of affect. For example, posting a GIF representing the obscure cult film *The Room* (Wiseau 2003) frames the poster as a film connoisseur and, because of the (unintentional) nonsensical nature of the film, the full meaning of the reaction can only be grasped if you have seen *The Room* or know a lot about it. Here the GIF functions as an intermedial hint for the already initiated. An example of GIFs strengthening the cultural affinity within, for example, a fandom is highlighted by Katharine McCain (2018). She explains how fans use GIFs to close the gaps between the original source medium (the *Harry Potter* book series) and the *Harry Potter* films. This, according to McCain, is done in three ways:

1. Using GIFs as a means of fixing apparent mistakes in the films,
2. Recreating significant, canonical scenarios that didn't make it into the films and
3. Creating new scenarios that help to continually expand the *Harry Potter* universe and keep the fandom alive (p. 114).

One example of an alternative plotline often explored by fans in GIFs and memes is a romantic relationship between Harry Potter and his nemesis, Draco Malfoy.

A GIF can function without any knowledge of the source media product from both the perspective of the poster and the perspective of the audience. But it still requires knowledge about the meaning of the gesture – eye-rolling as a conventional sign for 'I can't even' – or the operational aspects that qualify the GIF – how a GIF is used, the different types of GIFs, etc.

Transmediation

One of the most important intermedial features of the GIF is its transmedial and transformative nature. All GIFs that are created from a source media product both transmediate and represent that media product, which means that they reconstruct ideas, concepts and structural characteristics of another medium (see Elleström 2014, p. 14) and at the same time they represent, that is, point to, that medium. In these processes, the source media product – the film, TV series, news programme, home video, TV show, music video, etc. – is not only reproduced but transformed, and recognizing these changes is paramount if one wants to comprehend the essence of the GIF and its intermedial character. Table 16.1 below clarifies the differences between a source media product and the GIF as the target media product. This can serve as a starting point for an analysis of transmediation that transforms fragments of a source media product into a GIF.

Where the source media product is a stable artefact and presented to an audience in a one-way, top-down type of communication, the GIF is dynamic, user-generated and in constant dialogue with its source media product, other GIFs and other media products in general. A GIF only transmediates a tiny snippet of the original narrative or communicative situation, and without the original context, the meaning of the source medium is destabilized. New meanings can be added to the snippet, and it can be used in an infinite number of new contexts: 'GIFs create new meanings in the process of exchange. Their layers accrue, bearing traces of where they have been' (McCarthy 2017, p. 113). Miltner and Highfield (2017) assert that

Table 16.1 Transmediation from a source media product to a GIF

The source media product	The target media product GIF
One	Many
Complete	Fragment
A known originator	Usually anonymous
Hierarchic relation between producer and audience	User-generated; part of a participatory culture
One specific meaning in one specific context	Many different meanings in many different contexts
Progression	Repetition
Stable	Changeable and dynamic
Typically includes sound	Silent

> [t]he meaning of a GIF changes dramatically depending on who is using it and in what context. The perpetual embedding and re-embedding of GIFs in new conversations, listicles, and coverage of different topics highlight the content's malleability as it is repeatedly appropriated.
>
> (p. 5)

Popular GIFs are around for years and can disappear for a while only to resurface, and this process continues.

One example of a GIF that has taken on different meanings in different contexts is one that features the bald little boy from the film *The Matrix* (1999) who can bend spoons with his mind, but then tells Neo: 'Do not try and bend the spoon. That's impossible. Instead, only try to realise the Truth … there is no spoon … Then you'll see that it is not the spoon that bends, it is only yourself' (Matrix.fandom.com, n.d.). The scene is dramatic and dignified, which makes it funny to use in less serious contexts, such as in a list on BuzzFeed.com (Dunlap 2018) about 'The 17 Best and Worst Things About Having a Tall and Skinny Boyfriend', where number five is 'Finding a comfortable way to cuddle is one of the biggest challenges in your relationship'. 'There is no spoon' here means that it is difficult to 'spoon' when there is a big size difference. Natalie Brown (2017) lists '25 Hilarious April Fool's Ideas People Have Actually Tried', and number 21, called 'A *Matrix*-level mall prank' is illustrated by the spoon GIF:

> You need at least three friends to help you and some poor stranger to play it on:
>
> ★Go somewhere crowded like the mall or something.
> ★Pick your victim.
> ★Spread out and follow that person around, and periodically have each person you're with pass them and say, 'Wake up', 'You're in coma', 'This is a dream'. 'None of this is real', etc.
>
> (Brown 2017, n.p.)

In 2017, a Reddit user posted the spoon GIF with the following caption: 'HIFW [How I feel when] I Go to Bed Every Night as a Single Person' (www.reddit.com 2017). Here as well, the spoon refers to 'spooning'. As we can see, over time, the scene from the film has resurfaced online in GIF form, taking on new meanings in different contexts. Still, this GIF would not be funny if we did not know the original meaning and context of it. The contrast between the philosophical and moving scene in *The Matrix* and contexts involving dating, making out and pranking strangers in the mall is what makes the GIF funny. This is often the purpose and effect of GIFs and memes (here denoting captioned still images): to make fun of the source media product or the person they represent, sometimes in an affectionate manner but sometimes – for example, in political contexts – not so much. Nothing is sacred to the grassroots internet culture.

Another example of irreverent representation is what can be called the art GIF, a type of GIF that represents and perhaps, to borrow a term used by Bolter and Grusin (1999), refashions famous paintings, since it adds movement to the static artworks, thereby realizing the old dream of the moving painting (Gradinaru 2016, p. 181). In the following example, Edward Hopper's famous painting *Nighthawks* (1942) is transmediated into the GIF format (Useumorg 2016). The GIF is zoomed in to the couple sitting together at the diner. Close to the man's head, a notification of a new message pops up. Directly thereafter, two dialogue boxes, 'confirm' and 'ignore', appear close to the woman's head. The computer pointer clicks on the ignore box and the two boxes reappear. The GIF zooms in on the aspects of social media contact administration that lack emotional closeness and commitment. The GIF is a subtle play with the themes of loneliness and isolation that are attributed to Hopper's work and an effective way to refashion them in a social media context.

Temporality and stillness

Since a GIF is constituted of a small snippet from its source media product, and since it is repeated *ad infinitum*, the relation between progress and stillness is complex. Repetition is a paradoxical device, since it conveys both movement and stasis; there is movement, but it never goes beyond the depicted seconds, which provides it with a sense of stillness: 'By removing their original context and adding the perpetual repetition of a single action, they also become atemporal' (Brown 2012, p. 8). Alessandra Chiarini (2016) describes it as follows:

> Made up of individual stills repeated to generate a short cyclical animation, often intermittent and potentially inexhaustible, GIF-images tend to reveal, via a series of small shocks, the paradoxical nature of the moving image which turns out to be connected on many levels to stillness.
>
> (p. 2)

Hampus Hagman (2012) notes that the purpose of the GIF is not to tell an unfolding story but the opposite: the purpose is to remain in the moment. Therefore, even when what is transmediated to a GIF is part of a larger narrative (such as GIFs made from films or TV series), the result of the transmediation is anti-narrative; the transfer totally changes the spatiotemporal characteristics of the source medium. Regarding art GIFs, the situation is somewhat more complicated. The source media product, the painting, is materially static, but after it is transmediated to the GIF, it contains movement. How that movement affects the source media product, the painting, depends on the temporality it conveys rather than the temporality of its interface. A painting is materially static but can depict or indicate movement in various ways, for example, by means of blurring effects, stretched out shapes, characters depicted as being in the middle of an action, etc. Take, for example, Vincent van Gogh's painting *The Starry Night* (1889): the sky appears to be in motion due to the spiral-shaped, whirling clouds surrounding the glowing stars. GIFs made from this painting (and there are many) often focus on the sky, amplifying the sense of movement already inherent in the spatiotemporal modality of the painting.

A painting can also convey a specific sense of stillness and motionlessness. All still images are static in the material modality. However, still life paintings and portraits are examples of artworks that often convey a particular sense of stillness. Even Edward Hopper's paintings are often described in such terms. In these cases, the repetitive movement of the GIF can emphasize the sense of stillness already inherent in the painting, since repetition in itself is not progressive but the opposite: it halts time and hinders narrative development. Thus, as Bolter and Grusin (1999) point out, the result of the transmediation can be negotiated as *reform*:

> We have adopted the word to express the way in which one medium is seen by our culture as reforming or improving upon another. This belief in reform is particularly strong for those who are today repurposing earlier media into digital forms.
>
> (Bolter and Grusin 1999, p. 59)

GIFs can be studied from various perspectives, and we have here concentrated on a few of them: performativity, transmediation and temporality. These are all inherently intermedial issues. Studying GIFs from these perspectives will provide you with a deeper intermedial understanding, as well as an understanding of the complex character of the GIF.

Intermediality and social media: Conclusion

The two examples discussed demonstrate the extent to which social media are a context for the *new* to emerge out of the *old*. New media types, new media products, novel types of human communication and new spaces for interaction are created one after the other and provide us with unprecedented opportunities for action and agency. This vitality is, to a considerable extent, generated through intermedial relations and multimodal configurations.

These intermedial relations rarely exist independently but are interwoven together, as you saw in the macro level of social media entertainment and in the micro level of GIFs. Existing media types and media content are transformed into new forms through various types of transmediation and media representation and the coexistence, combination and integration of different media creates the reality of social media.

Perhaps it is possible, now more than ever, to feel the way in which media is an extension of our human bodies and minds as we experience a sense of community by regularly checking on and engaging with our favourite blogger or as we outsource our bodily and facial gestures to GIFs, which can sometimes express them better than we would ourselves ;-)!

Note

1 For the sake of brevity, we won't go into a detailed discussion and definition of the concept of platforms here, but the interested reader is advised to consult Burgess (2015), van Dijck et al. (2018) and Gillespie (2010).

Further Reading

Berryman, R. and Kavka, M. 2018. Crying on YouTube: Vlogs, self-exposure and the productivity of negative affect. *Convergence: The International Journal of Research into New Media Technologies*, 24(1), pp. 85–98. doi:10.1177/1354856517736981

Burgess, J. 2015. From 'broadcast yourself' to 'follow your interests': Making over social media. *International Journal of Cultural Studies*, 18(3), pp. 281–285. doi:10.1177/1367877913513684

Burwell, C. and Miller, T. 2016. Let's Play: Exploring literacy practices in an emerging videogame paratext. *E-Learning and Digital Media*, 13(3–4), pp. 109–125. doi:10.1177/2042753016677858

Craig, D. and Cunningham, S. 2019. *Social media entertainment: The new intersection of Hollywood and Silicon Valley*. New York: New York University Press.

Ferchaud, A., Grzeslo, J., Orme, S. and Lagroue, J. 2018. Parasocial attributes and YouTube personalities: Exploring content trends across the most subscribed YouTube channels. *Computers in Human Behavior*, 80, pp. 88–96. doi:10.1016/j.chb.2017.10.041

Gillespie, T. 2010. The politics of 'platforms'. *New Media & Society*, 12(3), pp. 347–364. doi:10.1177/1461444809342738

Glas, R. 2015. Vicarious play: Engaging the viewer in Let's Play videos. *Empedocles: European Journal for the Philosophy of Communication*, 5(1–2), pp. 81–86. doi:10.1386/ejpc.5.1-2.81_1

Hillrichs, R. 2016. Poetics of early YouTube: Production, performance, success. *Academia.edu*. https://www.academia.edu/27036096/Poetics_of_Early_YouTube_Production_Performance_Success [Accessed 1 October 2021].

Page, R. 2018. *Narratives online: Shared stories in social media*. Cambridge: Cambridge University Press.

Sjöblom, M. and Hamari, J. 2017. Why do people watch others play video games? An empirical study on the motivations of Twitch users. *Computers in Human Behavior*, 75, pp. 985–996. doi:10.1016/j.chb.2016.10.019

Snickars, P. and Vonderau, P. eds. 2009. *The YouTube reader*. Stockholm: National Library of Sweden.

van Dijck, J. 2013. *The culture of connectivity: A critical history of social media*. New York: Oxford University Press. doi:10.1093/acprof:oso/9780199970773.001.0001 [Accessed 16 December 20].

References

Introduction

Carr, C.T. and Hayes, R.A. 2015. Social media: Defining, developing, and divining. *Atlantic Journal of Communication*, 23(1), pp. 46–65.

Helles, R. 2013. Mobile communication and intermediality. *Mobile Media & Communication*, 1(1), pp. 14–19.

Jurgenson, N. 2012. When atoms meet bits: Social media, the mobile web and augmented revolution. *Future Internet*, 4(1), pp. 83–91.

Kember, S. and Zylinska, J. 2012. *Life after new media: Mediation as a vital process*. Cambridge: MIT Press.

O'Sullivan, P.B and Carr, C.T. 2018. Masspersonal communication: A model bridging the mass-interpersonal divide. *New Media & Society*, 20(3), pp. 1161–1180.

Schwartz, R. and Halegoua, G.R. 2015. The spatial self: Location-based identity performance on social media. *New Media & Society*, 17(10), pp. 1643–1660.

Media transformation on YouTube: Social media entertainment as an intermedial practice

Allmer, T. 2015. *Critical theory and social media: Between emancipation and commodification*. New York: Routledge.

BBC Newsbeat. 2019. PewDiePie cancels $50,000 donation to anti-hate group: 'I messed up'. *BBC News*. https://www.bbc.com/news/newsbeat-49686018 [Accessed 5 February 2021].

Bolter, J.D. and Grusin, R. 1999. *Remediation: Understanding new media*. Cambridge, MA; London: MIT Press.

Burgess, J. 2015. From 'broadcast yourself' to 'follow your interests': Making over social media. *International Journal of Cultural Studies*, 18(3), pp. 281–285. doi:10.1177/1367877913513684

Burgess, J. and Green, J. 2009. The entrepreneurial vlogger: Participatory culture beyond the professional-amateur divide. In P. Snickars and P. Vonderau, eds., *The YouTube reader* (pp. 79–107). Stockholm: National Library of Sweden.

Craig, D. and Cunningham, S. 2019. *Social media entertainment: The new intersection of Hollywood and Silicon Valley*. New York: New York University Press.

Enli, G. (2015). *Mediated authenticity: How the media constructs reality*. New York: Peter Lang.

Gillespie, T. 2010. The politics of 'platforms'. *New Media and Society*, 12(3), pp. 347–364. doi:10.1177/1461444809342738

Gilmore, J.H. and Pine, B.J. 2007. *Authenticity: What consumers really want*. Boston: Harvard Business School Press.

Graham, M. and Dutton, W.H. 2019. *Society and the internet: How networks of information and communication are changing our lives*. Oxford: Oxford University Press.

Graham, M. and Dutton, W.H. 2019. *Society and the internet: How networks of information and communication are changing our lives*. Oxford: Oxford University Press.

Navas, E., Gallagher, O. and Burrough, X. 2014. *The Routledge companion to remix studies*. New York: Taylor & Francis Group.

Navas, E., Gallagher, O. and Burrough, X. 2021. *The Routledge handbook of digital humanities and remix studies*. New York: Taylor & Francis Group.

Nightingale, R. 2017. 12 Engaging vlogs you need to start watching today. *Make Use Of*. https://www.makeuseof.com/tag/vlogs-to-watch/ [Accessed 12 December 20].

Page, R. 2018. *Narratives online: Shared stories in social media*. Cambridge: Cambridge University Press.

Roose, K. 2020. Rabbit hole. *The New York Times*. https://www.nytimes.com/column/rabbit-hole [Accessed 4 February 2021].

Snickars, P. and Vonderau, P. 2009. Introduction. In P. Snickars and P. Vonderau, eds., *The YouTube reader* (pp. 9–21). Stockholm: National Library of Sweden.

van Alphen, E., Bal, M, and Smith, C.E. 2009. *The rhetoric of sincerity: Cultural memory in the present*. Stanford: Stanford University Press.

van Dijck, J. 2013. *The culture of connectivity: A critical history of social media*. New York: Oxford University Press. doi:10.1093/acprof:oso/9780199970773.001.0001

van Dijck, J., Poell, T. and de Waal, M. (2018). *The platform society: Public values in a connective world*. Oxford: Oxford University Press.

Media referenced

Jawed, K. 2005. Me at the zoo. https://www.youtube.com/watch?v=jNQXAC9IVRw [Accessed 30 April 2020].

PewDiePie. n.d. PewDiePie channel. https://www.youtube.com/user/PewDiePie/featured [Accessed 2 October 2021].

PewDiePie. 2019a. I challenge the Ender Dragon in Minecraft (Ending) – Part 30. https://www.youtube.com/watch?v=YVxaK8WQhJo [Accessed 2 October 2021].

PewDiePie. 2019b. I raid an end city in Minecraft (Epicly) – Part 31. https://www.youtube.com/watch?v=oLAw5EGe1zY&list=PLYH8WvNV1YEnLCzUDWueIZQXDNhqLKywk&index=15 [Accessed 30 April 2020].

PewDiePie. 2019c. I slept in the Nether in Minecraft – Part 5. https://www.youtube.com/watch?v=YuihlgsgNSo&list=PLYH8WvNV1YEnLCzUDWueIZQXDNhqLKywk&index=41 [Accessed 30 April 2020].

PewDiePie. 2019d. Im actually having ... FUN? In MINECRAFT (Hacked) – Part 2. https://www.youtube.com/user/PewDiePie/featured [Accessed 30 April 2020].

PewDiePie. 2019e. Married in Minecraft epicly – Part 29. https://www.youtube.com/watch?v=GYpOapkr5MA&list=PLYH8WvNV1YEnLCzUDWueIZQXDNhqLKywk&index=17 [Accessed 30 April 2020].

PewDiePie. 2019f. Minecraft stream REPLAY. https://dlive.tv/p/pdp+zfVewDDWR [Accessed 30 April 2020].

PewDiePie. 2019g. Minecraft the series. https://www.youtube.com/playlist?list=PLYH8WvNV1YEnLCzUDWueIZQXDNhqLKywk [Accessed 30 April 2020].

PewDiePie. 2019h. This building will change Minecraft FOREVER Minecraft – Part 34. https://www.youtube.com/watch?v=2D2vWXt1uII&lc=UgySMbts1ZZx0mGilXZ4AaABAg [Accessed 30 April 2020].

GIFs

Boissoneault, L. 2017. A brief history of the GIF, from early internet innovation to ubiquitous relic: How an image format changed the way we communicate. *Smithsonianmag.com*. https://www.smithsonianmag.com/history/brief-history-gif-early-internet-innovation-ubiquitous-relic-180963543/ [Accessed 26 May 2020].

Bolter, J.D. and Grusin, R. 1999. *Remediation: Understanding new media*. Cambridge, Massachusetts: MIT Press.

Brown, K. 2012. *Everyday i'm tumblin': Performing online identity through reaction GIFs*. Chicago: School of the Art Institute of Chicago.

Brown, N. 2017. 25 Hilarious April Fools' Ideas people have actually tried. *Buzzfeed.com*. https://www.buzzfeed.com/nataliebrown/ingenious-april-fools-ideas-guaranteed-to-make-you-laugh [Accessed 26 May 2020].

Chiarini, A. 2016. The multiplicity of the moop: The dialectics of stillness and movement in the cinemagraph. In Adriano D. Aloia, Francesco Parisi, eds., *Snapshot culture: The photographic experience in the post-medium age*. Milano: Vita e Pensiero. https://www.academia.edu/25013824/The_Multiplicity_of_the_Loop_The_Dialectics_of_Stillness_and_Movement_in_the_Cinemagraph_in_SNAPSHOT_CULTURE_THE_PHOTOGRAPHIC_EXPERIENCE_IN_THE_POST_MEDIUM_AGE_Comunicazioni_Sociali_no_1_Gennaio_Aprile_2016 [Accessed 8 December 2020].

Dunlap, Connor 2018. The 17 best and worst things about having a skinny boyfriend. *Buzzfeed.com*. https://www.buzzfeed.com/connorrdunlap/things-that-will-make-anyone-whos-dated-an-awkwardly [Accessed 11 May 2020].

Elleström, L. 2014. *Media transformation: The transfer of media characteristics among media*. Basingstoke; New York: Palgrave Macmillan.

Gradinaru, C. 2016. The technological expansion of sociability: Virtual communities as imagined communities. *Academicus International Scientific Journal*, 7(14), pp. 181–190.

Hagman, H. 2012. The digital gesture: Rediscovering cinematic movement through GIFs. *Refractory: Journal of Entertainment Media*. http://refractory.unimelb.edu.au/2012/12/29/hagman/ [Accessed 14 February 2020].

Kattenbelt, C. 2010. Intermediality in performance and as a mode of performativity. In S. Bay-Cheng, C. Kattenbelt, A. Lavender and R. Nelson, eds., *Mapping intermediality in performance* (pp. 29–37). Amsterdam: Amsterdam University Press.

McCain, K. 2018. *Transforming Harry: The adaptation of Harry Potter in the transmedia age*. Detroit: Wayne State University Press.

McCarthy, A. 2017. Visual pleasure and GIFs. In P. Hesselberth and M. Poulaki, eds., *Compact cinematics: The moving image in the age of bit-sized media* (pp. 113–122). New York: Bloomsbury Academic.

Miltner, K.M. and Highfield, T. 2017. Never gonna GIF you up: Analyzing the cultural significance of the animated GIF. *Social Media + Society*, July–September, pp. 1–11.

Tolins, J. and Samermit, P. 2016. GIFs as embodied enactments in text-mediated conversation. *Research on Language and Social Interaction*, 49(2), pp. 75–91.

Media referenced

Matrix.fandom.se. n.d. Spoon boy. *The Matrix wiki*. www.matrix.fandom.com/wiki/Spoon_Boy [Accessed 7 April 2021].

The Matrix. 1999. There is no spoon GIF. 14 September 2016. https://media.giphy.com/media/3o6Zt0hNCfak3QCqsw/giphy.gif [Accessed 7 April 2021].

Useumorg. 2016. Nighthawks by Edward Hopper (detail and GIF). 4 April. https://blog.useum.org/post/142231645538/nighthawks-by-edward-hopper-detail-gif-to [Accessed 7 April 2021].

Wiseau, T. 2003. *The room*. Los Angeles: Wiseau Films.

www.reddit.com. 2017. HIFW I go to bed every night as a single person. *reddit.com*. 17 March. https://www.reddit.com/r/HIFW/comments/5zwi62/hifw_i_go_to_bed_every_night_as_a_single_person/?ref=readnext [Accessed 7 April 2021].

17 A toolkit for the intermedial analysis of computer games

Péter Kristóf Makai

This chapter is a companion to Part I's 'Media and modalities – Computer games'. In that chapter, we surveyed how intermedial theory elucidates the complex interplay of different media modalities that create a transmedial operation key to the aesthetics of the video game medium: simulation. In this chapter, we will proceed to the more practical matter of answering the question: 'how do I begin analysing video games intermedially?'

The first half of the chapter will set out a series of research steps and sample questions that intermedial scholars will want to pursue to make sense of video games through the lens of their relationship to other media. We will then provide two analyses in greater detail to show how different media, namely animation and literature enrich our understanding of video games. For simplicity's sake, we chose to include only single-player games to give prospective intermedial scholars of games a clearer idea of what a basic intermedial analysis of a game might entail. Note that although single-player games are methodologically easier to deal with, multiplayer games make up a significant portion of games played today, and they have unique aesthetic forebears. Both case studies featured here contain two parts: a general section that explores what a qualified media type (cartoons or novels) contributes to the computer game medium as a whole, followed by two case studies (of *Toonstruck* and *80 Days*) that demonstrate how the intermedial connection is realized in a particular game. The two case studies are games with strong narrative drives, which makes them easier to compare to other narrative media, but a lot of games do not feature a story, and thus might benefit from other perspectives.

The kind of analysis performed here is not meant to be definitive or the only way of approaching the intermedial nature of games, but rather a way to showcase the capabilities of the intermedial toolbox. Don't forget: your research question might take you down a very different path. The purpose of this chapter, then, is to inspire as much as to instruct; for it is only when we make our tools do unexpected things that we can feel that we have properly learned their use.

You are welcome to consult your own scholarly traditions and research methodologies to provide new insights into the phenomena surrounding games and gaming. What follows is a set of research procedures that will help you

DOI: 10.4324/9781003174288-20

investigate games using intermediality theory. This approach is geared towards the comparative view, and is most adept at highlighting the changes that occur when media are being adapted, updated, translated or remediated, or transformed in some other way.

To begin with, please note the scale of each of the phenomena to be investigated:

- A game moment (a portion or element of gameplay that is significant)
- A game mechanic (a set of repeated actions or principles of simulation in one or a number of games)
- A media product (a single stand-alone game)
- A game series (several connected titles)
- A game genre (a set of games with similar mechanics)
- The video game as a medium (a set comprising all existing and possible games)
- An intellectual property franchise (games and other media delivering a coherent set of experiences)
- Social event(s) that centre around games or gaming
- Cultural context(s) in which games are embedded

Identify the particular phenomenon, delimiting it clearly and precisely, including a description of the modalities of media that are relevant to the investigated phenomenon:

- Material: the physical interactions involved in the gaming phenomenon
- Sensory: the use of sights, sounds, tastes, smells, haptics and proprioception in the gaming phenomenon
- Spatiotemporal: the structuring of space and time in the gaming phenomenon
- Semiotic: the use of icons, indices and symbols in the construction of meanings within the gaming phenomenon

Decide which kind of intermedial relationship you are investigating:

- Media representation happens when a medium becomes the subject of a representation in a different medium. This could take many forms, such as:
    - A simple representation of qualified media, e.g. game characters talking about an in-game map
    - A complex representation of qualified media, e.g. film characters acting as if they were in a game
    - A simple representation of a media product, e.g. a game soundtrack featuring a jingle used by a radio station
    - A complex representation of a media product, e.g. a game using a soundtrack of licensed songs to evoke a particular era, genre convention or aesthetic

The intermedial analysis of computer games 311

- Media combination happens when more than one medium is being used to convey a particular experience or meaning in a video game. They could include:
    - A simple combination of qualified media, e.g. a game using visual and audio effects to represent a character's health
    - A complex combination of qualified media, e.g. a game that allows players to collect material clues, take photographs and record audio to catch a killer
    - A simple combination of media products, e.g. the player playing a song in *Guitar Hero* (2005) by pressing buttons on the controller in sync with visual input on the screen
    - A complex combination of media products, e.g. a game in which characters from different media franchises meet, such as *Super Smash Bros* (1999)
- Transmediation happens when the same form or content of media is mediated in a different technical medium. This can be found in any of the following:
    - A simple transmediation of qualified media, e.g. the depiction of a scanned photograph in a game, or a screenshot of a game state
    - A complex transmediation of qualified media, e.g. making a video recording of someone playing a game, or the film *Hardcore Henry* (2015)
    - A simple transmediation of a media product, e.g. a cameo appearance of a film character in a game, or a shot of someone playing a particular game on film
    - A complex transmediation of a media product, e.g. adapting a whole film into a game, or vice versa
- Media simulation may not be unique to the computer as a technical medium, but it is certainly the prime medium for simulations today. Media simulation happens when a target medium mimics the processes of mediation or the operations of a source medium that allows for creative mediation or the creation of novel media products. The following are some examples of this:
    - A simple simulation of qualified media, e.g. a minigame in which players control a brush to produce any painting they like
    - A complex simulation of qualified media, e.g. a game that simulates the workings of the film or news industry
    - A simple simulation of a media product, e.g. a game mechanic that simulates hacking scenes from *The Matrix* (1999)
    - A complex simulation of a media product, e.g. a game in which the players play as if they are the crew of a spaceship in the *Star Trek* universe, such as *Star Trek Bridge Crew* (2016)

Compare how the phenomenon in the source medium has been modified in the target medium on the basis of the four modalities of media and bring in other points of analysis that befit the argument you are making. Your interests might lie in what gets lost during transmedial operation, in how transmedial operations reflect on the medium itself, in how each medium expands a universe of a story, in how different media are used to engage their users, or in the way transmedial media products are tied to commercial and cultural values of the day.

A note on documenting observations

While, in principle, nothing can stop a researcher from simply playing games and then relying on their general impression of how play went to make generalizations about the behaviour and the representational artefacts of the games you study, it is worth keeping in mind that the dynamic nature of computer games makes the researcher's experience ungeneralizable in many ways. Nonetheless, even if you decide that your expert knowledge is enough to investigate the intermedial phenomena in question, it is important to document your findings.

Documenting your time with the game can be as simple as taking written notes, or you may opt to record your play session in some format. These may include taking screenshots or video footage of in-game events with dedicated software. The usefulness of these observations might bring out unusual behaviours of the program, which are unique to your playthrough, so before you attribute particular significance to an occurrence, you should compare your own play sessions with other players' experiences.

Since most games challenge you directly, you might face particular obstacles that are difficult (if not impossible) to overcome in the time frame allotted for gameplay in your research schedule. To cut down on time and effort needed to get to the phenomena you wish to study, you might consider the use of paratextual aids, such as walkthroughs, strategy guides, downloading save files of characters at various stages of progress or even editing your own save files. Crowdsourced encyclopaedias of game media franchises offer helpful lexical information you can access at a moment's notice.

There is a wealth of information about how people play the games you study in various media. Recorded play sessions of other players are available in text-based, screenshot-illustrated or video-recorded formats on sites like the Let's Play! Archive, YouTube, Twitch or other websites, which might illuminate the game for researchers in new ways. However, researchers must note that these recorded sessions are also curated to particular gaming audiences, and more often than not, feature the content creator prominently, who might structure the play session towards a preconceived narrative in mind. Content creators are seldom neutral, disinterested players, and they often rely on gameplay to attain status in their gaming communities, or they might use attention-grabbing production strategies for engaging audiences to secure views and earn income from their creative endeavours. In these instances, the researcher's personal experience will be a good compass in determining which elements of the play session are present in the original game and which are added intentionally by the content creator for effect.

Discuss the phenomenon and situate your analysis in the relevant scholarly context or discourse:

- Disciplinary discourses, e.g. game, film, literary (or other media) studies, computer science, biology, narratology, cultural studies, communication, sociology, history, etc.
- Theoretical approaches, e.g. Marxist theory, feminist studies, critical race theory, critical disability theory, queer theory, etc.
- Methodological considerations, e.g. ethnographical studies of players, statistical methods for quantifying media reception, qualitative analysis of representations, etc.

As noted above, not all of these procedures might be equally important for every line of research. Intermedial analysis is not a checklist process in which all points should be covered in equal length and depth. The researcher is always free to omit, rephrase, modify or otherwise adapt these aspects of inquiry to suit their needs.

Animation: *Toonstruck*

Animation in computer games

Almost all video games are animated. Whether it is via a sparkling animation of a gemstone or the elaborate motion-captured facial performance of a real actor, the worlds of computer games come alive as a result of the painstaking work of animators. Animated entertainment has always been a heavily technical accomplishment, a home for innovation and a form of visual expression that captures the hearts and minds of its viewers. Video games are no different. This section describes how animation is created in games and shows the complex medial connections between animation that is designed for theatrical cartoons and a game that takes place in a cartoon world.

Let us begin with a brief explanation of *game animation* from the perspective of the technical media of display involved in the creation of moving images on the computer (Cooper 2019). All art in video games was originally 2D; since the 1980s, 3D graphics have also been available, but they only began to be widely used in the mid-1990s. Both kinds of graphical output are made from binary data. There are two major forms of organizing that data into images: *raster graphics* and *vector graphics*. In a raster image file, a (usually rectangular) *bitmap* defines the position and colour of each constitutive part, called *pixels* (from pictures, abbreviated as *pix*, and *el*, short for element), in a mathematical matrix. Vector graphics are created using vector paths by setting geometrical coordinates that describe lines and curves, which may then be assembled to form more complicated shapes. This way of defining shapes is more data-efficient, but they are best suited to create more abstract, geometrically definable images. Unlike vector graphics, raster images can be photorealistic, and individual elements can be easily manipulated.

The difference between the two ways of storing image data has implications for computer animation. Most early games and today's 2D games tend to use raster animation, which is created by displaying one bitmap after another in separate frames. In contrast, a few arcade and early PC games (such as *Lunar Lander* (1979) and *Another World* (1991)) used vector graphics because of their scalability and memory efficiency. With the advent of optical storage media, such as LaserDiscs and CDs, designers could also begin to record live-action performances, which ushered in an era of full-motion video games, bringing recognized actors to the computer screen. Notable examples include *Wing Commander III: Heart of the Tiger* (1993), starring Mark Hamill, John Rhys-Davies and Malcolm McDowell in lead roles, and *Phantasmagoria* (1995), featuring Steven W. Bailey, Jeff Rector and Douglas Seale. In full-motion video games, lifelike video footage is digitized by compressing the visual data into bitmaps – here, gameplay consists of choosing which animated clip is played as the player explores different paths of a branching narrative (one recent example is *Black Mirror: Bandersnatch* 2018). At the time of writing, 2020, games use 2D raster graphics or some form of 3D. In 3D, artists use vector graphics to create wire-mesh models made of polygons, on which bitmapped textures are laid and then the models are animated and rendered into the 2D image you see on the screen. The models are then made to move similarly to the principles used in stop-motion animation to capture movement, except that the computer calculates each frame in real time or slightly ahead of its display. Nonetheless, even stop-motion animation is used in games, a great example being *The Neverhood* (1995).

Some of the principles of hand-drawn animation are the same as those used in 2D animation on the computer. Backgrounds are more static and detailed than animated foreground figures in both, and are shot on separate layers. Traditional cel animation, as used in theatrical cartoons, exploits the persistence of vision to flash 24 frames per second (fps), which produces the illusion of smooth movement for the eye, but the mind can be satisfied with just 12 fps to perceive something as animation, which is why TV animation is often 'shot on twos' (i.e. with half the frames) to cut costs. Similarly, in 2D games, backgrounds are also treated as separate from foreground objects, such as characters, whose bitmap images, called 'sprites', have livelier animations and move about independently of backgrounds. 2D platformers, for example, feature noticeable parallax scrolling, in which background layers closer to the player scroll at a quicker pace than layers further back. These similarities soon become notable in our case study, which reflects on cartoon animation as both an industry and a representative tradition.

Toonstruck

Toonstruck (1996) is a perfect example of a game where traditional animation and computer animation meet. It is also a self-reflective game in which animation is central to the plot and gameplay. As such, *Toonstruck* transmediates the animated cartoon as a medium. It mixes a filmed live-action actor playing the protagonist, Christopher Lloyd, with a hand-drawn game world, much like *Who Framed Roger Rabbit?* The player is put into the shoes of one Drew Blanc (Lloyd), an overworked animator at a cartoon studio known for Fluffy Fluffy Bun Bun (voiced by Tress MacNeille), which tells the story of a saccharinely cute rabbit's adventures in Cutopia. After falling asleep at the drawing board, Drew ends up within the cartoon world he helped to bring to life. He needs to wake himself up to escape from Cutopia, but to do that he must protect its residents from the evil Count Nefarious (Tim Curry). He is tasked by Cutopia's King Hugh (David Ogden Stiers) to build the Cutifier to defeat Nefarious. The simplicity of the plot and the game's visual appearance and soundscapes, as well as the logic governing the action, are exactly what we expect from Saturday morning cartoons, except that the player *enacts* the story, thinking of solutions to Drew's problems, rather than just sitting back and watching.

As scholars, we can use the intermedial approach to analyse several aspects of the game's use of different media in meaning-making. For example, we can highlight how *Toonstruck* uses cartoon animation and the conventions of the medium to provide medium-relevant clues to the logic governing the world of the computer game and to analyse the puzzle design of the game. Puzzles always leave strategic gaps in the semiotic game world, which the player must anticipate and subsequently perform. *Toonstruck*'s intermedial connections between television cartoons and games cue players in to a very particular form of lateral thinking by transforming the cartoon world into a world in which the player has agency and prompts them to utilize intermedial forms of thinking. By using intermedial terminology, we can specify how that effect is achieved, how it informs puzzle design and how specific cues serve as elements of the design process. This, in turn, highlights the cybernetic process of give and take that takes place between machines and humans – a feedback loop that requires semiotic manipulation and intermedial operations to produce the main aesthetic effect: the cognitive challenge of the player in the service of telling a story. Thus, *Toonstruck* becomes more than the sum of its parts: both a cartoon and a game, it is a memorable experience and one of the top 100 adventure games ever released.

Toonstruck is a graphical adventure game, which is a submedium of the *qualified media type* we call the video game. This means that players who know adventure games can expect certain ways of presenting information on the screen and performing actions (hence the name 'point-and-click' adventures). Adventure games have a narrative, which the player explores by moving around in the game world, talking to characters, facing obstacles. The main challenge of adventure games is to get around those obstacles by solving brain-teasing puzzles, either via finding the right items scattered around the game world and using them on other objects, or talking to characters who might provide additional bits of story or give verbal hints on how to solve the puzzle.

Materially, *Toonstruck* exists as computer code in the real world and exists as a program running on the technical medium of display, the home computer. It is programmed by lead programmers Douglas Hare and Gary Priest and programmers Michael Gater and Kevin Olson. Originally, *Toonstruck* was released on two CDs in a jewel case. Although certain data are copied onto the hard drive to make the game run, Disc One or Two needs to be in the drive for the game to be played. At the time of writing, 2020, the game is available as a downloadable programme on digital distribution platforms such as Steam or GOG, with no discs required. Because it is an old game written for DOS, the program needs to be run in an *emulator*, ScummVM, which is a virtual machine that mimics the behaviour of older computers.

Within the game, the cartoon logic of the world means that matter behaves rather differently from our expectations: most obviously, living people cannot inhabit a cartoon world. Christopher Lloyd's performance had to be transmediated (a bitmap sprite of his recorded actions had to be created) to make him a playable character. Drew is filmed in 3D then rendered in 2D, and the cartoon characters are already 2D. Thus, *Toonstruck* is both a complex transmediation of hand-drawn animation and a game that features a media representation of live-action performance.

Drew can easily store many, many more objects on his person than would be feasible for a real human being. This is a convention of most adventure games. And yet, in many puzzles, objects behave in a way that conforms with our expectations: mallets can hit objects, butter makes surfaces slippery, portcullises cannot be drawn up without significant force and so on. It's as if cartoon physics operates on the sole criterion of being moderately inconveniencing to the protagonist. Therefore, the game represents the physical affordances of objects and exploits them in puzzles, but it eschews simulating their full materiality for the sake of easy storage. Material interactions are brought to life with hand-drawn animation, and the possible set of interactions between objects and characters is encoded in the game itself.

As with most computer games, the players' *sensory* engagement with the game is visual, auditory and haptic, given that they control the game with a mouse. Therefore, the cartoon world is presented 1) in a visual format through static images (where Drew is, what he has, whom he is talking to) or animation (what he does, why he cannot perform the player's command, etc.), 2) with accompanying audio, such as background music (for ambience), spoken dialogue (for sharing the verbal knowledge of the characters) or sound effects (to highlight less visible events or to underscore interactions), while players 3) haptically communicate their intentions concerning what to do next (by moving the mouse and clicking on in-game objects).

Visually, *Toonstruck* is notable for being hand-drawn, animated by the Rainbow Animation and Nelvana studios and imitating the styles of Don Bluth, Chuck Jones and John Kricfalusi. The game also features animated and full-motion video cutscenes to put game events into a narrative context without interference from the player, thus providing essential narrative beats, such as transitions between the major regions of the game. The three game worlds Drew explores, Cutopia, Zanydu and the Malevolands, feature distinct visual styles and colour palettes. Cutopia has a rich pastel colour scheme with a lot of curved geometry that is pleasant to look at. Zanydu has jagged, energetic lines, dynamic arrows that lead the eye and a primary RGB colour scheme with its complementing colours. The Malevolands are made up of grotesque lines and pointed ends jutting outwards; a dark palette using shades of grey, green and purple dominates.

One puzzle actively challenges the player to pay attention to colour. In Zanydu, phones do not dial numbers but colours; to call someone, a colour sequence must be pressed. In order to win a prize in a phone-in game, the player must answer questions about what colour different Zanydu objects are. However, some colours do not have designated buttons – instead, players must use the logic of additive colour theory to 'mix' the right answer.

The visual conventions of animation also feature in another puzzle: Drew at one point must obtain a star-shaped object. However, there are no persistent pickup-able stars anywhere in the game. To progress, the player must recognize that hitting a cartoon character on its head with a boxing glove makes that character 'see stars'; this means that the character is shown knocked-out and a short animation plays with stars circling about their head, which then disappears. But if players are quick enough, they might notice that the cursor changes shape when they hover it over the stars, indicating that they can indeed be picked up. This requires a form of lateral thinking, since other objects are persistent and always available to the player – the puzzle exploits the representational conventions of the animated cartoon, but in this simple case of media transformation, the stars have now become interactable objects that conform to the logic of the adventure game.

One of the defining characteristics of *Toonstruck* is its distinctive audio profile (for sound in film, see Chapter 4). The voice acting is provided by a star-studded cast of Hollywood actors and high-profile animation voice-acting talent. The game is notable for being one of the first games to use sound effects and compositions from an actual production music library, APM, including songs such as 'Happy-Go-Lively' by Laurie Johnson, 'Workaday World' by Jack Beaver and 'Little Symphony – Spooky Scherzo' by Sam Fonteyn, as well as pieces of classical music, such as Tchaikovsky's '*Danse des petites cygnes*' and Rossini's overture to *La Gazza Ladra*. These are examples of *media representation*: the game features sound effects and popular music that have previously been used by animation studios as parts of their soundtrack to strengthen the player's sense that they are in a cartoon world.

One of the puzzles is specifically audio-based. Count Nefarious's castle is protected by elaborate security technology, including voice-activated door locks. To get inside a room, Drew must modify his voice to match the squeaky tones of Nefarious's henchmen. This is achieved by obtaining a balloon from another room, quickly inhaling helium at the door and stating the name of the henchman before the effects of the helium wear off. The puzzle uses the real-world knowledge of the material behaviour of helium, and it simulates its effects by distorting the voice of Drew when the player uses the balloon on Drew.

In terms of the *spatiotemporal* modality, *Toonstruck* the program is accessible on a PC and nowadays on Windows-compatible mobile devices, but it is not a location-based game. On average, it takes eight hours and thirty minutes to complete the game, allowing for leisurely exploration and the exhaustion of all dialogue options. In general, saving games serve an important function: it can break gaming sessions into manageable chunks of time. The freer the player is to save a game, the easier it becomes to correct one's mistakes. Earlier adventure games frequently featured death scenarios that would end the play session, requiring the player to restore an older saved game, and proceed from an earlier stage of progress. By the early 1990s, some adventure game companies have established conventions of design that avoided the player character's deaths. *Toonstruck* belongs to the category of games in which the player cannot be locked out of winning the game and thus having to restart due to character death or breaking the intended sequence of events to beat the game.

Toonstruck has a frame-narrative structure and is set in the real world of an animation studio, but the playable portion of the game takes place in Drew's dreams, a spatial representation of the cartoon worlds that he draws: Cutopia, Zanydu and the Malevolands. In-game, space is displayed as discrete scenes (called rooms). Rooms represent interior and exterior locations, similar to the proscenium theatre stage, with exits towards the left, right, up (or 'behind the curtains') and down (towards the audience). This is not so much a case of media representation as an instance of media simulation: the logic and the workings of black box theatre are being transmediated to form a new set of genre conventions in the adventure game.

Because *Toonstruck* tells a well-defined story in a chronological fashion, the story of the game progresses through 'Acts' (i.e. chapters) that determine which parts of the game world are accessible. Major storyline events are related as non-interactive cutscenes, also marking events when new areas become available. Initially, Drew arrives in Cutopia, and as the player proceeds, will eventually gain entry into Zanydu and the Malevolands. The player can travel between these three lands once they unlock the areas. The final portion of the game is set in an entirely different location, Count Nefarious' Castle, from where the player cannot access any of the other areas previously visited, thereby signalling that a showdown is at hand.

The story takes place in an undefined period of time: we know time passes, but it does not pass in an orderly fashion. Cutopia is flooded with permanent daylight, while the Malevolands are enveloped in perpetual darkness. In Zanydu, the official time is dictated by the town hall clock, which has stuck, ergo officially time does not pass. One puzzle, however, requires the manipulation of the clock: to get inside an important building, Drew needs the security guard to leave and to go home. To achieve that, Drew has to position the clock hands to 6pm, which signals the end of the guard's shift. This puzzle works because time is only represented in the game world; it is not simulated – the time of day only changes by fiat. Some obstacles, however, require timing, such as fleeing into hiding places when Nefarious's henchmen are seeking out

Drew and Flux; here, it takes time for animations to finish, which sets the time window for our heroes to hide.

Semiotically, *Toonstruck* uses the above three modalities to deliver a story about the animator Drew Blanc. Players can interact with the world through a semiotic representation of the player: the in-game avatar, Drew Blanc, whom the player controls with the mouse. Because Drew is a photorealistically rendered image of Christopher Lloyd, there is an indexical relationship between Christopher Lloyd's body as recorded and its actions as Drew Blanc. Game-world objects look similar to but not the same as real-world objects; that is, mallets are recognizably hammer-like, butter looks squishy, an ice cube looks as if it is melting. Iconic representations of inventory objects give clues to the players about their applications by referring to their affordances in the real world. However, the iconic ambiguity is resolved by a short textual description of the object at the bottom of the screen, the symbolic specificity of the words helping players to contextualize the objects. Meanwhile, characters' conversations are represented in text, symbolically, as audible dialogue performed by recognized voice actors who mimic speech impediments and give typically exaggerated vocal performances that might make it hard to pick up what is being said, especially for non-native speakers. Nonetheless, the indexical quality of the voice acting relates the voices to earlier performances in another media, which cements *Toonstruck*'s connection to the Saturday morning cartoon.

Some objects are shown to be interactable (when the player moves the mouse cursor over them, an animation plays, and the object's name appears in text at the bottom of the screen) while others are not (as noted above, this aspect is a helpful clue when trying to solve the 'stars' puzzle). When the player engages in talking, conversation options show up at the bottom of the screen as icons in coloured bubbles: the default option for small talk, for example, is an ice cube that melts as the characters go through their available dialogue. It is the literalization of a metaphor, thereby showing both an iconic and a symbolic component to conversations. Drew also has a companion character, a toon called Flux, who talks and walks, but some puzzles require the player to use Flux as an object (e.g. as a bowling ball to score a strike). This shift between the two categories of character and object prompts players to shift their view of the materiality of everything in the game.

Most puzzles require the player to pay attention to what is happening on the screen and what characters say, as their dialogue might include hints on how to solve a particular puzzle. An example of this is that one of the things Drew needs to build the Cutifier is a cloak, and the only person who has one is the Carecrow (he is a scarecrow acting stereotypically campy, hence the name). But he will part with his cloak only if Drew can find him the costume of his dreams. Finding the right costume requires browsing through the costume shop's selection. The Carecrow says:

> I want something I can wear all day long, and all year 'round – but it doesn't have to be out of this world. I don't want to have a hair out of

place. Nothing too sappy, and not too many bells or whistles. I don't want a big top – and definitely no cross-dressing.

To solve the puzzle, the player must interpret these desires in terms of which costumes the Carecrow's needs exclude from the costume shop's catalogue, shown as pictures. Here, the player must translate the verbal descriptions into visual terms, giving a cross-modal solution to the puzzle. Of the 12 costumes, the pyjamas, the tutu, the Easter Bunny and the Santa costume, the astronaut suit, the hunter and Viking outfits and the jester, the policeman, the pope and the clown costumes all have iconic attributes that exclude them, which leaves Drew with the only correct solution: the harlequin costume – a very fitting outfit for a Carecrow.

***Summary:* Toonstruck**

This section intended to demonstrate that video games in general, and graphical adventure games in particular, use animation to represent events of their storyworlds on the monitor, and as such, they rely on the principles of animation originally devised for the silver screen and the television set, along with new technological solutions afforded by the computer game medium. The case study of *Toonstruck* highlights how the audiovisual presentation of the game evokes the Saturday morning cartoons throughout the game world, how they inform game design, and how the genre of the graphical adventure game conventionalizes the player's interaction with the game world. Analysis of the game using the four modalities underscores that the choices of the game designers facilitate immersion into the game world, and also cue in the player to use the logic of the animated cartoon to solve certain puzzles. Together, they reinforce Burst Studios' creative effort to bring the experience of a human inhabiting a cartoon world to the player, an old premise of animation that originates from the earliest of Disney shorts, and live on to this day.

Playable literature: *80 Days*

Computer games and literature

Casting our historical net wide, we can discover many coin-operated antecedents to the pleasures of digital gaming (Kocurek 2015). Even prior to computers dedicated to video gaming, oscilloscopes and mainframe computers were being used to display purely visual games, like William Higginbotham's 1958 program, *Tennis for Two*, or Steve Russell's 1962 game, *Spacewar!*. But a curious tradition of games emerged in the early days of computing, which did not use graphics at all: they were purely textual. There are several names for these programs, each highlighting a different aspect of mediality. The initial term in the industry was simply 'adventure game', named not for its fictional content but to signal that the game was 'like *Adventure*', the earliest of its type.

Later to be called a *text adventure* to signal its difference from newer graphical games like *Toonstruck, Adventure* was written by Will Crowther and amended by Don Woods between 1975 and 1976 (Crowther and Woods 1975-6). It was an interactive exploration of a cave that was filled with fantastic beasts and magic and was influenced by the creation of *Dungeons and Dragons* (1974), the first role-playing game of fame (Barton and Stacks 2019, 34–8). The cave featured in the game is a faithful textual replica of the Bedquilt region of the Mammoth Caverns in Kentucky, which Crowther, an avid caver, helped survey (Jerz 2007).

A textual adventure consists of snippets of texts displayed on the computer screen, which constitute parts of a narrative. Because these snippets tell a coherent story with vivid, literary descriptions of scenes and events, and since the player is constantly prompted to type in what they want to do in the game world, this type of game is also called *interactive fiction* (Montfort 2003). Text adventures all feature a system for processing natural language, called a *parser*, which interprets player input that is phrased as two-to-four-word imperative structures, such as GO NORTH or USE MATCH ON LAMP. Every text input invites a response from the machine, and if the correct input is used, the story progresses with another snippet of text. Parsers usually have a limited vocabulary that treats synonyms differently, meaning players will have to correctly intuit the actual command needed to progress. The goal is to explore and navigate the space by removing obstacles and to reach the final room (such as an exit from a maze).

Some works of interactive fiction feature such finely crafted language, clever riddles and emotional storylines that they can rightfully aspire to the lofty title of *electronic literature* (Hayles 2008). They can also be called *hypertext fiction* (Ensslin 2007), because the snippets of text are meant to be read in a non-linear fashion, with some words forming hyperlinks to other snippets. Finally, some video game scholarship refers to text adventures as *ergodic literature*, coined by Espen Aarseth (1997) from the Greek words *ergon* (work) and *hodos* (path), suggesting that it takes effort from the players to read the work by carving out a path in the text that matches the order in which they read the snippets. As pieces of fiction or literature, many of the tools of literary theory can be fruitfully applied to investigate text adventures. Therefore it should not come as a surprise that literary theorists were among the first game studies scholars.

On a more general level, text is central to conveying information in games. Even in titles where text is secondary to the audiovisual and interactive elements or kept to a minimum, text is used in game menus to configure the software to the player's taste. Text often shows up on user interfaces as a verbal representation of the player's commands, as button names or as tooltips that disambiguate the meaning of otherwise purely visual icons. Spoken dialogue can be represented in text, and for many games, this might be the only medium available to represent speech, since employing voice actors is expensive. Last but not least, in-game objects can also be textual, such as signs, notes, letters or books. Some gamers object to lengthy textual descriptions, especially in more action-oriented gameplay, because reading text *does* stop the flow of events, forcing a spell of passivity on the player. Nonetheless, the right amount of text facilitates gameplay by giving the player relevant cues about what action to perform and how the story is developing and also provides verbal feedback on the success and failure of actions taken; in addition, it mediates sensory information that would otherwise be impossible to convey (such as smell, touch, pain and heat perception).

The choice of font can matter a great deal. Distinctive fonts used in game menus and logos can create new visual meanings: Sprint 2 says 'retro gaming' like no other font, *The Price Is Right*'s PriceDown font today is more readily associated with the *Grand Theft Auto* universe, the use of Morpheus and Friz Quadrata now immediately evoke the UI of *World of Warcraft* (2004), while Caslon Antique is the font of choice for many games set in the Renaissance and the early modern periods. This just goes to show that written language is not only a form of symbolic signification but also has important iconic aspects: how it is typeset can convey mood and attitude and can evoke distinct eras. Fonts are so characteristic that they signify actual characters in the game *Undertale* (2015): the character Papyrus uses the eponymous font for dialogue, whereas Sans, Papyrus' brother, speaks in the font Comic Sans, and provides comic relief.

Games often play with text and textuality, even when they are graphical, further underscoring their iconic functions. Players have to quickly type in words as they appear on the screen in *The Typing of the Dead: Overkill* (2013) to dispatch zombies. *Alan Wake* (2010) has a dream sequence in which the protagonist, a writer of horror fiction, must shine his torch on words that appear in the game world to transform them into actual objects – a shift from symbolic to iconic representation is brought on by the player. Similarly, in *Scribblenauts Unlimited* (2012), players can create any object by typing it in, and it then becomes part of the game world. Finally, *Type: Rider* (2013) is literally a game about typography, in which the player controls a colon (the punctuation mark) and must jump from platform to platform in a world constructed by characters and book-related objects, taking the player through the history of typography. These are just some of the many creative uses of textuality in games, but perhaps they give you a good idea of how textuality can be transmediated and made into integral elements of gameplay.

80 Days

One shining example of how computer games adapt the conventions of literature is the textual adventure game *80 Days* (2014). *80 Days* is a postcolonial rewriting of Jules Verne's (1872) *Le Tour du monde en quatre-vingts jours*. Set in an alternative historical vision of 1872, the game adopts the genre conventions of steampunk fiction (VanderMeer and VanderMeer 2008): steam machines are the primary source of energy, technological inventions take centre stage, automatons exist, airships are a major form of transportation and ideas important to Victorian society are re-examined under the critical lens of the twenty-first-century political imaginary. As such, *80 Days* is both a complex transmediation of Jules Verne's fictional universe and a re-righting (see Chapter 13 for further discussion) of the colonialist assumptions of imperial adventure.

The player is placed in the role of Passepartout, who is hired by Phileas Fogg to help him win his famous wager at the Reform Club. Passepartout has full control over where and how the duo travels. Instead of re-enacting the novel's itinerary of London–Suez–Bombay–Calcutta–Hong Kong–Yokohama–San Francisco–New York–London (which would be a case of media representation), the player can visit over 150 cities across the globe (which makes this more of a media simulation). Passepartout also has control over what they take with them: objects can be bought and sold in the cities, which might include maps, gifts or valuable artefacts. A basic economic system is implemented in the game, providing a gameplay challenge: travel is expensive and the player's funds are limited, so to pay for tickets, Passepartout must buy artefacts at low prices and sell them at high ones as they travel. Time is also an important constraint: although the game doesn't end if the duo does not reach the Reform Club in 80 days, it does result in Fogg losing his wager.

80 Days is an exquisitely crafted piece of playable literature. At a total of 750,000 words, if it could be read in its entirety, it would be longer than *War and Peace*, the *Lord of the Rings* or the first five books of the *Harry Potter* series. However, on any given playthrough, only a fraction of the text will be ever read by the player; the part that relates to the journeys they take and the cities they actually visit. Because the game is a piece of interactive fiction, the player makes choices about what the characters will do or say by highlighting and clicking on one of several options presented in a text box. The game's text is cut up into small snippets of text. Game studies scholar Espen Aarseth (1997, pp. 75, 119, 154) calls these *textons*, discrete pieces of text as they are stored in the game files; then, during play, these textons appear on the screen according to the display logic of the game, which Aarseth calls a *scripton*. This highlights the fact that there are important differences between what is encoded in the game and what players actualize during gameplay. There is an ambiguity in Aarseth's formulation, however: his terms may also be interpreted to distinguish between textons as single units of texts and scriptons as one particular combination of scriptons in chronological order as experienced by the player. To elucidate this latter concept: in *80 Days*, a circumnavigation usually touches 20–5 cities of the 150-odd ones available, and every city has a handful of scenarios and events that may occur, some of which are mutually exclusive. As such, the possible scriptons are several orders of magnitude higher than the textons.

The style of the narration encountered in the game mimics the prose of Victorian authors; it is full of choice archaisms and period-appropriate slang – language in its finest livery. Passepartout peppers his story with French colloquialisms, and while both he and his master speak certain foreign languages, they are almost never represented in text. As an adaptation, it takes significant liberties with its source material, but there are plenty of references to other literary works: in Nassau, the player can attempt to travel to the moon at the insistence of Michel Ardan, the French adventurer from Verne's *De la terre à la lune* (Verne 1865), they can embark on a journey to the North Pole with assistance from Otto Lidenbrock, the German professor from *Voyage au centre de la terre* (Verne 1864), and they may rub shoulders with Captain Nemo from *Vingt mille lieues sous les mers* (Verne 1869–70) aboard the *Nautilus* if they opt to travel from Bhayi to Saint-Denis. These would be examples of complex media representations, since they are not only present in the story, but Passepartout can have conversations with the characters; these are original dialogues. Fogg and Passepartout can even meet Jules Verne himself aboard the Amphitrite Express, a submersible train that crosses the English Channel underwater. These efforts to incorporate the whole oeuvre of Jules Verne is a result of the radical opening up of the storyworld, giving more options to the player but also constituting a gesture towards creating a transfictional world that connects characters in the same way hypertexts link together separate texts (for more on transmedial worlds, see Chapter 13).

In terms of the *material* modality, *80 Days* is presented as a computer program with a unique graphical interface that enables the manipulation of an in-game map and the contents of Passepartout's coffers and the text to be displayed using light waves and represented auditorily using sound waves to deliver an atmospheric score. The originally intended technical medium of display was the iOS 7, which entailed making a series of design choices to suit touchscreens, such as having a sparse user interface, specific fonts for easy readability, a font size appropriate for touching, and a simple but striking visual style. Later, the game was ported for Android, Windows, Mac OS X and the Nintendo Switch. Its code was written in '*ink*', a mark-up language of the developers' own devising that supports branching narrative creation and can be integrated into the Unity engine. The use of *ink* allows the story of *80 Days* to branch out into different event sequences based on the player's previous choices and conditions that the game tracks. Because it is just code, the story is also much easier to expand than a printed novel, whose text seldom changes as radically as a game narrative's. A major update of the Windows edition introduced over thirty new cities and several new storylines (some 250,000 additional words) to users old and new, challenging players to explore them. This just goes to show that a scholar cannot assume that a game will remain the same after he or she has conducted their analysis.

In the *sensory* modality, the game communicates with the player visually through the use of icons and images, verbally in text, that is, in menus, the user interface and the main text box where the narrative is displayed, and auditively via the game's sound effects and soundtrack (no dialogue is recorded), whereas the player gives haptic feedback via the touchscreen.

Visually, the art style of the game is, anachronistically, art deco, which communicates the idea to the player that the game world is not going to be faithful to the period either; instead, it evokes a more retro-futuristic atmosphere. The style was chosen by Jaume Illustration for more practical reasons as well: the iOS 7 update changed how user interfaces appeared, so the flat look and the use of primary colour highlights were a natural fit for the new environment. Despite the geometric look, the graphics were not created in a vector editor, but produced as bitmaps. The eye-pleasing pastel colour scheme changes as the globe spins and day turns into night, while vehicles are shown as black-and-white silhouettes to make them stand out, but leave the details to the imagination.

In terms of audio, Laurence Chapman provides an orchestral soundtrack that evokes the epic feel of adventure films, particularly the Indiana Jones series. Musical stings play as new routes are unlocked. Sound effects accentuate the character of each locale: in Maghreb countries, we hear the noise of the souks; in rural regions, we hear crickets chirp; and at the North Pole, icy winds blow. The soundscape shifts as the players travel, with culture-specific instruments entering the ambience as Fogg and Passepartout visit cities in different regions of the world.

Spatiotemporally, the software is playable on mobile and desktop devices, which means that the games are portable; this also means that texts come in shorter bursts of reading so that play sessions can be terminated at any point. An average circumnavigation of the globe takes about two to three hours of solid reading, which is rather short for a game, but due to the branching narrative style, this brevity is ideal for repeated playthroughs. Even so, it is extremely unlikely that any player has read every piece of text the game has to offer.

Within the game, however, space and time are the main challenges. Aside from the titular eighty days in which to complete Fogg's journey, trains, ships and other transport options run at certain times of the day, and if Passepartout spends too much time buying and selling in the market, the player might miss an important connection. Time passes while travelling and also when exploring the cities. The only time when the clock is not ticking is when a large piece of text is displayed, which the player can read at their own pace to enjoy the quality of its writing. Also, Fogg must sleep comfortably during the night or risk compromising his health – and, as an ill Fogg cannot travel, it costs precious days to nurse him back to health.

As for the issue of space, the game encompasses all major continents with the exception of Antarctica, and the player is free to choose their route across the globe. In topological terms, the cities are laid out in a graph structure, with the cities as nodes and the trips as edges. Similar graphs could be drawn in other pieces of interactive fiction, which shows this title's connections to the genre. Likewise, many nineteenth- and twentieth-century board games using the theme of travel have used a graph-like structure to provide players with an opportunity to plan their journeys across the board. While a few routes are two-way, most journeys steadily push Fogg onwards, largely to the east, which further connects the gameplay to the family of board games called race games, and it fits thematically with Fogg's wager. Cities are more densely packed in Europe and South East Asia, while the longest journeys are the voyages crossing the Atlantic and the Pacific. Sometimes disaster strikes during a journey, and detours or route changes are a significant part of the game's challenge. In this way, the game represents the original novel's unforeseen circumstances, even though they happen in a deterministic fashion, as the end result of conditions tracked by the game.

A *semiotic* reading of the game may note that ostensibly the game takes place in a world that has the same geography as our world, represented on a stylized globe (an *iconic* relationship), with the same city names as on our planet referring to the game locations (a *symbolic* relationship), and when Fogg and Passepartout visit a city they see images of famous landmarks, drawn from photographs to match the art style of the game (an *indexical* relationship). Even so, reader-players will soon realize that this world is not exactly the same as Earth was in 1872: it has diverged from our history in important social, political and technological ways.

For example, several vehicles used for travel have no equivalent in our world: the moving city of Agra takes a real-world referent, the Indian city of Agra, but uses the genre conventions of steampunk fiction to reinvent it as a pneumatically moving city (a mixture of *symbolic* codes from fact and fiction). Similarly, submersible trains and mechanical palanquins are more or less plausible inventions that have no real-world referents, but they evoke the atmosphere of an alternative 1872, where the horizons of the future seemed limitless. Meanwhile, other modes of transport, such as the Bożek car or the Trevithick steam carriage, are inventions that have actual, albeit obscure references in the real world and appear faithfully (an *indexical* relationship): the Czech-Polish József Bożek and the Englishman Richard Trevithick, respectively, did create steam-powered vehicles, even if they are relegated to the annals of history.

Similarly, as an alternative history, the game's storyworld is a combination of accurate geopolitical entities and events on the one hand and clearly fictional additions on the other. For example, in the British, Ottoman and Chinese Empires, Prussia and France are present as world powers, but in this world, Prussia has invaded and occupied a significant portion of France with a superior force of automaton soldiers. Paris has held many world expositions during the relevant era, but the one Fogg visits in 1872 can only be fictional. The most crucial change to our world stems from the authors' anti-colonial world-building philosophy: the non-Euro-Atlantic world is a much more formidable, dominant force in the alternative history when compared to the allohistorical timeline. The resulting storyworld showcases a nuanced, intricate webwork of different empires, oppressive regimes, republics, small communes or resistance movements, most of which resent the European colonial powers.

Summary: 80 days

As this short analysis demonstrates, the design team of *80 Days* used a variety of media to construct the storyworld that is meant to take the player on a fantastical journey inspired by Verne's globetrotting adventures. The visuals, sounds and writing liberally borrow from the literary genre of steampunk science fiction to reinforce a sense of living in an alternative 1872, where history plays out differently from events in our world. This supports the artistic philosophy of the team, which reimagines the political landscape of Earth from an anticolonial perspective. The alternative setting also helps the team to tell many different, sometimes mutually exclusive stories about Fogg and Passepartout's adventures, which illustrate, on a different level, that the course of history is not set in stone. All artistic choices contribute to a central vision of how the small decisions of individual humans can make a difference in the world, a theme that is explored in many computer games.

References

Aarseth, E.J. 1997. *Cybertext perspectives on ergodic literature.* Baltimore: Johns Hopkins University Press.

Barton, Matt and Stacks, Shane. 2019. *Dungeons and desktops: The history of computer role-playing games 2e.* Boca Raton: A K Press/CRC Press. https://www.routledge.com/Dungeons-and-Desktops-The-History-of-Computer-Role-Playing-Games-2e/Barton-Stacks/p/book/9781138574649

Black Mirror: Bandersnatch. 2018. Directed by David Slade. Written by Charlie Brooker. Netflix.

Cooper, J. 2019. *Game anim: Video game animation Explained.* Boca Raton: CRC Press.

Ensslin, A. 2007. *Canonizing hypertext: Explorations and constructions.* New York: Continuum.

Hayles, N.K. 2008. *Electronic literature: New horizons for the literary.* Notre Dame: University of Notre Dame.

Jerz, D.G. 2007. Somewhere nearby is a colossal cave: Examining Will Crowther's original *Adventure* in code and in Kentucky. *Digital Humanities Quarterly*, 1(2). http://digitalhumanities.org//dhq/vol/1/2/000009/000009.html [Accessed 3 December 2020].

Kocurek, Carly A. 2015. *Coin-operated Americans: Rebooting boyhood at the video game arcade.* Minneapolis: University of Minnesota Press.

Montfort, N. 2003. *Twisty little passages: An approach to interactive fiction.* New York: MIT Press.

The Matrix. 1999. Directed by Lana Wachowski and Lily Wachowski. USA: Warner Bros. Pictures.

VanderMeer, A. and VanderMeer, J. 2008. *Steampunk.* San Francisco: Tachyon Publications.

Verne, J. 1864. *Voyage au centre de la terre.* Paris: Pierre-Jules Hetzel.

Verne, J. 1865. *De la terre à la lune.* Paris: Pierre-Jules Hetzel.

Verne, J. 1869–70. *Vingt mille lieues sous les mers.* Paris: Pierre-Jules Hetzel.

Verne, J. 1872. *Le tour du monde en quatre-vingts jours.* Paris: Pierre-Jules Hetzel.

Games referenced

80 Days. 2014. iOS and PC. Inkle Studios.
Adventure. 1975–6. PDP-10. Will Crowther and Don Woods.
Alan Wake. 2010. PC. Remedy Entertainment.
Another World. 1991. Amiga, Atari. Delphine Software, Interplay and The Removers.
Lunar Lander. 1979. Arcade. Atarti. Atarti Inc.

Phantasmagoria. 1995. PC, Sega Saturn. Sierra On-Line.
Scribblenauts Unlimited. 2012. PC. 5th Cell.
The Neverhood. 1995. PC, PlayStation. The Neverhood, Inc. and Riverhillsoft.
The Typing of the Dead: Overkill. 2013. Wii, PlayStation3, PC, iOS, Android. Headstrong Games.
Toonstruck. 1996. PC. Burst Studios.
Type: Rider. 2013. PC, PlayStation 4, iOS. Agat Films & Cie – Ex Nihilo.
Undertale. 2015. PC, OSX, Linux, PlayStation, Nintendo Switch. Toby Fox.
Wing Commander III: Heart of the Tiger. 1993. MS-DOS, macOS, PlayStation. Origin Systems.
World of Warcraft. 2004. Windows, macOS. Blizzard Entertainment

Index

Note: page numbers in **bold** indicate a table

2D 31, 32, 35, 313, 314, 316
3D 30, 32, 34, 35, 37, 314, 316
400 Blows 171
80 Days 309, 320–327
9/11 attacks 166, 233

accessibility 78, 283
acting 28, 36, 145, 208, 216, 262–263, 296; voice acting 317, 319
actor(s) 13, 17, 19, 28, 31, 36, 140, 143–144, 153, 155, **174**, 205, 216–217, 225, 257–263, 269, 290, 292, 313–315, 317; as agents 93–95, 248; voice actor(s) 45, 52, 73, 80, 276, 278, 319, 321
adaptation 3, 105, 112, 130, 133, 139–140, 142–147, 152–156, 159, 265, 267, 269, 271–274, 289, 323; film adaptation 3, 6, 104, 138–140, 142–145, 147, 149, 152, 159, 184, 231, 265; novel-to-film adaptation 139, 142–143, 152, 159; opera adaptation 142, 152–155; theatre-to-film adaptation 139; stage-to-stage adaptation 142; *see also* appropriation; transmediation
adaptation studies 5, 139, 142–143, 152
adjustment strategies 139–140
Adventure 320–321
advertisement 8, 10–11, 18, 138, 162, 173, 217, 219, 276
aesthetic experience 74, 129, 168
aesthetic hierarchies 13
aesthetics 7, 11, 36, 59, 63, 71, 78, 79, 104, 132, 167, 176, 178–179, 215, 235, 239–240, 309
affordance 12, 45, 53, 140–141, 163, 191, 267, 284, 287, 289, 298, 316, 319

Agamben, Giorgio 203
agency 69, 70–71, 75, 80, 168, 220, 236–239, 245–246, 260, 262, 273, 304, 315
agon 216–217
AI 77, 225
Alan Wake 322
Alborta, Freddy 189–191
algorithms 48, 51, 87, 284, 286
Allianz Arena 215
All Quiet on the Western Front 235
alternative facts 226
ambiguity 24, 184, 187–188, 233, 319
American Gothic 151
American Psycho 170, 191
analogue 65, 70, 74, 96, 165–166, 170, 228, 233
animation 32, 114–115, 293, 298, 303, 309, 313–320; animated (feature) film 29, 35, 113, 116; animated television series 266; computer animation 314; hand-drawn animation 314–216; stop-motion animation 314
Animatograph 262
Another World 314
Anthropocene 237, 242, 246
Apocalypse Now 117
Appoggiaturas 125
appropriation 265, 267, 272–274
Arab spring 13
Arcade Fire 132
architecture 9, 20, 76, 255, 258, 260; architectural space 10, 129, 256–257, 261, 263
Argento, Dario 37
Aristotle 232, 234, 258
The Arrival 108

Index

art deco 324
artefact 72, 76, 123, 213, 301, 312, 323
artificial intelligence *see* AI
The Art of the Fugue 182
Assassin's Creed: Odyssey 72–73
Astruc, Alexandre 36
As You Like It 198
Atonement 113
audiobook 3, 42–43, 45–46, 52–53, 138
audio drama 268, 274–275
audiovisual experience 30, 103, 123
audiovisual narration *see* narrative
auditory imagery *see* imagery
auditory narrative *see* narrative
auditory perception 52, 123, 170, 178–180
auditory text 30, 34, **38**, 42, 45–46, **53**, 57–58, **66**, **75**, 89, **97**
Augustine 150–151
Austen, Jane 143, 145, 147, 231
Austenmania 147
Austin, J.L. 200
auteur 36
authenticity **66**, 112, 166, 168, 202, 207–208, 215, 220, 226–227, 230–231, 234, 250–252, 287–298
autobiography 235
auto-fiction 235
avant-garde 12, 36–37, 229; neo-avant-garde 48
Avatar 30
avatar 77, 162, 319
Ave Maria 124–126
The Avengers 112

Bach, Johann Sebastian 10, 63, 183
Bailey, Steven W. 314
Bal, Mieke 200
Balázs, Béla 36
Baldwin, Cecil 274–279
ballet 121, 156
Bardot, Brigitte 234
Barone, Eric 73
Batman 112
Batman Returns 29
Baudrillard, Jean 170
Bayern München 215, 220
Bayreuth Festival Theatre 255
Bazin, André 32, 36
Beatles 168, 256
Beat poet(s) 131, 205, 208, 222
Beaver, Jack 317
Bechdel, Alison 110–111
Beckham, David 217

Beethoven, Ludwig van 56, 183
Bejeweled 70–71
De bello judaico 155
Beyoncé 126, 132–133, 168
Biblique des derniers gestes 163, 188–189, 191
The Birds 113
The Birth of a Nation 36
Bizet, George 128, 154
Black Mirror: Bandersnatch 314
blog 107, 109, 269, 288–289, 292–293
Blue Velvet 210
blu-ray 30
Bluth, Don 316
board game 69, 78, 325
body genres 37
body language 3, 7, 13, 18, **66**, 140, 208, 293, 299
body movement 22, 65, 131, 159
Bohemian Rhapsody (movie) 32
Boléro 121
Bolter, Jay 14, 303–304
Bordwell, David 177
Bourdieu, Pierre 11
Braille 46
Bridget Jones's Diary 147
Brontë, Charlotte 265, 273
Brontës 143
Brothers Grimm 9
Burgess, Anthony 182–184
Burgtheater 262
Burtt, Ben 117
Butler, Judith 200

camera 17, 30, 32–33, 36, 86, 146–147, 170–171, **174**, 178, 207, 210–212, 215, 218, 228, 233–235, 245–246, 251, 289, 290, 292–294, 298–300
Campos, Augusto de 48
Campos, Haroldo de 48
Camus, Albert 232
caption 18, 72, 90, **96**, 108, 112, 282, 299, 302
Carey, Mariah 58
Carmen 128, 154
Carson, Ann 142, 149–152
Carson, Rachel 226, 237–239
Casablanca 28
catharsis 215
Catherine the Great 273
causality 188
CD 43, 56–57, 64–65, 79, 168, 314, 316
Celan, Paul 181
celluloid 28, **38**
censorship 37, 63, **174**

CGI 35, 245
Chamoiseau, Patrick 163, 188–189
Chapman, Laurence 325
character recognizability 270–271
Che Guevara 189–190
chick flick 147
choreography 217
cinema: as medium 16, 28, 30–32, 34–38, 141–143, 145–146, 167, 169, 171–180, 235, 246; as space 12, 28, 245; *see also* film
cinemascope 34, 37, **174**
cinematic novels 38
cinematic writing 163, 169–170, 176, 178
cinematography 28
Ciorba, Aldo 117
circularity 187, 210
cliffhanger 177
cli-fi *see* climate-fiction
climate crisis 9, 235–237, 243–244; climate catastrophe 245; climate change 9, 197, 236–7, 243–246, 252; climate disaster 246; ecological crisis 236, 240; ecological disaster 243, 246; global warming 9, 237
climate-fiction 231, 236–237, 243–244, 246
A Clockwork Orange 182–184, 188
CNN 92
co-creation 287
cognition 38, 75
cognitive experience 171
cognitive import 277
cognitive perception 21
cognitive space 59
cohesion 91–92, 177, 247–248, 259–261; *see also* internal coherence; narrative coherence
Coleridge, Samuel 234
comedy 38, 147, 245, 255–256, 259, 278; stand-up comedy 50, 198–199
comics 6, 10, 17–19, 42, 44, 48–49, 51, **53**, 106–112, 133, 267, 272, 285; comic book 49, 78, 107, 266; comic strips 107; *see also* graphic novel; graphic narrative
comics studies 5, 108
commercialization 36, 170, 219, 286–287
commodity 87, 217, 219, 227
communication: communication channels 9, 13; artistic/aesthetic communication 7, 197, 234; digital communication 89, 167, 247, 298–300; embodied communication 203; face-to-face communication 3, 7, 17, 45; interactive communication 217; interpersonal communication 283, 290; mobile communication 284; multimodal communication 6; mass communication 9, 93, 95, 283; masspersonal communication 283; mediated communication 11, 204; non-verbal communication 203; one-way communication 95; scientific communication 229, 238–239; knowledge communication 231; transmedial communication 230; truthful communication 236, 252
community-building 287, 292, 295, 298
comparative close reading 141, 146, 150, 156
computer game 8, 11, 16, 51, 69–79, 81, 162, 197, 309, 312–313, 315–316, 320, 322, 327; *see also* video game
Conan Doyle, Arthur 233, 267–268, 270
concept album 167–168, 183
Confessions 150–151
confirmation bias 231, 251
conformance 124, 126
constructedness 32
consumer culture 213, 219
content creator 287–290, 293, 298, 312–313
context *see* social context
contextuality 96
Convergence Culture 266
The Conversation 175
Coppola, Frances Ford 175, 272
co-presence 50–51, **53**, 198, 201; co-present audience 208, 210, 212, 217–218, 220, 259; co-present spectator 258
copyright 64, 271–272, 274
Corpse Bride 113
Cottingley Fairies 233
couleur locale 158
counterpoint 182
Counter-Strike 77
COVID–19 92, 229, 252
Coyote and the Roadrunner 175
Cranor, Jeffrey 274, 278–279
crime fiction 118, 175, 178, 270
Critical Terms for Media Studies 7
cross-modal capacities 47
cross-modal translation *see* translation
Crowther, Will 321
Crypt of the NecroDancer 74
cultural capital 78, 131, 168
cultural text 256, 260, 265, 268, 274, 280
Cumberbatch, Benedict 268–269
Curry, Tim 315

Index

dance 10, 13, 22, 56, 62, 64–65, 127, 148, 153, 155–156, 158–159, 198, 201, 238
Danish Dogma manifesto 235
Danse des petites cygnes 317
da Vinci, Leonardo 11
The Day after Tomorrow 226, 243–246
The Death Fugue 181
DC Comics 267
decoding (in comics) 110, 112
deep fake 225, 228, 230
Deep Purple 270
democratization 286
Dench, Judi 144
Derrida, Jacques 200
deus ex machina 258
dialogue 28, 30–31, 34–35, **38**, 48, 73–**75**, 80, 82, 89, 108–109, 114–115, 118–120, 122–123, 139, 142, 144–146, 153, 159, 169, 172, 217, 257, 278, 301, 303, 316, 318–319, 321–322, 324
Dichterliebe 125
Dickens, Charles 143
Dickinson, Adam 240
diegesis 118, 122, 163–164, 168–169, 259
diegetic world 119, 121, 123, 162, 245, 269, 275, 277
digital code 72, 74
digital dualism 284
digitality 284
digitalization (music) 64
digital media 9, 10, 13–14, 43, 45, 53, 72, 87, 90, 96, 165–166, 248
digital mediascape 132, 269
discourse 36, 57, 81, 89, 123, 143, 170–171, 179, 216–217, 226–227, 233–239, 241–242, 244, 246, 250, 252, 256–257, 268, 273, 291, 298, 313
disinformation 9, 197, 226, 236, 248, 252
Disney 260, 268, 320
Disneyland's Royal Theatre 255
dissemination 35, **38**, 43, **66**, 72, **75**, 87, 94, **96**, 107, 147, 221
dissemination devices 17
docudrama 235, 237
docufiction 37
documentary 4, 9, 32, 118, 130, 234–235, 237–238
Dogme 95 films 114
Don't Look Back 130
Downey Jr., Robert 267
Dracula 271–274
Dungeons and Dragons 321
Duras, Marguerite 181

Durham Peters, John 228
DVD 30, **38**
Dylan, Bob 11, 130–131

e-book 3, 43, 46–47, 53, 73
ecocriticism 236, 238
ecological discourse 237
ecopoetry 226, 240–241
editing 30, 32, 36, 44–45, 69, 117, 170–171, 175–176, 178, 277, 286, 290, 295–296, 298, 312; sound editing 117, 212, 296
Egan, Jennifer 163
Eilish, Billie 58
Eisenstein, Sergei 36
ekphrasis 148–151, 159
ekphrastic poem 142, 149, 151
ekphrastic text 112, 148, 151
Elementary 267–268, 270
e-literacy *see* literacy
Ellens dritter Gesang 124
Elleström, Lars 15–16, 20, 80, 139, 148, 202, 231–232
ellipsis 176–177
Ellis, Bret Easton 170, 191
embodied reading 46
embodiment 21, 46, 244, 246
emergence 199
Emmerich, Roland 244
emoji 282, 284, 299
Encyclopaedia Britannica 235
entanglement 199, 201, 262
enunciation 126
Es waren zwei Königskinder 251
exhibition 167, 237
exoticism 158
expressions: facial 7, 18, 202, 207, 225, 300; verbal 202, 203; non-verbal 203; guttural 202; emotional 61, 202

Facebook 16, 87, 282–284, 298, 303
face recognition 225
faction 232
facts 226–227, 232–235, 238–242, 244, 246, 248–251, 273, 279; *see also* truthfulness; alternative facts
Fahlström, Öyvind 48
fake news 9, 94, 225, 236, 247–248, 252, 286
fan art 267, 275
fan communities 267, 279
fan culture(s) 63, 270, 285
fandom 299, 300
fan fiction 51, 267, 300

fansumers 219
fashion 9
fiction 43, 95, 107, 188, 226–227, 232–235, 237, 240, 247–248, 251, 260, 262, 266, 321, 326; *see also* crime fiction; faction; musicalized fiction; non-fiction; science fiction
fidelity 139, 143, 231
film: action film 38, 52, 296; adventure film 81, 243, 246; art-house cinema 37; auteur cinema 37, 172; colour film 29, 34; digital film 28, 30; educational film 34, 36; experimental film 29, 238; feature film 29, 35, 105; film noir 38; heritage film 143; Kodak colour film 29; montage film 37; narrative film 29, 36, 37, 299; silent film 29, 31, 173; splatter film 38, 178; talkies 29; western 36; *see also* animation; adaptation
film adaptation *see* adaptation
Film Form: Essays in Film Theory 36
film music 30, 33, **38**, 65, 129, **174**, 298
film studies 5, 142
film theory 32, 36
filter bubbles 286
Fink, Joseph 274, 276, 278–279
Fitzgerald, F. Scott 171–172
flash fiction 109
flash mob 255, 261, 263
The Flying Dutchman 255
focalization 118, 178
Foley sound *see* sound
folk tales 42, 49, **53**
font 90; in game 322, 324
Fonteyn, Sam 317
football (as performance) 198–199, 201, 213–221
form 7, 11–12, 14, 16, 36, 42, 60, 69–70, 104, 110, 118, 125, 141, 169, 182, 184, 234, 239, 256, 261, 289, 311
Fortnite 77
found object art 164
Fox News 92, 245
framing 36, 92, 147, 167, 175–176, 184, 198–199, 208–209, 235, 244, 285
Frankenstein 270–273
The Frankenstein Chronicles 273
Freeman, Martin 269
French New Wave 172, 235
Fria Tider (Free Times) 248–249
Friday, or, The Other Island 273
Frost, Robert 239
fugue 13, 181, 183
Fun Home, a Family Tragicomic 110

game *see* computer game; video game
game animation 313; raster graphics 313–314; vector graphics 313–314
game manual 79
game mechanics 77–78
Game of Thrones 265, 267, 272
gameplay 71–73, 76, 78–80, 289, 294–298, 310, 312, 314–315, 322–323, 325
game retellings 79
game series 310
game studies 71, 76, 321, 323
gameworld 71, 76, 81, 318–320
gaming experience 71, 74, 79
Gargantua and Pantagruel 50
Gater, Michael 316
Gatiss, Mark 269
La Gazza Ladra 317
Genette, Gérard 265, 273
genre 4, 234, 285, 287–289, 291, 293; film 30, 31, 35–38, 114–115, 117, 143, 147, 170–172, 175, 178, 180, 235, 237, 246; game 75–76, 79, 81–82, 310, 318, 320, 322, 325, 326; literature 19, 51, 118, 143, 148, 163–164, 178, 238–240, 242, 273; music 59–60, 66, 124–125, 129, 152, 182–183, 186 news 89, 96 performance 209, 211, 213; radio 118; theatre 256, 259
gentrification (in adaptation) 143
Geostorm 243
Gesamtkunstwerk 11–12, 129
gesture 10, 18, 46–47, 50, **53**, 202–208, 211–212, 220, 292, 299–301, 304
Ghosh, Amitav 237
Gibbon, Dave 19
GIF 3, 5, 282–283, 285, 298–304; reaction GIF 298–299
Gilgamesh 49
Ginsberg, Allen 131, 205, 207–212
The Girl with the Dragon Tattoo 176
Godard, Jean-Luc 234
GOG 316
Goodbye to Berlin 170–171
The Good Dinosaur 32
Goodreads 285
Google 94, 132, 276
Google Earth 132
Gone with the Wind 265
Glennie, Evelyn 56
Globe Theatre 255–256, 261
Gomringer, Eugen 48
Grady, Cristopher 109
Grand Theft Auto V 70–71

334   *Index*

graphic narrative *see* narrative
graphic novel 11, 17, 19, 44, 78, 197, 110, 133, 141, 266–267, 271–272, 274
Grass, Günter 163, 185–186, 188
The Great 273
The Great Derangement: Climate Change and the Unthinkable 237
The Great Gatsby 171
Greek drama 10, 257
Greenberg, Clement 12
Gren, Jonas 226, 240, 242
Griffith, D. W. 36
Grusin, David 14, 303–304
Guitar Hero 311
Gulf War 214
gutter 108, 110, 112

Håfström, Mikael 37
Haggard, Henry Rider 272
Hamill, Mark 314
Hamlet 198–199, 270
Hammett, Dashiell 143
Hansel and Gretel 9, 23
Hanslick, Eduard 59, 65
Hardcore Henry 79, 311
Hare, Douglas 316
harmony 60, 62–63, 125, 154, 182, 210
Harry Potter 266–267, 271, 300, 323
Harry Potter: Wizards Unite 81
Hartnett, Josh 272
hashtag 282, 284, 303
Heidegger, Martin 240
Heine, Heinrich 125
Hermann, Bernard 246
Higginbotham, William 320
High Fidelity 162
Hillsborough stadium 216
Hitchcock, Alfred 31, 173
Hollywood 9, 29, 33, 35–38, 78, 90, 117, 141, 226, 234, 243, 245–246, 271–272, 317; Hollywood blockbusters 9, 35, 225, 243–244, 271
Holocaust 181, 186, 188
Homer 148
homo ludens 214
Homo Ludens: A Study of the Play Element in Culture 214
hook (cinematic transition) 177
Hopper, Edward 142, 149–152, 303–304
Horace 11
Hornby, Nick 162
horror 31, 37–38, 81, 158, 163, 173, 175, 177–180, 184, 225, 234, 244–245, 278, 297, 322

House M.D. 269–270
Howl and Other Poems 205
How to Do Things with Words 200
Hughes, Ted 240
Huizinga, Johan H. 214
Hume, David 232
Hutcheon, Linda 139
Huxley, Aldous 182–184
hyperlink 91, 95, 321
hyper-medium/hypermedium 13, 200
hyperreality 170, 246
hypertext 265, 324
hypertext fiction 321
hypertextuality 96
hypotext 265

Ibrahimović, Zlatan 217, 220
icon 23–24, 32–33, **38**, 48–50, 59–61, **66**, **75**, 80, 82, 91, **97**, 109, 114–115, 119–125, 128, 131, 139–140, 146, 148–151, 172, 176, 188, 277, 284, 298–299, 310, 319–322, 324, 326
iconicity 35, 48, **53**, 228
identity **38**, 61, **75**, 147, 189, 198, 200, 214–216, 218, 225, 255, 259, 299–300
Iliad 148
image: mental image 6, 151, 278; moving image(s) 17–18, 28, 30–32, 35, **38**, 46–**47**, 65, 69, 74–**75**, 87, 89, 91, 95–**96**, 103, 105–106, 121, 130–131, 133, 139, 141, 146, 171, **174**, 282, 299, 303, 313; still/static image(s) 6, 17, 49, 139, 148–149, 284, 302, 304, 316; sound and image 29–31, 112–113, 130, 211; text and image/ word and image 4, 6, 10, 17–18, 42, 47, 49, **53**, 89, 103, 106–110, 112, 141, 148, 229, 269
image-based media 165
image-processing 225
imagery 131, 173, 182, 241; auditory 46, 57, 63, 182; verbal 91; visual 119–121, 123
image theatre 256
IMAX 34
immediacy 95–96, 179, 212, 220, 227, 290–291
immersion 45, 235, 244, 246, 320
improvisation 50, 63–64, 169, 186–187, 205–206
Inception 79
Independence Day 233
independent cinema 37

index 23–24, 31–33, **38**, 48–49, **53**, 61, **66**, **75**, 82, 91, **97**, 109, 115, 120, 131, 216, 228, 230–231, 235, 247–249, 251, 277, 284, 310, 319, 326
indexicality 49, 231, 233, 249, 251
Indigo 273
infosphere 247–248
Instagram 282–284
interaction: human/social 16, 24, 42–43, 50, 52, 59, 75, 77, 109, 113, 119–120, 198, 201, 209, 238, 247, 256, 259–260, 283–284, 287–288, 292, 296–298, 304; in/between media 3, 4, 6–7, 10, 14, 24, 28, 103, 107–110, 119, 124, 128, 164, 197, 204, 212, 217, 227, 230–231, 252, 258, 316; with media 17, 24, 42–43, 45, 51, 71, 73, **75**, 80, 82, 95–96, 165, 199, 201, 204, 212, 239, 310, 320
interactive fiction 321, 323, 325
interactivity 51, 95–96, 215, 287–288, 291, 293, 295, 298
interart studies 5, 197
intermediality 3–5, 10, 15, 38, 72, 81, 108, 130, 133, 198, 282–283, 289, 298–299, 304, 310
intermedial literacy *see* literacy
intermedial performativity *see* performativity
intermedial reference 104, 162, 169, 175, 209
intermedial relation 3–5, 8, 14–15, 22, 24–25, 101, 106, 110, 112, 199, 210, 213, 282, 304, 310; *see also* media combination; media representation; media transformation; transmediation
intermedial theory 8, 133, 173, 197, 255, 267, 309
internal coherence 226, 232, 234–235, 247
interpictoriality 188
Interstellar 243
intertextuality 48, 251
intertextual reference 128, 151, 162, 175, 179, 251
intertitles 31, 175
Intolerance 36
intonation 3, 7, 46, 58, 202–203, 207
The Irishman 225
Isherwood, Christopher 170–171
Italian neorealism 235

James Bond films 271–272
Jandl, Ernst 209

Jane Eyre 265, 273
Jay–Z 126, 133
Jazz 168, 181, 183
The Jazz Singer 29
Jelinek, Elfriede 184
Jenkins, Henry 266
Johnson, Laurie 317
John the Baptist 155
Jones, Chuck 316
Josephus, Flavius 155
journalism 4, 86, 91, 93–94, 217, 238, 250
journalistic authority 93, 227, 247
Joyce, James 162, 181
Jurassic Park 32, 35

Kaddish and Other Poems 205
Kafka on the Shore 171–172
Kairos 220
Kant, Immanuel 13
Karim, Jawed 291–292
Kill Bill: Volume 1 173
kinetophone 29
King, Stephen 179
Kittler, Friedrich 7, 57
Kjellberg, Felix *see* PewDiePie
Knightley, Keira 144–145, 147
Körkarlen 31
Kornfeld, Theodor 50
Kracauer, Siegfried 32
Kraft, Åsa Maria 240
Kricfalusi, John 316
Kron, Lisa 112
Kubrick, Stanley 175, 184
Kung Fu Panda 33
Die Kunst der Fuge 63

Lady Gaga 126
Lamentation of Christ 190
Langer, Susanne 60
Laocoon 12, 300
Larsson, Stieg 174, 176
The League of Extraordinary Gentlemen 272
League of Legends 77
legend 49–50, **53**, 155, 159
Leitch, Thomas 139–140, 143, 146, 152
Lemonade 132–133, 168
Leone, Sergio 117
Lessing, G.E. 12, 200
Let's Play 79, 285, 289, 291, 293–294, 297, 312
Letterboxd 285
Levinas, Emmanuel 225
libretto 153, 155–156

336   *Index*

light (as or in media) 29–30, 36, **38**, 198, 206–207, 210, 215, 228, 260
linguistics 7, 22, 200, 203; linguistic pragmatics 200
literacy 8, 133; e-literacy 282; intermedial literacy 7, 110, 252, 282, 297; media literacy 9
literary studies 5, 10, 108, 142
literary theory 48, 321
literature: children's literature 6, 17–18, 44, 49, **53**; digital literature 46, 48, **53**; *electronic literature* 321 ergodic literature 321; expressionist literature 36; hyperlink novels 51; narrative literature 26, 162, 167, 240; oral literature 50, **53**; Twitterature 51, 53; *see also* fiction; narrative; novel; poetry
literaturoper 156
Little Richard 203
live-action 32, 35, 103, 114, 314–315
liveness 119
Lloyd, Christopher 315–316, 319
The Lodge 37
Logan, John 271–273
Looney Toons 115
The Lord of the Rings 143, 154, 267, 323
Love Actually 147
Lovecraft, H.P. 272
Lowry, Malcolm 172–173
LP (long-playing record) 138, 167–168
Lumière brothers 29, 35
Lunarbaboon 109–112
Lunar Lander 314
Lunch, Lydia 205–206, 208, 210
Lynch, David 210
lyrics 10, 57–59, 61, 64, 103, 123, 126–128, 131, 133

McDowell, Malcolm 314
McFadyen, Matthew 144
McLuhan, Marshall 7, 9–10, 14, 25, 88
MacNeille, Tress 315
Mad Max: Fury Road 243
Mad Men 269
Madrigal 125
magic lantern 29
Magritte, René 18
Mahābhārata 49
Malmö Opera 255, 259
The Maltese Falcon 143
Manifesto 32
Las Manos de Orlac 172–173
Mantegna, Andrea 190
Martin, George R.R. 265

Marvel 267, 274
Mash-up 267, 271
mass media 4, 6, 7, 87, 89, 91, 95–**96**, 214, 283; *see also* communication
Materazzi, Marco 217
material interface 21, 45, 80, 103
materiality 48, 63, 65, 78, 96, 115–116, 167–168, 176, 214, 216, 219, 221, 228, 261, 316, 319
material modality *see* modality
material mode 32–33, 131
The Matrix 81, 266, 302, 311
Maus 107
Mbappé, Kylian 217
meaning-making 3–4, 14, 18, 21, 24, 44, 58, 60, 63, 65, 69, 103–104, 106–107, 109, 128, 199, 216–217, 282, 315
meaning multiplication 108–109
media and communication studies 5–6, 282
media archaeology 6–7
media border 4, 7, 13, 142, 197, 269
media combination 8, 10, 14, 19, 31, 51, 58, 65, 103–107, 109, 112, 118–122, 129–131, 197, 269, 285, 294, 304, 311; intermedial combination 103, 106, 112, 133, 289; media integration 7, 10, 31, 38, 58, 65, 69, 103–104, 106–107, 109, 113, 117–118, 284–285, 304
media interaction *see* interaction
mediality 11, 42, 50, 262, 320
media logic 89
media product 4–10, 14–22, 24, 28, 31, 52, 64, 69, 71–74, 76–79, 86, 89– 91, 103–106, 112, 118, 122, 133, 138–144, 148–151, 154–155, 160, 162, 164, 171–173, 197, 199, 201–202, 205, 207, 210–216, 218–219, 221, 226–230, 235, 241–242, 247–248, 252, 256, 259, 263, 266, 268, 274, 280, 282, 285, 290–291, 296, 299–304, 310–312
media representation 103–105, 112, 141, 149, 162, 164, 166, 172, 174, 180, 188–189, 201, 211–212, 215, 288–289, 298, 304, 310, 316–318, 323, 324; diegetic media representation 10, 163, 172, 173, 175; illusion 29, 169, 180, 262, 263, 277, 314; imitation 169; structural media representation 163, 169, 172
media revolution 13
mediascape 129, 132, 269
media technology 7, 218, 259

mediation 7–8, 14–17, 24, 96, 112, 138, 199–200, 202, 211, 213, 231, 261–262, 285, 311
mediatization 199, 211, 213, 262
media transformation 4, 8–9, 13, 103–104, 112, 118, 130,133, 138, 143, 152, 159–160, 169, 199, 211, 226, 231, 285, 288, 294, 317
media type: basic media 4, 9, 13, 17–23, 28, 30, **38**, 42–43, 45–46, 48–49, 51–**53**, 56, 57, **66**, 69–70, 74–**75**, 87, 89–91, **96**, 103–104, 106, 108–109, 112, 123, 130–131, 133, 138–141, 146, 155, 164, 171–172, **174**, 201, 203, 211–212, 228–229, 252, 255–256, 262, 282, 284–285, 299; qualified media 4, 7–11, 16–19, 24–25, 28–29, 34, 36, **38**, 42, 48–**53**, 56, 58, 62, 65, **66**, 69, 71–72, **75**–76, 81–82, 89–90, 103–104, 106–107, 110, 118–119, 122–123, 127, 129–131, 133, 138–142, 147, 149, 162, 164–168, 171–172, 188, 197, 199–202, 211, 213–214, 218, 226, 228–229, 231, 233, 235, 239, 246–247, 252, 256, 263, 270, 288–289, 298, 309–311, 315
medium specificity 11–14, 104, 140–141, 146, 150,155, 160; contextualized medium specificity 14
Méliès, Georges 36
melisma 125
melodrama 37, 153
melody 10, 33, 58, 103, 123–125, 184
meme 3, 6, 18, 286, 300, 302
memory 43–44, 46, 50, 86, 190–191, 261, 282
Mendes, Sam 272
Le Mépris 234
metaphor 14, 47, 59, 61, 91, **97**, 180–181, 206, 214–215, 260, 187, 289, 319
Michelangelo 11
Mickey Mousing 33
microblog 51
Microsoft Kinect 73, 80
Midsommar 37
A Midsummer Night's Dream 255–256
Millennium trilogy 174
mimesis 258, 260
mise en abyme 251
mise en scène 36
Mission Impossible 175
Mitchell, Margaret 265
Mitchell, W.J.T. 3, 7, 12, 15

mixedness 6, 284; mixedness of media 7, 15; hybridity 284
modality: material modality 20, 22, 30–31, **38**, 46–47, 49, **53**, 58, **66**, 72, 74–**75**, 90, **97**, 108, 127, 139, 257, 259, 304, 324; semiotic modality 20–22, 32, 35, **38**, 47–49, **53**, 58–59, 63, **66**, **75**, 91, **97**, 106, 108, 122–123, 125, 131, 133, 148, 202, 156, 258, 260, 263; sensorial modality 21–22, 30, 34–35, **38**, 45–50, 52–**53**, 58, **66**, 71, **75**, 90, **97**, 103, 106, 108, 118, 123, 129, 148–149, 169, 199, 202, 258; spatiotemporal modality 21, 32, 35, **38**, 47, **53**, 58, **66**, **75**, 81, 90, **97**, 123, 197, 214, 220, 256–257, 260, 262–263, 304, 318
Moderato Cantabile 181
mods (modifications) 74
Moggach, Deborah 144
monologue 30, 118–121, 159, 206, 296
Monroe, Marilyn 270
monster narrative 267, 271–272
montage 170–171, **174**–180, 296
Moore, Alan 19, 272
Morrison, Toni 168, 181, 183
motet 125
motif 120, 157–158, 180–181, 183, 187–188, 242; leitmotif 155, 157–158, 181
mousiké 11, 62, 65
MP3 43, 56, 65, 138
Müller, Thomas 220
multimodal communication *see* communication
multimodality 96, 108, 200, 213; multimodal analysis 18, 104, 203; multimodal context 45, 50–51; multimodal integration 19, 69, 89; multimodal medium/media 214, 256
multimodal studies 4, 6–7, 15, 21, 107
multivoicedness 183–184, 187–188
Murakami, Haruki 171–172
Murch, Walther 117
music: absolute music 59–60, 65; ambient music 59; art music 10, 13, 56, 59–**66**, 183–184, 197; baroque music 180; black metal 202, 205; blues 60; classical music 121, 126, 128, 181, 183, 186–187, 317; East Asian music 33; folk music 56, 62, 64–**66**; instrumental music 13, 65, 148, 153, 159, 182; jazz 59–60, 63, 169, 180–181, 186–187; orchestral music 12, 78; pop(ular)

music; 10, 22, 56, 59, 62, 64–**66**, 103, 107, 124, 126–128, 162, 165–168, 183, 198, 203, 289, 317; punk 164–167 rap music 61; rock 22, 58, 124, 131–132, 163–167, 180, 183, 201, 205, 208–209, 270; vocal music 57–58, **66**, 130; waltz 64
musicality 58
musicalized fiction 169
musical meaning 59–61, 63
musical notation 56–58, 63; sheet music 56–57, 59, 62, 64, **66**; written music 57, 64
musical structure 60–61, 66, 154, 157, 169, 180–181, 184–188
musicology 5, 59, 63
music theatre 65, 152–153, 156–158
music video 106–107, 128–133, 213, 301
Das musikalische Opfer 63
Muybridge, Edward 35
My Neighbor Totoro 113, 116
myth 36, 49, 92, 217, 274

Naishuller, Ilya 79
narrative 6, 19, 28, 31, 42, 45–46, 49–51, **53**, 59, **66**, 70–71, **75**–76, 78–79, 88, 92–93, 103–107, 109–110, 112, 118, 124–126, 128, 138–141, 145, 149–150, 152, 154–155, 162, 168–169, 171–172, 175–176, 182–185, 187–188, 212, 217, 226, 233, 235–236, 238, 244–245, 247–249, 263, 266–267, 279, 293, 301, 303, 312, 314–316, 321, 324; audiovisual narration 171–172, 175–176; audiovisual narrative 31, 113, 139, 175; auditory narrative 107, 123; cinematic narration 145; factual narrative 7, 91, 247; fictive narrative 235, 239; graphic narrative 106–110; graphic narration 42, 44, 141; literary narrative 43; macro narrative 251; pictorial narration 188
narrative coherence 296–297
narrative conflict 10, 181
narrative event 74, 118–123
narrative form 88, 248
narrative media 118, 309
narrative pattern 91, 93, 247
narrative strategies 239, 250
narrative structure 13, 35, 118–119, 145, 163, 176, 178, 181, 183, 246, 318
narrative studies 118; narratology 108, 118, 266, 273
narrative time 176, 276

narrative voice 168, 178, 258
narrativization 110
narrator 14–51, 112, 119, 144, 146, 154–155, 162, 170–171, 173, 179, 187, 189, 190, 250, 269, 279
Naudin, Julien 117
Nazism 187; Nazi Germany 186; Nazi propaganda 14; Nazi SA 185, 187
Neistat, Casey 286
Nesbø, Jo 163, 168, 170, 174–179
The Neverhood 314
new journalism 250
news: commentaries 89; digital news 96; editorials 89, **96**; feature 89, **96**; newspaper articles 6, 9–10, 13; news story 88–93, 95, 227, 247–248, 251
news media 4, 9, 17, 69, 86, 89–90, 93, **96**, 226–227, 229, 246–248, 252, 286
news values 92, **96**
New Testament 155
Nickelodeons 35
Nighthawks 303
Nintendo Wii 73
Nolan, Christopher 79
non-fiction 107, 227
nonsensical sound 203
nostalgia 166, 246
notational system 45, 57–58
novel: cinematic novel 38, hyperlink novel 51; illustrated novel 18; postmodern novel 45, 170; *see also* fiction; graphic novel; narrative
novelization 78, 279
novelty (in news) 88, 91–92, 94

objectivity 93, 227, 234–235, 251–252
odorama 35
Old Testament 159
Olson, Kevin 316
onomatopoeia 23, 59
opera 10, 22, 36, 58, 128–129, 138–139, 142, 152–159, 255–256, 260
opera studies 5, 152
Oper und Drama 158
orality 50, **53**, 202–207, 212
orature 50
ostinato 180
othering 215
Outkast (hip hop group) 127

Paget, Sidney 269
painting 11–13, 16, 18, 22, 29, 48, 104, 138–139, 142, 148–152, 159, 162–163,

188, 190–191, 262, 265, 303–304, 311; abstract painting 48
palimpsest 265, 267, 273–274
Palimpsests: Literature of the Second Degree 265
panel (comics) 108, 110, 112
pantomime 198–199, 255
Paradoxia 205
Paragone 11
paratext 79, 130–131; paratextual media 175
Parents Music Resource Center (PMRC) 62
parody 256
parser 321
Passion Impossible – 7 Day Emergency Call for Germany 262
Peirce, Charles Sanders 23, 80
Pennebaker, D.A. 130–131
penny dreadful 273
Penny Dreadful 267, 270–273, 280
Penny Dreadful: City of Angels 271
perception 21, **38**, 65, **75**, 87, 92, 95–96, 148, 152, 171, 178, 220, 225–226, 232, 235, 237, 261, 322; audiovisual perception 172, 178; auditory/aural perception 52, 104, 123, 170, 178–180; cognitive perception 21; external perception 230–231, 233, 252; perception of interaction 283; perception of truthfulness 226, 229; sensorial perception 24; sensual perception 21, 218; spatial perception 47; visual perception 48, 57, 109, 122, 179
performance: live performance 56–57, **66**, 153, 198, 201, 211–212, 214, 218–219, 221, 268, 278; mediatized performance 119, 199; oral performance 50, 130; staged performance 255, 260; street performance 205; theatre performance 90, 198, 229, 261–262
performance art 205, 261
performance studies 8, 197–199, 201–203, 213
performative event 199, 263
performative space 198, 202, 204, 208–211, 213, 256, 259, 263
performative time 209
performativity 199–201, 298–299, 304
performer 46, **53**, 63, 65–**66**, 126, 182, 198–199, 201–204, 208–210, 213, 256–257, 260, 263, 279; performer's body 201, 204, 213
persona 126, 293, 298

personae (pop music) 126
personalization 283
PewDiePie 286, 288, 291, 293–298
Phantasmagoria 314
phenakistiscope 29
photography 5, 23–24, 29, 49, 90–91, **96**, **97**, 112, 133, 148, 162–164, 188–191, 210, 226, 228, 230, 233, 251, 262, 284, 295, 311, 326; analogue photography 228, 233
physicality 284
pictorialism 169
picture book 3, 5
The Picture of Dorian Gray 271
Pignatari, Décio 48
Pilate, Pontius 243
plagiarism 188, 272
Plague, Inc. 70
platform 69–70, 72, 77–78, 80, 94, 107, 109, 277, 282–288, 291, 293–294, 297, 322 ; digital distribution platform 69, 72, 78, 316 ; media platform 77, 217 ; social media platform 94, 286, 291, 298 ; streaming platform 56, **66**
Plato 13, 62, 226, 232, 245
plot 35, 37, 81, 104–105, 138, 140, 152, 154–156, 164, 167, 173, 175–176, 181–184, 186, 188, 231, 234, 246, 259, 269, 272–273, 276, 315
Podbay 277
Podbean 277
podcast 238, 268, 274–279, 286
Podolski, Lukas 213
poetic language 51, 233, 241
Poetics 232, 258
poetry: baroque poetry 50; concrete poetry 48, **53**; digital poetry 44, 51, **53**; epic poems 49, **53**; spoken poetry 50; *see also* ekphrasis; ecopoetry
poetry performance 204–205, 212
poetry reading 204–205, 210; lyrical performance 204–205, 207, 209, 210; poetry slam 205; spoken word performance 205, 208
Point Counter 182
point of view 104, 170–171, 176, 178–179, 246, 250
pop music *see* music
popular science 226, 237–239; popular science narrative 238, 252
porn 37, 38
The Portable Henry Rollins 205
post-dramatic theatre *see* theatre
post-truth 226; *see also* truthfulness

A Prairie Home Companion 275
praxis 203, 217, 258
prestige adaptation 143–144
The Price Is Right 322
Pride and Prejudice 4, 115, 142–147, 274
Priest, Gary 316
Princess Mary's Gift Book 233
printing press 43, 46, 50, 53, 94
propaganda 14, 37, 236
proscenium theatre *see* theatre
Psycho 31, 33, 173
Pussy Riot 221
Pythagoras 62

quadrivium 63
qualifying aspects (of media) 31, 34–38, 49, 62, 70, 76, 91–92, 204, 210, 228–230, 287, 288 contextual qualifying aspects 34, **174**–175, 208 operational qualifying aspects 34, 52, 113, 117
Quick 37

Rabbit Hole 286
Rabelais, Francois 50
radio drama 106–107, 114, 118–119, 123, 133, 275
Rajewsky, Irina 162, 169
Rapacioli, Paul 249
Ravel, Maurice 121
realism 119, 237, 244
recognition effect 249–251
Rector, Jeff 314
recycling 285, 287–289, 291, 298
Reddit 302
refugee crisis 249
Relotius, Claas 249–250
Remarque, Erich Maria 235
remediation 95, 138, 256
Remediation. Understanding New Media 14
Renaissance 11, 19, 50, 61, 65, 125, 156, 190, 322
re-righting 273, 323
rewriting 45, 268–269, 273, 322
rhyme 46, 51, 56, 127
Rhys, Jean 265, 273
Rhys-Davies, John 314
rhythm 3, 13, 46, 52, 58, 62, 121, 123, 154, 183, 185–187, 201, 207–208, 210–212, 241, 277–278, 292
Ricoeur Paul 233–234
Rihanna 123, 128
The Road Not Taken 239
Robin Hood 274

Robinson Crusoe 273
rockumentary 130
romantic era 65, 241
Rollins, Henry 205–206, 208, 210
Rondo 186–187
Rosefeldt, Julian 32
Rossini, Gioachino 317
Royal Albert Hall 207, 209
The Rules of Attraction 175
Run, Lola Run 79
Russell, Steve 320
Ryan, Marie-Laure 266

Salomé 142, 155–159
Ein Sanduhr 50
Saussure, Ferdinand de 22
Schauspielhaus Hamburg 262
Schlingensief, Christoph 262–263
Schubert, Franz 124–126, 128
Schumann, Robert 125
Schwitters, Kurt 182
science fiction 35, 38, 81, 234, 238–239
Scorsese, Martin 225
Scott, Walter 124, 126, 128
Scribblenauts Unlimited 322
scripton 323
sculpture 11, 13, 20, 70, 164, 233, 265
ScummVM 316
Seale, Douglas 314
semiosis 258, 266
semiotic modes 18, 32–33, 35, 60, 108–110, 282
semiotic resources 123
semiotics 22, 36
sensorial modality *see* modality
sequentiality 38, 47–49, **53**, 58, **75**, 90, 123, 149
Shakespeare, William 19, 143, 198, 255, 261, 273–274
Shakira 123
Shelley, Mary 271
Sherlock 267–268
Sherlocked 268–271
Sherlock Holmes 233, 267–271, 274, 280
The Shining 175
Shire, Warsan 132
Shoot the Pianist 171
Shore, Howard 154
Showboat 117
Sibelius, Jean 63
sign 19, 22–24, 60, 82, 261, 277 *see also* icon; index; semiosis; symbol
sign system 18, 22, 148, 150

Silent Spring 226, 237–239
The Simpsons 61
The Sims 71
simulation 70–71, 74–76, 79, 81, 169, 309–311, 318, 323
Sjöström, Victor 31
The Snowman 163, 170, 174–178, 180
Snow White 29
Snow White and the Seven Dwarfs 35
Snyder, Gary 240
soap opera 297
social context 6–7, 17–18, 35–36, 50, 52, 96, 103, 140, 146, 164
social media entertainment 285, 287–291, 293–294, 297–298, 304
Socrates 72
Solibo Magnifique 189
sonata 13, 182–184
Sonate in Urlauten 182
song 43, 46, 57–59, 64, **66**, 68, 103, 106–107, 123–132, 138, 153, 162, 164, 168, 181, 186, 198, 213–214, 251, 270, 310–311, 317; singing 58, 63–64, 106, 133, 153, 158 *see also* music
A Song of Ice and Fire 265
Sortie de l'usine Lumière à Lyon 29
sound: Dolby digital sound 29; Dolby Stereo sound 29; electronic sound 113; Foley sound 33, 113, 117; interiorized sounds 179; library sound 33, 113–114; mental sound 6; mono sound 29; non-verbal sound 30, **38**, 202; organized sound 4, 13, 16–18, 20, 30, **53**, 57–59, 62, **66**, 75, 104, 106, 131, 138, 140, 164, 181–183, 187, 202, 211; verbal sound 66; *see also* auditory text
sound design 112, 117, 146
sound editing 117, 212, 296
sound effect 28, 30, 33, **38**, **53**, 69, **75**, 89, 103, 106, 112–117, 119–121, 123, 127, 133, 146, 171, **174**, 178–179, 212, 258, 277, 316–317, 324–325
sound effect (in comics) 108–109
sound mixing 117
soundscape 80, 114–115, 119–120, 154, 181–182, 208, 215, 315, 325; background sound 114; keynote 114–116; signal sound 114–115, 117; sound mark 114–115, 119
sound studies 114
soundtrack 30, **38**, 74–**75**, 79–80, 91, 117, 130–131, 154, 156, 181, 310, 317, 324–325

sound waves 9, 18, 20, 22, 28, 33, **38**, 45, 57–59, 63, 65–**66**, 74–**75**, 90, **97**, 103, 181, 276, 324
source media product *see* transmediation
Spacewar! 320
spatiotemporality 122, 199, 208
speech act 200
Der Spiegel 249–250
Spiegelman, Art 107
Spielberg, Steven 35
Spotify 138, 168, 277
Stardew Valley 73
The Starry Night 304
Starship Troopers 175
Star Trek 274, 311
Star Trek Bridge Crew 311
Star Wars 29–30, 117, 266, 268, 271, 274
Statue of Liberty 245–246
Steam (platform) 72, 316
steampunk fiction 322, 326
Stein, Gertrude 10
Stevenson, R.L. 271
Stiers, David Ogden 315
stillness 150, 152, 298, 303, 304
Stockhausen, Karlheinz 62
Stoker, Bram 271–273
Stone, John 151
storage (devices and media) 17, 28, **38**, 43–44, 57, **66**, 72, 80, 167–168, 314, 316
Storck, Adam 124, 126
The Stork 247, 249
storytelling 37, 49–**53**, 70, 72, 91, 145, 184, 187, 250, 266, 268–269, 297; transmedia storytelling 266, 269; transmedial storytelling 266
storyworld 20, 22, 33, **38**, 48, **53**, 70–71, 81, 104, 147, 256, 260–261, 266–276, 280, 320, 324; transmedia storyworld 274; transmedial storyworld 8, 197, 265–267
The Strange Case of Dr Jekyll and Mr Hyde 271
Strauss, Richard 142, 155–159
stream-of-consciousness 173
Stromae 128
A Study in Scarlet 268
subgenre 178, 204–205
sublime; apocalyptic sublime 244–246
submedia 19, 30, 74, 112, 118, 234, 239, 256, 291
Subterranean Homesick Blues 130
subvocalization 46
Super Smash 311

342 *Index*

surrealism 36
suspense 175–177, 179
suspension of disbelief 234–244, 260–261
Swedish Film Institute 36
Swedish Golden Age 37
symbol 23–24, 32–34, **38**, 48, **53**, 59–60, **66**, **75**, 82, **97**, 109, 115, 119–120, 123, 125, 127–128, 131, 139, 148–150, 157, 159, 162, 167, 184, 220, 241, 245, 260, 263, 277, 284, 299, 303, 310, 319, 322, 326
symbolism 156, 256

tableaux vivant 143
Tan, Shaun 108
Tarantino, Quentin 173
target media product *see* transmediation
Tchaikovsky, Pyotr Ilyich 317
technical media/medium of display 4, 7, 16–21, 24, 28, 31, 34, **38**, 42–46, 51–52, 56, 57, 72, 87, 89, 91, 94, **96**, 103–104, 107, 122, 138, 141, 164, 167–168, 171, **174**, 202, 209, 210–211, 214, 252, 256–257, 259, 263, 284, 313, 315, 324
Technicolor 34
television series 112, 118, 133, 147, 265–269, 271–275, 296, 297, 300, 301, 303; anthology series 271
The Tempest 273
temporality 47, 76, 90, 110, 243, 276, 303; simulated time 81; virtual time 22, **38**, **53**, 59, **66**, **75**, **97**; virtual time-space **38**, **53**, **97**, 258, 259 *see also* spatiotemporality
Tennis for Two 320
Tesori, Jeanine 112
Texaco 188
texton 323
textuality 322
theatre: image theatre 256; music theatre 65, 152–153, 156–158; post-dramatic theatre 255, 257–258, 260–263l proscenium theatre 257, 259–261, 318; theatre contract 261; theatre performance 90, 198, 229, 261, 262; *see also* performance
theatre studies 5, 201, 263
theatron 257
theme (in music) 105, 128, 158, 168, 182, 183
theme park 139, 266, 309
thriller 52, 163, 175, 178
Thurman, Uma 173

TikTok 283
timbre 58, 60, 123, 154
The Tin Drum 163, 185
Tolkien, J.R.R. 81, 143
Toonstruck 309, 313–321
To the Lighthouse 162
Le Tour du monde en quatre-vingts jours 322
Tournier, Michel 273
Toy Story 29
tragedy 51, 256, 259
La Trahison des images 18
transfiction 265–268, 270–271, 280; *see also* storyworld
translation 6, 112, 124, 126, 157, 174, 211; cross-modal translation 21, 57; intersensorial translation 21
transmediality 12–13, 104, 140–141, 146, 150, 157, 160, 267–268
transmedia(l) storyworlds *see* storyworld
transmediation 8, 103–105, 112, 138–144, 148, 155–156, 159, 190, 199, 201, 210–212, 237, 239, 242, 285, 287, 289, 291, 293, 298, 301, 303–304, 311, 316, 323; source media product/source medium 104, 138–144, 148–152, 154–155, 160, 241–242, 299– 303; target media product/ target medium 104, 138–141, 143–144, 148–149, 152 155, 160, 241, 301, 311–312
Tranströmer, Tomas 180–181
travelling concept 200
travel log 288–289
La Traviata 154
A Trip to the Moon 36
Truffaut, François 171
trust: credibility 228–229, 241–243; media distrust 226; reliability 226; trustworthiness (of media) 93, 293 trustworthy media 233
truth claims: objective truth claims 230, 234–235, 240, 242–243, 246–247; subjective truth claims 230–231, 234–235, 240, 242, 246–247, 252
truthfulness 9, 189, 225–232, 234–235, 238–240, 242, 244–247, 251–252
truthiness 93
Tumblr 283, 299
Tutti Frutti 203
Twin Peaks 275
Twitch 294, 312
Twitter 51, 87, 128, 269, 282–283, 298
Tykwer, Tom 79
Type: Rider 322

The Typing of the Dead: Overkill 322
typography 3, 7, 10, 44, 48, 104, 109, 322

Ulysses 162, 181
'Umbrella' (song) 128
Undertale 322
Under the Volcano 172
The Unforgiven 107, 118–120
Universal Monsters franchise 272
Ut pictura poesis 11–12

van Gogh, Vincent 304
VAR (video assistant referee) 218–219
Varney the Vampire 273
vaudeville 143, 153, 208
Verdi, Guiseppe 154
Verne, Jules 272, 322–324, 326
VHS 30, **38**
video game 69–72, 74, 76–78, 80–81, 104, 213, 266, 286, 288, 293–294, 309–311, 313–315, 320–321; adventure game 73, **75**, 315–318, 320, 322; arcade games 80, 81; ARG alternate reality games 81; casual game 78; console games 80; full-motion video games 314; indie games 78; LitRPG 79; massively multiplayer games 77; multiplayer games 69, **75**, 77, 309; offline game 78; online game 77, 78, 81; role-playing game 321, 69, 71; single-player games 69, **75**, 77, 78, 309; software-as-a-service game 78; strategy game 79
Vingt mille lieues sous les mers 324
vinyl 167
virtual space 22, 32–33, **38**, 58, **66**, 80
virtual time *see* temporality
virtuoso opera aria 153
A Visit from the Goon Squad 163, 165, 167, 183
visual album 132–133
visual arts 12, 44, 148
visual imagery *see* imagery
vitality (of media) 285, 304
Viva Vaia 48

vlog 286–291
Volksbühne 262
von Trier, Lars 117
Voyage au centre de la terre 324
VR 75, 81

Wagner, Richard 12, 129, 156–158, 181, 255, 257
Waking the Dead 118
Wall-E 117
Warner, Marina 273
Watchmen 19
Waterworld 243
webcomics 107, 109
Webtoons 107
WeChat 283
Weibo 283
Welcome to Night Vale 268, 274–275, 278–280
Western Motel 142, 149, 151
Who Framed Roger Rabbit? 315
Wide Sargasso Sea 265, 273
Wilde, Oscar 142, 156, 271
The Wilderness Downtown 132
Williams, Linda 37
Wing Commander III: Heart of the Tiger 314
The Witness 74
Wonder Woman 112
Wood, Grant 151
Woods, Don 321
Woolf, Virginia 162
word music 182
World of Warcraft 322
worldness 70, 72
Wright, Joe 142, 144, 146–147

Yeats, William Butler 201
Yorick's skull 270
YouTube entertainment 283, 285

Zavattini, Cesare 36
Zidane, Zinedine 217
Zirimu, Pio 50
zoetrope 29, 35
zoopraxiscope 35

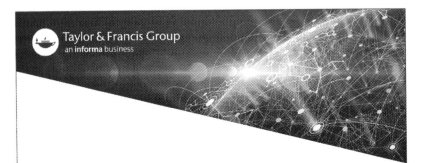

Printed in the United States
by Baker & Taylor Publisher Services